Ace the PMI-ACP® exam

A Quick Reference Guide for the Busy Professional

Sumanta Boral

Apress®

Ace the PMI-ACP® exam: A Quick Reference Guide for the Busy Professional

Sumanta Boral
Delhi, India

ISBN-13 (pbk): 978-1-4842-2525-7 ISBN-13 (electronic): 978-1-4842-2526-4
DOI 10.1007/978-1-4842-2526-4

Library of Congress Control Number: 2016961522

Managing Director: Welmoed Spahr
Lead Editor:Celestin Suresh John
Technical Reviewer: Karthik Jonnalagadda
Editorial Board: Steve Anglin, Pramila Balan, Laura Berendson, Aaron Black, Louise Corrigan, Jonathan Gennick, Robert Hutchinson, Celestin Suresh John, Nikhil Karkal, James Markham, Susan McDermott, Matthew Moodie, Natalie Pao, Gwenan Spearing
Coordinating Editor: Prachi Mehta
Copy Editor: Karen Jameson
Compositor: SPi Global
Indexer: SPi Global
Artist: SPi Global

Distributed to the book trade worldwide by Springer Science+Business Media New York, 233 Spring Street, 6th Floor, New York, NY 10013. Phone 1-800-SPRINGER, fax (201) 348-4505, e-mail `orders-ny@springer-sbm.com`, or visit `www.springeronline.com`. Apress Media, LLC is a California LLC and the sole member (owner) is Springer Science + Business Media Finance Inc (SSBM Finance Inc). SSBM Finance Inc is a **Delaware** corporation.

For information on translations, please e-mail `rights@apress.com`, or visit `www.apress.com`.

Apress and friends of ED books may be purchased in bulk for academic, corporate, or promotional use. eBook versions and licenses are also available for most titles. For more information, reference our Special Bulk Sales–eBook Licensing web page at `www.apress.com/bulk-sales`.

Any source code or other supplementary materials referenced by the author in this text are available to readers at `www.apress.com`. For detailed information about how to locate your book's source code, go to `www.apress.com/source-code/`. Readers can also access source code at SpringerLink in the Supplementary Material section for each chapter.

Printed on acid-free paper

Dedicated to my Dad, who knew that I was working on this book but, unfortunately, couldn't stay on to see it published.

Contents at a Glance

Contents

About the Author

Sumanta Boral is an ardent evangelist and faculty of Agile practices. He has played roles ranging from hands-on development, technical leadership and coach for several teams, helping them in successful implementation of technology-based solutions that involved cross-functional and geographically distributed teams. During the last 16 years of his illustrious career, he has served several organizations around the globe in telecom and banking domains delivering dozens of projects of various complexities. Presently, Sumanta is working as a Vice President of a division in a UK-based bank that caters to innovative technology solutions for the commercial and private banking business. He has been extremely successful at growing the Agile center of excellence in his organization from scratch, imparting training on project management and Agile/Scrum, thereby building capability in teams based out of multiple locations.

This book is backed by his rich experience in project management and work done on transformation and adoption of Agile practices in an enterprise framework. Sumanta is PMP® certified and has a variety of Agile certifications, namely, PMI-ACP® from PMI® and Certified Scrum Professional (CSP®) and Certified Scrum Master (CSM®) from Scrum Alliance®.

Acknowledgments

Taking a first step toward something always comes with its share of challenges and potential rewards. It was always my dream to write a book, but I hardly believed that I could really do one on my own. Until it was Apress persuaded me to give it a try. This is my first venture in writing a book. I had experience in writing blogs, developing training course materials, writing critics for other books and that's about it.

I was not even sure if I would be able to devote time and do justice. But then an official contract with the publisher, once signed, does wonders. Days, nights, weekends and holidays magically disappear. The brain is cluttered with several strings of thoughts running continuously - but all towards one goal. How should I make it easy for the reader to understand nuances of Agile better? How do I make sure that they are able to clear the PMI-ACP® certification with ease? How do I equip the reader to become better Agilists and contribute meaningfully to their projects and their organizations?

Well, honestly, this is just an attempt and I am far from perfection that one would expect from a well-endowed and accomplished author. But, in creating this piece of work, I must give credit to a virtual team that's been around me.

- First, is my dad, who left me while I was in the middle of writing the book. Having been in the teaching profession, I suppose I naturally inherited a fraction of his style and the traits of knowledge sharing. Even as he was battling cancer, he encouraged me to carry on. I wish he could have seen this.

- My wife, who amid a lot of things, made sure that distractions and interruptions were at bay and I got the freedom to use whatever time was available.

- My daughters who patiently accepted my 'misses' in taking them to their music classes, to the park, or to the shopping mall. I got to make up for it some time and with dividends.

- My current and previous organizations where I got an opportunity to see, feel and try things, often with varying degrees of success and failures. I have been closely associated with many erudite and nerdy colleagues who had 'done that and been there before.' I would especially mention Pawan Mehta, Chander Prakash Thareja, Atulya Mahajan and Vandana Ohri who teamed up with me to build the Agile center of excellence in my organization and help spread the spirit of Agile. Coaching a wide variety of teams and imparting training has truly been a great form of personal enrichment that I must acknowledge.

- Not many times do teachers and trainers have regard for students that create their caricatures and that too while sitting in the class. Vivek Jain, a cartoonist by hobby, attended one of my PMP® training classes and created a beautiful sketch of me and then showed it in class. I had spotted his talent and thought he could be handy. And indeed, what an awesome contribution he has made for most of the figures and sketches that you see in the book. Wherever I struggled with a pictorial description of a concept, he came up with ideas and often a basket of them, giving me the enviable luxury of choice. I was blessed by his multitalented personality - that of a product owner, a business analyst, a tester, a teacher and most important a trusted friend. I heartily appreciate how he managed the schedule the book demanded, working crazy hours with me.

- While I was preparing for my PMI-ACP® exam, I was assisted immensely by Sachin Arora, currently working as a project manager at a premier organization. He happened to get certified before I did and I benefited from his study notes and learning from his experience. Sachin helped me with the content review and contributed to the quizzes in the book. It was truly beneficial to have someone like him by my side.

- I owe thanks to Karthik Jonnalagadda and Kshitij Agrawal for helping me tremendously with lots of valuable and thought-provoking review comments. Much of the quality of the book that you see is attributed to their own profound experience in the subject and their rich experience of clearing the PMI-ACP® exam and guiding other aspirants. I heartily appreciate their time and of course, being available at short notice to help me out.

- I referred to a variety of books during my preparations for the PMI-ACP® exam. They all play a significant role in my Agile education, which has helped me considerably during my professional pursuits. On the top of my list is Mike Cohn, Alastair Cockburn, Mary Poppendieck, Mike Griffith, Esther Derby, Alan Shalloway and Andy Crowe.

- I should also mention the entire Apress team who have been involved in the whole publishing process. Celestin, in particular, approached me to write the book in the first place. Admittedly, the book would not have been here without him. He kept the conversation going on throughout these several months. Then Prachi, who kept a tab on my progress but unfortunately always forgot to save my number to her phone. Thanks to her for sending gentle reminders and tying the strings together. Then Laura, for doing such a brilliant job in reviewing and actually showing me how to differentiate between writing a document and a book. She is a true gem.

Beyond the acknowledgments above, truly there are a lot more resourceful people who have contributed in various capacities and often remain behind the scenes. I bow to them and wish my heartfelt thanks. Your contribution lives on in the pages to follow.

Foreword

"Ace the PMI-ACP® exam" is a very strong reflection of Sumanta's belief, learning and versatile professional experience with various large-scale global organizations. He has played key roles around Project and Product management and using flavors of PMP and Agile methodologies. All of his exposure, including theoretical concepts and ground-level real-time work, makes him write his experiences for the benefit of the wider community.

Sumanta and I have worked together for a few years and share a common passion around Agile methodologies. We have collectively been responsible for capability development in global organizations. And 500+ hands-on Agile educates are an outcome of hard work that has gone into developing people and, in turn, ourselves respectively. Be it professional conversations or offline coffee conversations, Agile seems to be one of the topics we can discuss till coffee sugar overtakes our senses.

Sumanta has structured the book across 9 chapters and these are linked appropriately. I admire the way he emphasizes Chapter 3: Value-Driven Delivery, which is a buzzword and soon will become the basics of professional education. Like everyone else who is continuously learning and developing, I also admire the way he has focused on "Continuous Improvement" in Chapter 8.

This book is a good collection of concepts and working examples. Apart from focusing on the PMI-ACP® exam, I strongly believe that this book will help the reader to become more professionally equipped with Agile methodologies.

With Best Wishes for Sumanta and all the Readers,

—Pawan Mehta,
Head - Data Governance,
Maersk Line,
A. P. Moller Maersk Group

I have worked in a number of technology leadership roles always striving and hopefully succeeding, to build flexible and Agile organizations that are responsive to internal and external customers in an ever-changing world. In one of these roles I met and worked with Sumanta for a number of years for a multinational bank. Sumanta was a strong and passionate advocate of Agile practices. So when he said he was writing a book on Agile I was very happy to hear that others would benefit from his Agile expertise and, more important, from the battle scars he received from adopting these practices in staunch waterfall environments.

Sumanta's passion and knowledge of the field helped introduce Agile practices in a number of complex environments. He did this through the practical application of Agile techniques and principles, helping new practitioners identify opportunities to embark on an Agile journey. Sumanta is already well versed at passing on his knowledge and experience. I have seen firsthand the benefit of Agile and Scrum training he has authored and designed. This has produced outstanding feedback from 250 technology professionals who proceeded to establish Agile practices in their own working environments, shifting from long-standing waterfall methodologies.

Through this book, the reader will benefit from these experiences and will be taken through the journey from understanding the original concepts of Agile, through the core content that allows the reader to progress through Agile qualifications. The content draws significant experiences of using Agile in the real world and it is tailored based on the feedback from the many people Sumanta has mentored in this field,

I wish all the readers the best of luck on a long and successful Agile journey, knowing that this book will give you a great head start.

—Steve Grice,
CTO Elevate,
United Kingdom

Excellent self-study guide and 'must read' for PMI-ACP® certification. This brings the essence of different Agile frameworks and concepts in a way that is not only helpful for certification exam but also in practical Agile implementation.

—Kshitij Agrawal,
Senior Manager,
Amazon

With this book, Sumanta has taken the leap to help aspiring Agile professionals wishing to learn more about Agile processes and, specifically, prepare for the PMI-ACP® certification. Going through the chapter extracts, I found the content very well-written and explained in a lucid manner to help people understand what the much-abused buzzword of 'Agile' is all about. There are a lot of misconceptions in the minds of the laymen about Agile processes and this book would be a ready reckoner to get up to speed and move from traditional processes to Agile. From people who think that Agile means not having any plans to those who are a little more experienced in Agile processes but want to better understand the various intricacies, this book should help them become more well-versed in the methodology and move along the road to Agile adoption.

In my view Agile is about the mindset, more than any specific process or set way of doing things. Being Agile means adopting a collaborative approach that seeks constant feedback and actively engages with the end user. If you take that away from the book and can adopt the true Agile mindset, your money would have been well spent. Happy 'being Agile'!

—Atulya Mahajan,
Development Manager,
IHS Markit

I was lucky to partner with Sumanta during evangelizing Agile practices at an organization level, beginning with training programs for 'Agile and Scrum' and various workshops, contests and coaching interventions for technology teams across various cities in India and the UK. From the first event itself, Sumanta impressed me with his energy, enthusiasm and knowledge of the subject and it was not a surprise that we got excellent ratings consistently. When I learned that he was planning to write a book, I was not sure if he would be able to complete it, knowing that he is extraordinarily busy anyway. Sumanta proved his commitment yet again. I was fortunate to go through some of his work before anyone of you. I was amazed by the fact that some of the most difficult topics were covered with such simplicity. If you are a beginner or a pro, you will find this book interesting and useful. If you are planning to go for PMI-ACP® certification, you have the best book in your hands. Thank you, Sumanta.

—Chander Thareja,
CEO and Founder,
Intellemind Technologies Pvt. Ltd.

It's been more than two thousand five hundred years, when Heraclitus, the Greek philosopher observed that - 'the only constant is change.' The human civilization continued to evolve adapting to the changing environment unconsciously but surprisingly the conscious mind continued to emphasize on an extremely rigid and sequential approach to man-made projects. The last fifty years in human civilization with the rapid increase in the usage of computer based technology in every aspect of life has brought tremendous change in our environment, lives and most importantly the way we think.

The realization that quick iterations, with end user involvement in a supportive fail-fast environment is the most effective way to churn out successful deliveries - is a great gift that we have given to our conscious mind. And 'Agile' is an appropriate name to the process of achieving it. Underneath this commonsense Agile methodology the process needs to be robust to ensure its success. Hence the importance of the Agile PMI-ACP® certification.

About four years ago when I was heading the Compliance Technology function in a UK headquartered global bank - I was challenged to adopt Agile methodologies in all of my programs. Bogged down with operational commitments, managing teams of various sizes working on diverse technologies, I couldn't fathom how and where to start with Agile. That's when I got introduced to Sumanta who by then already had built a reputation in the bank with his expertise in implementing Agile. Not only just advising how to adopt Agile, he arranged training courses with his team of certified Agile practitioners and helped the whole team to come up to speed from the basics to the advanced concepts. I was impressed with Sumanta's lucid delivery of the complex concepts and felt confident as my team adopted Agile seamlessly into the daily way of working.

This book is another example of Sumanta's commitment and love for Agile and showcases his deep knowledge and understanding of Agile. I appreciate this effort of sharing his learnings to the wider world in a step-by-step guide toward achieving the PMI-ACP® certification, which I believe will be invaluable to anyone wanting to make a successful career in an information technology-based career.

—Kausik Ghosh,
Compliance Advisory: Strategy & Innovation,
Barclays,
United Kingdom

Introduction

As observed from numerous surveys worldwide, the IT industry over the last decade has radically evolved in the way software is developed and provisioned to meet the changing requirements of the environment. Agile methodologies are continuously gaining popularity over the traditional project management practices. Organizations are naturally trying to accelerate their business by being flexible and responsive to change. So whether it's a company building a software product for internal or external markets, or are trying to sell IT services, we are seeing a trend of adoption of Agile practices. Such is the power of the iterative and incremental style of progress, Agile practices are also finding relevance in many other non-IT domains. Hence knowledge of this subject has become much in demand these days.

Certifications boost the career of the exam takers, as it, in most cases, indicates knowledge, interest, proficiency and pursuit of excellence in the particular subject. One of the premier institutes of Project Management - PMI® has outlined the requirements of the Agile Certified Practitioner (PMI-ACP®) certification exam that was formally launched in 2011.

This book helps in providing all the information and guidance required to prepare for the PMI-ACP® examination. The book augments a certification aspirant's professional experience and skills with the knowledge of tools, techniques and practices that are required for the examination. Beyond certification seekers, the content in this book are for all Agile practitioners on whom organizations rely to deliver projects effectively and efficiently for their customers.

Audience of this book

The audience for this book primarily includes IT professionals who wish to prepare for and pass Agile Certified Professional (ACP®) exam from the Project Management Institute (PMI®). The contents can also be referenced by those who would be pursuing the Certified Scrum Master Certification (CSM®) from Scrum Alliance® and also a variety of other Agile certification courses in the market.

Apart from certification seekers, the book will also cover good ground for people using or learning to use various flavors of the Agile methodologies and its tools and techniques. As an author, I would expect this book to become a popular asset in corporate and academic libraries.

If you are a PMI-ACP® aspirant, this book will augment your professional experience and skills with the knowledge of Agile tools and techniques that are required for the examination. The content covered in this book is necessary and sufficient to supplement your knowledge on Agile and aligned to the PMI-ACP® course outline. This book contains the best of learnings from all the 12 reference books enlisted by PMI®, as well as documented and working knowledge from sound practitioners with whom I have been associated during my professional experience. This is invaluable for professionals like you who are extremely busy in their day to day work lives, but still want to devote enough attention to master the key concepts, practice hard and clear the PMI-ACP® exam.

Incidentally, even if you are not aspiring for the PMI-ACP® right away, this book will still serve as a ready reckoner for the key concepts in Agile and will, in a nutshell, expose you to the variants of Agile methodologies - namely Scrum, XP, Lean and Kanban. So, whether you are a beginner or a seasoned practitioner, this book will appeal to you, enrich your learning journey and add to your toolbox as an Agile professional.

Brief Content of this Book

This book is a comprehensive, step-by-step and one-stop guide for the Agile Certified Exam (ACP®) from the Project Management Institute (PMI®). Salient features of this book include: 100% coverage of the exam topics as detailed in the course outline and the course handbook, practice exam questions and tips for passing the exam.

This book will include the following topics:

- All contents covered under the PMI-ACP® outline that details the domains, tasks, tools and techniques and knowledge and skills.
- Understanding of the Agile manifesto and principles.
- Understand facets of Agile project management including planning, prioritization, estimation, release planning, retrospectives, risk management, communication management, stakeholder management and contract management etc.
- Agile metrics and means of demonstrating progress.
- People management aspects like Agile coaching, servant leadership, negotiation, conflict management.
- Overview of Agile methodologies including Scrum, XP, Lean and Kanban.
- Practice questions as quizzes in each chapter and three full-length mock exams in the appendix.

The PMI-ACP® exam

If you are planning to apply for the PMI-ACP®, the first thing you should do is read the PMI-ACP® Handbook from the PMI® site. The link is: `http://www.pmi.org/-/media/pmi/documents/public/pdf/certifications/agile-certified-practitioner-handbook.pdf`

You will see a lot of details in there, but here are some of the highlights.

Process

Figure 1 shows the different stages on the way to become PMI-ACP® certified.

Figure 1. *Diagram of stages to become PMI-ACP® certified*

Let us look at each of the stages very briefly.

PMI® Membership

PMI® membership is not mandatory for PMI-ACP® certification seekers. However, I would recommend considering membership as it comes with several benefits like a discount on the PMI-ACP® exam fee and access to a lot of learning resources for professional development. It also helps you to earn Professional development units (PDU's) that are required to maintain your certification.

Presently, the annual PMI® membership comes to about 129$, plus a 10$ membership fee. Check `pmi.org` to see if you can avail other forms of membership at discounted rates.

Eligibility

The next step is to determine the eligibility criteria set by PMI®. There are 4 aspects, all of which you would need to satisfy (Figure 2).

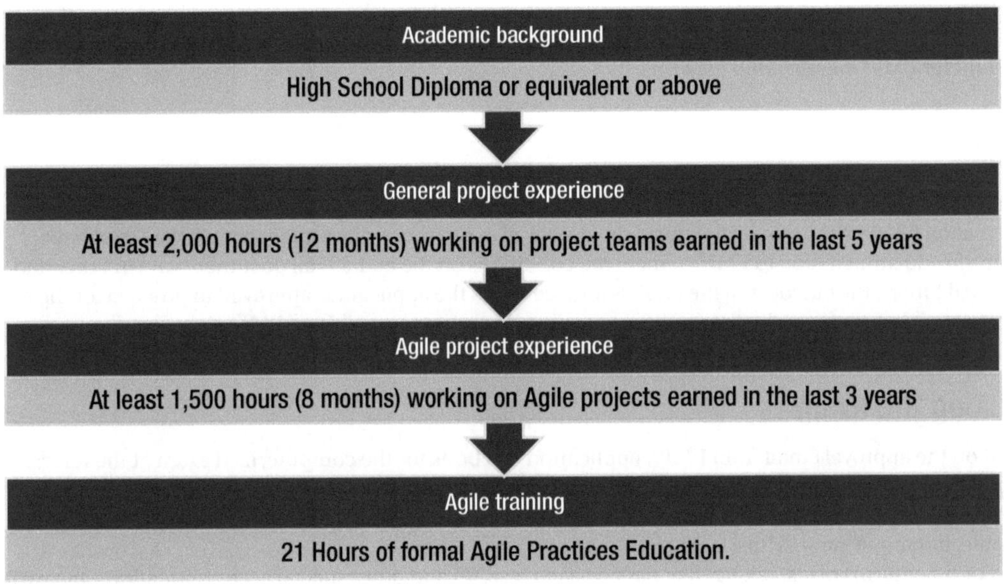

Figure 2. *PMI-ACP® certification exam eligibility criteria*

Application

Once the eligibility is determined, your next formal step in the pursuit of the PMI-ACP® certification is to submit a formal application form, preferably through the online portal `pmi.org`.

The PMI-ACP® application form consists of 4 sections:

- Personal section - for your name (as you would like to be printed on the certificate), communicable address, email address, contact numbers.
- Educational qualification - that meets the eligibility criteria.
- Professional experience - detailing general project and agile experience (in non-overlapping hours) that meets the eligibility criteria. You would need to mention the name and contact details of a supervisor or a colleague of yours who can bear testimony to your working experience.
- Education course - demonstrating attendance of 21 hours of formal Agile training, through one or more means as listed in the course handbook.

You do not need to submit any other form of documentation with the application form, but keep them handy for reference. Keep your supervisor's informed, whose name you have specified on the form, as that can be handy if your application form is picked up for audit.

The application form once submitted gets reviewed by PMI® within a week or two.

Payment of exam fees

Once the application form is reviewed one needs to make the payment.

The preferred mode to opt for is the Computer based testing (CBT) at a registered local Prometric test center. The exam fees are $435 for a PMI-member and a $495 for a non-member (you are getting a 60$ discount for PMI® membership here).

Audit

Some applications might be picked up for a random audit to verify the correctness and genuineness of the information filled on the application form. In almost all cases, the audited applicant is asked to submit supporting documentation to PMI® to meet the conditions on the audit. If all documents are in order and furnished timely, the outcome of the audit is a success and the applicant is approved to proceed for the exam.

If not picked up for audit, the applicant receives an approval email from PMI® right away.

Booking the exam

Based on the approval email from PMI®, application can book for the computerized exam at the relevant Prometric test center. It is generally recommended that the applicant should book the exam once he is almost fully prepared and a week or two in advance. Rescheduling and cancellation of exam booking is possible, but might come with a cost.

For other forms of test taking (like paper-based testing) and other special accommodations, please refer to the PMI-ACP® course handbook.

Taking the exam

The final step is taking the examination at the scheduled date. The test center asks for the exam appointment letter (that also has the proof of payment) and valid identification of the test taker. The exam is a closed-book format. All forms of materials like books, bags, calculators, food materials, or cellphones etc. are prohibited from the exam room. Smaller articles like a car key or a wallet could be stashed away in a locker if the facility is provided at the test center. Be mentally prepared for an 'airport-like' frisking. The Test center administrator will provide the test taker with erasable / laminated sheets of scratch paper and marker pens for use during the exam which needs to be returned after the exam. The whole test taking session will be monitored by a video camera. There are no scheduled breaks during the exam, but the test taker is allowed to take unscheduled breaks with permission from the Test center administrator.

From my experience, I observed that the test was rendered on a secure software running on a Windows® PC with a mouse and a keyboard. The test is complete when the test taker chooses to end the exam or the 3 hour time limit expires. Once the exam is finished (and the optional survey form is filled), the results are available on the screen immediately. The Test center administrator will also give you a printed copy of your score sheet that you can take home with you. You may leave the exam room and the premises of the Prometric test center immediately after that (don't forget to pick up your belongings).

If the outcome of the exam is a fail, the applicant can opt for retaking the exam up to three times in a calendar year. Each reattempt comes with a separate examination fee.

Scoring

There are two universal unknowns with the PMI-ACP® exam.

1. No one knows what the passing score is. Test takers simply get to know whether they passed or failed. But it is sometimes rumored that the passing score is somewhere around 70%.
2. No one gets to know their absolute score of the exam they just undertook.

Apart from the pass / fail notification on the score sheet printed out by the Test Center Administrator, the test taker will see their attained proficiency levels in each of the domains that were tested during the examination. The proficiency levels are: Proficient, Moderately Proficient and Below Proficient.

After passing

If the applicant passed, they can call themselves PMI-ACP® certified from then and there. You would expect to receive a congratulatory letter and a certification package with the formal certificate from PMI®. The soft copy of the certificate will also be available for download from the PMI® site. The name of the certified professional is also entered into an online certification registry: `https://certification.pmi.org/registry.aspx`

Maintaining the PMI-ACP® credential

The PMI-ACP® certification is valid for 3 years. To renew your certification, you will need to follow the requisites of the Continuing Certification Requirements (CCR) Program, details of which are available at: `http://www.pmi.org/-/media/pmi/documents/public/pdf/certifications/ccr-certification-requirements-handbook.pdf`

To be eligible for a renewal, you will have to earn 30 PDU's (professional development units) in Agile topics during the last 3 years and pay a renewal fee. No other form of exams are required anymore. If you do not choose to renew, then your certification is temporarily suspended for a year before it expires.

Format of the exam

The duration of the PMI-ACP® exam is 3-hours. Before the exam there is a tutorial and at the end there is a survey, both of which are optional and usually take 5-10 minutes to complete.

There are 120 multiple-choice questions. Out of 120 questions, 20 are unscored (pretest) questions which do not affect the score and are used by PMI® to test validity of future questions. These 20 questions are spread randomly throughout the exam and the test taker will not be aware of the same.

The rest 100 questions carry 1 mark each. For each question, only 1 out of 4 choices are correct. There is no negative marking, so never leave any question unanswered. Each question is presented sequentially on the screen one at a time, with an option to go to the previous or next question. If you are unsure of the response for a particular question, you can 'mark' it and proceed to the next question. Marked questions can be reviewed after the last question is attempted. Each screen also has a button to pull-up an on-screen calculator, irrespective of whether the question is a numerical one or not.

Every exam taker in the world is almost guaranteed to be presented with a random and unique set of questions. The set of questions are statically allocated to you at the beginning of the exam. This means that correctness or incorrectness of an answer to a question does not determine the difficulty level of the next question.

Syllabus of the PMI-ACP® exam

Now let us talk about the syllabus of the PMI-ACP® exam as enlisted in the course outline.

Domains

The whole syllabus of the exam is divided into 7 domains, which is also how the chapters of this book is aligned. For the purpose of traceability, the organization of this book is shown in Table 1.

Table 1. *PMI-ACP® certification exam domains*

Domain #	Domain Name	Percentage of questions in the exam	Chapter # in this book
Domain I	Agile Principles and Mindset	16%	1 and 2
Domain II	Value-driven Delivery	20%	3
Domain III	Stakeholder Engagement	17%	4
Domain IV	Team Performance	16%	5
Domain V	Adaptive Planning	12%	6
Domain VI	Problem Detection and Resolution	10%	7
Domain VII	Continuous Improvement (Product, Process, People)	9%	8

Note that the percentage column is just for indicative purpose showing the distribution of emphasis on each domain. In reality the questions on the exam might cover topics that need knowledge from multiple domains at the same time. Under each domain a set of tasks are listed and described in the PMI-ACP® course outline.

Apart from the 7 domains, all certification seekers will be tested (with a few questions) and have to adhere to PMI®'s Code of Ethics and Professional Conduct. This is available at: `http://www.pmi.org/-/media/pmi/documents/public/pdf/governance/code-of-ethics-and-professional-conduct.pdf?la=en`

Tools and techniques

Each of the following tookits have tools and techniques under them which have been covered in various chapters in the book as follows. If you are looking up for a particular tool or technique you can use the Table 2 or the index of this book.

Table 2. *Tools/techniques covered on the PMI-ACP® exam by chapter*

Toolkit Name	Chapter # in this book
Agile Analysis and Design	4 and 6
Agile Estimation	6
Communications	4 and 5
Interpersonal skills	4 and 5
Metrics	3
Planning, Monitoring and Adapting	1, 2, 6
Process Improvement	8
Product Quality	7
Risk Management	7
Value-Based Prioritization	3

Knowledge and skills

As per the PMI-ACP® course outline, like tools and techniques, there is an equal emphasis on knowledge and skills areas. These are covered in various chapters of this book as shown in Table 3:

Table 3. *Knowledge and skills on PMI-ACP® certification exam by chapter*

Knowledge and skills	Chapter #
Agile values and principles	1 and 2
Agile frameworks and terminology	1 and 2
Agile methods and approaches	2
Assessing and incorporating community and stakeholder values	4 and 5
Stakeholder management	4
Communication management	4 and 5
Facilitation methods	4
Knowledge sharing/written communication	8
Leadership	4
Building agile teams	4
Team motivation	5
Physical and virtual co-location	4

(*continued*)

Table 3. (*continued*)

Knowledge and skills	Chapter #
Global, cultural and team diversity	4 and 5
Training, coaching and mentoring	8
Developmental mastery models (for example, Tuckman, Dreyfus, Shu Ha Ri)	5
Self-assessment tools and techniques	8
Participatory decision models (for example, convergent, shared collaboration)	4
Principles of systems thinking (for example, complex adaptive, chaos)	1 and 8
Problem solving	7
Prioritization	3
Incremental delivery	1, 2 and 3
Agile discovery	8
Agile sizing and estimation	6
Value based analysis and decomposition	3
Process analysis	8
Continuous improvement	8
Agile hybrid models	8
Managing with agile KPIs	3
Agile project chartering	3
Agile contracting	5
Agile project accounting principles	3, 6
Regulatory compliance	3
PMI®'s Code of Ethics and Professional Conduct	9

How to use this book? – a word from the author

Congratulations! You have come so far – so you know what it takes to become PMI-ACP® certified. You are about to embark on reading the book and taking the first step towards clearing the exam. The PMI-ACP® exam is not difficult, but you cannot take it lightly too. Supplement your professional knowledge in working on Agile projects with the theory presented in this book.

Your preparation should be steady and not rushed. You should make sure that the concepts sink-in and you validate your learning by recapitulating, taking some notes, highlighting areas of the book and answering the quizzes at the end of every chapter. I have written the book based on my personal experience of clearing the PMI-ACP® exam few years ago. It is a form of knowledge sharing and giving back to the Agile community in our software industry.

Before you start reading the book, here is a bit of guidance for you:

- Preferably read the book in the same sequence as it is written. Although there are cross-references between chapters, you will notice that the book assumes that you are growing in knowledge of the theory as you traverse one chapter after next. Finish the chapter that you have started with before you start the next one.

- Chapter 2: Agile methodologies is a special chapter. You will notice that there are no domains in the PMI-ACP® course outline that are dedicated to Scrum, XP, Kanban and Lean. But you have to know these specific topics very well to be able to clear most of the questions in the exam. So read it thoroughly and if necessary flip back and forth into this chapter while trying to co-relate to concepts presented elsewhere in the book. I have tried to liberally provide cross-references across chapters to help you.
- Read the book at your own pace. Considering that you are a busy professional who aspires to get certified soon, I would recommend that you spend about 2 hours daily reading and practicing, with slightly more time over the weekends. However do not penalize yourself or put yourself under stress if you miss the rhythm for a day or two. Each chapter should not take more than 4-5 days to read and you should be able to complete the first reading of the entire book in less than 4 weeks. This, of course, depends your speed of reading and prior understanding of the topics.
- If you are reading the book for the second time for revision, then carefully focus at the last section in each chapter called "Focus for the exam". Within the chapters, I have also inserted a "Exam Watch" icon to highlight the topics that you are likely to see on the exam. So pay special attention to them.
- As you read each chapter, you will come across references and footnotes at the bottom of some pages. These are for your reference and I leave it to your discretion whether you want to spend time going deep or not. It might be useful for your learning style, but don't digress too much.
- As you read the book, relate to your own professional experience. That will help in learning and retention of concepts. PMI® requires you to have Agile project experience and that is for a good reason. You will get some scenario-based questions in the exam. Unless you are able to correlate the theoretical concepts with those scenarios, you will struggle to get the right answer.
- You will notice that throughout the book I have consistently used the example of a team building a web portal for a Library Management System. This is purely hypothetical and used for anecdotal purposes. If you feel appropriate, substitute that with an example that you can closely relate to. You are very welcome!
- This book contains the best of the 12 reference books recommended by PMI® in the PMI-ACP® course reference material. Those books are excellent sources for reference, but since I have referred to the key concepts from them already, you don't necessarily need to toil and spend further time on them. If you have luxury of time, then of course, go for it. Otherwise, remember that this book is necessary and sufficient.
- Attempt the quizzes at the end of each chapter once you read the chapter fully. I believe that some theory is best understood and remembered in the form of questions and answers, rather than reading paragraphs of content. So don't be surprised, if you see a question which is not covered in the preceding content. Anyway, if you get the answers right, well done! If you got it wrong, remember the keyword FAIL which stands for 'first attempt in learning'. Simply go back and revise the topic again and you should be on your way.

- At the end, is the appendix section of the book, I have provided two memory aids for you - all acronyms and formulae. There are quite a few acronyms that you will come across in the Agile vocabulary, so knowing what they stand for and used in which context, will easily help you clear few questions on the exam. Unless you are a mathematical geek, you will find the list of formulae helping you recap and clearing the mathematical questions in the exam. Note that there will be very few mathematical questions in the test, but if you see any, I want you to score full marks. Period.
- Once you are well prepared for the exam, you should attempt the three full-length mock tests given in the appendix of the book. Practice them with all seriousness as you would on the real exam - seclude yourself from distractions, clock your speed, complete within the stipulated 3 hours and calibrate your score. Learn and understand from the incorrect answers, but do not attempt the mock exams more than once, since obviously, an improved score might give you false confidence. I expect that you score 85% in these mock exams which will signal that you are ready for the real exam.
- Beyond this book, you will need to fulfil all the eligibility criteria laid out by PMI®. You will probably have to reach out to a PMI® Chapter in your region or contact a PMI® registered education provider (R.E.P.) to provide you a formal 21-hour course. Apart from that, try to refrain from looking up arbitrary content over the web. There are, perhaps, petabytes of information related to Agile topics and the PMI-ACP® exam. So do not confuse yourself or put yourself under undue stress with an overwhelming amount of preparation to do. As I told you, this book should be necessary and sufficient. Rest assured, you are in safe hands!
- Finally, I am very open to feedback. So if you have any, please feel free to pass them on.

CHAPTER 1

Domain I: Agile Principles and Mindset

Cause change and lead;

Accept change and survive;

Resist change and die.

—Raymond John Noorda (CEO of Novell between 1982 and 1994)

The PMI-ACP® certification recognizes an individual's expertize in Agile practices by putting equal focus on knowledge and skills as well as Agile tools and techniques. The Tools and Techniques area that spans 50% of the exam covers topics like estimation, planning, adapting, quality, metrics, communication, value-based analysis and prioritization to name but a few. The other 50% is dedicated to knowledge and skills. The discussion around these topics will constitute this book. But first and foremost, we need to understand the foundation concepts of the Agile framework; its contrasts with traditional (waterfall-based) project management; and most important, the Agile Manifesto and its guiding principles.

1.1 What Is Agile?

In the realm of software development, Agile is a philosophy. Agility is a mindset.

Agile, by itself, is not a methodology. It embodies practices, tools and a culture that allow the business and the technology team to closely collaborate and thrive in a zone of rapidly changing requirements and to deliver working code in an incremental and iterative manner. As an alternative to traditional project delivery that mostly uses a sequential or waterfall model, Agile uses a timeboxed approach to frequently deliver product increments and seek continuous feedback from the users, thereby being able to refine the system. The Agile philosophy is inherently lightweight and encourages teamwork between a set of cross-functional, self-organized and empowered members to deliver high-quality software.

The popular methodologies that follow the Agile values and principles include Extreme Programming (XP), Scrum, Kanban, Lean, Crystal, Dynamic Systems Development Method (DSDM) and Feature-Driven Development (FDD). These values and principles are stated in the Agile Manifesto, which is explained in detail later in the chapter. And the details of the methodologies themselves are described in Chapter 2: Agile Methodologies.

S. Boral, *Ace the PMI-ACP® exam*, DOI 10.1007/978-1-4842-2526-4_1

1.2 History of Agile

Although this section is not a topic for the exam, it is worthy to observe the evolution of different software development methodologies. The 1990s saw rapid proliferation of demand for software systems to manage evolving business needs. For a pretty long time, teams took the comfort of heavyweight waterfall-based processes to deliver software. But it was quickly realized that the lag between conceiving an idea to the delivery of the product must be reduced to withstand fierce competition in the market.

Most Agile practitioners regard the making of the Agile Manifesto in 2001 as the most important and initial milestone of the Agile journey.

However, that is not the case, as the Agile Manifesto was authored by experts who were advocating various lightweight methodologies for delivering software. And some of them existed several years before the manifesto was crafted.

It started out in 1974, when E. A. Edmonds wrote a paper on the adaptive software development process. And some of the roots can be traced back to Toyota's production system.

The 1990s saw more action.

- The Theory of Constraints was published by Goldratt in 1992, which spoke about identifying bottlenecks in a system and targeting all efforts to remove the same.
- In the mid-1990s, Jeff Sutherland and Ken Schwaber introduced Scrum to the world. Scrum delivered software through short timeboxes iterations that are preceded by a planning game and ends with a demo and retrospective. Scrum, is arguably, the most prevalent methodology that is followed in the Agile community.
- Around the same time, Kent Beck and Ward Cunningham started work on Extreme Programming, commonly referred to as XP. XP, to quote Kent Beck, "is a lightweight methodology for small-to-medium-sized teams developing software in the face of vague or rapidly changing requirements."
- Also in the mid-1990s other methodologies or frameworks also sprung up - namely Unified Framework (the most common adaptation being Rational Unified Process or RUP), Dynamic Systems Development Method (DSDM), Feature-Driven Development (FDD) and Alistair Cockburn's Crystal family of methodologies.

What was common between the various flavors was the lightweight, but sufficient practices and emphasis on close collaboration and communication between the delivery teams and business users. Each of them advocated people-centric ideas to frequently deliver valuable software to business. However, the term "Agile" was only coined in 2001 when a set of these experts came together, represented their areas and wish lists and came up with the Agile Manifesto.

It is now time to look into the Agile Manifesto in detail, the first important topic from the PMI-ACP® exam point of view.

1.3 The Agile Manifesto

On February 11-13, 2001, The Lodge at Snowbird ski resort in Utah witnessed a meeting between seventeen advocates of lightweight methodologies, seeking to discuss and identify any common ground for software development.

The meeting was attended by the following:[1]

Kent Beck	Mike Beedle	Arie van Bennekum
Alistair Cockburn	Ward Cunningham	Martin Fowler
James Grenning	Jim Highsmith	Andrew Hunt
Ron Jeffries	Jon Kern	Brian Marick
Robert C. Martin	Steve Mellor	Ken Schwaber
Jeff Sutherland	Dave Thomas	

During the meeting a few things happened:

- The word "Agile" was chosen to lay emphasis on ways that software development is expected to react to changing business circumstances. Other alternatives considered were 'lightweight' and 'adaptive'.
- The seventeen attendees formed a group and christened themselves as "The Agile Alliance."
- Each of the experts spent time listening to others and presenting their nuggets of wisdom based on their individual experiences that started several years ago before this meeting was decided. There were discussions around Extreme Programming (XP), Adaptive Software Development, Scrum, Feature-Driven Development, Dynamic Systems Development Method (DSDM) and many others.
- The Agile Software Development Manifesto emerged. The manifesto had four core values and is discussed in the next section.
- Along with the Agile Manifesto, the experts also agreed on twelve detailed statements that further explains agility.

In spite of a variety of experiences and individualism in the meeting, it is to be understood that the experts were not interested in merging all that was discussed and creating a brand new methodology to propose to the external world as a one-size-fits-all model. The real intent was to find an alternative to traditional project management practices that tends to, unfortunately, focus on documentation and the façade of process paraphernalia. The fact that the outcome of the meeting was a set of agreed core values and guiding principles led to discovery of a larger set of Agile practices and as advocated, tailored to meet the necessary but sufficient needs of the domain, business and technology needs of the world.

The meeting in 2001 and the Agile Manifesto had a widespread and significant impact to software engineering, project management, contract management, career paths for many, tooling and corporate strategy. We will explore more of these throughout the book, but for now, let us focus on the four core values of the Agile Manifesto and dissect each phrase of it.

[1]Information sourced and adapted from `http://agilemanifesto.org/`

1.3.1 Four Core Values of the Agile Manifesto

The Manifesto for Agile Software Development states:

> We are uncovering better ways of developing software by doing it and helping others do it. Through this work we have come to value:
>
> **Individuals and interactions** over processes and tools
>
> **Working software** over comprehensive documentation
>
> **Customer collaboration** over contract negotiation
>
> **Responding to change** over following a plan
>
> That is, while there is value in the items on the right, we value the items on the left more.

1.3.2 The Agile Manifesto Explained

The Agile Manifesto is a popular reference within the Agile community and is also an important topic for the PMI-ACP® exam. You can expect a few questions in the exam on this topic. A few generic points to remember on the framing of the Agile Manifesto:

- To begin with, let us focus on the first line. The word "We" evidently refers to the Agile Alliance group consisting of practitioners of lightweight software development.
- The second half of the sentence that says "doing it and helping others" emphasizes that the four values were arrived by seasoned practitioners who believe in being hands-on and then sharing the learnings that they gathered during several years of continuous involvement.
- As shown in Figure 1-1, the rest of the Manifesto is presented in a format of "We value A over B." This means that while there is value in doing B (e.g., processes), they would rather advocate A (i.e. interaction) any day as a better way of developing software. To quote Jim Highsmith:[2] "In order to succeed in the new economy, to move aggressively into the era of e-business, e-commerce and the web, companies have to rid themselves of their Dilbert manifestations of make-work and arcane policies. This freedom from the inanities of corporate life attracts proponents of Agile Methodologies and scares the begeebers out of traditionalists."

[2]Refer `http://agilemanifesto.org/history.html`

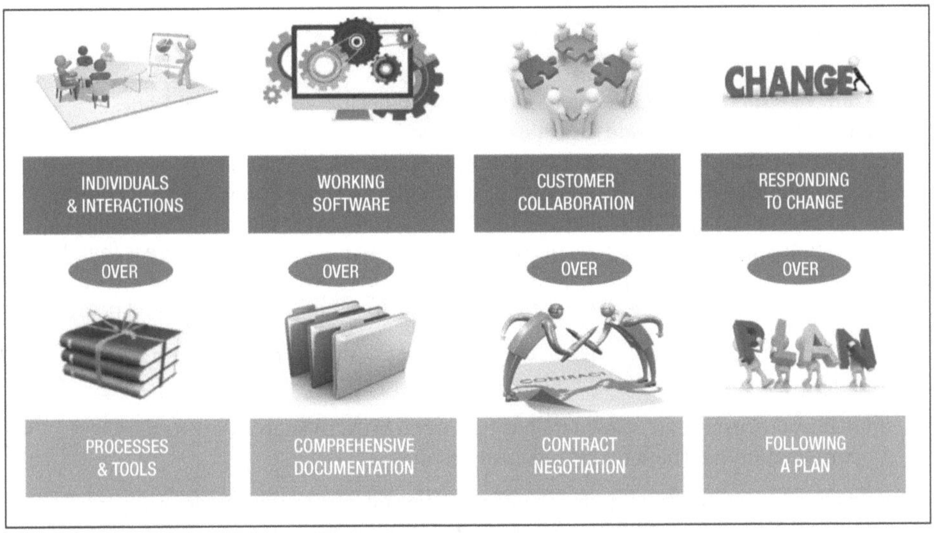

***Figure 1-1.** The Agile Manifesto*

- The Agile Manifesto, although simple, is not prescriptive. It is indeed powerful in terms of focus on people and value-based delivery and welcoming changes.
- The four values are also not independent and go hand in hand.

Let us now look into each of the four values one by one.

1.3.2.1 Individuals and Interactions over Processes and Tools

This value emphasizes the people in the team and the interactions within them rather than a heavy-process mindset and an armory of project management tools.

The appreciation comes from the fact that in contrast to operations or manufacturing industries, software engineering being an inherent knowledge-based work cannot afford to undermine the power of collaboration and individuals talking to each other. The value doesn't say that processes are an overhead or cannot help in delivering projects, nor does it say that Agile projects (of any scale) are completely devoid of processes and tools. But, be it trawling requirements from customers, elucidating scope to analysts and developers, triaging and troubleshooting defects, it is the people who plays the dominant role. So the focus should be on people and not on just fulfilling the 'heavy-weight' process requirement that might not be even applicable to all real-world situations. This value states that processes and tools might be helpful, but without effective collaboration between individuals in an Agile project team delivery is not possible. It is never realistic to assume that fool-proof processes will be as effective as face-to-face conversations and periodic interaction between the users who define the project, express their needs and experience, set its acceptability criteria and go on to use them. Agile teams are empowered to tailor the process based on what they consider as essential in the specific context of their project (and the organization) and evolve the same through periodic introspection.

1.3.2.2 Working Software over Comprehensive Documentation

This value reminds us that until the software is delivered to production, it adds no value to the customer. The only measure of a usability of a product is feedback based on working code, as Alistair Cockburn puts it, "Running code is ruthlessly honest."

To understand this value, let us consider the example of a screen development for a web page. In traditional methodologies the analysts will spend a lot of time specifying and designing the 'look and feel' of the screens by trying to anticipate the needs of the end user. Writing such a detailed document is tedious and is not cherished by most. But the underlying assumption here is that the document, if sufficiently detailed, will provide all the necessary inputs that a developer will ever require to build the web page. This has a few anticipated problems though, as mentioned below:

- It is almost impossible for a person to *initially* specify *exactly* how a screen should look like or be perceived by an end user.
- In reality, end users can change their minds frequently, so keeping up-to-date documentation is a challenging and costly affair.
- Considering the fact that significant effort is invested in creating a supposedly 'rock-solid' and elaborate document, this can give a false sense of progress. Projects are initiated to deliver valuable software and until that is available, we have built up a huge backlog of detailed specification documents ('work-in-progress' items) that does not contribute tangible value.
- If more some reason the project is terminated in the middle of the project, what will be left behind is a pile of documents that yields no value to the end user. Even if there was a few working screens, they could have added some benefit.

In contrast, frequent delivery of working software gives more comfort at measuring progress for the users and developers alike and provides an opportunity for inviting and incorporating real-time feedback, which is extremely valuable. Not a fraction of this value can be realized by showing a document or even securing a sign-off on a document.

However, before we leave this point, we have to appreciate that to a fair extent, documentation is required. For example people might move (e.g., get reallocated to other projects or leave a company) and it is important that the knowledge of the system stick around so that the product can be maintained, supported in production, or enhanced based on evolving needs. Or for that matter, there are reports and documents that go out to regulators and used to fulfill legal and compliance requirements. Agile teams, like others, should still invest effort behind producing these essential documents and factor them in the list of deliverables on their backlog. Project documents that are created solely to transfer information between various team members working on the same project is not considered efficient and hence discouraged. In summary, this value recommends 'barely sufficient' documentation for Agile teams.

1.3.2.3 Customer Collaboration over Contract Negotiation

This value focuses on building a relationship based on trust that spans across organization boundaries between the customer and the vendor or service provider of the software. In traditional projects, contracts are rigid, in the sense that both sides are coerced (or legally bound) to obey the elements of scope, time and cost (also called *The triple constraints*). In the realistic event of a change in any of these three parameters, a sophisticated change control process, takes over. Approvals of such change controls take a long time and at times, could make the progress frustratingly slow. A typical dialogue between a customer and a project manager, in the event of a change is shown in Figure 1-2.

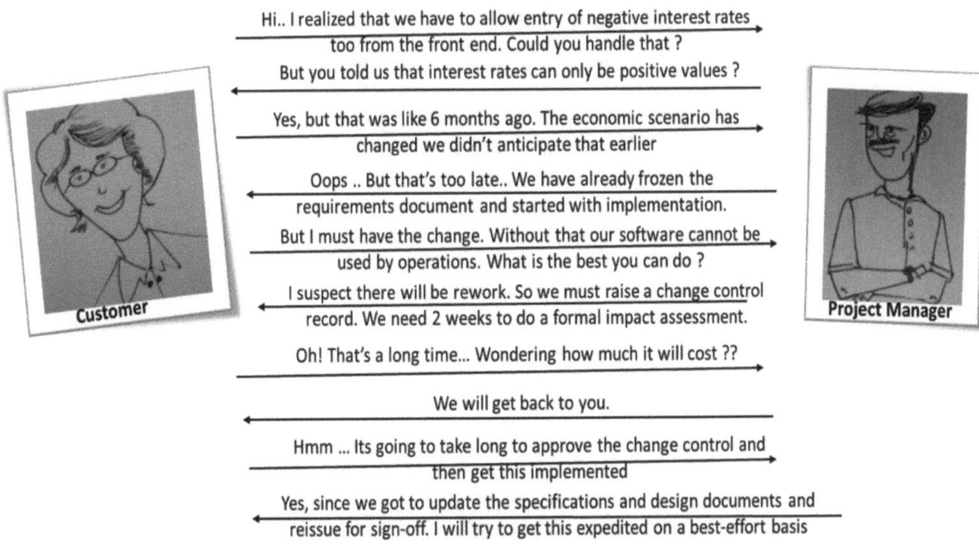

Figure 1-2. *Handling a change in traditional projects*

As an alternative approach, it is anticipated that, by its inherent nature, software development will be affected by changing business conditions or technology solutions from time to time. Rather than negotiating with the customer on the scope and enforcing rigorous change management (which is often unfortunately seen as change suppression) techniques, it is in the interest of both the customer and the vendor to collaborate, be flexible and drive toward a common goal. This gives rise to a more trusted relationship and could be facilitated by more creative and proactive provisions made upfront in the Agile contract itself. (We shall deal with the details of Agile contracting later in the book.) Alistair Cockburn[3] goes on to the extent of commenting that "Good collaboration can sometimes make a contract unnecessary".

1.3.2.4 Responding to Change over Following a Plan

The final value embodies the fact that Agile acknowledges and embraces change and not treat that as an exception.

Traditional projects invest a substantial effort in developing a detailed project plan, consisting of detailed schedules, allocation and critical paths. The project team is supposed to follow this plan from start to finish. And in the event of a change, re-planning and re-baselining needs to be done to make sure that the plan is up to date and reflects the changes.

In the case of Agile projects, upfront detailed planning is considered counterproductive and inefficient because of the uncertainties involved. A fair amount of planning happens just in time or at the last responsible moment. This is also called *Rolling Wave Planning*. Development is timeboxed into finite iterations (say one month) and it follows the principle of rolling wave planning. This means that the work items for the upcoming iteration is well detailed out and the others are left coarse-grained. Once the iteration is over, only then is the next iteration planned out. And this gives an opportunity to look around and see if there are any changes in scope or prioritization that need to be attended to. Figure 1-3 shows the effect of change between traditional and Agile projects.

[3]Reference to the book by Alistair Cockburn, *Agile Software Development: The Cooperative Game*, 2nd ed. (Upper Saddle River, NJ: Pearson Education, 2006).

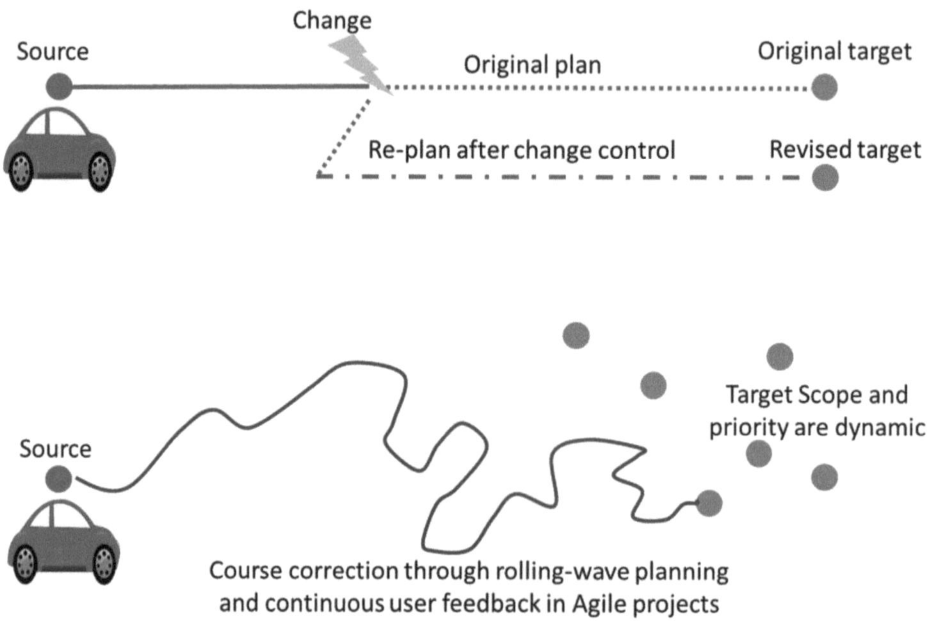

Figure 1-3. *The effect of change on traditional projects versus Agile projects*

Such is the emphasis on responding to customer feedback, which several companies these days proactively monitor social media and derive analytics from several streams of unstructured chatter. Based on these analytics, they take decisions to transform their product, take corrective actions or add features, sometimes ahead of other planned deliverables.

1.4 The Twelve Agile Principles

The authors of the manifesto also came up with a set of twelve principles that supplement the Agile Manifesto and explain agility. Like the core values in the manifesto, these principles are very important to be understood and is helpful from the PMI-ACP® exam perspective. There could be tricky questions where one or more choices could appear to be correct, but by applying the core values and these principles, you should choose the best answer or eliminate the wrong ones.

It is also important to realize that different Agile methodologies (we talk about them in Chapter 2) are based on these values and principles. While the practices and characteristics could be unique, the generic principles still hold up well.

The original text of principles (in bold-faced font below) are from the source:

`https://www.agilealliance.org/agile101/12-principles-behind-the-agile-manifesto/`

Here is what it states and its explanation:

1. **Our highest priority is to satisfy the customer through early and continuous delivery of valuable software.**

The first principle is admittedly the most important one and hence worthy on spending some time on it. Customers seek software to add value to their business – whether it is to secure market share, increase their profit margins, stay in business, or even respond to regulatory laws. Such is the importance, that Agile development prioritizes delivering to business over anything else like processes, documentation and so on.

The word "early" is important. Agile aims at delivery to business as early as possible, even if it is in the form of chunks of prioritized features that add value. The intent is to ratify the requirements, receive feedback, incorporate them and also retrospect on internal processes.

The next significant word in this principle is *"continuous."* Agile delivery maximizes flow; ruthlessly removes waste; and, by following a continuous operating rhythm, ensures that valuable software is with business and adequate provisions are there for instant feedback and, course correction (let's say reprioritization). So how does Agile achieve this? In contrast to traditional software development life cycle, Agile does a little bit of analysis, development, testing, build, integration and deployment at frequent timeboxed intervals called iterations. These iterations could be anywhere between 2 to 4 weeks, although projects might want to choose a number that best suits themselves. This means that customers get valuable software delivery continuously, that is, at regular predictive intervals. Once in the hands of the customer, the software is likely to generate revenue and if the circumstances change (e.g., due to economic, competitive, or regulatory reasons), an immediate feedback and course - correction can be requested without going through lengthy processes of change management as prevalent in traditional waterfall methodologies.

The final word to focus on this principle is *"valuable."* Agile development does not require a detailed specification of features and programs to be built. As we will see later on the book, it works on a backlog that is maintained by a person whose job is to ensure that the maximum ROI (return on investment) is realized for every iteration. This backlog is prioritized continuously and the ones that are highest in value get picked by the team to deliver, bearing their capacity in mind. This means that at any point in time, the features or components that are deemed most valuable are being worked upon. There is also a latent upside in this. In the event that the project's funding dries up, or the sponsor considers the project not viable to proceed, it will still be left with a working version, albeit with limited functions. If this were to happen in waterfall projects during the development phase, all that we would be left with is a project plan (that is now obsolete), requirement specifications, high-level and low-level design documents and half-cooked (read untested) code, with unrealized value.

2. **Welcome changing requirements, even late in development. Agile processes harness change for the customer's competitive advantage.**

The second principle share one thing in common with the first one – the customer focus. And it also ties back to the core value in the Agile Manifesto that favors "Responding to change over following a plan." As previously discussed, the onerous change management processes in waterfall project management practices prohibit agility. It could, particularly, prove to be fatal where the organization's inability to make quick and important changes to their software leads to a loss to its competitors at the marketplace.

Agile methodologies, on the other hand, accept and expect changes continuously, some of which could be late breaking. Some of these changes could cause significant deviation from the past and might need the architecture and design to evolve rather drastically. Agile project management does not require comprehensive documentation of change controls, lengthy approval processes and re-baselining of project plans. By virtue of the principle of continuous and frequent delivery principle and the use of timeboxed iterations, it takes the changes in the stride. Note that it doesn't mean that Agile doesn't analyze the functional and nonfunctional impact of the changes adequately. It does it, but just that the process followed is lightweight and adaptive.

3. **Deliver working software frequently, from a couple of weeks to a couple of months, with a preference to the shorter timescale.**

The third principle seriously gets into numbers. Agile advocates short bursts of development in contrast to thorough and detailed implementation that can span over months or years. The realization is that change is inevitable during the course of large projects and without early and continuous feedback we could be on the wrong track very soon, leading to sunk costs.

In this context, Agile follows a strategy called *"Fail-fast."* The word "fail" obviously brings about a negative connotation. But what it means is doing something (say a proof-of concept or a prototype), soliciting rapid feedback from real users and then incorporating the same until the most usable version is built. This particularly works in situations that are uncertain (up to a limit, of course) and the requirements are volatile; and it is found that a sample prototype will help to arrive at the decision around the requirements. Needless to mention, it saves a lot of time and money.

Note that none of the Agile methodologies are prescriptive in choosing the duration and leaves it to the project team to pick what suits them the best and paying due consideration to the pace at which business can accept the incremental changes. Agile practitioners resort to tools that help them track, manage versions, build, integrate and deploy changes to keep up with the pace and maintain continuum.

Finally, there is another subtle benefit of short cycles. A short cycle makes business committed and engaged to the affairs of the project. They partake in requirements clarification, planning and giving feedback to the team at frequent intervals. In fact, in an era of rapid development, it is difficult and discomforting for a customer to sanction a project for a year and not stay in touch all the time. We shall see more on this during the discussion on the choice of iteration length in Chapter 6: Adaptive planning. This is a perfect segue into the next principle.

4. **Business people and developers must work together daily throughout the project.**

This principle is somewhat hard to achieve, but it is strongly recommended since the software to be delivered is for the business. Whether it is the iteration planning session or the demo at the end of every iteration, the presence of business users alongside the development team is invaluable. We've experienced how face-to-face communication is the richest form and how other means like documentation (and their approval or sign-off process), e-mails and dozens of conference calls can slow down the process of information interchange. And not to forget the camaraderie it brings about between the technology and the business community that are working toward a shared goal.

However, there are some known challenges and Table 1-1 shows how Agile teams look to mitigate them.

Table 1-1. *Communication challenges and how Agile teams look to overcome them*

Communication challenges	Some strategies to overcome them
The Agile team and business may not be co-located. This is a realistic problem where • A software is being built to serve multiple lines of business, often at various geographical locations. • The software has many components that are being codeveloped by developers based out of multiple locations, often in different time zones.	In such cases the Agile team should find a common time and use forms of technology like video conferencing to bring the virtual team together on a frequent basis and use collaboration tools for synchronized progress. It should be emphasized that however, dispersed the team is, it is a common goal that all are aiming for. It might be helpful to bring the team together physically, especially at the beginning of the project as that is a form of team building, helps to remove some cultural barriers and communication.
The business people might have limited availability and their 'daily' meeting commitment may not be fulfilled.	As prevalent in XP, if the onsite customer is not present for a particular event, the role can be filled with product managers, domain experts, interaction designers and business analysts. These are called proxy users. It is not ideal, but helps to move forward. Note that it is also recommended that the onsite customer or the proxy user should remain intact throughout and not change frequently.

5. **Build projects around motivated individuals. Give them the environment and support they need and trust them to get the job done.**

Project are for the people and by the people. And this Agile principle stresses a people-centric approach. In fact, this gels well with the first core value in the Agile Manifesto that favors "Individuals and interactions over processes and tools." Different Agile methodologies have different roles like coach, Scrum master, etc., but at the heart of it is the belief that motivated people are a critical success factor in an Agile project. Agile teams are self-organized and they are empowered to make decisions as a group. Indeed, because of this, whether it is requirements collection, release planning, or estimation, it is the collaboration and group consensus that plays the dominant role. Mention should also be made of the "*swarming*" tendency prevalent in Kanban teams, where team members look to help each other and finish items that are in a work-in-progress state *before* they accept new work, thereby maximizing the flow and throughput.

This principle is fairly contrasting with traditional role of project managers where they hire or source specific skill-sets and typically, armed with a detailed project plan, follows a command-and-control style to get work progressed. With the increase of popularity of Agile methods, classic project management roles are often compared against those of Agile leaders like Scrum masters. The contrast is that Agile leaders steer away from any element of micromanaging. Agile leaders look to bring in a motivated bunch of people, create an atmosphere that is transparent and collaborative, encourage synergies among team members, remove roadblocks in the reaching the project-specific goals, pursue a journey of continuous improvement and take pride in what gets delivered.

6. **The most efficient and effective method of conveying information to and within a development team is face-to-face conversation.**

We have spoken about this principle while discussing the earlier ones. We will talk further about *tacit knowledge* and *osmotic communication* that is common in Agile teams where team members rely on information picked up by just being collocated. Indeed such is the emphasis of co-location and face-to-face communication, Agile team are found to frequently arrange themselves, furniture and logistics around themselves. Examples are writable walls (of course, erasable too), board or spaces where sticky notes can be put up, pair programming desks and boards radiating information on metrics and progress.

Finally, like all other values and principles, this one is not prescriptive. Agile experts do realize that as projects scale, the need for communication (and documentation) becomes heavier. So the communication methods should be tailored to the specific needs of the project.

7. **Working software is the primary measure of progress.**

In line with the core value of Agile Manifesto that favors "Working Software over comprehensive documentation," the authors cannot stop repeating the value of working code. Of all the metrics to measure and report progress, only working software is worth the investment. Documentation in the form of project plan, requirements specification and design may be useful, but not as valuable as working software. The real test of working comes through the validation and acceptance process; and unless this is achieved, the software does not add real value.

It is to be realized that the same documents become an overhead and liability in the event of a change. Especially from the product management point of view, documentation carried over from one project to next, it becomes extremely difficult to maintain and could easily become obsolete. In the later chapters we will talk about "*definition of done*" where a team marks a work item as complete only when the product increment passes the acceptance criteria. On Agile projects, it is extremely unlikely to see completed or signed-off documents as 'doneness' criteria - and for obvious reasons.

8. **Agile processes promote sustainable development. The sponsors, developers and users should be able to maintain a constant pace indefinitely.**

This is an interesting and important principle. It calls for a sustainable pace of development, such that the team is happy, motivated and is able to leverage good working relationships between one another and business.

From all of the discussions so far, it creates a perception that Agile is characterized by repeated iterations of extremely rapid planning, estimation, development, testing and deployment and of course, often with elements of rework as the inevitable change strikes. While all this happens, it is important to note that the pace should be just right, so that people do not get burned out easily. Motivated people are the critical success factors for a project and it is no secret that a disturbance in the work-life equilibrium (because of long hours or frustrating rework or a poor build process) could actually lower the productivity drastically. In extreme cases, people might choose to leave, leading to loss of productivity and incurring the burden of hiring and onboarding.

There are a few things that Agile teams do (or often like to do):

- In daily meetings, the team capture the mood of people with the help of, the over-simplistic style of smileys depicting a range of emotions like mad, sad, or glad. The 'team barometer' is an important aid to understand whether the team is under stress for a prolonged duration of time or not.
- If the team discovers that they have under-committed work during an iteration they can talk to the product owner and transparently share the situation. This is generally, not a problem because the team might choose to pick up more work items from the backlog.
- In the opposite scenario if the team discovers that they have over-committed, then also they can speak to the product owner and explain the situation. Of course, a little bit of stretch effort from a passionate and committed Agile team member is not a bad thing. But the problem can arise if and when it repeatedly becomes a necessity thus burning out people, making them cut corners as far as quality is concerned and disturbing their work-life balance.
- At frequent intervals (e.g., retrospectives) teams get together to inspect and adapt. They identify what works, what doesn't and agree to improve the situation. Issues around sustainable pace of development are important topics to discuss during team retrospectives. The team could make simple decisions like something that takes the manual drudgery out and helps to repeat an activity (e.g. an automated build) many times during the development life cycle.
- Realistically test if people are enjoying what they are doing; and given a chance, would they really want to continue what they are doing?
- Share ownership and celebrate achievements as a team.

9. **Continuous attention to technical excellence and good design enhances agility.**

The synonyms of Agile are adaptive and maneuverability. This principle essentially, goes one level deep and makes note that a clean design (let's say object-oriented one) is easier to change. Since in Agile all the requirements are not known upfront, there is no way that a full-blown architecture and design can be built in day one. Hence the design and the code should be kept as simple, efficient so that it can be evolved and updated easily.

In this context, let us introduce the term of "*technical debt.*" As with any legacy system, design and code becomes complex over a period of time. This is inadvertently, as a result, of making hasty and tactical changes for one project after the next, without paying much attention to the overall simplicity of the design in mind. The result is that design and code becomes more difficult to change, leading to lengthy effort and costs, as well as risks and uncertainties incurred in dealing with unknowns. This is called technical debt. And like financial debt, this accumulates and grows interests over time, which implies that it worsens unless some corrective actions are undertaken.

Agile teams understand the need for keeping a balance between feature development and curbing the complexities arising out of technical debt by following some practices like the following:

- *Refactoring code* as in Extreme Programming - this is a practice where the developers continuously look at opportunities to reorganize, clean up and ensure that the code is in a maintainable state. All this is done without impacting the functionality or behavior. However, this comes with a cost but is worth the effort.
- Invest behind tools like SQALE (Software Quality Assessment based on Lifecycle Expectations), which helps to evaluate the technical debt. Based on a set of rules configured, such tools can precisely measure the nonfunctional attributes of code like reusability, portability and maintainability. And more importantly, produce an estimate of the level of effort involved to remove a particular debt such that the team can factor it in during their estimation process.
- Invest behind automation testing for their regression cycles such that the impact of change can be easily and quickly detected and addressed.

10. **Simplicity—the art of maximizing the amount of work not done—is essential.**

Given a chance, why would someone *not* want to keep things simple? It's because *it is hard* to keep things simple. Producing something simple that can adapt itself is not easy. The normal human tendency, as far as software development, acts just the opposite. Developers can be casually taking pride in creating more and more rich features, often to an extent that some of them may never get to be used. Not only does these prolong the project and create more opportunities for defects in the system (hence, prolong further to remove the defects), but it also contribute to technical debt. As discussed in the previous section, technical debt compounds the difficulty in adapting to future changes.

This concept is well articulated in the literature on Lean, details of which we will cover in the following chapter. The Lean philosophy is aggressive about eliminating waste and thereby maintaining focus of the team only on essential tasks that add value to the customer.

Another example of practicing simplicity is seen in Agile teams who frequently come up with *Minimal Marketable Features* (MMF). This is the smallest piece of the product that can be built and implemented, yet it adds value to the real user.

11. **The best architectures, requirements and designs emerge from self-organizing teams.**

In this principle, the authors believe that like requirements, design and architecture should also evolve. They found little value in doing and signing off on an architecture too early in the project, such that it is very difficult to adapt it to changes as anticipated during the course of the project.

The experts also advocated that the team who is working on the project is the best-placed to do the design and architecture themselves, rather than designated architects who are external to the team and do a one-off job and hand it over to the development team. It is known from experience that in some instances, an initial architecture could be too difficult to implement in a constrained environment and hence may not be accepted by the developer at all. Moreover since the initial architecture rarely remains as-is and is subject to change on the fly, the architects and designer (who were external to the team) may disown them at a later stage.

With all this, the experts reckoned that self-organizing teams know what the right approach is, are aware of the nuances of the system and its interfaces and take pride in adjusting the same from time to time. They can start with simple architectures at a fraction of the cost and gradually evolve them as they build more features to it. Such a team does not need to be told or 'sold a design,' but rather feels motivated to own the system development from start to finish. And of course, if there is a problem, they can always step back, introspect and adapt.

In what we have stated above, there is an underlying assumption and rather an important one. It is assumed that the developers are good at coming up with simple designs and also have the innate capability to read and learn what is in there and ultimately refactor as needed. They are also good at unearthing nonfunctional requirements about reusability, performance, stress, reliability and scalability.

12. **At regular intervals, the team reflects on how to become more effective, then tunes and adjusts its behavior accordingly.**

This principle is the fundamental one, without which Agile teams cannot improve. In traditional projects, a lessons learned exercise is part of project closure formality and the value of the document collated is questionable. If there are no two project that are run under identical conditions, will the lessons learned from one be applicable to the future project? With so many projects being churned out year after year, will a future team member really have the time and patience to dig up old lessons learned and choose what is applicable to him/her?

Agile projects embody a practice called *retrospectives* at the end of each iteration. This is a forum where the team takes the opportunity to reflect on their own - what is going well, what needs to change and what should be stopped. At the end of the retrospective meeting, the team agrees and comes up with a list of activities that they commit to improve from the next cycle. The flavor of instant application of the ideas are hugely beneficial; and of course, since the team came up with the ideas themselves, they are the best judge to measure and assess its benefit themselves.

As we now close this section, we realize that the core values and the principles work hand in hand. You will notice that we have intentionally introduced a few terms from the Agile vocabulary in this section. This is just to remind you that the rest of the book really uses the core values and principles as the foundation. So, while you continue reading the rest of the chapters and get exposed to more terms, feel free to introspect on what values and principles of Agile they are related to. If you do this exercise well, you are guaranteed to score heavily on this topic. It is the base, so it means a lot for you!

1.5 The Declaration of Interdependence

The Agile Manifesto gained popularity ever since it was published in 2001. With that, a number of people from the leadership and management cadre expressed a need to explore applicability of this manifesto to project and product management for communities outside software engineering. It is told that a few product managers, project managers and leaders came together and formed the Agile Project Leadership network (APLN) in 2005. They started with the Agile Manifesto and came up with a set of six principles based on it. This is called the Declaration of Interdependence (DOI).

The DOI is mostly aimed at leaders and project managers. The DOI states:[4]

Agile and adaptive approaches for linking people, projects and value

We are a community of project leaders that are highly successful at delivering results. To achieve these results:

We **increase return on investment** by making continuous flow of value our focus.

We **deliver reliable results** by engaging customers in frequent interactions and shared ownership.

We **expect uncertainty** and manage for it through iterations, anticipation and adaptation.

We **unleash creativity and innovation** by recognizing that individuals are the ultimate source of value and creating an environment where they can make a difference.

We **boost performance** through group accountability for results and shared responsibility for team effectiveness.

We **improve effectiveness and reliability** through situationally specific strategies, processes and practices.

[4]Refer to `www.pmdoi.org`

You are somewhat unlikely to find a question in the PMI-ACP® exam on DOI, but it is still worthwhile to understand the concepts. So let us now explore each of these a little more.

We increase return on investment by making continuous flow of value our focus. - This emphasizes the concept of "value-driven delivery," where each piece of feature development is backed by the highest business value, which in turn maximizes the ROI at any point of time. As Lean philosophy teaches us, value realization comes by decreasing the batch size and inventory. It can be pursued by elimination of waste (e.g., non-value added processes) and striving for continuous improvement.

We deliver reliable results by engaging customers in frequent interactions and shared ownership. - In contrast to prolonged requirements eliciting phase in traditional methodologies, this focuses on collaborative culture between the customers or business users and the team to understand the requirement, their evolution over a period of time and being open to incorporate feedback without any onerous change management process.

We expect uncertainty and manage for it through iterations, anticipation and adaptation. - Rather than create and follow a rigid plan and undergo substantial efforts to replan in the event of a change, this statement focuses on just-in-time planning for short iterations, anticipating change, reviewing at the end of each iteration and then adapting to change for the subsequent iteration. Another way to manage uncertainty is to get team members cross-trained in different skills or technology such that they are equipped to help the team tide over hurdles, thereby smoothing the flow.

We unleash creativity and innovation by recognizing that individuals are the ultimate source of value and creating an environment where they can make a difference. - This statement encourages leaders to create an environment that fosters positivity, stimulation, productivity and reward.

We boost performance through group accountability for results and shared responsibility for team effectiveness. - This is a radical statement where teams are empowered to make decisions on their own rather than being asked to follow a decision. Being a part of a decision-making process themselves, a team is more likely to exhibit a greater degree of commitment and ownership for the outcome of the project.

We improve effectiveness and reliability through situationally specific strategies, processes and practices. - This statement reminds us that there is no "one-size-fits-all" approach. Instead Agile processes, tools and techniques might need tailoring based on the environment and circumstances.

1.6 Comparison between Waterfall and Agile Methods

So far we have covered the values and principles in Agile and during the discussion, we have often contrasted between the waterfall and Agile methods. We take a closer look at both in this section.

1.6.1 Waterfall Method

In the case of waterfall methods each phase follows the other in linear sequence. The analysis phase can only start when the requirements phase is completed. Once analysis is done, the high-level design phase can start. Similarly when design is completed, implementation can begin. When implementation is over, testing begins. And finally once testing gets over, the team can proceed to deployment. The observation over here is that there is no provision to go back from one step to its previous step(s). The analogy is with the flow of water in the direction of gravity - hence the name waterfall.

In the waterfall method, there is a lengthy process of requirement collection and analysis that is documented and then handed over to the design team. Once the scope is finalized, the project manager prepares a project plan to deliver the solution. Throughout the project, metrics are collected and are compared against the baseline version. If there are variances found (e.g., in parameters of cost or time), corrective actions are taken and the plan is updated accordingly.

If during testing, defects are raised and those trace back to the design or requirements, fixing them is rather costly. Same is the situation when a change is introduced in a later phase. Once a change request is approved, it might take considerable rework and effort to alter the design and implementation.

1.6.1.1 Application of Waterfall Method

Waterfall models are well suited for projects that have clear, unambiguous, well-understood requirements that are unlikely to change. By tracking well-defined milestones (through quality gates) like design signed-off or code review done, it is relatively easy to monitor the progress of waterfall projects.

1.6.1.2 Limitations of Waterfall Method

There are a few notable limitations of the traditional waterfall-based software development:

- Since the phases follow each other serially, the **total time required to complete the project is the sum of the times required to complete each phase**. This means that projects that are constrained on a shorter schedule are likely to suffer unless they exploit some type of concurrent development strategies like fast-tracking. Fast-tracking, however, carries with itself the risk of rework.
- There are **no provisions of going back**. Trying to do so, especially in the case of fixing a defect, or addressing an approved change control is an effort-intensive and costly affair. Hence waterfall methods are not suitable where requirements are fuzzy, ambiguous and expected to evolve or change over a period of time.
- There is also a **considerable time lag between when the specifications are written and business gets the software**. During this intervening time, the customer may not be regularly engaged and it is quite possible that the design or implementation has deviated from the stated or unstated goals of the customer. Moreover, scope changes as a response to evolving business conditions, which are quite usual, are difficult to accommodate.
- **Creating a detailed project plan with schedules and milestones takes a considerable effort upfront**. More effort is spent in keeping the plan up-to-date and rebaselined in the event of a change request.

1.6.2 Agile Methods

As described in the previous sections on core values and principles, Agile methods were crafted to address some of the pitfalls of waterfall methodology. This is illustrated in the following Figure 1-4. Instead of sequential phases, Agile methods have fixed timeboxed iterations or sprints where there is analysis, design, development and testing - the ultimate outcome of which is a product increment that can be deployed for customer use. The team seeks feedback from the customers continuously and collaborate to add features, refactor the code and incorporate feedback incrementally. Because of this working style, Agile projects are able to respond to change more flexibly and keep the product features thriving and up-to-date with the latest developments in the industry.

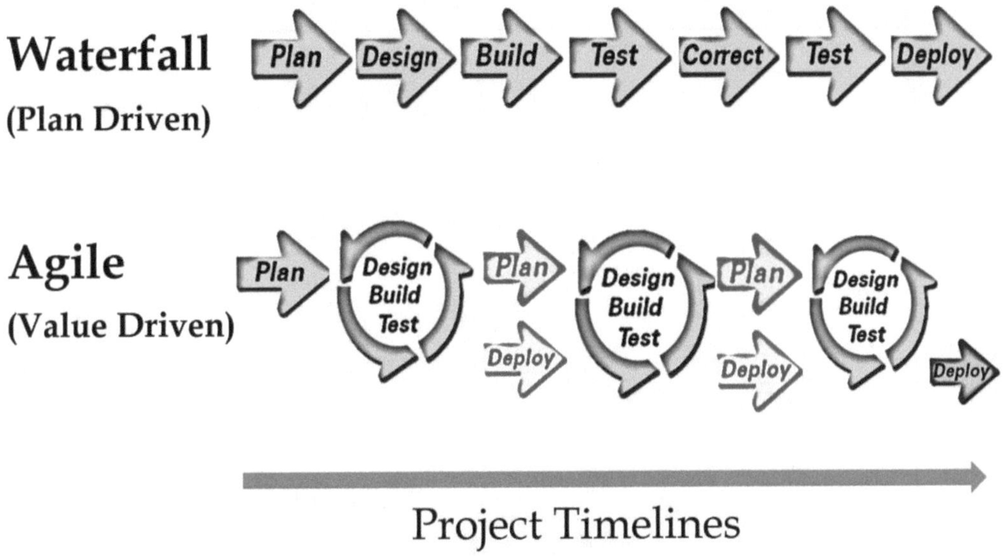

Figure 1-4. *Contrasting Waterfall and Agile methods*

1.6.2.1 Application of Agile Methods

Agile methods are particularly suited where the scope of the project is expected to evolve and there is lack of a clear view of the final product or expectations of the customer in the beginning. It is particularly true when a product undergoes cycles of rapidly changing requirements or standards to meet the demands of the environment.

Let us now look at an adapted version of Stacey's matrix in Figure 1-5 to understand the complexity of the situation and where Agile methods could potentially work best. Stacey has plotted certainty of the requirements against the perceived agreement from stakeholders.[5]

[5]Refer to Ralph D. Stacey's book *Strategic Management and Organisational Dynamics: The challenge of complexity to ways of thinking about organisations.* (New York: Pearson, 2011).

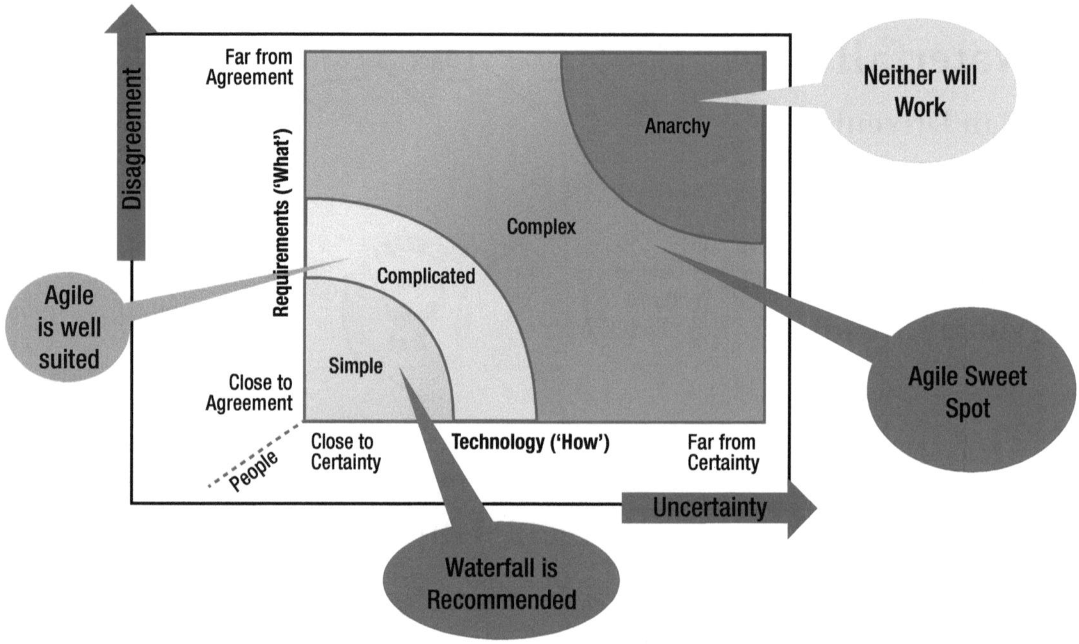

Figure 1-5. *Stacey's matrix*

At the bottom left corner is the zone that is called "simple." This is the region where requirements are fairly certain and there is good consensus around. Best practices prevail and rational decision-making is based on established facts. Traditional project management, which is waterfall-based and follows a plan works the best in this situation.

Slight north of this zone is the area that denotes high levels of disagreements, but certainty on how the results are achieved. For such an area the decisions take a political hue and coalitions, working relationships, negotiations and compromises dominate.

To the right of the "simple" zone is the area with a high degree of consensus about a goal is there, but certainty of the means of achieving the goal is lacking. Typical examples will be where organization set a five-year vision, but it's hard to detail out minute steps on a project plan.

At the extreme right corner is the zone of "chaos" or anarchy indicated by high levels if uncertainty and disagreement. It is hard to believe whether any methodology would work in this case. Organizations would rather withdraw or avoid such a situation until stability comes back.

The middle of the matrix, probably the largest space, is the zone of complexity. This is typically characterized by moderate levels of uncertainty and disagreement. Agile works pretty well in such domains that are complicated and complex, as it requires a custom approach and being able to maneuver based on evolving conditions. This area is considered the *Agile sweet spot.*

1.6.2.2 Benefits of Using Agile

We've covered a lot of ground in this chapter. Let us now try to summarize the perceived benefits of using Agile methodologies.

- Increase wallet share quickly - by incremental delivery it is possible to realize some business benefits even though the full product has not been built.

- Reduce cost of making a change - by anticipating change and being able to quickly adapt.
- Speed up delivery - by continuous focus on elimination of waste, limiting work in progress and relentless pursuit of continuous improvement.
- Generate value from the user's perspective - by ensuring that only the items that brings the maximum ROI are implemented first.
- Reduced Risk - by following a 'fail-fast' strategy (explained above) and not planning too far ahead.
- Ensure visibility and transparency - by encouraging active user involvement and soliciting feedback from the user after every iteration.
- Increasing quality - by producing frequent and incremental code builds that allow the opportunity to detect and fix bugs quickly.
- Increased motivation in the team - because it break silos between "us" and "them" and the team members are empowered to take decisions.

1.6.2.3 Limitations of Agile Methods

While we have spoken favorably about Agile methods so far, there are some criticisms that can be heard among the software development community. Again, this is not a topic for the exam, but helps to understand the overall concepts presented earlier in the chapter.

Some of the common topics of debate are:

- When applied in large and complex projects, Agile methods make it **difficult to provide an estimate**. The high-level estimates of costs and schedule are usually enablers for a project to be sanctioned and approved.
- Agile Manifesto demands **'daily' collaboration with users**. In many cases, especially for projects with long duration, this may not be practically possible. It is possible to substitute with proxy users, but that has a potential to go wrong.
- Experienced and cross-functional resources are required for project deliveries and decision-making. This could **make it hard for specialists and new joiners** to get easily integrated with the team. New joiners, particularly, could have a hard time owing to lack of documentation and tacit knowledge takes time to build.
- By lowering the emphasis on documentation, there could be a **tendency to avoid documentation altogether** and that could create a challenge for knowledge retention and ongoing support and maintenance of the project.
- In a spirit for delivering rapidly, the team could be inclined to **take hasty decisions without a thorough analysis** assuming that there is always an opportunity to "refactor" or change later. This could lead to considerable rework and potential increase of costs.
- Agile **testers are kept busy throughout the project**, in contrast to traditional projects where they are brought in close to completion of code. This could effectively increase the cost, but that might get compensated by quicker delivery timelines.

- **Agile projects are intense** with lot of timeboxed activities to accomplish in a short iteration. This could take a toll on the team. Moreover teams used to deliver agreed scope upfront (as in traditional projects) can struggle delivery a continuous train of iterations and responding to change. So it is important that the team strives for a sustainable pace where a healthy balance is maintained.
- Agile methods succeed when the team is equipped with **sophisticated technology tools** that do automated testing, version management, continuous build and integration and automated release management. Adoption of such tools could be costly and make a steep learning curve for teams. This could be an upfront investment, which, if not used after the life cycle of the project could prove to be wasteful.

1.6.3 The Comparison - Traditional vs. Agile Project Management

In the previous section we have seen the strengths and weaknesses of waterfall and Agile methodologies. The discussion around Stacey's diagram also provided a rough guidance of which method could suit in which scenario.

Traditional projects are plan driven with the scope being agreed first and the schedule, cost and the resources being derived out of it. The project manager, during the course of the project, measures metrics related to scope, time and cost and calculates the variance against the baselined plan and plans for corrective actions, as required to bring the project back on track.

In contrast, Agile projects progress with a fixed duration for its iteration and that has a fixed capacity, hence cost. However, the scope that can be delivered during a particular iteration is dynamic. Out of a backlog of features, the one with the maximum value are prioritized, estimated and the team commits to deliver them. Here the decision is taken by the self-organized and self-empowered teams.

This difference is depicted in Figure 1-6 below:

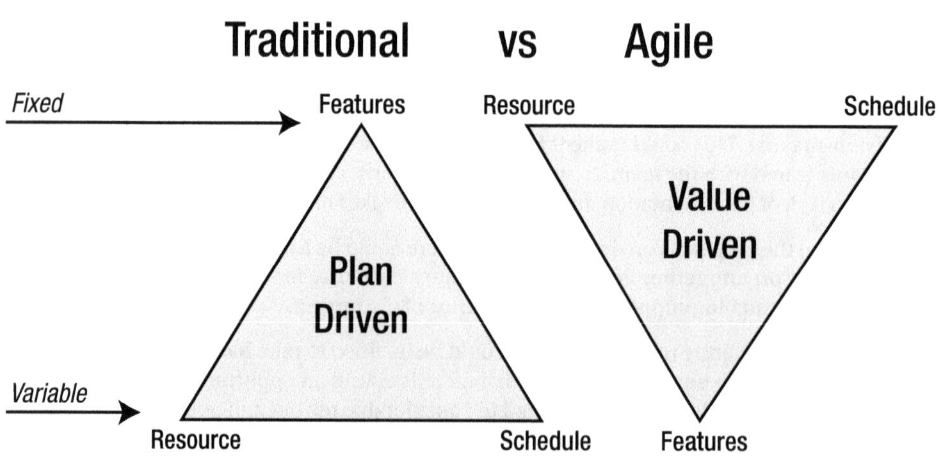

***Figure 1-6.** Traditional vs. Agile project management*

Table 1-2 gives a quick rundown of the comparisons between Traditional and Agile project management.

***Table 1-2.** Comparison between traditional and Agile project management*

Aspect	Waterfall or traditional project management	Agile project management
Focus	Focus on processes, tools and best practices.	Focus on individuals - team members and users.
Scope management	Scope, time and cost are the three constraints. Generally scope is agreed and then schedule and cost estimates are derived.	Iterations are time bound (2-4 weeks), but the scope of each iteration varies based on priority and capacity to deliver.
Change management	Focus on lengthy change management processes that include impact analysis, reviews and approvals.	Flexible to accept change in scope or change in priorities.
Architecture and design	Upfront architecture and design deliverables.	Architecture and design emerge from a collaboration between teams.
Planning	Follows a detailed project plan that is baselined after every change.	Follows a rolling wave planning strategy, where only the current iteration is planned out in detail and the rest is left at high level.
Delivery	Customers get to see the working product at the end, that is, once the project implementation is over.	Customers can see incremental versions of the product after each iteration and they collaborate with the team on a daily basis.
Contracting	Contracting principles are rigid, as in fixed-price projects.	Contracting principles are kept flexible to accommodate anticipated changes. Time and Material contracts are more prevalent.
Review and intermittent feedback	No formal mechanisms to capture user feedback during the middle of the project.	Formal review sessions are held to solicit user feedback and incorporate them.
Process improvement	Lessons learned exercises are held at the end of the project and uploaded to the organization's process assets or knowledge base.	Retrospectives are held after every iteration, providing the team an opportunity to inspect and adapt in the very next iteration.
Documentation	Focuses on comprehensive documentation of requirements, analysis and design artifacts.	Emphasis on working code. Barely sufficient documentation is encouraged.
Team size	Team size could be very large and geographically distributed.	Small co-located teams with sizes of 6-8 people are found to produce the most optimal results.

(*continued*)

Table 1-2. *(continued)*

Aspect	Waterfall or traditional project management	Agile project management
Project phase	Project phases are completely sequential, with each phase producing an output (also called Quality Gates) into the next phase.	Follows incremental and iterative style with each iteration having a flavor of analysis, development, testing, integration and deployment of a working product increment.
Leadership style	Generally needs a command-and-control of project management.	Needs a participative leadership style, with most of the decisions based on group consensus.
Skills of resources	Team members are specialists with unique domain and technology skills.	Team members are cross-functional and self-organizing in nature.

1.7 Focus Areas for the Exam

- ✓ Understand the basic concepts of Agile.
- ✓ Agile Manifesto - you need to know the exact words used in the four values and their significance.
- ✓ Light history about the making of Agile Manifesto and the Agile Alliance.
- ✓ The 12 guiding principles of Agile. When in doubt for a question or a given situation, you should always fall back on the 4 values of the Agile Manifesto and the 12 principles.
- ✓ Basic awareness of the Declarations of Interdependence, which is for project leaders and managers.
- ✓ Characteristics, application and drawbacks of waterfall methods.
- ✓ Characteristics, application and drawbacks of Agile methods.
- ✓ Comparison between waterfall and Agile project management - the former being plan driven and the latter being value driven.

Quizzes

1. Which of the following is an Agile Manifesto value?

   A. Individuals and interactions over contract negotiation

   B. Working software over comprehensive documentation

   C. Customer collaboration over processes and tools

   D. Working solutions over comprehensive documentation

2. What is valued more than Processes and Tools?

   A. Individuals and interactions

   B. Working software

   C. Customer collaboration

   D. Responding to change

3. Which of the following Agile Manifesto values deals most closely with WIP (Work in Progress)?

   A. Individuals and interactions over processes and tools

   B. Working software over comprehensive documentation

   C. Customer collaboration over contract negotiation

   D. Responding to change over following a plan

4. Which Agile Manifesto value is concerned with team empowerment?

   A. Individuals and interactions over processes and tools

   B. Working software over comprehensive documentation

   C. Customer collaboration over contract negotiation

   D. Responding to change over following a plan

5. Which Agile principle targets to satisfy a customer with great software?

   A. Working software over comprehensive documentation.

   B. Our highest priority is to satisfy the customer through early and continuous delivery of valuable software.

   C. Deliver working software frequently, from a couple of weeks to a couple of months, with a preference to the shorter timescale.

   D. Working software is the primary measure of progress.

6. How do we achieve motivated people on the team?

   A. Business people and developers must work together daily throughout the project.

   B. Build projects around motivated individuals. Give them the environment and support they need and trust them to get the job done.

   C. The most efficient and effective method of conveying information to and within a development team is face-to-face conversation.

   D. Individuals and interactions over processes and tools.

7. Which of the following is not a value stated in the Agile Manifesto?

   A. Individuals and interactions over processes and tools

   B. Working software over comprehensive documentation

   C. Customer communication over contract negotiation

   D. Responding to change over following a plan

8. What is the Agile term for the technique of creating a group of rules that govern how team members interact?

   A. Standard Operating Procedures

   B. Teaming Agreements

   C. Working Agreements

   D. Rules of Engagement

9. In what year was the Declaration of Interdependence (DOI) published?

   A. 1974

   B. 1990

   C. 2001

   D. 2005

10. Spot the Agile Manifesto value from the following choices:

    A. Individuals and processes over interactions and tools

    B. Interactions and processes over individuals and tools

    C. Individuals and interactions over processes and tools

    D. Individuals and tools over processes and interactions

11. Agile Manifesto values ________________

    A. Well-crafted software over comprehensive documentation

    B. Working software over comprehensive documentation

    C. Working software with as little documentation as possible

    D. Working solution without documentation

12. Which of the following is an Agile Manifesto value?

    A. Creating a plan over following a plan

    B. Following a plan over constant changes

    C. Responding to change over following a plan

    D. Steadily adding value over responding to change

13. Timeboxed means?

    A. Working with teams in a box.

    B. Working with a fixed time schedule for planned activities.

    C. Adjust the time to complete as many as possible activities.

    D. Allow flexibility of scope after an agreed sprint goal.

14. Which of the following Agile principle shows "Architecture and design emerge from a collaboration between teams"?

    A. The best architectures, requirements and designs emerge from self-organizing teams.

    B. Business people and developers must work together daily throughout the project.

    C. Build projects around motivated individuals. Give them the environment and support they need and trust them to get the job done.

    D. Continuous attention to technical excellence and good design enhances agility.

15. According to the manifesto, communications are best managed through:

    A. Daily Stand-Up meetings

    B. Face-to-face communications

    C. Video conferencing

    D. Documentation stored on SharePoint

16. Which of the following is an Agile principle per the Agile Manifesto?

    A. Delivering incremental change

    B. Ensuring that business people and developers work together

    C. Ensuring that business people and developers hold daily retrospective meetings

    D. Delivering comprehensive documentation

17. Agile Project Management:

    A. is an execution-biased model

    B. is a planning-and-control-biased model

    C. is a planning-biased model

    D. is a planning-and-execution-biased model

18. What happens if the development team cannot complete its work within its timebox?

    A. The timebox is adjusted permanently to reflect reality

    B. The timebox is extended temporarily.

    C. The iteration should be abandoned.

    D. The timebox is unchanged, but the unfinished work is carried forward to the backlog.

19. Which of the following is an Agile principle as per the Agile Manifesto?

    A. Defect reduction

    B. Simplicity

    C. Test-driven development

    D. Removing waste

20. The Agile Manifesto was created at a meeting at:

    A. A rugby match, February 2001

    B. A ski resort in Europe, February 2001

    C. A ski resort in Snowbird, Utah, USA, February 2001

    D. A ski resort in Snowbird, Utah, February 2000

Answers

1. B
2. A
3. B
4. A
5. B
6. B
7. C
8. C - Working Agreements refer to the standards and rules that each Agile team abides by to work together during the course of the project.
9. D - The Declaration of Interdependence was published 4 years after the Agile Manifesto in 2005 by a group of Agile practitioners to help implement guidelines set forth in the Agile Manifesto.
10. C
11. B
12. C
13. B
14. A
15. B
16. B
17. A
18. D
19. B
20. C

CHAPTER 2

Domain I Continued: Agile Methodologies

In this chapter, we will discuss some of the popular Agile methodologies. For the PMI-ACP® exam, the first four methods, namely, Scrum, Extreme Programming (XP), Lean and Kanban are very important. Awareness of some of the other methodologies like Feature-Driven Development (FDD), Dynamic system development method (DSDM) and the Crystal Family of methodologies is required since they embody some unique Agile practices that are commonly used in other methodologies.

So, while these methodologies follow the same set of guiding principles (Agile Manifesto) in general, they have certain specific characteristics that make them unique. It is up to the organization and the team to choose the flavor that suits best. Success of a methodology used in a project depends on a variety of factors ranging from the nature of the project to the organizational culture and the people involved.

While reading this chapter, you will come across quite a few terms that are described later in other sections of this book. So, if you feel like it, you can quickly look up the keywords from the index of this book and jump to the proper section where the terms are defined, described, or elaborated with examples.

2.1 Generic Flavor of Agile

Before getting into the discussion about specific methodologies, let us quickly review the common characteristics of most Agile methods, as also illustrated in Figure 2-1.

- Agile methods are timeboxed, iterative and incremental in nature. The duration of the iterations could be in the range from 2 to 4 weeks.
- The software requirements from the customer are broken down into user stories and stored in a backlog. This backlog is continuously prioritized such that the stories of the highest value are implemented before the lower priority ones.
- The team decides on a release plan based on the overall roadmap of the product and commits to deliver incremental value in every iteration.
- Before every iteration, the team estimates the most important stories and based on the capacity, plans to complete them before the timebox expires. During each iteration, the team works collaboratively to analyze, design, code, test and deploy the working software.
- The team produces barely sufficient documentation and embraces change along the way, although changes midway into the iteration are prohibited.

S. Boral, *Ace the PMI-ACP® exam*, DOI 10.1007/978-1-4842-2526-4_2

- At the end of each iteration, the team gives a review or demonstration of the working software and solicits real user feedback to further refine the product in later iterations.
- The team also retrospects on the ways of working on the project and works to improve upon the tools and processes used in the project.

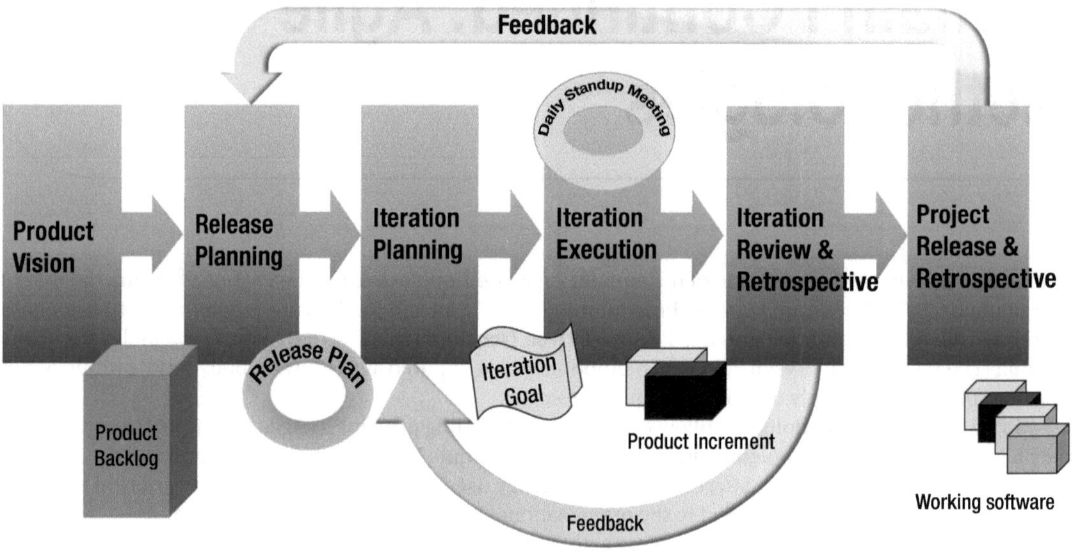

Figure 2-1. *Generic flavor of Agile methodologies (like Scrum and XP)*

It is now time to deep dive into the methodologies, starting with the most popular one called Scrum.

2.2 Scrum

2.2.1 Origin of Scrum

Scrum is one of the most popular Agile methodologies that focuses on iterative and incremental development of software. As quoted below, the origin of Scrum goes back to 1986, when the authors described a new approach to commercial product development that would increase speed and flexibility. In contrast to the traditional project life cycle, which is mostly sequential in nature, the authors made an analogy to the game of rugby (Figure 2-2) as follows:

Figure 2-2. *Scrum and the game of rugby*

"The 'relay race' approach to product development may conflict with the goals of maximum speed and flexibility. Instead a holistic or 'rugby' approach - where a team tries to go the distance as a unit, passing the ball back and forth - may better serve today's competitive requirements."

—Hirotaka Takeuchi and Ikujiro Nonaka, "The New Product Development Game," *Harvard Business Review*, January 1986

In the mid-1990s Jeff Sutherland and Ken Schwaber used and coined the word Scrum.

2.2.2 Pillars of Scrum

As the following Figure 2-3 illustrates, Scrum methodology is based on three pillars - Transparency, Inspection and Adaptation.

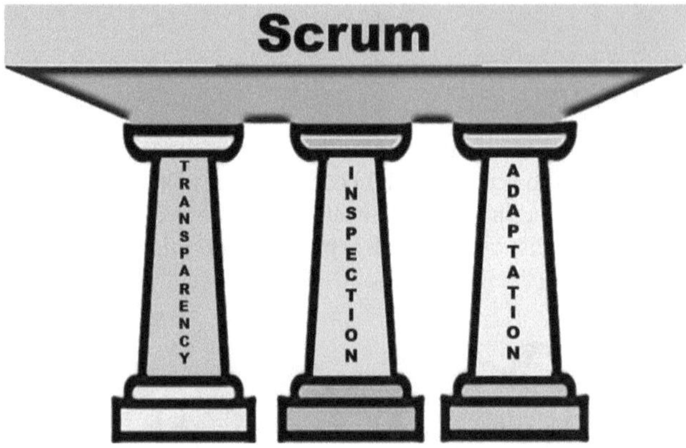

Figure 2-3. *Three pillars of Scrum*

2.2.2.1 Transparency

The outcome of Scrum is transparent and visible to stakeholders, thereby fostering a very open and collaborative culture. This requires creating a common standard or definition that is understood and agreed by all in the team. Examples of such are the use of burndown charts, impediments log, convention of daily stand-up meetings, or a 'definition-of-done' between the development team and the user accepting the work.

2.2.2.2 Inspection

The members of a Scrum team frequently inspect how the project is progressing toward its goal and keeping a check on the variances. Examples of opportunities for inspection are sprint reviews and sprint retrospectives that are explained later in the chapter. During these events the project team inspects and reflects on the project metrics like escaped defect rate or burndown charts or user feedback.

2.2.2.3 Adaptation

Adaptation is the 'secret-sauce' how Scrum teams continuously strive for improvement.
All ceremonies of Scrum has feedback loops, where the team comes together and optimizes the product or the process of making it. Such an adjustment happens in real time.

2.2.3 Characteristics of Scrum

Scrum methodology consists of three phases:

Scrum Phases

Pre-game – Sprint planning

Development – Sprint execution

Post-game – Integration, sprint review and sprint retrospective

The chief characteristics of Scrum, as introduced in Figure 2-4, are as follows:

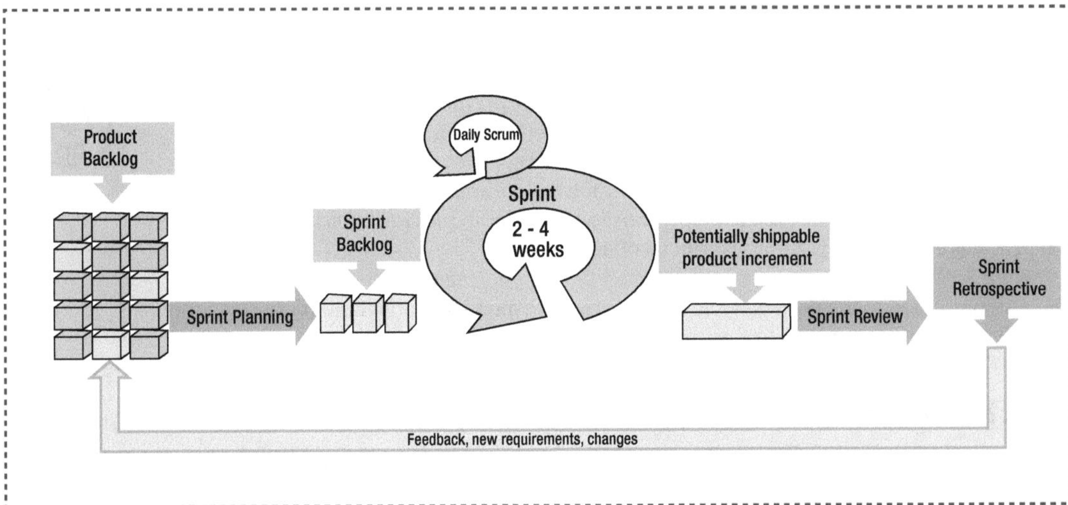

Figure 2-4. *Scrum methodology in a nutshell*

Scrum is an Agile process that allows us to rapidly and repeatedly deliver actual working software every 2 weeks to 4 weeks, called *Sprints*. A sprint (or iteration) represents the "timeboxed" effort and the basic unit of development in Scrum. The duration of the sprint is decided in advance and is kept fixed throughout the project.

During each sprint the product is designed, coded, integrated, tested and delivered.

The business sets the priorities and the team self-organizes among themselves to determine the best way to deliver the highest priority features.

Let us now deep dive into the Scrum framework, which is commonly expressed as $3^3 + 1$, in more details. As seen in the following Figure 2-5, there are 3 roles, 3 +1 ceremonies and 3 artifacts in Scrum. In this section, we will also get introduced to quite a few new terms, which will be defined and described in later sections of this book.

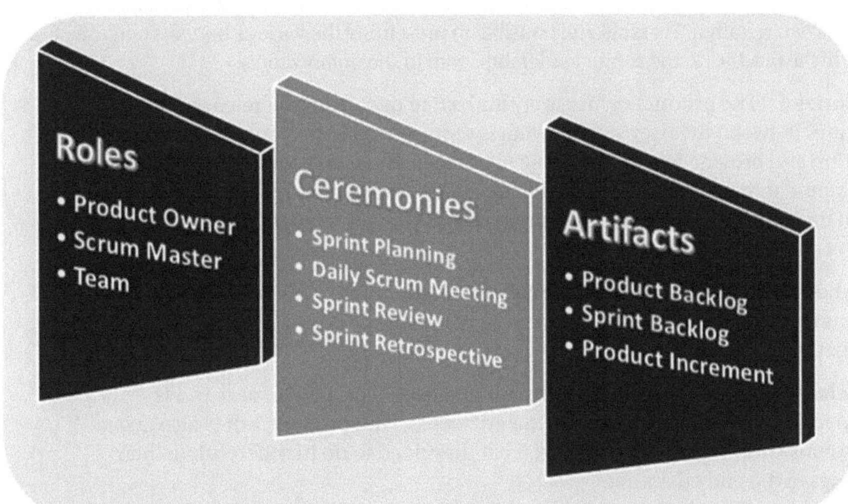

Figure 2-5. *Scrum $3^3 + 1$ framework consisting of Roles, Ceremonies and Artifacts*

2.2.4 Scrum Roles

There are three primary roles in Scrum, namely, the Product Owner, Scrum Master and the Development Team. In the context of the *'chicken and the pig fable',*[1] Scrum consists of the above three core roles or pigs, who are totally committed to the project and accountable for its outcome. The chickens are the roles outside these three. They provide consultancy or are informed of its progress. This analogy is based upon the contrast that the pig provides bacon, which is a sacrificial offering (since the pig must die in order to provide meat) versus a chicken that provides eggs, which is a non-sacrificial offering.

For a Scrum project, Scrum Master, Product Owner and Team are considered as people who are committed to the project while customers and executive management are considered as involved but not committed to the project.

2.2.4.1 Product Owner (PO)

The product owner represents the voice of the customer and defines the features of the product and their priorities based on market value. He or she is primarily responsible for the profitability of the product (ROI) and will work with the sponsor of the project to ensure that the project is funded as required. The product owner also works out the release date and the constituent features in each release by determining the priorities and the inputs from the rest of the team. Maintenance of the product backlog, writing of high-level user stories and their acceptance criteria are also part of his or her core responsibilities. The PO may not participate in all daily stand-up meetings, but mandatorily attends the first half of the sprint planning meeting where he or she clarifies the requirements to the team and ensures that all have a common understanding.

The abbreviation CRACK, which stands for Committed, Responsible, Authorized, Collaborative and Knowledgeable, is often used to describe an effective product owner. Here is what they mean:

- **Committed** - The product owner is committed to the cause of the project and is determined to keep the team focused on its objectives.
- **Responsible** - The product owner is responsible to maximizing the ROI for the deliveries during each iteration. He is also responsible for maintaining a prioritized backlog of features requested by the users and providing clarifications to the development team as and when required. He is also responsible in presenting the various benefits and use cases of the product to the senior leadership team in the organization.
- **Authorized** - The product owner is authorized to decide on the release plan, the priorities between the user stories, what is required to be delivered during an iteration and provide feedback during the demos. By working together with the development team and the Scrum Master, he also has the authority to terminate a sprint midway if he sees that the sprint goal is no longer relevant in the context of the project or the organization.
- **Collaborative** - The product owner collaborates with the Agile team during the various ceremonies that guide the team to iteratively deliver the features of the product.
- **Knowledgeable** - The product owner is considered a domain expert and is knowledgeable of not only the anticipated needs of the product, but is also aware of the competition in the market and what they need to do to differentiate their offerings to the end customer.

---

[1]Refer to `https://en.wikipedia.org/wiki/The_Chicken_and_the_Pig`

2.2.4.2 Scrum Master

The Scrum Master plays the role of the servant leader[2] in a Scrum team and is responsible for upholding the Scrum values and practices. This role is distinctly different from the traditional team lead or project manager who follows the command-and-control style. He participates in the daily Scrum meetings and enables close cooperation across all roles and functions making sure that the team is self-organized, cross-functional and productive. When a new member joins the team, the Scrum Master helps the person to be onboarded through coaching and be acquainted with how Scrum is implemented in the project. Wherever possible, the Scrum Master works to remove impediments and shields the team from external interferences. The Scrum Master is also responsible for helping the product owner maintain the backlog and reiterating the goal of the project to the development team.

2.2.4.3 Development Team

The development team is responsible for developing the product in potentially shippable increments at the end of each sprint. The team typically consists of five-nine members possessing cross-functional skills to do analysis, architecture, design, development, testing, deployment and documentation. It is essential that the team be self-organizing, self-managing, with ultimate accountability of the outcome of the project. The team members are also empowered to make decisions via group consensus on aspects like planning, estimation and choice of metrics to track. Ideally the team members should be working full time on the project and the composition of the team should change only between sprints.

2.2.5 Scrum Ceremonies

Scrum has four meetings that mandate participation from all members of the Scrum team.

2.2.5.1 Sprint Planning

Each sprint starts with a planning meeting lasting for eight hours usually, where the tasks for the sprint are identified, estimated and committed to deliver in that sprint.

- During the first half of the sprint planning meeting, the Product Owner discusses the highest priority items from the Product Backlog (that are likely to go into the Sprint backlog) and clarifies any questions that the team might have around them.
- In the second half of the meeting, the team breaks down the user stories from the sprint backlog into tasks, does a very high-level design and estimates the tasks (using a technique like Planning Poker).
- The outcome of the sprint planning meeting is the sprint backlog or the sprint goal, which contains the team's commitment to deliver during that sprint. The commitment is based around the priorities, estimates and the team's capacity to deliver.

---

[2]Refer to Chapter 4: Stakeholder Engagement for the theory on servant leadership.

2.2.5.2 Daily Scrum Meeting

Scrum discourages unnecessary meetings. During the beginning of each workday in the sprint, all team members come together at the same place and at the same time for the stand-up meeting. The duration of the meeting is generally timeboxed to 15 minutes. There is no provision for sitting in the meeting, so all participants have to stand, hence the name 'stand-up'. Standing up in the meeting makes sure that the meeting finishes on time, team members remain energetic, focused and do not digress into topics that are not are on the agenda. The stand-up meeting is also sometimes called a *daily huddle*.

During the meeting, each team member answers three questions:

> What did you do since yesterday?
> What will you do today?
> Are there any impediments?

Note that the meeting in the above format is not equivalent to a status reporting to a management, but a collaborative effort between peers where information is exchanged and commitments are made in an open and transparent manner. This meeting should not be used for problem solving or detailed discussion on any particular topic that might derail the meeting.

2.2.5.3 Sprint Review

A sprint generally ends with a half-day sprint review. This is a meeting where all relevant stakeholders are invited and the team gives a demo of the working software and invites real-time user feedback. Some of the feedback could translate into work items that need to be entered into the product backlog or a change in priorities among the work items.

2.2.5.4 Sprint Retrospective

This is the last formal ceremony of a sprint and the team reflects and reviews what happened during the past sprint. This meeting, typically, lasts for about 2 to 4 hours and is attended by all on the team. The retrospective is facilitated by the Scrum Master or a retrospective leader appointed from another team.

Each member of the team ponders the response of three main questions, namely:

> What should we START doing?
> What should we CONTINUE doing?
> What should we STOP doing?

The outcome of the discussion is a series of action items that reflect the team's desire to continuously learn and improve the ways of working. The action items are ranked in order of urgency and importance and the team commits to implement them from the next sprint. We will discuss further about retrospectives in Chapter 8: Continuous Improvement (Product, Process, People).

2.2.6 Scrum Artifacts

This section represents the deliverables from the different roles in a Scrum team.

2.2.6.1 Product Backlog

This is the list of requirements that is generally managed and ranked continuously by the product owner based on the considerations like business value, risk, dependencies and required date of delivery. It can contain business requirements, features, defects and nonfunctional requirements that are required for a working product. Ideally each item in the product backlog should be represented in the user story format. This list is dynamic and the team makes sure that the most valuable items (that give the highest ROI) are detailed out and worked on first. The entries in the product backlog are called Product Backlog Items and the product owner constantly keeps it in a prioritized order.

2.2.6.2 Sprint Backlog

As we have seen earlier, during the onset of a sprint, the Scrum team gets together for the sprint planning meeting. At this meeting items from the product backlog are prioritized and based on their estimates size or complexity are slotted into the timeboxed sprint. This list of items is called the sprint backlog. The development team commits to complete these prioritized items and deliver a potentially shippable increment at the end of the sprint. As each day progresses, the team members are expected to update the sprint backlog on the amount of remaining effort, thereby making it visible how close the current estimate matches to the original estimate.

2.2.6.3 Definition of Done

In the spirit of transparency and to remove any ambiguity, the Scrum teams should upfront determine when a work item of the sprint backlog can be marked as complete. This can also be looked upon as the "exit criteria" that consists of a checklist of activities that need to be completed as part of the work item. For example, the following could be part of the *doneness criteria*:

- Code review is completed and all changes incorporated
- Code is checked into the right branch in version control
- Code is fully integrated and built with no errors
- Code coverage tests were completed
- Code passed the regression test suite with no failures
- Code passed the acceptance criteria laid down by the customers

Different Scrum teams can agree with different definitions of done, but once agreed it should be kept consistent across several iterations that the team works on. The definition of done also drives release and sprint planning, estimation, execution and sprint review. Only items that meet the doneness criteria should be presented in the sprint review and the leftover part should be returned back to the product backlog to be reprioritized and reworked later.

Another related phrase that is sometimes used in Scrum teams is *definition of ready,* which denotes a set of "entry criteria" that must be fulfilled before a story is picked up in a sprint. Satisfying these entry criteria help in ensuring that the team is able to face relatively lesser number of obstacles on the way and the chances of a successful completion during the sprint are higher than otherwise.

Examples of criteria under *definition of ready* are as follows:

- If a story has external dependencies, then they must have been resolved.
- If a story needs to develop a user interface, then the prototype has been fully designed, reviewed and agreed.
- The size of a story should be lesser than a predetermined threshold.

However, the team would have to be cautious that these criteria do not turn the Agile project into stages that mimic steps of a waterfall, like analysis of all requirements have to be completed before design can start.

2.2.6.4 Product Increment

This is the most important Scrum artifact. At the end of the sprint, the component should not only pass the acceptance criteria laid down by the product owner, but also fulfill the team's *Definition of Done.* The product increment must be of high enough quality to be given to users. Note that each iteration produces a version that is integrated with or that is on top of the existing product.

2.2.6.5 Burndown Charts

The burndown chart depicts the progress of the team against a committed goal, expressed in number of story points remaining to be implemented in the current sprint. The team makes sure that the burndown chart is updated in real time and is always displayed in a public viewing space. We will cover burndown charts extensively in later chapters.

2.2.7 Further Discussion on Scrum

Before we leave this section, it is worthwhile to touch upon a few topics around Scrum that are frequently discussed among the Agile community. This section is not required for the PMI-ACP® exam, but is presented to aid learning and bridge between theory and practice.

2.2.7.1 Difference between a Project Manager and Scrum Master

It is to be noted that the classic role of a project manager is not defined as one of the roles in Scrum. That leads to thinking that project management, a role that existed in classic software development projects is no longer relevant for a project running Scrum. The closest role in Scrum is that of a Scrum Master. However, there are far more differences between a PM and a Scrum Master as illustrated in Table 2-1 below.

Table 2-1. *Comparison between the roles of a Project Manager and a Scrum Master*

Project Manager	Scrum Master
Takes accountability to accomplishing the project objectives of time, cost and scope.	Focuses on making sure that the Scrum principles are upheld and adhered to in the team and that the team is aligned to the sprint goal.
Follows a more authoritarian approach and a command-and-control style.	Follows a more participative leader style and a facilitator (e.g., facilitates ceremonies like sprint planning, estimation sessions, daily stand-ups, review and retrospectives).
Focuses on a plan-driven approach - tracking and monitoring variances in metrics around time, cost and scope and taking corrective actions.	The planning and tracking is done by the entire team. Follows more of an inspect-and-adapt style.
Allocates tasks to the team members based on their skills, competence and availability. Proactively tracks risks, issues and dependencies.	Scrum Master doesn't have to allocate tasks as the team is both cross-functional and self-organized. However the Scrum Master looks to mitigate risks by removing impediments that block the progress of a project.
Could play the role of line manager / appraiser of the project team.	Generally doesn't have line management responsibilities. Plays the role of a servant leader. Takes a people-centric approach and acts as a mentor or coach.
Primarily interfaces with the sponsor and user representatives to collect requirements at the beginning of the project and ensure acceptance of the completed product towards the end of the project.	Continuously collaborates with the sponsor and the users, supports the product owner to make sure expectations are met, by delivering in increments and soliciting feedback at regular intervals.
Follows rigorous change control procedures to ensure that there is no scope creep and the team stays track on the documented plan.	Works as part of the team to anticipate change and follow a rolling wave planning method.
Relies on sophisticated status reports to communicate progress periodically to sponsors and stakeholders.	Encourages team to use information radiators to emanate data indicating progress and have open spaces where osmotic communication can flow.

From the above discussion, it is to be concluded that the Scrum Master does not replace the project manager role. Both the PM and Scrum Master roles could coexist, complementing each other, especially in large and complex projects consisting of multiple products, teams or running across organizational boundaries.

2.2.7.2 Scaling Scrum

As we have seen earlier, the optimum size of Scrum teams are 7 ± 2 members. However, for large and complex projects, teams need to scale. The factors for scaling could include the geographical dispersion of the team, type of application and its dependent components and the duration of the project.

Scalability is achieved through a team of teams, which in Scrum terminology is called *Scrum-of-Scrums*. A Scrum-of-Scrum meeting follows the same format as that of daily stand-ups, but is generally held at a less frequent interval (say weekly) and the duration is longer (say thirty minutes). Also the focus is on the dependencies between delivery streams from different teams.

As the above Figure 2-6 illustrates Scrum-of-Scrum can be used with 500+ person projects at an enterprise level.

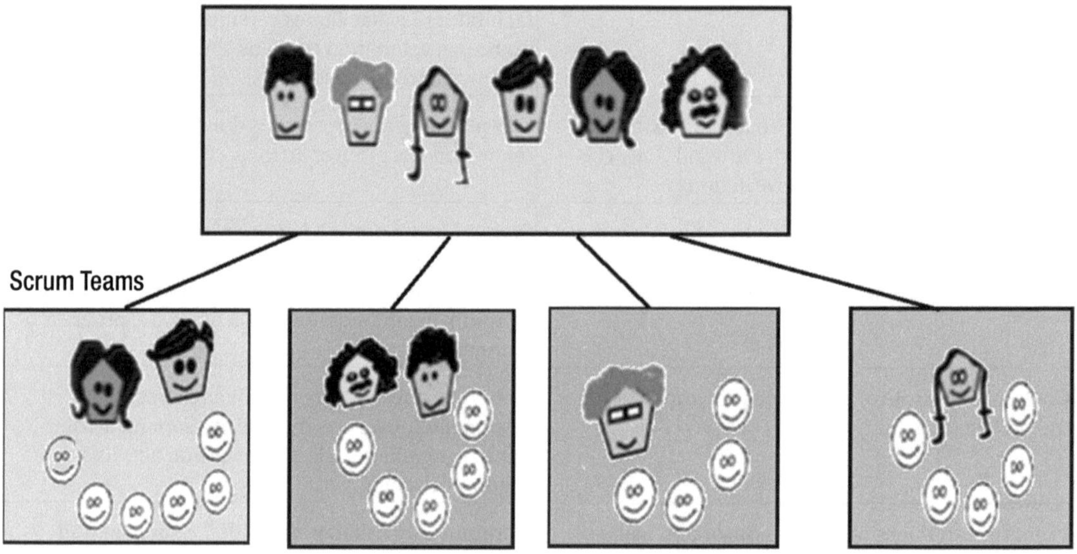

Figure 2-6. *Scrum-of-Scrums*

Another framework to achieve scalability at the enterprise level is the **Scaled Agile Framework** (SAFe®)[3] as defined by Dean Leffingwell. This method is becoming increasing popular as far as adoption of Agile practices at an organization level is concerned. This topic is outside the purview of the PMI-ACP® exam.

There is also the concept of **Meta Scrum**, which is applied where different Scrum teams working on different features of a product come together. This meeting can happen once a month and is generally facilitated by the Chief Product Owner or the Chief Scrum Master. The representatives of different teams look to resolve blockers and dependencies between teams and track whether the release plans conforms to the overall roadmap of the product.

[3]Refer to `http://www.scaledagileframework.com/`

2.3 Extreme Programming (XP)

Extreme Programming, also commonly abbreviated as XP was created by Kent Beck in the 1990s. XP is described as a lightweight software-development discipline that organizes people to produce higher-quality software more productively.

Like Scrum, XP performs a bit of analysis, design, development and testing in each short timeboxed iteration. The outcome of each iteration is a potentially shippable product increment. Each iteration has a planning session, execution session and culminates in a review or demo and a retrospective.

However, compared to Scrum, XP projects have shorter iterations that range between 1 to 3 weeks. The shorter iteration not only enforces discipline and focus, but also practices efficiency with sound engineering practices like pair programming and test-driven development.

XP is found to work best in scenarios where the project environment is uncertain and requirements are volatile. It is also favored where a team is working with a new domain or technology, but still expected to deliver rapidly in response to changes.

2.3.1 Core Values in Extreme Programming

XP has five core values as described in Figure 2-7.

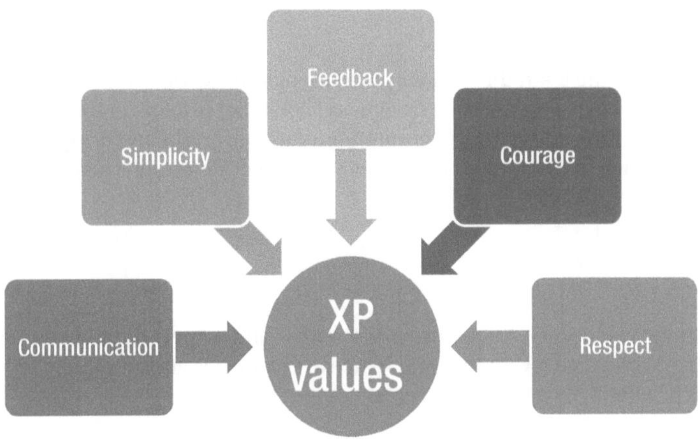

Figure 2-7. *Core values in XP*

Let us take a closer look at these values in the next section.

2.3.1.1 Communication

This value focuses on one of the key success factors in a project, that is, smooth communication and collaboration between the XP team and the customers who sit together. The co-located team, the on-site customer and the daily stand-up meetings help to maximize this value, something not achievable through comprehensive documentation prevalent in traditional waterfall-based projects.

2.3.1.2 Simplicity

XP projects are characterized by simple design and code that is flexible enough to accommodate changes as the requirements evolve. XP projects steer away from the need of an upfront complex architecture and design or any forms of addition of features that do not directly add value to the customer (also called *goldplating*). This is also termed as the "You aren't gonna need it" (YAGNI) approach. Instead XP relies on the cross-functional team to design iteratively, refactor the code and remove technical debt, thus eliminating any forms of waste. Another aspect of simplicity is that XP advocates plan at the last responsible moment, thereby making sure that there is no wastage of effort that goes in detailed planning and estimation upfront.

2.3.1.3 Feedback

The iteration length in XP is generally 1 to 3 weeks. This implies that XP cycles provide ample opportunity to review the product and get feedback from the end user. Rapid feedback also comes through outcome of continuous build, integration and running of automated test cases. It also follows the concept of fail-fast and fail-early, which work particularly well when the requirements are evolving.

2.3.1.4 Courage

XP projects instill courage in the team through empowerment to make decisions. Another example, as seen above, is to focus on a simple design and code that is relevant for today and not think too far ahead in the future, as the future requirements are uncertain and likely to change. A final example is the courage to throw away code that is no longer required, irrespective of the amount of effort that has already been spent.

2.3.1.5 Respect

Respect is a very essential value when XP teams work together and respect differences and diversity. XP teams have collective ownership and hence everyone has accountability for the design, code, success of a build, or passing of a regression test suite.

2.3.2 XP Roles

Like Scrum, XP relies on a cross-functional team that converts user stories into pieces of working software at the end of each timeboxed iteration. This section introduces some of the roles seen in XP teams, as shown in Figure 2-8.

Figure 2-8. *Roles in Extreme Programming*

2.3.2.1 The Whole Team

The XP team is a co-located, self-organized and cross-functional team. Like Scrum, they also go through the ceremonies of planning, daily stand-up meetings, demo and retrospective in each iteration. An XP team can consist of 5 to 20 *full-time* team members having diverse and complementary skills. Often in matrix organizations, it is common to see *fractional assignment* of resources where they are required to contribute to multiple projects at the same time. XP project does not recommend this as it involves a lot of thrashing and context switching, which is counterproductive and limits the amount of valuable work getting done.

2.3.2.2 XP Coach

Since the XP team is self-organized and self-empowered, explicit leadership or the management layer is often found to be unnecessary. So in contrast to traditional management roles, the XP Coach plays a supporting role for the team's success. The coach oversees discipline and ensure that the XP principles (discussed in the next section) are followed in the team. Coaches set up conditions for energized work and also enable the team to interact with the rest of the organization.

2.3.2.3 On-Site Customers

On-site customers are responsible for defining the user stories (requirements) and their acceptance criteria (determining whether they are "done"). They are considered as domain or product experts and are responsible to see that the right product with the maximum business value is implemented by the team. The most important activity for the on-site customers is that of release planning, where they take into account the project vision, maximize ROI in each iteration, mitigate risks and provide real-time feedback at the end of every release. If the on-site customer is not present or does not commit full-time involvement (as required ideally), the role can be filled with product managers, product owners, user-interface designers, domain experts and business analysts who are called *proxies*. The word "on-site" implies that the customers or their proxies *sit together* with the rest of the team to ensure that communication flows freely. The sheer presence of a co-located customer creates a sense of ownership for the product and its features and makes a significant difference to the success of the project and realization of benefits.

2.3.2.4 Programmer

The XP team consists of multiskilled teams of 4 to 10 developers that practice pair programming (described later in the section on XP concepts). They self-assign stories or tasks out of the iteration backlog and proceed on implementation of the same. Each team should have at least one senior programmer, designer, or architect so that the team can work toward an incremental design and architecture. The team also practices test-driven development, continuous integration, automation testing and reduces technical debt by refactoring the code as required. As far as continuous integration is concerned, the XP team strives to complete the build and integrate the new features into a complete package in less than *ten* minutes. Programmers, although can specialize in a particular component of the system based on their skill-sets, but they have a collective ownership of the code (described in the section on XP concepts below).

2.3.2.5 Testers

As James Shore writes, the thumb rule is to include one tester for every four programmers. In some cases XP teams may not have dedicated testers at all and in that case the programmers and the on-site customers are expected to fill the role by using strategies like Test-Driven Development, automated regression testing, or exploratory testing.

Testers assist the on-site customer in writing the acceptance test criteria, executing them and communicating their results back to the programmers. Unlike traditional methodologies, XP testers do not perform long manual regression cycles. Instead they use techniques like exploratory testing to help the team identify whether it is successfully preventing bugs from reaching finished code. Testers also look at nonfunctional requirements like usability, performance, stability, resilience and ability to handle long periods of load and stress.

2.3.2.6 XP Tracker

This role helps to keep track of the progress of the team at an iteration or release level. The tracker should ideally collect information and metrics from the information radiators at public places and report them as required without disturbing the rest of the team. Sometimes the tracker can also facilitate activities within the team and help with external communication.

2.3.2.7 Sponsor

The sponsor funds the project, hence is a very important stakeholder of the project. The team should regularly engage with the sponsor, provide demos to show tangible evidence of progress and ensure that the product roadmap is aligned to his expectations.

Although above we have listed some commonly found XP roles, other roles might be relevant and important based on the situation. Some of such roles can include the business analyst, domain expert, user-interface designer and architects.

2.3.3 Core XP Practices

At its core, XP has twelve high discipline practices as shown in Figure 2-9. We shall see each of them in some more detail in the next sections.

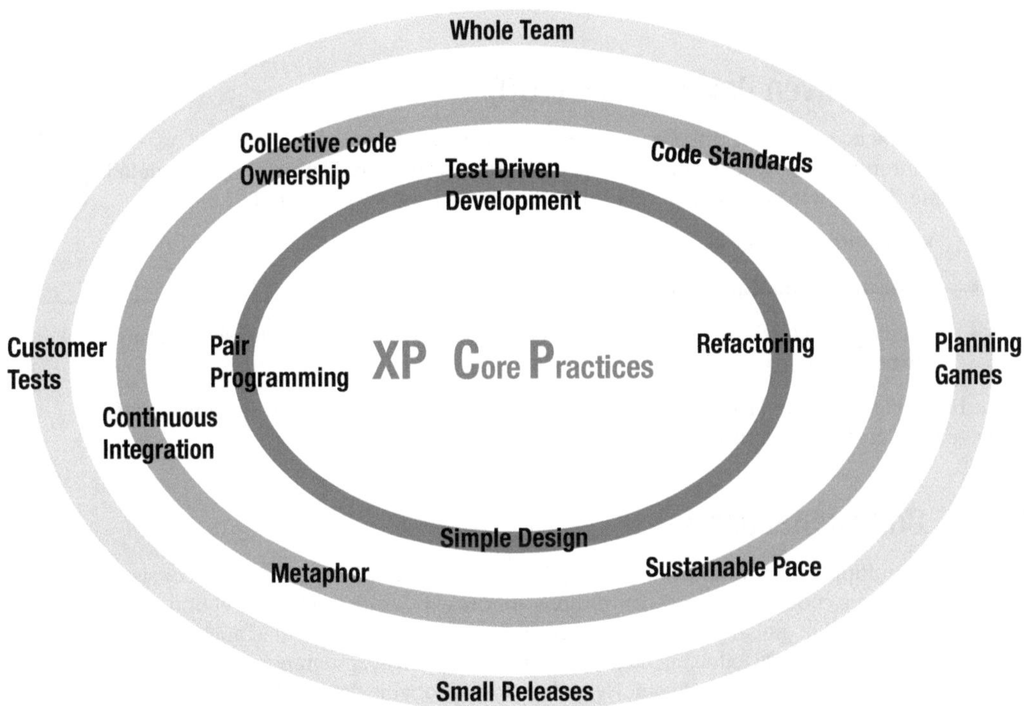

Figure 2-9. *Twelve core practices in XP*

2.3.3.1 Planning Game

The main planning process in XP is called the Planning Game and consists of planning at two levels - Release planning and Iteration planning. In both these levels, there are three phases, namely, exploration, commitment and steering.

In case of release planning, programmers and customers jointly decide what all requirements can be delivered into production and when. This is done based on estimates, risks, priorities and the capacity of the team to deliver. However, this is a rough approximation, hence the plan is likely to be adjusted based on changes.

In case of iteration planning, XP team members pick the most valuable user stories from the backlog, break them into tasks, estimate them and commit what they can deliver during the iteration.

2.3.3.2 Simple Design

XP teams do not create big designs and architecture up front, which could be challenging for very complex projects. They start with a simple design and let it emerge and evolve through the iterations, keeping pace with rapidly changing requirements. The code is frequently refactored to keep it maintainable and free of technical debt.

Keeping design simple sometimes is easier said than done. Often the team encounters uncertainties about design and implementation choices, especially if they are using a new piece of technology. At this time, XP teams conduct a small experiment or proof-of-concept exercise called *spike*. The outcome of the spike helps the team understand the validity of the hypothesis, gauge the complexity of the solution and feels more confident to estimate and build (or not to build) something based on the experiment.

2.3.3.3 Test-Driven Development (TDD)

XP follows the practice of writing unit test cases before the code is produced. These unit tests are run in an automated fashion during the build and integration stage. TDD is covered in detail later in Chapter 7: Problem Detection and Resolution. But the primary steps of TDD include:

- Write the unit test case first, which will fail to begin with.
- Write the minimal amount of code to pass the test.
- Refactor the code by adding the needed functionality, while continuously ensuring the tests pass.

The benefit of following TDD is that the programmer is forced to write only that amount of code that passes the test, nothing more than that, since it is wasteful.

2.3.3.4 Coding Standards

Since there are multiple programming pairs at play, it is extremely helpful to adhere to a consistent style and format of the code, like naming conventions, modularity, error logging, exception handling. or use of local or global parameters. These coding standards are decided and agreed before development begins. By following these conventions rigorously, programmers make it simple to understand each other's code quickly or detect any probable defects. It also helps to fulfill the principle of collective ownership of code discussed below.

2.3.3.5 Refactoring

As XP teams look to rapidly churn out working code, it is quite possible that overall complexity[4] of the code increases over a period of time, making it hard to change and maintain. There could be duplicate code, residue of unused functionality, undefined parameters, or excessively long files. All these contribute to technical debt, which is found to increase over time.

---

[4]One of the metrics used in this context is called Cyclomatic complexity. There are sophisticated methods like SQALE (Software Quality Assessment based on Lifecycle Expectations), which can help to identify technical debt in code based on rules and extrapolate the effort in remediating them.

Few of the practices to remove technical debt include:

- Ensuring that code is not duplicated, such that for a change of logic, one and only one place needs to be touched.
- Ensuring that all declared variables in scope are defined and used.
- Ensuring that variables, constants, methods are given names that are readable and easy to understand.
- Ensuring that a particular method or function is not excessively long that is difficult to follow.
- Removing unnecessary temporary variables.
- Using proper visibility modifiers like private, protected and public based on the context.
- Removing unreachable code or logic that is unused under present circumstances.

By refactoring, the programmers look to improve the overall code quality and make it more readable without altering its behavior. This makes the design and code efficient and takes less of an effort to maintain. There are a few commercial software editors like Eclipse and Visual Studio that have options to automatically refactor code.

For people that are new to pair programming, there are a few obvious questions that get asked from time to time. The following Table 2-2 reflects how a XP team deals with such situations.

Table 2-2. *Questions about XP practices*

Questions	How XP teams address them?
We have two programmers working on the same piece of code. Isn't the productivity halved?	If coding was simply a matter of typing text on the keyboard, the question around productivity would have been valid. However, building software is a far more complex affair. Having one concentrate on logic and write syntactically correct code and unit tests, while the other thinking ahead about the design, refactoring and other aspects of the strategy leads to a better quality of maintainable software.
Do we get rid of code reviews and inspections? They have shown in the past to improve code quality.	Not necessarily. For an effective code review, it makes sense for the reviewer and the author to closely collaborate and share the context such that both syntactic and semantic elements are covered. With pair programming reviews are more real-time because the two are inextricably involved as the code is written.
What if programmers are not comfortable pairing with each other? Should a manager enforce pairing?	Yes, some programmers are habituated to their personal space and may not be comfortable with someone watching over their shoulders. So it might make sense to begin with a small experiment for a few weeks to see if it works or are plagued with challenges. As programmers start to see benefits through mutual cooperation and the variety of perspectives on the table, pair programming session could actually add to the fun quotient. Choice of partners should be flexible and on-demand rather than assigned by managers.

(*continued*)

Table 2-2. (*continued*)

Questions	How XP teams address them?
Will it help if I encounter attrition in the team?	Indeed. With pair programming we automatically disseminate more knowledge across the team. This is vital for a collective code ownership, where, it is more likely that more than one developer would be knowledgeable and available to troubleshoot a bug or fix a production issue. This is also handy if there is attrition in the team and the need for an elaborate knowledge transition phase during exit is not called for.
Do we have to follow pair programming all the time?	This is more of a choice left to an individual or a team. If the work item is trivial or repetitive, then there is no need. Otherwise for production code that has a longer shelf-life it makes sense to utilize pair programming and benefit from it.
Ok, we got the programmers sit together. Do we need anything else?	A comfortable workspace with adequate lighting, ventilation and space on the desk and chairs are required from a logistics point of view. If a session becomes exhaustive or monotonous, it is important the pair switches their roles or take a break. Note that in case of virtual teams, some degree of pair programming could be achieved with the use of collaborative software and video conferences, but the benefits might be limited.

2.3.3.6 Pair Programming

This is one of the most important practices in XP. Pair programming consists of two programmers working on the same code and its related unit test case suite, at the same workstation (so one screen and one keyboard).

One of the programmers plays the role of the **pilot** and focuses on writing clean code that compiles and runs. The other programmer plays the role of the **navigator** and mostly focuses on the big picture; reviews the code being written by the other; and looks for opportunities to simplify, improve and refactor the code as required.

While such happens, it is important to keep the conversation going about aspects like simple design choices, test-driven development and the overall direction. Every hour or so, the pair is allowed to switch roles. The pairs of programmers are also not fixed and they are frequently swapped such that over time everyone gets to know about the code base for the whole system and fresh perspectives also emerge.

2.3.3.7 Collective Code Ownership

By following this practice, XP teams can take collective ownership of code (and thereby of successes and failures of the system) and there is no key-man dependencies at any point. So, if there is a defect or a production issue, pretty much any programmer can be called upon to fix it.

2.3.3.8 Continuous Integration

In XP, pairs of programmers work concurrently on local versions of the code and so there is a need to integrate changes made every few hours or at the most on a daily basis. After each code compilation and integration step, all the tests are executed automatically for the entire system. If the tests fails, they are fixed then and there, so that any chance of defect propagation and further problems are avoided down the line.

In order to maximize productivity, XP advocates a *ten-minute build*. The build should be comprehensive - performing compilation, running automated tests, updating configuration files and deploying changes to the runtime environment.

2.3.3.9 Small Releases

Small releases help in maintaining quality as the need for testing a large and complex feature at the end of a very long period of development is not there.

A cross-functional team in XP practices small releases containing Minimal Marketable Features abbreviated as MMF. This helps the team as well as the on-site customer to demonstrate visible progress and focus only on the least amount of work just in time, but having the highest priority.

As far as releases are concerned, the working software should be in a deployable and usable state at the end of the iteration. By this time, the programmers would have completed coding for the user story, performed integration, run all relevant test packages, fixed the defects, refactored the code, checked into version control, compiled and built the executable and got acceptance from the customer. Analogous to the definition of done in Scrum, such completed user stories are said to be *"done done."*

2.3.3.10 System Metaphor

The system metaphor is a simple ubiquitous story that the whole team could relate to and use for easy communication and explanation of design or achitecture. XP teams could come up with a story or a real-life analogy that involve a sample workflow or a component in the system and conveys how the system would work or ought to be built. At a more granular level it could be a naming convention used in design and code and is created to have a shared technical view based on real-life examples. This makes it convenient for everyone in the team to relate to the functionality of the particular component by just looking at its name. For example, by looking at the function name `debit_customer_account()`, it is possible to guess what the function is expected to perform.

2.3.3.11 On-Site Customer

The on-site customer writes the user stories and defines the acceptance test cases for them. This topic has been discussed in the previous section on XP roles.

2.3.3.12 Sustainable Pace

This is a people-centric practice in XP which advocates that a forty-hour working week. XP iterations are generally intense sessions and might require some periods of stretch. But it is equally important for the team members to be properly rested so that their efficiency and productivity is optimal. It is to be observed that the previous practices like TDD, continuous build and integration and refactoring of code help to proactively improve the quality, stability and predictability of the working software, which in turn contributes to the sustainable place that XP teams strive for.

Another way in which XP looks to maintain a sustainable pace is to introduce slack time during the iteration. This time is kept not to do actual development, but to act as a buffer to deal with uncertainties (such that commitments still can be met). Teams can use slack time to pay down technical debt by refactoring code, or do research to keep up pace with the latest in their domain and technology.

By embracing this principle, XP teams stay motivated, have a healthy work-life balance, perform at their best and are able to continue at this pace as long as possible.

Before we leave this section, it is worthy to note that among the twelve practices, the most important ones (from the perspective of adoption to XP) are the following:

- Planning Game
- Small Releases
- Test-Driven Development
- Pair Programming
- Refactoring
- Continuous Integration

2.3.4 XP Success Factors

For a team to adopt XP and practice the same to deliver projects, a few critical factors should be there. Without this adoption, XP will not succeed.

- Active support from management.
- Co-located team, open spaces, workstations that can accommodate pairs of programmers.
- Presence of on-site customer or his proxy.
- Buy-in and lots of positive energy and courage from the team.
- Team of the right size (ranging from four to twelve programmers) and skill composition.
- Adoption of most (if not all) principles.
- Pursuit for continuous improvement.
- Ease of access to an experienced XP coach.

2.4 Lean

We now cover one of the most important topics in this chapter - Lean. From a PMI-ACP® exam perspective also, you can expect quite a few questions on the fundamental principles of Lean. As far as software development methodology is concerned, Scrum and XP top the popularity chart, but is closely followed or augmented by principles of Lean. Application of Lean philosophies can also be seen in Kanban and Scrumban (which, loosely speaking, is a hybrid of Scrum and Kanban).

2.4.1 Origin of Lean

Lean has its roots in the manufacturing industry. The origin of Lean goes back to the late 1940s when a Japanese businessman Taiichi Ohno introduced what was called the Toyota Production System (TPS) to deliver value to business with the use of pull-based systems that eliminate all forms of waste. This was later popularized as the Lean Manufacturing and ever since, has been adopted in various sectors like health care, construction, financial services, communication, fast-moving consumer goods (FMCG) and software services. There were two key observations. The first being that Taiichi listed seven forms of wastes that do not contribute any value to business and this is applicable in many real-life situations. We will discuss this in the next section. Secondly, the emergence of Toyota as one of the largest manufacturers in the automobile industry is a testimony of the values these principles bring in.

However, it was in 2003 that Mary Poppendieck and Tom Poppendieck first introduced the application of Lean principles to software development in their book called *Lean Software Development*. Ever since then, Lean and its principles have been popularly adopted by the Agile fraternity. Lean frequently complements other practices like Scrum by minimizing work in progress and maximizing flow in the system by eliminating all forms of waste. Lean focusses on a well-orchestrated effort between the business users, project teams and management to deliver a stream of valuable features (considering priority and urgency of the need), at a sustainable pace and with optimal quality. As Mary Poppendieck summarizes,[5] "we learned that by focusing on value, flow and people, you got better quality, lower cost and faster delivery."

2.4.2 Seven Forms of Waste

Lean uses value stream mapping[6] to analyze and identify all forms of waste and ultimately eliminate them from the system. In the context of TPS, Taiichi identified the seven forms of waste, which are also called *muda* in Japanese. The different wastes are illustrated in Figure 2-10 and described as follows:

1. **Transport** - unnecessary movement and handling of goods and people. The example in software domain is where resources are partially allocated to multiple projects at the same time. Context switching between projects leads to unproductivity and ultimately slows things down.

2. **Inventories** - storage of parts that are either excess or awaiting consumption and often runs the risk of degrading in quality or becoming obsolete. For example any code that has not been delivered to production does not yield value to the customer.

[5]Refer to *Lean Software Development: An Agile Toolkit* authored by Mary Poppendieck and Tom Poppendieck. (Salt Lake City, UT: Addison-Wesley Professional, 2003).
[6]Value stream mapping is discussed in Chapter 4.

3. **Motion** - unnecessary motion of employees, artifacts, or equipment. The example in software context is handoffs of documents between role families (i.e. from analyst to a developer to a tester). Often in this case tacit knowledge in the team never gets transferred, unless people are in the same room and able to freely communicate.

4. **Waiting** - for an upstream process (e.g., instruction, approvals, etc.) to produce and deliver that is to be consumed by the next process. Delays in a project are passed on to the customer as he/she has to wait that much of time before value can be realized.

5. **Overproduction** - of things that are not demanded by the actual users. An example is extra features (*goldplating*) that the developer feels *might* be required in future, but not needed now. Such code might look harmless up front, but in the long run adds to technical debt, contributes to complexity, act as a potential point of failure and also needs to be maintained for life.

6. **Overprocessing** - doing non-value added tasks and relying on inspections rather than preventive measures up front. Taking the example of documentation, Lean recommends that we produce barely sufficient documents that are short, kept at high level and can be easily understood and referenced by the team or the customer.

7. **Defects** - from a variety of sources including rework, scrap, or incorrect documentation. Lean recommends that we build often, integrate often, test often and deploy often.

An easy way to remember the seven wastes is by the acronym **TIMWOOD** (working anticlockwise fashion in Figure 2-10).

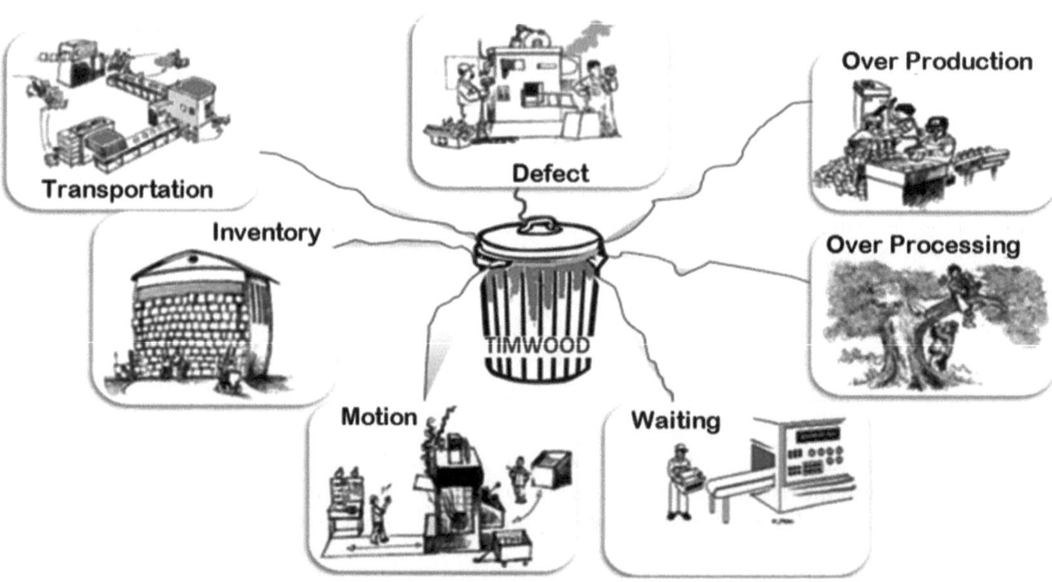

Figure 2-10. *Seven wastes in Lean*

2.4.3 Lean 5S Tool for Improvement

Lean uses the 5S technique that was used for Just-in-time manufacturing. The goal of 5S is to produce a workplace that is well organized, clean, efficient and effective.

As Figure 2-11 shows, 5S stands for:

- Sort (Seiri) - remove unnecessary materials from the workplace.
- Set in order (Seiton) - arrange all items in a proper sequence, which facilitates a smooth flow.
- Shine (Seiso) - periodically inspect the workplace and keep it clean.
- Standardize (Seiketsu) - follow standard practices and processes at the workplace.
- Sustain (Shitsuke) - maintain order, discipline and good working conditions.

Figure 2-11. *Lean 5S tool*

For the PMI-ACP® exam, only the English words sort, set in order, shine, standardize and sustain will suffice.

2.4.4 Principles of Lean Thinking

Figure 2-12 below illustrates the set of seven popular principles in Lean.

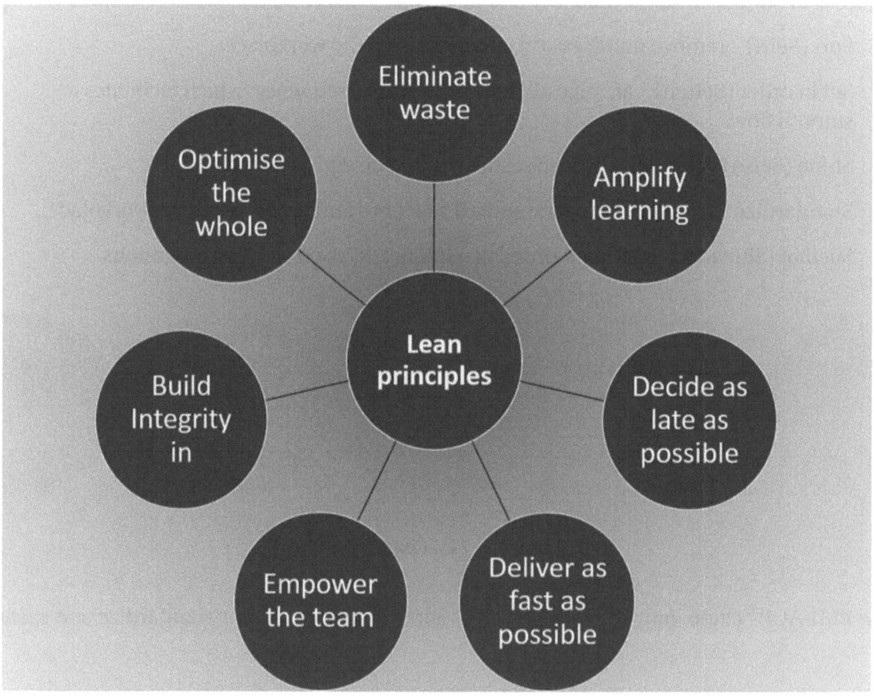

***Figure 2-12.** Seven principles in Lean*

2.4.4.1 Eliminate Waste

In the earlier section, we observed the different forms of waste (*muda*) that Lean discards. In software development such wastes could manifest in the form of

- extra documentation that the customers do not need;
- handoffs between different roles like analysts to developers, developers to testers and testers to release management teams;
- unnecessary features and complexity in code (tangles, loops, tight coupling, high cyclomatic complexity;)
- code that is not tested, built and integrated;
- blockers in processes like approvals and sign-offs;
- ineffective meetings like those without a clear agenda, an expected outcome and timekeeping;

- defects and other visible quality issues;
- management overhead like status reports;
- allocating resourcing on multiple projects and switching them back and forth between them;
- idle time waiting for upstream systems to produce or downstream systems to consume data or interim deliverables.

All forms of waste, as described above, are ruthlessly removed from the value stream, thereby ensuring that there is a continuous flow end to end.

2.4.4.2 Amplify Learning

The concept of value stream map, which emphasizes that identification and elimination of waste is not a one-off activity. It is a continuous activity that the team pursues throughout. An approach to get it right the first time may not work in a scenario where customer needs are evolving and priorities are likely to change. Hence Lean culture embodies a practice of continuous learning and seeking opportunities to improve. Ultimately the goal of a software developer is to *discover* the customer needs and engineer a solution to deliver the same.

As we saw in Scrum and XP, short iterations that produce code and testing whether it confirms to requirements helps in this continuous learning process. Not only does this help to solicit early feedback and refactor accordingly, but also gives the team an opportunity to reflect and make their processes more effective and efficient. Another way to amplify learning is to make brief experiments or *spikes* to reduce risk or uncertainty.

Lean managers steer away from any forms of micromanaging like assigning tasks and tracking them. Instead they work with the team members, coach them, support their learning journey and encourage them to solve problems on their own.

2.4.4.3 Decide as Late as Possible

Lean follows what is called just-in-time planning because when requirements are expected to change and there is insufficient visibility what the end looks like, detailed project planning and upfront commitment are considered a waste of time and effort.

Lean looks to *defer commitment* and delay decision-making until the *last responsible moment*, so that the team can benefit from maximum agility. This is in complete harmony with the Agile Manifesto and its principles that we have covered in the previous chapter.

Lean thinking steers away from making premature decisions too early because they limit the team to technology-bound solutions or wastes time in keeping the plan up to date to accommodate changes. Factoring the escalating cost of change during SDLC, this is effort intensive - much of which generally yields little or negligible value to the customer. Instead, it plans and designs in a change-tolerant manner such that the team can iteratively adapt and refactor a complex system and respond to customer needs. Some of the techniques adopted are the use of abstraction, modularization of code, avoiding repetition in code (also called *DRY - Do Not Repeat Yourself*) and using a breadth-first approach to problem solving rather than depth-first.

2.4.4.4 Deliver as Fast as Possible

Considering a rapidly changing environment, longer is the latency between conception and consumption (of value from a system in production), more likely it is to deviate from the customer's needs. Often the speed (and of course, quality) at which a product or a feature delivered means a lot in terms of earned revenue, competitive advantage, or reputation of the customer in the marketplace.

Lean follows the principle described as *fast-flexible-flow*. By delivering in small iterations, Lean teams look to deliver working software to the customer, who, in turn, can look to realize value incrementally (rather than at the end of a very long project cycle) and provide feedback to the team. This feedback amplifies the team's learning about the domain and the customer needs better and plans to incorporate in the next iteration.

Another enabler for faster delivery is by using the concept of *pull-based system*, which means that the system produces only when the customer demands it. And hence there is no inventory of items waiting to be consumed. In contrast to Scrum, Lean teams do not commit to a set of stories at the beginning of the sprint. Instead they look to pick up a piece of work when they are done with the previous task. This helps to reduce work in progress (which, as we saw, is considered as a waste) and context switching between tasks. And, as per Little's Law,[7] lowering the WIP helps to maximize the flow (and throughput) through the system.

Incidentally while we use the word "fast," it is important to keep a sustainable pace, a value that is also iterated in XP.

2.4.4.5 Empower the Team

Lean is a people-centric philosophy that respects people at work, allowing them to adopt and adapt ways of working that maximizes value and seeks continuous improvement. In contrast to command-and-control style in traditional project management, this principle in Lean is based on the premise that an energized and intrinsically motivated bunch of workers, who are empowered to take decisions and have ultimate accountability of the product are the best suited for making technical decisions for a project. Such people actively deliver value, remove quality issues, refactor design and code, come up with new ideas and thrive in a culture of adaptation and continuous improvement (also called *kaizen*). The role of leaders now changes to set overall direction, aligning people to a common purpose and enabling motivation and giving team members the right to choose what is appropriate.

2.4.4.6 Build Integrity In

There are two flavors of integrity[8] in this principle.

One is the *perceived integrity* and is how the customer experiences the system and balances qualities like accessibility, reliability, economy, ease of use, its applicability and so on. As an example, consider some of the prevalent editors commonly used by programmers (like Eclipse[9]), which are very easy to use to connect to version control, kick off a build, do auto-styling, improve productivity by highlighting and autocorrecting errors even while typing and before compilation. Above all, this comes for free!

The other flavor is *conceptual integrity*, which is how the components of the system are coupled together that leads to flexibility, maintainability, extensibility and the aspects in perceived integrity. For example it is a matter of great satisfaction and convenience to us that today's smartphones can work as a phone, camera, music player and a GPS navigator. So one does not have to depend on or carry multiple devices.

Practices like incremental delivery in short iterations, simple and emergent design, refactoring of design and code, test-first development, coding standards, unit testing, automated testing, continuous build and integration act as enablers for this principle.

---

[7]Little's law and its application to limit WIP is described in the following section on Kanban.

[8]Refer to *Lean-Agile Software Development: Achieving Enterprise Agility* authored by Alan Shalloway, Guy Beaver and James R. Trott. (Salt Lake City, UT: Addison-Wesley Professional, 2009).

[9]Refer to `Eclipse.org`

2.4.4.7 Optimize the Whole

If we take the organizational context, Lean applies to many levels. These levels could range from product, sales, marketing, business community, technology teams, infrastructure and management - precisely anyone in the enterprise who delivers solutions for the end user. For this reason, Lean encourages system thinking. It focuses on the whole system from the beginning to the end - how its parts integrate with each other and how it can be continuously improved.

While the technical components are built, the big picture and customer focus is kept in mind. It is important that each team member focuses on the overall system performance and not be restricted to the area where they have a specialized skill like Java programming, or Oracle database development, or a user-interface design. Also in situations where parts of the system are being built by different teams (let's consider the situation of contracting and subcontracting), it is important that the entire team signs up for this principle, trusts each other, understands the core purpose of the system and embeds this thought process during any form of interaction with the system or its customers. The quotation from Poppendieck[10] in this context, "Think big, act small, fail fast; learn rapidly" is very relevant.

[10]Refer to *Lean Software Development: An Agile Toolkit* authored by Mary Poppendieck and Tom Poppendieck. (Salt Lake City, UT: Addison-Wesley Professional, 2003).

2.5 Kanban

2.5.1 What Is Kanban?

Kanban is a pull-based method for software development that aims at minimizing work in progress (WIP), maximize continuous flow and provide visualization of work as it flows through various life-cycle stages from inception (conceptual phase) to production.

The word Kanban is literally made up of two Japanese words: *Kan* which means visual and *ban* which means card. Put together Kanban means a visual card or signboard or a billboard.

The concept of Kanban has its origin from the just-in-time manufacturing system called Lean Production System[11] in Toyota. However, it was in 2010 that David Anderson, in his book *Kanban* formulated the application of Kanban to software engineering.

2.5.2 Principles in Kanban

Kanban software development is based on the following six simple, yet powerful principles.

2.5.2.1 Visualize Work

Visualization is one of the most important characteristics of Kanban. A Kanban team can simply start with writing a work item on a card or a sticky note and post it to a board. This board consists of a number of columns that the team comes up with to denote the different steps in which work flows, starting from the backlog all the way into production.

This board is called the **Kanban board**[12] and Figure 2-13 shows a simple illustration of the same.

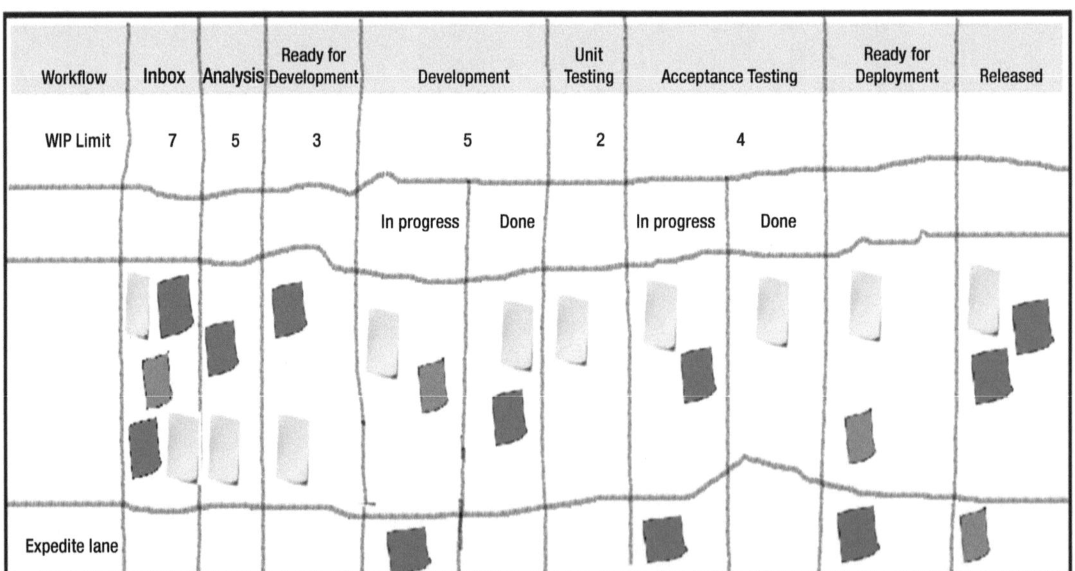

***Figure 2-13.** Example of a Kanban board*

[11]Initially it was called Toyota Production Systems abbreviated as TPS.

[12]Kanban board is an example of Information Radiator that we will discuss further in Chapter 4: Stakeholder engagement.

As seen in the above diagram, each column represents a queue of work items being worked upon. For example, when a work item is done with development, the testing team will pull it into the testing queue. At the same time, since the developer frees up, he can "pull" the next item from the "Ready to develop" queue to "Development in progress" queue and start to code it.

The work items can be described in the form of index cards[13] or sticky notes. Refer to the following Figure 2-14.

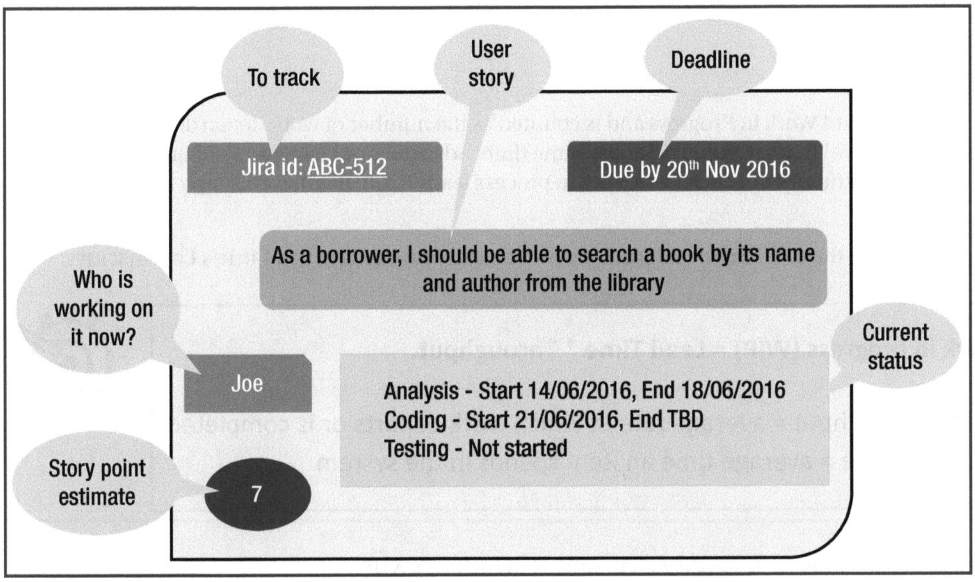

Figure 2-14. *Sample Index cards used in Kanban*

As seen in the above diagram, it is common to find the following attributes of the work item mentioned on the card:

- Work description, often in the form of a user story,[14] defect, technical debt, or a production bug (may be depicted with uniquely colored post-its).
- Name of the person assigned.
- Due dates by which the work must be completed.
- Tracking IDs by which more documentation and other discussions about the work item are captured in an electronic system.
- Progress indicators like the number of days elapsed, status of completion of previous steps like analysis and development, or whether it is blocked.

[13]Refer to the discussion on story cards in Chapter 6: Adaptive Planning.

[14]User stories are elaborately explained in Chapter 6: Adaptive Planning.

- Estimate of the work item. The Kanban board represents a low-tech but high-touch tool. It makes hidden work apparent, making it a powerful tool to organize, track and monitor status and remove unnecessary work in the team. Since information is shared real time, it leads to transparency showing who is working on what at any point in time.

Kanban boards are generally physical boards like whiteboards or 'writable' walls strategically placed at very visible locations. However, for the aid of the virtual team, electronic boards are also available. Examples of such boards are Jira[15] and Kanbanflow.[16]

2.5.2.2 Limit WIP

WIP is the abbreviation of Work in Progress and is counted as the number of work items (depicted on cards as shown above) that are going on at the same time. Advocates of Lean and Kanban are ruthless in limiting this number because less work in process leads to quicker flow through the system.

This theory is based on the mathematical formula based on stable systems called **Little's Law** that says:

Work in progress (WIP) = Lead Time * Throughput.

WhereThroughput = average rate at which work departs or is completed and Lead Time = average time an item spends in the system

In other words, in order to decrease lead time, we have to limit WIP.

Now in software development, what leads to WIP? The simple answer to the question is - anything that doesn't add to customer value (i.e. not delivered to the customer).

Examples are:

- requirements specified or analyzed, but not coded yet;
- code completed, but not integrated yet;
- code integrated but not tested yet;
- code tested but not delivered to production yet.

As the queue builds up with items in WIP, several problems can arise as shown in Figure 2-15 below.

[15]Refer to `https://www.atlassian.com/agile/kanban`
[16]Refer to `https://kanbanflow.com/`

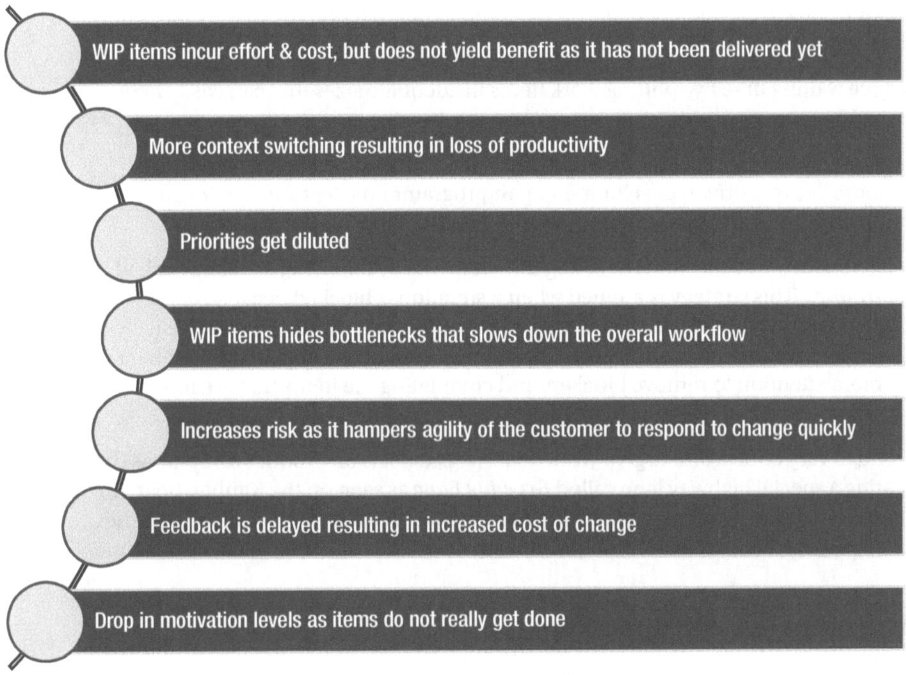

Figure 2-15. *Drawbacks of WIP*

Clearly WIP needs to be limited. Teams collectively and through repeated trials, decide upon WIP limits across each stage of the workflow. For example they choose that no more than three items will be under development at the same time, setting it a limit of three. Or no more than two items should be in the queue waiting to get deployed, giving that step a WIP limit of two. In the Kanban board shown above, the name of the columns are followed by the number in parentheses, which denotes the WIP limits for each column.

2.5.2.3 Manage Workflow

Let us now look at strategies that Kanban teams adopt to manage the workflow and restrict the number of work items below the agreed WIP limit.

- Pursuing a *just-in-time* planning strategy and avoiding temptation to add features (*goldplating*) that does not add value.
- Limiting the intake of work items by following the approach of "Stop starting and start finishing."[17]
- Having cross-functional skills within the team such that each one is able to help the other out.

[17]Refer to the book *Kanban in Action* authored by Marcus Hammarberg and Joakim Sunden (Greenwich, CT: Manning, 2014).

- Meeting daily to discuss the items on the Kanban board (compare to the daily stand-up ceremony in Scrum).
- Reduce waiting time by splitting work items in adequate sizes that can easily flow through.
- Avoiding rework by focusing on quality from the start and deploying technical practices like test-driven development, pair programming, test automation and continuous build and integration.
- By aggressively tracking and removing impediments by following a strategy called "*swarming.*" This strategy is applied when a situation is blocked because of the complexity and dependencies involved and people swarm around to resolve it quickly and restore the normal flow. The point to note here is that team members pay more attention to remove blockers and completing the items that are in WIP state over taking in new items to work.
- Attend to very critical and urgent work items (e.g., defects on production systems) by creating a special highway lane called *Expedite Lane* as seen on the Kanban board in Figure 2-13. Even items on the Expedite Lane are restricted by WIP limits so that the team is not working exclusively on production defects for an extended period of time.

2.5.2.4 Make Process Policies Explicit

Directly related to visualization is a need for explicit agreement on policies and procedures. Often in a team environment, it is easy to see people making assumptions or working in a particular style that could be inconsistent or conflicting.

Examples of explicit policies could be:

- The Kanban board itself where the team members are explicitly required to post their updates regularly.
- Entry and exit criteria as the work items move right from one column to another.
- The WIP limit where the team agrees to a capacity to deliver.
- Conventions for coding and code reviews.
- Measuring and decreasing technical debt.
- Guidelines for what work items belong to the "expedite lane."

By making policies explicit and clear, the conflicts and misunderstandings within the team are resolved. This, then, acts as a base for the team to divorce from personal judgment or emotional sentiments and collaboratively hold rational discussions on how to improve the policies.

2.5.2.5 Implement Feedback Loops

Like all flavors of Agile, this practice is about retrospective of the process itself. Taking off from the Lean philosophy, Kanban focusses on continuous improvement and visualization of the workflow aids in that objective. Unlike Scrum, Kanban does not have retrospectives at the end of the iteration. Instead the team is free to choose an interval when it thinks that holding the retrospective meeting will aim the optimal result.

Apart from retrospectives, Kanban also uses the *Ishikawa diagram or 5-why's technique*[18] to determine the root cause of a problem and explore opportunities to improve. A variation of this technique is called *Kanban Kata* originated from Toyota.

2.5.2.6 Improve Collaboratively, Evolve Experimentally

The practice uses scientific models such as Goldratt's Theory of Constraints and Lean to push the team toward further improvements. A visualized workflow, a limit for the WIP and a focus on moving work through your workflow aids in spotting improvement opportunities.

A simple example of this is setting up of the WIP limits. WIP limits are not hard enforced rules, but triggers conversation so that the team can adapt based on the project needs.

2.5.3 Kanban Metrics

Kanban team choose metrics that help them move forward, not to finger-point or penalize someone.

Some commonly used metrics include:

- Task Completion Rate (TCR) - Tasks completed per day
- Task Add Rate (TAR) - Tasks added or arrived per day. If TAR exceeds TCR, then the team has a continuous flow, the queue is never exhausted and the project is never completed
- Current Task Estimate (CTE) - Total number of active and pending tasks (i.e. represents remaining work)
- Days to complete = CTE / (TCR - TAR)

Some more Kanban metrics are discussed in detail in Chapter 3:

- Lead time
- Throughput
- Number of blocked items
- Rate of defects / escaped defects
- Rate at which delivery happens by due date

2.5.4 Application of Kanban

Kanban has a great appeal because it starts where one is now. And then it continuously looks to limit WIP, maximize flow and find opportunities to improve. Incidentally, because Kanban is "flow-based," it is important that the team does not see this as a never-ending game. It is imperative that the right cadence is chosen where the team can pause plan, review, inspect and adapt at regular intervals. Being a people-centric process, motivation is a critical success factor.

[18]Both 5 Why's technique and the process of retrospectives are described Chapter 8: Continuous Improvement.

As we observed, in contrast to Scrum or XP, Kanban does not have fixed-length sprints or iterations. In terms of practical application, Kanban is a very popular in operations, production support and incident management that needs response in a short amount of time and often governed by priority or severity based service-level agreements (SLA's).

While this section was for Kanban, it is also worthwhile to note that there exists another methodology called "Scrumban," which starts from Scrum and transitions to Kanban. Scrumban was introduced by Core Ludas in 2009.

2.6 Dynamic Systems Development Method (DSDM)

2.6.1 What Is DSDM?

The origin of DSDM methodology dates back to 1994 and was seen as an enhancement over the Rapid Application Development (RAD) method. It combines the project management and product management life cycle. Like Agile methods, DSDM uses iterative and incremental development cycles, but within an appropriate framework of project governance as prevalent in organizations.

2.6.2 Phases of DSDM

DSDM has three phases, namely: pre-project, project life cycle and post-project.

The project life-cycle phase, as shown in Figure 2-16, is further broken down into five stages called feasibility study, business study, functional model iteration, design and build and implementation.

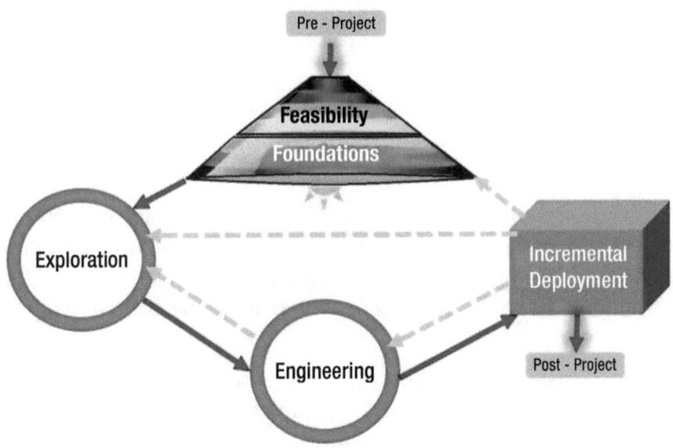

Figure 2-16. *Phases of Dynamic Systems Development Method (DSDM)*

There are a few Agile practices in DSDM that are popular like timeboxing, facilitated workshops, MoSCoW prioritization and prototyping. These are discussed in the later chapters of the book.

2.6.3 Principles in DSDM

There are eight principles in DSDM and they existed before the Agile Manifesto was created. They are listed as follows:

1. Focus on the business need
2. Deliver on time
3. Collaborate
4. Never compromise quality
5. Build incrementally from firm foundations
6. Develop iteratively
7. Communicate continuously and clearly
8. Demonstrate control

2.7 Feature-Driven Development (FDD)

Although slightly lesser known than the previous ones, Feature-Driven Development or FDD is a lightweight Agile methodology that aims to build a software in increments of features or functionalities. These features directly represent value-added functionality that a user wants to use.

The origin of FDD goes back to Jeff De Luca in the mid-1990s. Jeff described FDD as a model-driven process consisting of five activities listed in the following Figure 2-17.

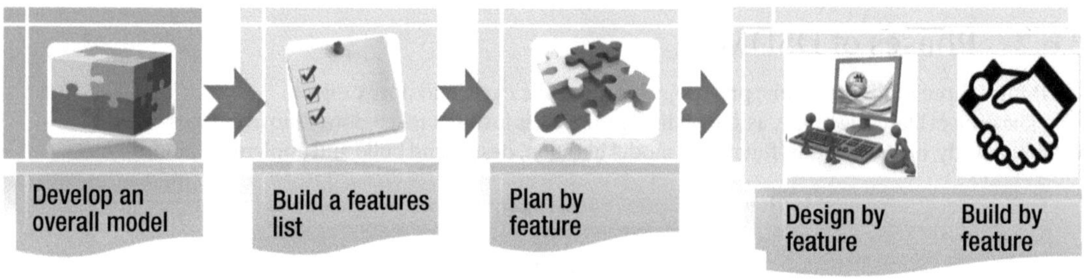

Figure 2-17. *Activities in Feature-Driven Development (FDD)*

1. Develop overall model - FDD is seen to have "modeling teams" consisting of domain experts and lead programmers who are responsible for coming up with an overall model of the system based on the scope. The model is further detailed into domain models for each component, which are then shortlisted following a peer review.

2. Build feature list - Based on the initial model the "feature team" identifies features and business activities. These are small pieces of functionalities expected by the customer and is analogous to user stories in Scrum. The features are intentionally kept small enough so that they can be fitted into a two-week iteration. Otherwise they are further broken down into smaller features.

3. Plan by feature - With a feature list in hand, planning starts in the form of assigning ownership of a particular feature or an area to an individual who takes care of the consistency, performance and conceptual integrity of the code to be implemented. Note that this is the opposite of the concept in XP of collective code ownership. The sequence in which features are worked upon is based on the complexity, capacity of the team and the dependencies between them.

4. Design by feature - The team then progress to detail out the design for a set of features than can be delivered in a single two-week iteration. The design is then reviewed and passed on for implementation.

5. Build by feature - During this stage the team codes, unit tests, reviews and builds the code. Like the earlier design review, code reviews ensure good quality and a defect prevention activity. The builds are orchestrated at regular intervals and gives a sense of visible progress that can be demonstrated.

Progress of a FDD project is tracked through defined milestones like domain walkthrough, design, design review, code, code review and build.

2.8 Crystal

Crystal is the name of a family of methodologies created by Alistair Cockburn in the mid-1990s. After years of research and looking into working practices of communication and community-based Agile projects, Alistair came up with Crystal.

Alistair, to quote from his book, *Agile Software Development: The Cooperative Game*: "The core Crystal philosophy is that software development is usefully viewed as a cooperative game of invention and communication, with a primary goal of delivering useful, working software and a secondary goal of setting up for the next game."

Compared to Scrum or XP presented above, Crystal is a *family* of methodologies described by colors, namely, Clear, Yellow, Orange, Orange Web, Red, Maroon, Blue, Violet and so on. The analogy is with the precious gemstone Crystal with progressive darker colors depicting heavier methodologies as required in larger projects. The choice of methodologies gives the people in the team flexibility to adopt to what suits them the best - in terms of communication, processes, policies, tools and techniques.

In the above Figure 2-18, the horizontal (X) axis denotes the team size varying from a small team of 2-6 members to a large team having 80-200 members. The vertical axis (Y) denotes the criticality of the system and the impact it has if it breaks down. The Y axis ranges from projects on systems whose breakdown would cause loss of comfort (C), loss of money within some tolerance (D), or more (E) and life critical (L).

		Crystal Methodologies				
		Clear	Yellow	Orange	Red	Maroon
Criticality of the Project	Life (L)	L6	L20	L40	L80	L200
	Essential Money (E)	E6	E20	E40	E80	E200
	Discretionary Money (D)	D6	D20	D40	D80	D200
	Comfort (C)	C6	C20	C40	C80	C200
		1 to 6	7 to 20	21 to 40	41 to 80	81 to 200
		Number of People involved in the Project				

Figure 2-18. *Choice of Crystal family of methodologies based on criticality and size of projects*

2.8.1 Principles and Characteristics of Crystal

Following are some of the key characteristics that are common among all flavors of Crystal. The keywords are marked in bold to aid memorizing for the PMI-ACP® exam.

- **Small teams** interacting with each other and forming their own way of working to deliver the product.
- Producing **running code more frequently** to the user by developing in **short increments** of duration of 1 to 3 months.
- **Continuous improvements** by holding pre- and post-increment **reflection workshops.**
- Using richer and **osmotic communication** within **co-located** team members, taking precedence over documentation.
- **Personal safety** in being able to trust and openly discuss a question or throw an idea among a group of people without fear of retribution or anything adverse.
- **Focus** on the goals of the project and the individual tasks in hand.
- Providing the team an opportunity to pause and adapt their ways of working based on the prevailing conditions.
- **Ease of access to business or expert user** who is around to clarify a scenario or suggest solutions to problems.
- Sound **technology practices and an environment** that supports automation of testing (e.g., for regression), version control, continuous build and integration.
- **Reduce intermediate work products**, overhead and bureaucracy to the least sufficient and required amount irrespective of the size of the projects.
- **Adaptable and amenable** since it permits using of practices from other methodologies like pair programming in XP or a daily stand-up from Scrum.

2.8.2 Crystal Processes

The Crystal framework is cyclical, consisting of three processes, namely, chartering, delivery cycles and wrap-up.

The chartering phase starts with *Exploratory 360°*. During this phase most of the setup tasks are done, the core team is built, the business value of the project is checked, the project and technology plans are formulated and the team defines and agrees to the standards to be followed.

During the delivery phase, the team could look to start with a *Walking skeleton*, which is a tiny implementation of the system that performs a small end-to-end function and is demonstration. This gives a sense of *early victory* and the much needed confidence to the team. The team continues to develop, test, integrate and release product increments. As discussed above, Crystal permits use of practices like daily stand-up meetings from Scrum, pair programming from XP and reflection workshops on the way.

Finally, in wrap-up phase, the team completes the project and reflects on it.

2.8.3 Members of Crystal Family

For the purpose of the PMI-ACP® exam, knowing the concepts on principles and processes of Crystal are enough. The next few sections cover some basics of the members of the Crystal family of methodologies. This is generally not seen in the exam, although the concepts are useful.

2.8.3.1 Crystal Clear

This is the lightest of the Crystal methods and applicable to a small team such as three-eight members seated in one or adjoining office and working on systems that are life critical. The roles required are sponsor, senior designer cum programmer, another designer cum programmer who is relatively junior and a user. Like all other members of the Crystal family the focus is no people-centric processes that bring efficiency, regular reflection workshops, documentation that is 'barely sufficient' is needed and close proximity to the real user. The team leverages important tools like configuration management systems and information radiators like a printable whiteboard. Teams are free to 'borrow' practices like daily stand-up, timeboxing and pair programming from other methodologies discussed in this chapter.

2.8.3.2 Crystal Orange

This level is applicable for medium-sized teams of thirty-fifty people located in the same building working on a medium-sized project that could last for 1 to 2 years. With a slightly larger team size, the team needs are organized into role families that do planning, monitoring, design and architecture, coding and infrastructure and testing activities. Incremental and frequent delivery approaches are still followed, but the iterations could get longer and extended to three-four months. Similarly this methodology requires more documentation.

The Crystal Orange web variation of the above is targeted toward teams delivering code and features to the Web continuously.

2.8.3.3 Crystal Red

In this level the team size is much larger, about seventy-eighty people working on systems that are likely to be life critical. The team needs to be organized into subteams to allow better management and control. The methodology shifts to a heavier side with more documentation and elaborate processes like design and code reviews.

2.9 Focus Areas for the Exam

- ✓ Awareness of the generic Agile processes.
- ✓ Emphasis on Scrum, XP, Lean and Kanban.
- ✓ Scrum - features, three pillars.
- ✓ Different functions played by each role in Scrum, what happens during each Scrum ceremony and significance of each artifact.
- ✓ Awareness of the differences between a classic project manager and that of Scrum Master.
- ✓ Core values of XP.
- ✓ XP roles like XP coach, whole team, tracker and on-site customer.
- ✓ Twelve core practices in XP and their significance.
- ✓ Origin of Lean and seven forms of waste (acronym to remember is TIMWOOD).

- ✓ Lean 5S tool and seven principles.
- ✓ Literal meaning of the word Kanban, visualizing flow using the Kanban board.
- ✓ What are the drawback of having too much WIP and ways to limit WIP.
- ✓ Six principles in Kanban and their significance.
- ✓ Phases of DSDM and FDD at a very high level.
- ✓ Basic understanding of Crystal family of methodologies and how darker colors denote progressively heavier methodologies.

Quizzes

1. What are the core values in Extreme Programming (XP):

   A. Simplicity, communication, respect

   B. Simplicity, controlling, feedback

   C. Simplicity, controlling, respect

   D. Solution, communication, respect

2. The three Scrum pillars are:

   A. Transparency, Inspection, feedback

   B. Transparency, adaptation, progress

   C. Check, Feedback Progress

   D. Transparency, Inspection, adaptation

3. What are the three questions discussed or asked in Daily Scrum meetings?

   A. What has been achieved since the last meeting? What will be done before the next meeting? What obstacles are in the way?

   B. What has been started since the last meeting? What might get done before the next meeting? What obstacles are in the way?

   C. What has been started since the last meeting? What will be done before the next meeting? What obstacles are in the way?

   D. What has been achieved since the last meeting? What might get done before the next meeting? What obstacles are in the way?

4. Name the backlogs available in Scrum.

   A. Product backlog, iteration backlog

   B. Project backlog, iteration backlog

   C. Project backlog, sprint backlog

   D. Product backlog, sprint backlog

5. In Scrum, Definition of Done is NOT created by

   A. Scrum Master

   B. Product Owner

   C. Process Owner

   D. Development Team

6. Which of these are core practices in XP?

   A. Whole team, planning games, small releases

   B. One team, process game, small releases

   C. Whole team, planning games, quick releases

   D. One team, process game, quick releases

7. Lean principles:

   A. Eliminate waste, empower the team, build quality in, deter decisions, amplify learning

   B. Eliminate waste, empower the team, build quality in, deter decision, minimize learning

   C. Eliminate waste, empower the team, build quality in, defer decisions, amplify learning

   D. Eliminate waste, empower the team, build quality in, defer decisions, optimize learning

8. Which of the following are some of the planned opportunities for inspection and adaptation in the Scrum method?

   A. Sprint retrospective, velocity review meeting, daily Scrum meeting

   B. Sprint planning meeting, sprint retrospective, sprint risk meeting

   C. Sprint retrospective, daily Scrum meeting, sprint review meeting

   D. Sprint planning meeting, daily Scrum meeting, retrospective planning meeting

9. In Kanban, WIP stands for:

   A. Waste in progress

   B. Work in progress

   C. Waste in process

   D. Work is progressing

10. The core principles in Kanban are:

    A. Minimize the workflow, pull flow, make process polices explicit, improve collaboratively

    B. Visualize the workflow, manage flow, make process policies explicit, improve collaboratively

    C. Minimize the workflow, manage flow, make process polices explicit, improve collaboratively

    D. Visualize the workflow, pull flow, make process policies explicit, improve collaboratively

11. What does the word 'timeboxed' mean in the context of Agile?

    A. Fast

    B. Flexible

    C. Frequent

    D. Fixed

12. Which of these is NOT an Agile methodology?

    A. Extreme programming (XP)

    B. Scrum

    C. Crystal clear

    D. PMBOK®

13. A person who makes decision and practices Scrum to the core is performing what role?

    A. Pig

    B. Chicken

    C. Scrum master

    D. Scrum team

14. The MoSCoW prioritization technique is originated from which Agile technique?

    A. DSDM

    B. Feature-driven development (FDD)

    C. Scrum

    D. Extreme programming (XP)

15. Who determines how much of the product backlog can be delivered in the upcoming sprint?

    A. Product Manager

    B. Team

    C. Scrum Master

    D. Project Owner

16. Which of these method/practices demands a sustained level of customer interaction throughout the project and so has the role of an 'on-site customer':

    A. Waterfall method

    B. Agile project management

    C. Extreme programming

    D. Kanban

17. In the Kanban model, how do WIP limits help?

    A. Tracking becomes easy

    B. Prevents work piling up of tasks at the bottleneck

    C. Limits the size of product backlog

    D. Helps developers to choose tasks easily

18. The idea of timeboxing in Agile is to:

    A. Save effort and money

    B. Effectively prioritize work and provide incremental result

    C. Develop a mechanism to increase project scope

    D. Prevent schedule overruns

19. Which of these incorrectly describes a servant leader?

    A. Are stewards of their organization's human, financial and physical resources

    B. Participatory management style

    C. Have a natural feeling to lead first

    D. Focus on the needs of their colleagues and those they serve

20. In XP, frequent verification and validation is ensured through:

    A. Code reviews

    B. Pair programming

    C. Simplicity

    D. Automated test suite

21. During which meeting do team members synchronize their work and progress and report any impediments to the Scrum Master for removal?

    A. Brainstorming meeting

    B. Status Meeting

    C. Daily Scrum

    D. Sprint Retrospective

22. In an XP team, what is expected from the Project Manager?

    A. Help team work with the rest of the organization

    B. XP does not have a project manager role

    C. Provide domain expertise to team

    D. Responsible for defining the software

23. At what point of the project is the product backlog frozen and disallows any further changes?

A. Before the project execution starts

B. After we are done with the first few sprints and the review has happened

C. It is never frozen

D. Once the estimation and planning is done

24. A list of activities that is expected to be completed successfully by the end of a sprint is called:

A. Sprint checklist

B. Quality metrics

C. Definition of Ready

D. Definition of Done

Answers

1. A - XP core values are Communication, Simplicity, Feedback, Courage and Respect. Solution, controlling are made-up terms.
2. D
3. A
4. D
5. C - There is no such role as process owner.
6. A
7. C
8. C
9. B
10. B
11. D - Timeboxed term in Agile refers to completing work in a fixed and agreed time. If work is not completed in the timebox, it is returned to the backlog to be considered for a later timebox.
12. D
13. D - Scrum Team is owning the work and empowered to make decisions using Scrum practices.
14. A
15. B
16. C
17. B - WIP manages workflow, too many in-progress tasks can create bottleneck and delay others.
18. B - Timeboxing is the mechanism of working toward a short deadline with a specific goal and a defined budget.
19. C
20. D
21. C
22. A - A project manager in an XP team ensures that the team works well with the rest of the organization. A PM is more focused in managing external stakeholders.
23. C
24. D

CHAPTER 3

Domain II: Value-Driven Delivery

> *Wait wait — put your hands down. Listen: I know you have a thousand ideas for all the cool feature iTunes could have. So do we. But we don't want a thousand features. That would be ugly. Innovation is not about saying 'Yes' to everything. It's about saying 'No' to all but the most crucial features.*
>
> —Steve Jobs

This chapter pretty much takes over from where we left off in Chapter 1: Agile Principles and Mindset. We saw how Agile projects are value driven in contrast to being plan driven as in traditional waterfall-based projects. The concept of value-driven delivery manifests in every stage of an Agile project - initiation where the business case of projects are justified, incremental planning where customer values and risks are balanced and prioritized, monitoring and tracking with deliberate emphasis on real-time customer feedback and reporting value through a variety of visual indicators.

3.1 The Agile Triangle

In traditional projects, project managers balance the '*triple constraints*' of Scope, Time and Cost. These are labeled on the three vertices of the *Iron Triangle* as depicted in Figure 3-1. The triangle structure helps to represent the fact that all three constraints are tightly related to each other. Any one of these constraints if affected would impact the other two constraints simultaneously. The other factor that is also balanced is Quality and that is placed in the center of the iron triangle. For example, if scope is increased, then it will take longer to develop and cost more. If the project budget is reduced, then lesser scope can be delivered and the project is likely to finish sooner.

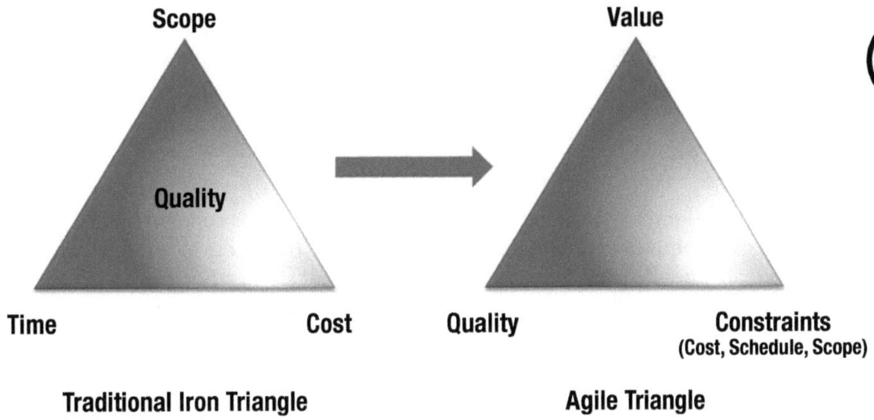

Figure 3-1. *The Traditional Iron Triangle vs. the Agile Triangle*

S. Boral, *Ace the PMI-ACP® exam*, DOI 10.1007/978-1-4842-2526-4_3

For Agile projects, however, the emphasis is on continuous value realization for the end customer. Jim Highsmith has suggested that the triangle structure be reused, but with a set of different vertices, namely - **Value, Quality** and the triple **constraints** of cost, schedule and scope. Notice that the focus shifts into the delivery of value-added features to the customer. The usability of the features and the benefits realized greatly depend on the quality of the product. In the third vertex, one of the constraints is the scope, which is variable as we have seen before. The schedule and the cost constraints are also variable and tend to respond and adjust to the pull or demand of value by the stakeholders.

3.2 Embedding Value-Driven Delivery in Agile Practices

In the first section we take a look at some of the ways that Agile teams realize values.

3.2.1 Deliver Value in Increments

Agile projects deliver in small increments with each increment consisting of the features of the products that are deemed to be of the highest business value. The choice of the work items delivered during a particular increment also factors in risk that need to be mitigated by the project team. At the end of each timeboxed iteration, the development team delivers a working version of the product that is of use to the customer.

3.2.2 Deliver Value Early

Overarching the iterations is the release plan where the team begins with delivering minimally marketable features (MMF's)[1] for early recognition of value. Early deliveries help teams to understand customers' requirements better, increase the confidence of stakeholders, pave way for course correction early on (if the direction of the project is not as expected) and also gauge the pace and capacity of the team to work together and turn user stories into working software. This is why there is a strong bias for just-in-time planning and working software as a measure for progress over detailed documentation and upfront detailed planning.

3.2.3 Value-Based Analysis

Agile projects consider both the business value of work items as well as the cost of delivering them. This is called *Value-based analysis* and forms a crucial input to the prioritization exercise. As we shall see in the next section, one of the goals of the product owner (as in Scrum) is to maximize the return on investment (abbreviated as ROI) in every timeboxed iteration. ROI is expressed as a fraction with the revenue or the business value in the numerator and the cost in the denominator. In other words, work items that have the highest fraction of the business value at the minimum cost of implementing it gets the highest priority. While computing the business value, the product owner should consider the payback period, the return year on year and the inflation-adjusted return.

3.2.4 Prioritizing Collaboratively

The product owner prioritizes units of work based on business value. This is collated in the product backlog. Each work item, based on its perceived complexity, is also estimated by the development team. During the planning sessions the team and the product owner / onsite customer sit together and collaboratively plan for the work to be delivered such that during each iteration the ROI is maximized. We will see some of the economic models like ROI, NPV and IRR later in this chapter.

---

[1]Release planning and MMF's are covered in detail in Chapter 6: Adaptive Planning.

3.2.5 Minimizing Non-Value Added Work

Agile teams relentlessly pursue elimination of non-value added work from the customer's perspective. It does so by coming up with a value stream map that contains all the steps in sequence that are required to deliver a product to the customer and remove anything that hinders or is deemed as waste. This ensures that value is handed over to the customer based on pull and as fast as possible.

3.2.6 Frequent Review Based on Stakeholder Priorities

At the end of every iteration, the team gets an opportunity to gain acceptance of the work done and solicit feedback from stakeholders, which in turn, leads to new requirements, enhancements, changes to existing requirements, or changes to priorities. This is invaluable as it helps teams to adapt to change seamlessly and mitigate escalating costs of change if introduced at a very late stage in the project. Agile teams carefully choose an iteration length trading off the number of days they can afford to go without feedback versus the overhead of iterating (planning, executing, regressing, reviewing, etc.). The culture of frequent feedback and review also creates a sense of engagement and empathy between the customers and the development team and helps them thrive in a zone of volatile requirements.

3.2.7 Focus on Quality

Defects erode value and limit the usability of a product. Defects also have a compounding effect as the cost of removal exponentially goes up with time and more and more features get built on top of it. While progressing on delivery, Agile teams are diligent in quality management. By following frequent verification and validation, the team ensured that functional and nonfunctional requirements are completed and defects do not propagate too far into later stages. There is a strong emphasis on test-driven development, automated regression, continuous integration and behavior-based acceptance testing.

3.2.8 Focus on Nonfunctional Requirements

While so far the discussions have centered on functional requirements that add values to the business, Agile teams also need to be attentive toward nonfunctional requirements that are like the quality attributes of the system and govern fitness for use. Considerations for nonfunctional requirements play a key role during architecture and design of the system.

Examples of nonfunctional attributes of a system include:

- Safety, security, privacy, compliance, usability, accessibility, performance
- Availability, reliability, resilience, backup, disaster recovery
- Portability, operability, interoperability
- Extensibility, maintainability, scalability

3.2.9 Continuous Improvement

Agile teams retrospect continuously. Agile teams look at opportunities to translate lessons learned and retrospectives during the previous iteration to be translated into action items for improvement from the very next iteration. They tailor their approach, processes and tools based on project environment, organizational characteristic and the capacity of the team to deliver. For example, they enjoy the freedom to do barely sufficient documentation that is essential to build and maintain the product or choose how heavy their methodologies should be based on the team size or whether they are co-located or not. We will cover this in more detail in Chapter 8 of this book.

3.3 Determining Value at Project Initiation

Projects are typically authorized as a result of one or more of the following strategic considerations:

- Market demand or requests from customer segments
- Strategic opportunity to seek competitive advantage
- Improvement of operational efficiency
- Technological advancement
- Legal and regulatory compliance requirements
- Environmental consideration
- Social need or safety need

However, it is through comparative benefit measurements that one project is chosen over the others. The same can be applied to selective choose features to be included in a particular project, because after all a balance needs to be maintained between time, cost and scope.

3.3.1 Economic Models for Project Selection

The following sections describe a few economic models such as NPV, IRR and payback period, which are used to compare one project over another. In some scenarios, considering the life cycle costs of the software product is also relevant because it factors not only building the product the first time, but also maintaining it down the line. Note that these methods are used irrespective of whether the project will be delivered through waterfall or Agile methodologies.

For the PMI-ACP® exam, the calculations of the formulae are not required. One should understand that these techniques are used to compare one project to another economically and which value is more favorable over the other.

3.3.1.1 Present Value (PV)

The concept of present value is based on time value of money by factoring in a rate of interest or inflation. PV is commonly expressed by the following formula:

$$PV = FV / (1+r)^n$$

Where FV = future value, r = interest rate and n = number of time periods.

As an example, consider two projects A and B that are producing a product such that:

1. Project A has a future value of $300 after 3 years, at an interest rate of 10%.
2. Project B has a future value of $500 after 5 years, at an interest rate of 10%.

Project A has a PV of $PV_A = 300 / (1 + 0.1)^3 = 300 / 1.33 = \$225$

Project B has a PV of $PV_B = 500 / (1 + 0.1)^5 = 500 / 1.61 = \$311$

Hence, in present value terms Project B is more profitable and should be favored over Project A.

3.3.1.2 Net Present Value (NPV)

Net present value extends the concept of PV by factoring in the initial investment as well as the revenue stream of future.

Net Present Value (NPV) = - Initial investment + ∑ Return of each year in today's terms.

As an example, again consider two projects A and B that are producing a product such that:

1. Project A requires an initial investment of $1000 and produces a return of $300 for the next 3 years. Assume a steady interest rate of 10%.
2. Project B requires an initial investment of $800 and produces a return of $200 for the next 4 years. Assume a steady interest rate of 10%.

Using the same formula of NPV, we can calculate the following:

Project A has a NPV of $NPV_A = -1000 + 300 / (1.1)^1 + 300 / (1.1)^2 + 300 / (1.1)^3 = -\$254$

Project B has a NPV of $NPV_B = -800 + 200 / (1.1)^1 + 200 / (1.1)^2 + 200 / (1.1)^3 + 200 / (1.1)^4 = -\$166$

Hence in terms of Net Present Value, Project B is more profitable and should be favored over Project A. In real-life situations, the upfront investment cost could be staggered over a few years or the rate of discounting be variable or inflation-adjusted year by year. Since we consider both cash inflows and outflows, NPV calculation is quite popularly used[2] to compute returns of a project.

3.3.1.3 Payback Period

Payback period is the number of time periods it takes to recover the investment in the project before it starts to accumulate profit. Note that in both the projects A and B in the above example for NPV calculation, break-even has not been reached even after 3 and 4 years respectively indicated by a negative NPV for the period of computation.

For the case of comparison, the lesser the payback period the better. So a project with payback period of 3 years is favored over the other with 5 years.

Let us look at another example illustrated in Table 3-1 below. In this project there is an investment of $10,000 in the first year and the project expects revenue from the second year onward.

Table 3-1. *Revenue projections for a project*

Year	Year 1	Year 2	Year 3	Year 4	Year 5	Year 6	Year 7
Cash inflows	-10000$	2000$	3000$	5000$	4000$	4000$	3000$

We see that at the end of the fourth year, break-even is reached since the total returns from Year 2 to Year 4 is $2000 + $3000 + $5000 = $10,000, which is equal to the initial investment. So the payback period of the project is 4 years. From the fifth year onward, the project becomes profitable.

A variation of payback period that factors in a rate of discounting (i.e. time value of future cash flow) is called *Discounted Payback period.*

[2]Microsoft Excel® has a formula to compute NPV

3.3.1.4 Internal Rate of Return (IRR)

IRR is defined as the discount rate at which the project inflows and outflows are equal. Simply stated, by considering a project's duration, cash flows at regular intervals and payback period the IRR is calculated. The actual computation of IRR is beyond the scope[3] of the PMI-ACP® exam. The only point to remember is that higher the IRR the better.

So a project with IRR of 12% is favored over the other with 8%.

3.3.1.5 Return on Investment (ROI) or Benefit Cost Ration (BCR)

ROI is the ratio of net benefits of the project to it total cost. As an example consider a project that costs $1000 and returns revenue of $1500. The net benefit is therefore 1500 - 1000 = 500. So the ROI is 500 / 1000 = 50%.

For comparison, the higher the ROI or BCR, the better.

Before we leave this section, be reminded that the formulae or computation of PV, NPV and IRR are not expected in the PMI-ACP® exam. They have been discussed above to aid in understanding and help in retention of the concepts. The following Table 3-2 helps in a quick recap that will help in answering most, if not all, questions on this topic in the exam.

Table 3-2. *Economic models for choice of projects*

Method	Project A	Project B	Which is better?	Why?
NPV	$82000	$65000	A	Higher the better
IRR	14%	22%	B	Higher the better
Payback period	3 years	4 years	A	Lower the better
ROI	50%	120%	B	Higher the better

3.3.2 Compliance and Regulatory Needs

Projects that are originated to serve legal, compliance and regulatory requirements are given the highest precedence. Such projects are deemed as mandatory for the organization as otherwise its license to operate could be compromised and it has to bear penalties or undergo legal action. For example, consider the case of banking regulations in global financial markets where trading and payment transactions are strictly prohibited in some countries because of sanctions against fraud and terrorist financing. In such scenarios, considerations of commercial value (like in terms of IRR, NPV and ROI) for projects may be secondary in nature.

Some of the common areas of compliance observed are:

- Sarbanes-Oxley Act (abbreviated as SOX) administered by U.S. Securities and Exchange Commission (SEC) to protect shareholder and general public from accounting errors and fraudulent practices in the enterprises and improves accuracy of corporate disclosures.
- Health Insurance Portability and Accountability Act (abbreviated as HIPAA) to improve portability and continuity of health insurance coverage in the group and individual markets and combat waste, fraud and abuse in health insurance and health care delivery.

[3]Like NPV, Microsoft Excel® has a formula to compute IRR.

- Dodd-Frank Wall Street reform and Consumer protection act to promote the financial stability of the United States by improving accountability and transparency in the financial system and protect consumers from abusive financial services practices.
- Basel I, II and III to lay down guidelines for capital adequacy, liquidity and risk management and disclosure requirements for financial institutions.
- BS7799 and ISO 27001 for Information Security Management.
- ISO 9000 for quality management standards.
- Federal Drug Administration (FDA) regulations.

3.3.3 Business Case Development

Armed with the calculations from the economic models, Agile teams get ready to prepare the business case document. This is an important document[4] that enlists the vision of the project, high-level statement of the project scope, expected cost and duration of the project and how the deliverables will be produced.

Following are some of the sections that can go into a business case document:

- Project background - to provide historical context to the reader, helping to set the stage.
- Project purpose - why the project is deemed as necessary by the organization. As we have seen earlier in the beginning of Section 2, a project could be born out of a customer need, a regulatory requirement, exploiting a business opportunity in the market, keeping up with technology advancement, or to bring in efficiency in the operations.
- Project scope - description of what the project plans to address and how it fits into the strategic vision of the company.
- Project stakeholders - people and organizations who would be impacted positively or negatively because of the project.
- Monetary factors - consideration of the potential to increase revenue that justifies the investment in the project. For example, the new project could result in increase in revenue coming from existing or new customer segments, or prevent a loss in revenue if the project is not executed. In this section the projections of cash inflow and outflow; life cycle costs of a product; and calculations of NPV, ROI and IRR are used to justify the project.
- Risks, issues and dependencies - consideration of factors that could have an adverse impact on the progress of the project or dependencies on internal and external bodies (e.g., clearance from municipal or government agencies).
- Business model - depicting a catalogue of services performed by the software on behalf of the business, activities under the services, qualitative and quantitative value proposition, customers served, resources utilized, channels of interaction and sources of revenue. One of the ways of depicting new or existing business models is through the business model canvas.[5]

---

[4]Refer to *Lean-Agile Software Development: Achieving Enterprise Agility* authored by Alan Shalloway, Guy Beaver and James R. Trott. (Boston: Addison-Wesley, 2009).

[5]Refer to `https://en.wikipedia.org/wiki/Business_Model_Canvas` as proposed by Alexander Osterwalder.

3.3.4 Agile Charters

Irrespective of whether the project follows the traditional waterfall-based or Agile methodologies, the project charter is one the earliest documents or artifacts that is produced in the project life cycle. Remember, that of all documents that Agile teams look to produce, the charter is the first and also a must-have.

During the chartering session, the stakeholders come together and aim to create a common understanding of the product, its vision, its mission and its goals. As a part of the chartering process, stakeholders experience a rich level of engagement and collective understanding of the many facets of the desired project or product. Once the project charter is approved by the senior leadership team in the organization, the sponsor gets to appoint a project manager (as in waterfall projects) who is authorized to expend funds to commence the project work and accomplish its objectives.

Charters for Agile projects are no longer than a page or two in length, so it is not expected to contain fine-grained project details, most of which may be unknown initially. However, it is a significant document that the participating stakeholders agree upon. Agile project teams rely on methods like adaptive planning, close collaboration with customers, short feedback cycles, iterative delivery methods, retrospectives to respond and adapt to the inherent uncertainties in project scope, priorities, technologies and risks.

Figure 3-2. *W5H acronym for the contents of a project charter*

The acronym **W5H**, as shown in Figure 3-2, is an easy way to remember the contents of a project charter.

The W5H questions mean to address the following in order:

- **What** is the scope of the project? - A high-level description of project goals and objectives, with an acknowledgment of the fact that scope may change during the course of the project. If the project envisions a product to be built, the product is given a name along with a compelling value proposition that states why the product is expected to thrive in the marketplace. This section of the charter also states the critical success factors and what the team will need to accomplish to reach the vision.

- **Why** is the project being undertaken? - The business justification or statement of the need of the project and what the desired end state is. If the product is expected to compete with other products known or already existing in the market, then this section states what differentiates it over the others. Take a note of the different reasons that an organization undertakes a project as described in the beginning of Section 2.
- **Who** will be impacted because of the project? - A list of the project participants and target users. Stakeholders of the project could be anyone or any organization who are actively involved in the project or whose interests may positively or negatively affected by the performance or completion of the project. For instance the sponsors, product manager, senior management, subject matter experts and the development team.
- **When** will the project start and end? - The start and end dates of the project, along with a high-level view of the milestones. Note that since in Agile projects the scope is expected to evolve, the duration and milestone dates can be further refined as the project progresses.
- **Where** will the project occur or deliver? - Details of work location or where the product will be deployed. This aspect of the charter factors in different skills and expertize at different location (consider the case of multinational companies) that would be involved in creating the product. The product could also be marketed and deployed to satisfy the needs of varied user segments across the globe.
- **How** will the project be executed? - A description of the approach or process such as incremental and iterative delivery, feedback loops that would be followed to engage stakeholders, factor in changes, perform acceptance of product increments, etc. At a very high level, the charter also includes how much of budget would be required by the project.

3.3.5 Product Vision and Elevator Pitch

At the beginning of the chartering session, the product vision is defined. The product owner or business sponsor takes the lead and explains, in fewer than 140 characters, what the product serves and why it is deemed as valuable. This statement is called the *elevator pitch* or the *elevator statement*. Note that the product owner is in the best position to come up with the elevator statement because he or she is responsible for driving the project, making sure that the return on investment is maximized and customers are able to realize benefits. The elevator statement acts as a commonly referred statement that anyone in the project team or organization can relate to throughout the project or product life cycle - starting from the junior staff in the development team to the senior executive in the marketing department. This helps to create a uniform view of the mission and vision of the product.

The format of an elevator statement looks like this:

For [target customer]
Who [statement of the need or opportunity]
The [product name] **is a** [product category]
that [The statement of key benefit which is a compelling reason to use or buy].
Unlike [primary competitive alternative],
our product [statement of primary differentiation]

When applied to our library management system, the elevator statement can take the form like this:

For [the avid book reader, student, research fellow and the librarian]

who [needs to search, borrow and read books and other electronic content]

the [library management system] **is a** [online portal]

that [provides a one-stop window to access thousands of books, magazines, publications, research material and electronic media].

Unlike [the older manual system],

our product [provides seamless integration to the student database for basic details regarding membership, connectivity to wallets for processing online payments and accessibility on mobile handheld devices]

The elevator pitch, thus created, articulates the vision of the project in a clear, focused and compelling manner that is understood by one and all. It is a common practice to print out the elevator pitch and stick it to the wall in the team's workspace to serve as a reminder to the team. For small projects, the business case document may be skipped and instead the project charter combined with the elevator statement serves the purpose.

For defining the product vision, a few more Agile tools can be used as follows:

- **Product vision box** - This is a collaborative exercise conducted at the beginning of the project between team members to visualize what all features of the product will attract or compel the user to buy or use the product. The goal of the exercise is to steer away from technical description of the product, but form a single and shared vision of the product across the team. The vision is still owned by the product owner, but the consensus helps to make sure that all team members are on the same page.
- **Flexibility matrix** - This is an Agile tool that determines the relative priority of some parameters by classifying them into fixed, firm, or flexible. In the following example (Table 3-3), it shows a project where the project budget is fixed, quality and compliance to audits is firm and the scope, schedule and ease of use are flexible. When the parameters compete, this matrix could act as a guidance of what could possibly give.
- **Product data sheet** - Like the elevator statement, this is a crisp one-page summary of the goals and objectives of the project that addresses the needs and expectations of the customer and the team. A typical product data sheet could contain the customers served, channels and interfaces, proposition of benefits, project milestones, high-level budgets, some high-level risks and potential challenges etc.

Table 3-3. *Flexibility matrix*

	Fixed	Firm	Flexible
Scope			✓
Schedule			✓
Quality		✓	
Cost	✓		
Ease of use			✓
Compliance to audits		✓	

3.4 Cycle Time

This section attempts to answer the question - How soon does it take to deliver value to the customer?

As we have seen in Chapter 2, Scrum and XP progresses delivery in iterations that are timeboxed for two-four weeks. Stories and features that can be accommodated in the iteration (i.e. meeting the definition of done) are delivered within the same iteration. However, if we look at Kanban or Lean there is no concept of timeboxing. Then how do we calculate how much time it takes to complete a particular story or feature?

This leads us to a very important concept of *cycle time*. Cycle time is defined as the average time it takes an item to get from the end of the queue to a state of being complete or done. For Kanban, this can be expressed in number of days and is calculated for each story by subtracting the date it took to complete the work item from the date when the work item arrived on the queue. These inputs are available on the story card for Kanban as we have seen in Figure 2-13 in the last chapter.

For example consider that you are visiting a supermarket to pick up a list of grocery items. You enter the store at 5 p.m., pick up a shopping trolley and then traverse through the various isles picking up items on your list or even randomly looking at the sales and promotions going on in the store. At around 6 p.m., you feel that you are done and head toward the checkout counters, but notice that there is a huge queue at each of the counters and it will take you probably 30 minutes or so before you get serviced. You also observe that the store has a special counter for customers who have fewer than 15 items to buy. You quickly hop on to the queue and by 6:15 p.m. you complete the payment transaction, packaging your items and head on your way. The total cycle time to shop was 1 hour 15 minutes.

3.4.1 Queueing Theory and Little's Law

The goal of Lean and Agile is to ensure that the cycle time be kept at a minimum. The origins of this strategy are based on the well-researched topic of queueing theory.[6] Applications of queueing theory have been found in many domains like supply and retail chains, transport systems, telecommunications, computing and networking.

Some of the key observations made from the queueing theory are:

- The maximum queueing delay is proportional to buffer size of the queue. This means that the longer the items are waiting to be serviced, the longer the average waiting time is.
- Queues tend to build up because of mismatch between rates of the producer (of work items) and the consumer (finisher of work items). The number of work items currently progressing in the queue is said to be in Work in Progress, commonly abbreviated as WIP.
- As system utilization increases, the cycle time increases nonlinearly. This is seen that if the highways are heavily utilized at 80%, it takes longer to drive across and can potentially result in a gridlock. If the utilization of the highway is lesser, at say 40%, there will be lesser delay in reaching the destination. This is depicted in Figure 3-3 below.

[6]Refer to `https://en.wikipedia.org/wiki/Queueing_theory`

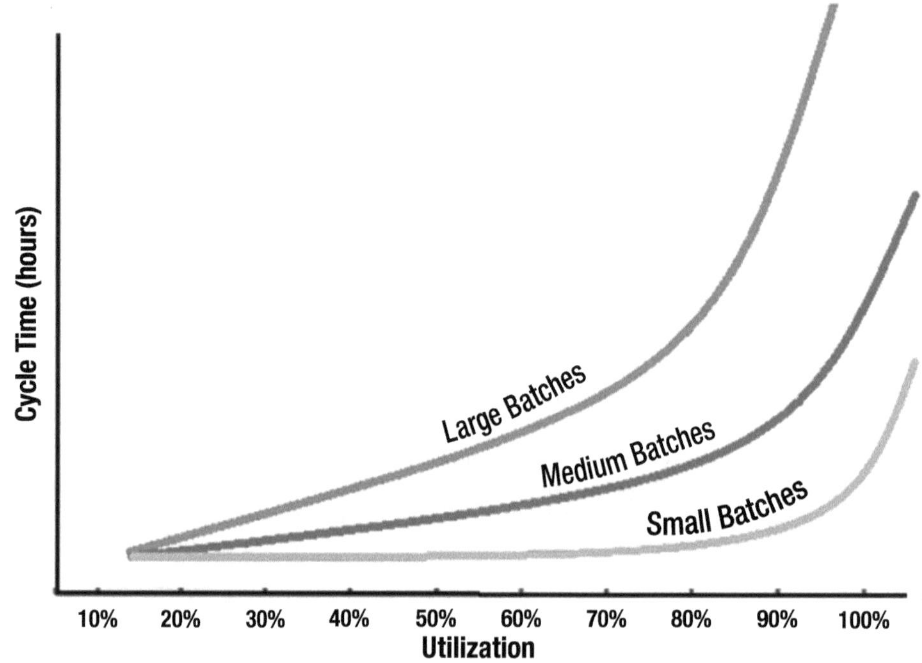

Figure 3-3. *Cycle time increases with larger batches and more utilization*[7]

The Little's Law states that the length of a queue (number of items in WIP state) is directly proportional to the duration of the time spent in the queue. Hence the relation between the cycle time and WIP is expressed by the following formula:

Work in progress (WIP) = Lead Time * Throughput.

where
Throughput = average rate at which work departs or is completed
and Lead Time = average time an item spends in the system

There is a very subtle difference between cycle time and lead time. Consider a software development project where code is developed and tested in iterations that are two-weeks long, however the features are queued up and wait for a release train that deploys to production once every 8 weeks. Taking only development activity into account, the cycle time is 2 weeks. But the total end to end time required to release the software to the end user is 8 weeks. In other words, depending on when the iteration ends, the maximum wait for the feature to be delivered is 8 weeks. This is the lead time.

[7]Refer to *Lean Software Development: An Agile Toolkit* authored by Mary Poppendieck and Tom Poppendieck. (Salt Lake City, UT: Addison-Wesley Professional, 2003).

3.4.2 How Do We Reduce Cycle Time?

The longer is the cycle time, the more delayed is the customer in getting value delivered to them. So it is in the interest of everyone to reduce cycle time in a system, thereby maximizing flow. There are a few commonly followed strategies to reduce cycle time.

- **Reduce variability in rate of arrival** - consider the example of a visa issuance office that would not have been orderly if there was no appointment-based system. In traditional waterfall-based projects the testing team feels burdened with large complex changes to test that requires a lot of test planning, a long execution cycle and inherent risks. In contrast, teams following Agile delivery continuously develop and test software incrementally. By following practices like test-driven development and automated regression throughout the development phase, the team ensures that the testing effort is evenly distributed over all iterations and feedback, if any are captured early.
- **Reduce variability in rate of processing** - by reducing the batch size teams ensure that there is continuous flow through the system. With smaller work packages, there is reduced risk of delivery, as even if one item is blocked for any reason, the others can continue to flow. Also, considering the highway example above, it is always advisable to leave a bit of slack in the team giving room to adapt to change or look at innovation and the creative side of things. This is a bit counterintuitive since managers traditionally want their resources to be busy all the time, but at the cost of increasing the cycle time for delivery for an overworked and fatigued team that is busy with a lot of work and rework.
- **Limiting work in progress** - we shall see more about this in the next section.
- **Removing blockers, waiting times** - generally larger work items are more prone to get blocked. By making work items smaller and similarly sized waiting times, there is better chance of flow. Also, in case of blockers, avoid picking up new pieces of work and get the team to swarm around each other to help move the item forward.
- **Investing behind smart engineering tools and practices** - tools like version control, continuous build and integration agents, code quality checkers and practices like test-first-development and pair programming helps teams to bring in more efficiency in the way they deliver software.
- **Investing behind a cross-functional team** - it helps to have a team with members possessing multiple specialties such that in times of need they can help each other. So if a tester is out sick, could the business analyst in the team chip in?

3.4.3 Limiting WIP

Advocates of Lean and Kanban are ruthless in limiting WIP because it leads to quicker flow through the system. This section continues from the discussion on Kanban in the previous Chapter 2. As visualized on the Kanban board in Figure 2-12, Kanban teams restrict the number of work items in a particular column (status) based on their capacity to deliver. The team ensures that they never take in more work than the WIP limit.

Although with a bias toward a lower value to improve lead time, the choice of the WIP limit is subjective. WIP limits should be decided by the team collectively based on the nature of the work items in the project, the team's composition and their combined capacity to deliver.

The recommended approach is to try a WIP limit, evaluate the resultant flow and then change it as needed. Note that both extremes of WIP limit are discouraged because of the following:

- Too high a limit - As we have seen above, having a very high WIP limit (or none at all) will mean that work will start piling up at the bottlenecks and reducing the cycle time for delivery. As a result, while resources will have high utilization, work items might stay idle.
- Too low a limit - If the WIP limit is too low, it might help to unearth the source of bottlenecks in the system, but means that a lot of resources might be idle as only too few work items are getting progressed at a time.

3.4.4 Cumulative Flow Diagram (CFD)

To see the relation between WIP and lead time, one can use a very powerful visualization called the *Cumulative Flow Diagram,* abbreviated as CFD. CFD's have become very popular in the Agile community because they are a valuable tool to track the performance of a workflow.

The CFD is easy to construct using the stacked area graph utility in Microsoft Excel® and conveys a lot of information that the team can use to visualize the flow of work, identify bottlenecks and come up with recommendations for process improvements. To see the application of a CFD, let us refer back to the Kanban board that we saw in Figure 2-12 (in Chapter 2: Agile Methodologies). The following Table 3-4 counts the number of work items that are displayed in each column of the Kanban board for each day for a period of 11 days. Such a piece of data can be easily collected during the end of the day or at the beginning of the daily stand-up meeting by visually inspecting the Kanban board and making a note in this table. Notice that the WIP limits are mentioned in parentheses next to the column headers.

Table 3-4. *Sample data from a Kanban board captured over time*

Date	Inbox (7)	Analysis (5)	Ready for Development (3)	Coding (7)	Unit testing (5)	Acceptance testing (4)	Ready to deploy	Done
1-Aug-16	4	2	1	4				
2-Aug-16	5	2	2	4				
3-Aug-16	6	1	3	3	2	2		
4-Aug-16	5	2	2	3	2	2		
5-Aug-16	6	1	2	2	5	2	2	1
6-Aug-16	7	2	1	4	4	1	1	2
7-Aug-16	4	2	2	5	3	2	0	4
8-Aug-16	4	0	2	5	2	3	3	4
9-Aug-16	2	2	0	7	3	3	2	4
10-Aug-16	6	1	3	4	2	4	2	5
11-Aug-16	7	2	2	5	4	2	2	6

When converted to a stacked area graph, the CFD looks like the following Figure 3-4.

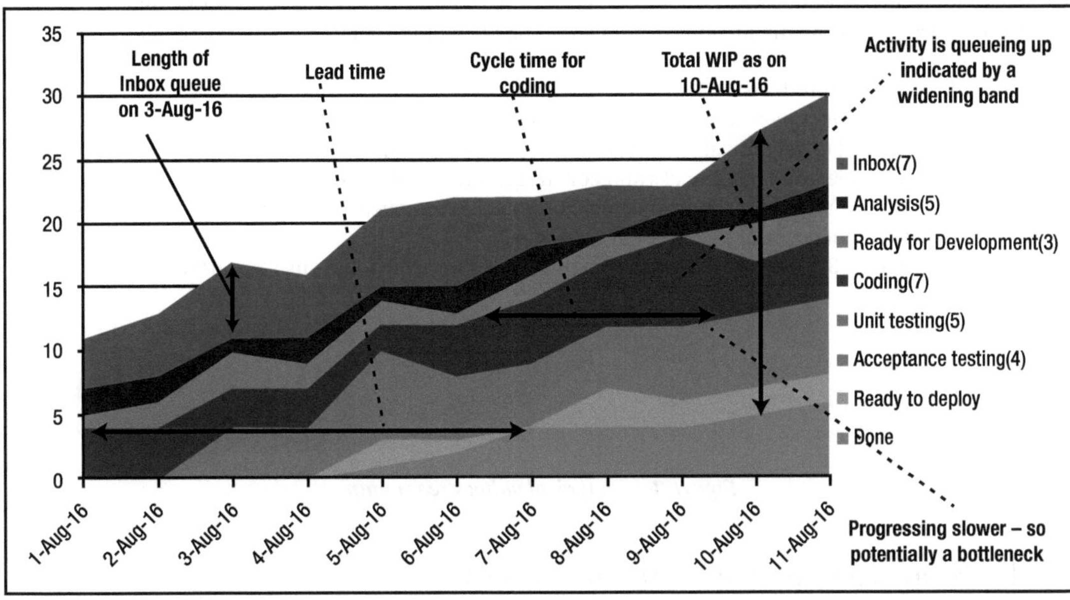

Figure 3-4. *Cumulative flow diagram (CFD) - based on the data in Table 3-4*

3.4.4.1 Observations from a CFD

- As annotated in Figure 3-4, the CFD provides us information about the lead time, cycle time for each activity (like coding), length of the items in a particular queue on a given date and the total number of items in a WIP state (i.e. not deployed / done) on a given date.
- Since cycle time can be derived from a CFD, this can be used to predict the completion date of a work item and so is commonly used as a forecasting technique.
- Also notice in Figure 3-4 that the stacked area for "done" keeps growing as more and more items are deployed into the production. This justifies the word 'cumulative' in the cumulative flow diagram.
- The area marked as "inbox" is expected to shrink when items get moved across to the later columns, but could also see a rise when newer work items get added to the backlog.
- It is easy for the Agile team to spot bottlenecks by a visual inspection of the CFD. Notice that in the above figure from around August 7, the graph area for coding widens, which implies that more and more work items are getting queued up waiting for the next process to take over. Now coding is followed by unit testing and we observe that it has a lower gradient, which implies that the activity is progressing at a slower rate than its predecessor. In such a case the unit testing activity is a bottleneck of the workflow. Now that the bottleneck has been identified, the next step for the team is to work together, understand the root causes and remove them. Strategies like test-driven development or an automated test suite might help to remove the bottleneck.

3.5 Value Stream Mapping

As we have introduced in Chapter 2 (section on Lean), Value stream mapping is a technique that has its origins from the Lean manufacturing industry. The Lean philosophy keeps the customer at the heart of every decision. It looks at value from the customer's perspective and delivers them in the form of features in products and services.

It begins with a *value stream map* that sequences all the steps and processes that are required or not required to get this value delivered to the customer. All non-value added activities that are considered as bottlenecks and constraints are identified by the team and eliminated one by one. Once that is done, the next bottleneck is removed and this cycle of continuous improvement goes on.

As shown in Figure 3-5, a typical value stream map could have the following steps from inputs to the output.

Figure 3-5. *A typical value stream map*

3.5.1 Steps to Create a Value Stream Map

Following are the steps required to create a value stream maps of a process.

1. Identify the product or service that needs to be analyzed.
2. Identify the steps, queues, delays and information flows in the process to come up with the value stream map of the process.
3. Create flow by identifying and eliminating all forms of wastes and their sources. Wastes imply delays, constraints, bottlenecks and non-value added tasks.
4. Create a new value stream map of the future state by eliminating the wastes identified in the previous step. This leads to an efficient process that responds to customer pull.
5. Develop a plan to reach the future state from the present state.
6. Pursue perfection by continuously reviewing the process so as to find opportunities to optimize it further.

The steps are depicted in the following Figure 3-6.

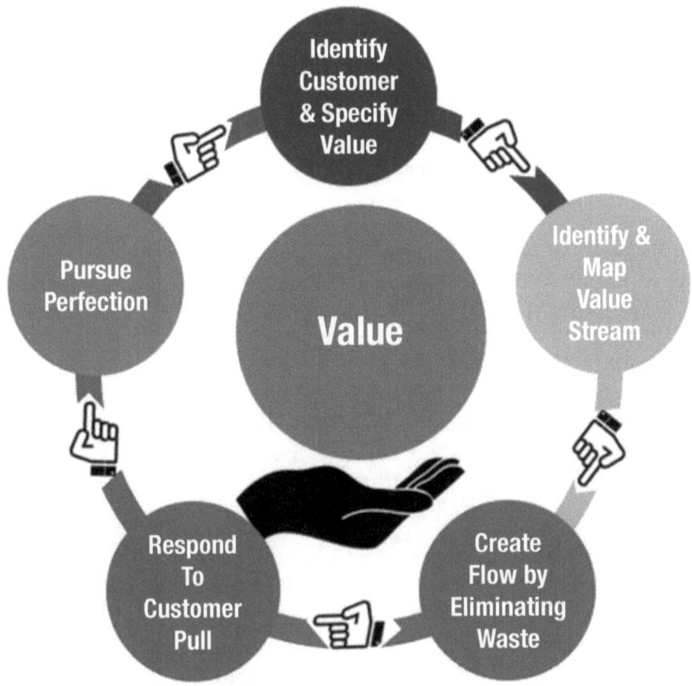

Figure 3-6. *Lean using the value stream map to identify and eliminate waste*

3.5.2 Example of a Value Stream Map

To understand this better, let us now look at an example of how the team delivers a change request. The whole sequence of steps starts from the user (originator of the change request) and again ends at the user (who receives the final product feature). In between several team members are involved, namely, the sponsor, analysts, developers, testers and so on.

In Figure 3-7 the value-added steps are shown in boxes. These steps are to assess the impact of the change, perform detailed analysis, complete the high- and low-level design and code change, perform different levels of testing, including interfacing with upstream and downstream application, build the final artifact and deploy the change into production for the user to use.

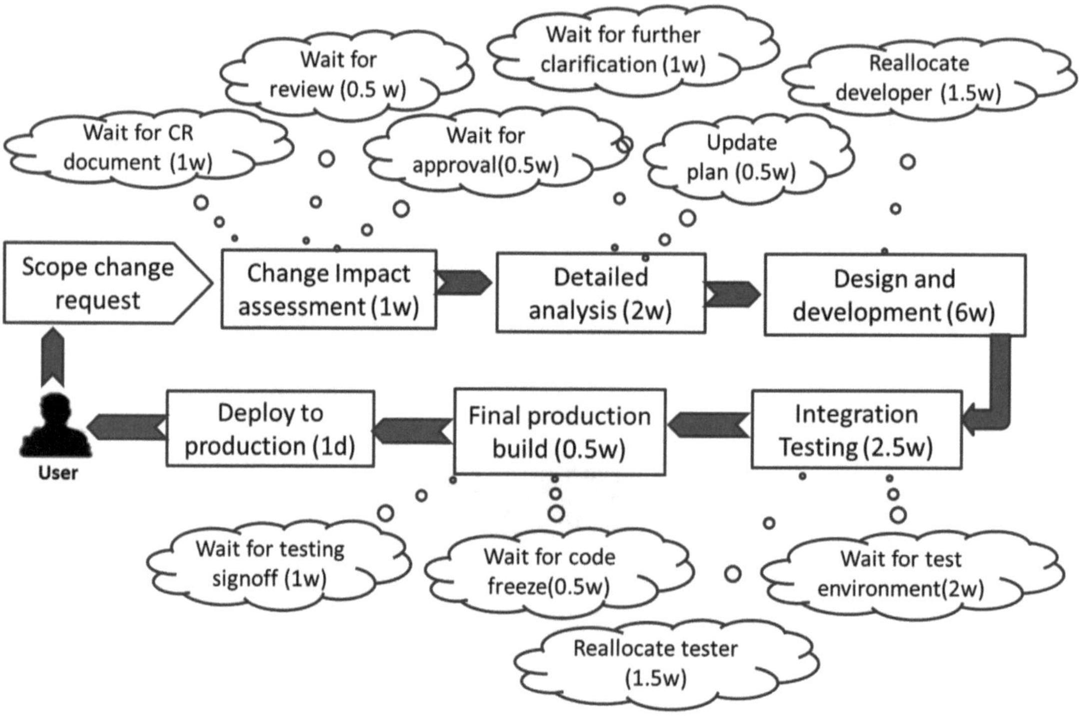

Figure 3-7. *Value stream map how the team handles a software change request*

The steps that are non-value added and considered as bottlenecks or idle waits are marked in the shape of a cloud. These are like waiting for documentation, review, environments to be ready for testing, approvals and sign-offs and task-switching to reprioritize and reallocate resources to look at the change control.

For each of the steps involved the estimated duration is indicated in parentheses. For example, design and development takes 6 weeks and is denoted by 6w next to the name of the task.

3.5.3 Computing the Lead Time

The value stream maps are a very powerful graphical representation of the processes involved, how the team is utilized and the current state of the project.

Coming back to Figure 3-7 again, let us try to compute the lead time to get the requested change delivered to the end user.

We see that the total duration of the value added tasks is 1w + 2w + 6w + 2.5w + 0.5w + 1d = 12 weeks approximately.

Total duration of the non-value added tasks is 1w + 0.5w + 0.5w + 1w + 0.5w + 1.5w + 2w + 1.5w + 0.5w + 1w = 10 weeks approximately.

The **total lead time = total duration of the value-added and the non-value-added tasks** = 12 weeks + 10 weeks = 22 weeks.

Therefore the **process cycle efficiency = Total value added time / total lead time** = 12/22 = 0.55.

In other words the above process is about 55% efficient and there is considerable room for improvement.

3.5.4 How Do We Compress the Value Stream?

The goal of the Lean / Agile system is to compress the value stream by eliminating waste. So all delays in the queue and time spent behind non-value added activities are treated as waste and eliminated. This is in line with Goldratt's Theory of Constraints that spoke about identifying bottlenecks in a system, targeting all efforts to remove the same and then proceeding with the next bottleneck and so on.

In the above example (Figure 3-7) we see about 45% waste. Given that situation, consider a few alternate options that can potentially lead to reduction of waste:

- Consider embracing iterative and incremental approach for product development that lets teams to respond and adapt to changes more seamlessly. This can significantly reduce the cost of change and remove most of the unnecessary overhead.
- Examine whether the detailed documents for the change control are required or not. Since this does not add customer value, consider removing it altogether or at most reducing it to a bare minimum.
- Challenge the need for multiple rounds of review and approval of the document. If the team has close proximity to the business user, makes sure there is rich communication that might make approvals redundant. This can also make the weekly or monthly review meetings hosted by the change board.
- Arrange for the user or a representative of the user to be co-located with the team, so that any clarifications can be sought in real time avoiding any forms of delay and waste (incurred in e-mails, documentation, or setting up audio calls with agendas and minutes published).
- Emphasize and pursue simple design approaches, refactoring of code and reducing technical debt in the code such that the estimates to make a design and code changes goes down.
- Consider pair programming to avoid the separate overhead of a peer code review.
- Consider test-driven development and automation of regression test cases so that the manual efforts involved in testing can be reduced to a great extent.
- Consider, wherever possible, working with full-time resources who are dedicated to one project and are not context switching between multiple projects.
- Consider using sophisticated tools that help in continuous build and integration. For example, invest behind a tool (like Teamcity and Hudson) that can trigger a build and run unit test cases on checking in code in to version control. This provides immediate feedback whether the recently developed code is correct and complete and reduces the probability of defect propagation.

Note that while considering the above options to make the processes more efficient and reduce cycle time, due attention should be provided to the cost aspect. Co-location, pair programming, dedicated resources, tools for version control and continuous integration could all come with a cost. The project team should be able to trade off between the available constraints and the value-driven delivery.

3.6 Value-Based Prioritization Techniques

All teams are constrained with time, costs and scope. By doing prioritization the team aims to make a trade-off between these constraints. We have seen in earlier sections of this book that Agile teams and business representatives work diligently to deliver the highest value to the customer as early as possible and at the lowest cost. This is achieved by consciously choosing the items or stories of the highest return on investment from the backlog and implementing the same in the available timebox.

Value-based prioritization is used during backlog grooming,[8] release planning and iteration planning. Some of the factors that are considered to arrive at the priority of a work item are as follows:

- Business Value in terms of incremental or retained revenue and customer satisfaction
- Legal, regulatory and compliance requirements
- Cost of implementation and ongoing maintenance
- Urgency and time sensitivity of the feature in the product
- Early adopters for a niche concept in the market
- Greatest return on investment (e.g., quick wins) and likelihood of success in marketing the product
- Inherent riskiness of the feature
- Stakeholder consensus
- Usability and reusability
- Amount of knowledge or experience gathered about the domain, technology, or the product

In the following section, we take a look at some of the prevalent techniques that Agile teams use for prioritization of work items.

3.6.1 Numerical Assignment

One of the simplest ways to prioritize business requirements in order of value is to rank them in priorities of 1, 2, 3, or High, Medium, Low and so on. This scheme is indeed simple as the name suggests, however should be used with caution. If there is no uniformity in justification of the priority value of an item, it could lead to a skewed distribution with too many items marked as priority 1. This is because, over time users will realize that the items with lower priorities may never get addressed and hence face starvation.

3.6.2 Analytical Hierarchical Process (AHP)

The Analytical Hierarchical Process (AHP) technique is a structure technique used for complex decision-making in a group environment. The details of the AHP technique are beyond the scope of the PMI-ACP® exam.

[8]Backlog grooming is discussed later in this chapter.

All that one needs to remember is that AHP takes a list of features and does a pairwise relative comparison based on some criteria. For example if there are three stories X, Y and Z, the comparison is done in pairs XY, YZ and ZX. Based on the evaluation criteria and the weight assigned to each criteria, a score is reached for each of the features X, Y and Z based on which the relative order is derived.

3.6.3 100 point or Cumulative Voting Method

The 100-point method is like an opinion poll for determining the priority of items in a group environment. Each participant in the group is given 100 points to be distributed as votes across the list of user stories (or product backlog items). The participant is at his or her free will to give as many votes or as few votes based on the items that seems most or least important in his or her perspective. After all participants finish voting, the votes are counted and the stories are sorted and ranked in descending order of the votes it received. The story with the biggest amount of votes is given the highest priority, followed by the one with the next highest votes and so on.

Let us have a look at the following example illustrated in Table 3-5. There are 6 stories that need to prioritize by a group of 5 stakeholders. Each stakeholder distributes 100 points across the stories. For example stakeholder #1 distributes 15, 20, 20, 10, 25 and 10 points across stories 1-6 respectively. This means that in her perspective story #5 is the most important closely followed by story #2 and #3. Note that for the stakeholder #3, only story #3 is required or relevant from his perspective, so he puts all his points on just one story.

Table 3-5. *Applying the 100-point method to force-rank stories based on their relative priorities*

Stakeholder list	Total votes per stakeholder	Votes for Story 1	Votes for Story 2	Votes for Story 3	Votes for Story 4	Votes for Story 5	Votes for Story 6
Stakeholder 1	100	15	20	20	10	25	10
Stakeholder 2	100	50	0	20	20	10	0
Stakeholder 3	100	0	0	100	0	0	0
Stakeholder 4	100	0	30	0	30	10	30
Stakeholder 5	100	0	0	40	50	10	0
Total votes distributed	**500**	**65**	**50**	**180**	**110**	**55**	**40**
Derived priority		**3**	**5**	**1**	**2**	**4**	**6**

Finally all the votes are summed up. Story #3, which received the highest number of 180 votes is given the highest priority, followed by story #4, #1, #5, #2 and #6. Notice that it is the relative rank of an item over another that is valuable to the team during planning, not the absolute position. It is generally advisable to perform the voting in private, so as to eliminate any possibilities of bias or undesirable influence ('halo effect') between each other. The 100-point method for prioritization is also called the Cumulative voting method and is simple, quick and hence popular.

One of the variations of the 100-point method is called the *Dot Voting* or *Multi-Voting* method where the users are given a predetermined number of dots (check marks, tally marks, or anything to indicate scoring) instead of 100 points. The users are free to place their dots on any feature as long as the total votes do not exceed their quota. At the end, the summing up of the *dot* votes, ranking and relative prioritization happens in the same way as the 100-point method.

3.6.4 Monopoly Money

In many ways, monopoly money is similar to the 100-point method. Here the project budget is given to the sponsors or users in the form of fake currency, as seen in the popular game of Monopoly. The users are then asked to distribute the money on the system features or functionalities that are valued or matter to them most. The aggregate of these values for each feature is ranked to determine the priority of the business features required. The trick is to keep the project budget intentionally much lower than the sum of all the estimated costs of the features of the system so that the users are forced to think hard about where to put their money on.

3.6.5 MoSCoW

The MoSCoW prioritization technique has its origin in DSDM.[9] It is an acronym that stands for the following (shown in Figure 3-8).

Figure 3-8. *MoSCoW technique for value-based prioritization*

Let us quickly have a look at what each phrase means.

1. **Must Have:**
    - Requirements that are fundamental for the working of the system. Hence they have the highest priority.
    - If even one such requirement is excluded or not delivered, the system will fail or be rendered unusable.
    - These requirements appear on top of the prioritized backlog and are most likely to make it to the backbone and walking skeleton[10] of a release plan.

[9]Refer to the discussion on DSDM in Chapter 2: Agile Methodologies.

[10]Refer to Release planning in Chapter 6: Adaptive Planning for a detailed explanation of backbone and walking skeleton that constitutes critical elements of a release plan.

- The keyword MUST also can be used as an abbreviation for **M**inimum **U**sable **S**ubset. This term is a close analogy of a minimally marketable feature (MMF).[11]
- Example of a must-have feature for a mobile phone is the ability to make and receive calls and an address book to store the list of contacts.

2. **Should have:**
   - Requirements that are important for the system to work correctly, reliably and predictably. Hence they have medium priority.
   - If such a requirement is excluded or not delivered, the system can continue to function with a workaround that could either be difficult, time consuming, or cause inconvenience.
   - Example of a should-have feature of a mobile phone is the ability to connect to a data network and being able to browse the Internet.
3. **Could have:**
   - Requirements that are somewhat useful or desirable, but not necessary.
   - If such a requirement is excluded or not delivered, the system continues to function properly, but the user experience can be affected adversely.
   - Their priorities are medium to low and are picked up for implementation provided there is sufficient time and money available.
   - Example of could-have features of a mobile phone is to be able to play music, click photos, or help in GPS navigation.
4. **Won't have:**
   - Requirements that are cosmetic or 'nice-to-have,' but are of least criticality.
   - If such a requirement is excluded or not delivered, the system is not impacted in any way.
   - Can be deferred for future or dropped forever.
   - Example of won't-have features of a mobile phone could be to act as pedometer that counts steps for a morning jogger.

The MoSCoW technique is a popular technique for prioritization and is commonly seen in the PMI-ACP® exam.

3.6.6 Kano Analysis Model

So far we have seen prioritization techniques based on business values. The inherent problem that will crop up over a period of time is that almost all features expected by the user will get categorized as high priority ones as anything that is of a medium or low priority would stand little chance of getting implemented ever. The Kano analysis model, introduced Dr. Noriaki Kano, addresses this concern by looking at perceived customer satisfaction while a user story or a feature gets implemented. Using the model, the product owner and the team are able to prioritize a product feature in one of the five categories mentioned below and expend resources to deliver them.

[11]MMF's are discussed in Chapter 6: Adaptive Planning.

Let us look at each of the five categories in conjunction to Figure 3-9[12] shown below that plots customer satisfaction (on a scale from high to low) against customer needs (on a scale of being implemented to not being implemented).

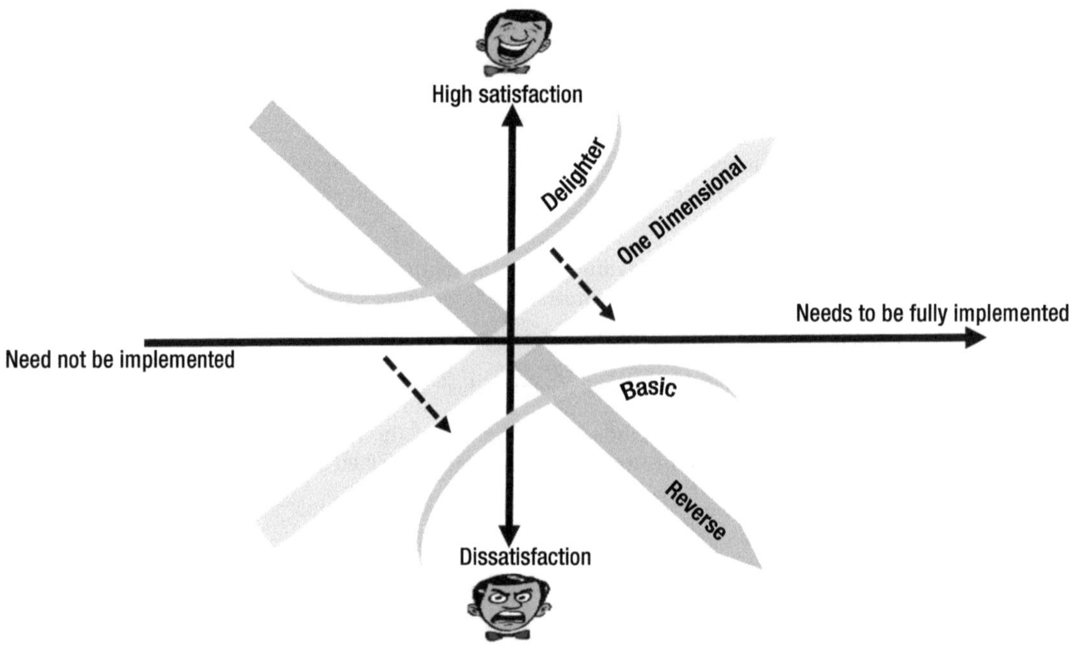

Figure 3-9. *Kano Analysis Model*

1. **Basic / Must-be**
   - Like the must-haves in MoSCoW, these features must be present in the product for the customer to be able to use them. Hence the customer implicitly expects these bare minimum functions and if they are absent the customer is extremely dissatisfied.
   - As a result the project team is expected to pay the maximum attention to these features, even if that means that no significant amount of revenue may be generated by those features.
   - Examples of such features are like being able to toggle the channel or volume buttons on a TV remote or being able to search a book from our library management system.
   - As shown in Figure 3-9 by the brown line below the X-axis, the presence of the features do not increase customer satisfaction, but its absence causes a lot of dissatisfaction.

[12]The figure for Kano analysis model is an adaptation of `https://en.wikipedia.org/wiki/Kano_model`

2. **Attractive/Delighters**

   - These features are neither requested nor expected by the customer, but when delivered lead to business benefits accompanied by a high degree of customer delight and appreciation.
   - Organizations and product teams invest effort behind such innovative features because they differentiate their product offering from their competitors, give high perceptions of customer-oriented behaviors, penetrate the market place quickly and increase their profitability.
   - As an example, being able to record a favorite TV show or a sporting event is a good attractive feature, as the viewer has an option to enjoy it later in case he/she missed when the TV channel telecasted the program or simply wants to play back again.
   - As shown in Figure 3.9 by the brown line above the X-axis, the presence of the features increase customer satisfaction exponentially, but its absence does not cause any grief or inconvenience as the customer never expected or asked for it.

3. **One-dimensional/Performance**

   - These features are explicitly requested by the customer. The more (or better quality) of these the greater is the positive impact on customer satisfaction. Conversely if these features are not implemented or function poorly when benchmarked with the product from a competitor, they have an adverse impact of customer satisfaction or retention. These features are analogous to the 'should-have' features in MoSCoW.
   - Organizations and product teams invest effort behind such features because they would like to stay competitive in the market and achieve customer satisfaction to retain revenue.
   - As an example, consider an online shipper who expects his purchased item to be delivered to his doorstep for free within the promised turnaround time of 3 days. If the item does not arrive by that time, there will be inconvenience caused. In some cases, the customer could also ask for an expedited (say overnight) delivery by paying an extra shipping fee, if that option is provided by the online retailer.
   - This is depicted in Figure 3-9 by arrow that goes linearly from the bottom-left quadrant to the top-right quadrant implying linear increase of customer satisfaction by implementing needed features.

4. **Neutral/Indifferent**

   - These are the features that the customer does not care about. So whether they are present or absent does not impact the customer satisfaction directly and so he/she is indifferent about it.
   - An example of this is a flight recorder also commonly known as black box in an aircraft. Most passengers on a commercial flight are oblivious about the presence or absence of a black box on the aircraft. But it is a regulatory and compliance requirement by the aviation industry that such a device be very much operational in the aircraft, collecting and recording flight parameters frequently and help in facilitating investigations during mishaps and accidents.

5. **Reverse**

   - These set of features when present cause customers to dislike a product and their absence causes dissatisfaction. In most cases, the customer would like to seek alternative and move to another product that does not provide the same set of features that it dislikes.
   - Logically this works in the direction opposite to the one-dimensional/ performance category, so the team should make a careful consideration whether to implement them or not.
   - This is depicted in Figure 3-9 by an arrow that goes linearly from the top-left quadrant to the bottom-right quadrant implying linear decrease of customer satisfaction if 'disliked' features get added.
   - An example of this is an old neighbor of mine who still uses the telephone to hail cabs because he doesn't feel comfortable using high-tech smartphones to use app-based taxi services.

Before we complete the discussion on the Kano Model, it is important to bear in mind that the stakeholder satisfaction and expectations evolve over time. Also market and economic conditions change as more and more competition emerges. What started out as a delighter could drift into a basic need for a customer. For example, when the Apple® iPhone® was launched the customers were delighted to have a phone, camera, music player and storage media all integrated into one device. But over the past few years, this has evolved from being a wish item to an expectation to a must-have feature on any smartphone product that the market is flooded with.

3.6.7 Wiegers' Method

The Wieger's method is a quantitative analytical approach to prioritization[13] that makes a weighted computation of value, cost and risk associated with a requirement. This method is only applied for features whose prioritization is negotiable - not the ones that are mandatory (e.g., to meet legal, compliance or regulatory requirements) or where it is a must-have (as in MoSCoW) or a one-dimensional requirement (as in Kano Model).

Some of the key steps of the Wieger's method are:

1. The customer representatives determine the value of a feature by considering the business benefits that it brings or the penalties if it does not exist and ranks them on a scale of 1 to 9 (with 1 being the lowest and 9 the highest). The business benefits are considered twice the weightage over the penalties.
2. The development team also estimates costs and technical risks associated with implementing the feature. The costs and risks are relatively ranked on a scale of 1 to 9 (with 1 being the lowest and 9 the highest) considering the complexity of the work involved and uncertainties in the form of resource availability or choice of technologies. Generally the cost and risks are weighted equally.
3. Finally the values are expressed in percentages and the priority computed using the formula: Priority of a feature = Value % / (cost % * cost weight + risk % * risk weight)
4. Finally the items are sorted in descending order of priority. As Wieger summarizes - "All other things being equal, those features that have the highest risk-adjusted value/cost ratio should have the highest priority."

[13]Refer to the article at `http://www.processimpact.com/` authored by Karl E. Wiegers.

Table 3-6 shows a sample illustration of prioritizing a list of features/user stories based on their value (benefit + penalty), estimated relative cost and technical risks. After applying the formula above, the stories are sorted in descending priority order. So the feature #1 has the highest priority followed by #4, #2 and so on. Feature #5 has the least priority and the team could choose to defer the same or not implement it at all.

Table 3-6. *Wieger's prioritization based on value, cost and risk*

Feature	Relative Benefit	Relative Penalty	Total Value	Value %	Relative Cost	Cost %	Relative Risk	Risk %	Weiger's Priority	Priority Order
Allow a student to search a book, novel or audio book	9	3	21	31.8%	15	22.1%	3	14.3%	1.1	1
Allow a student to borrow and reserve a book	6	3	15	22.7%	12	17.6%	4	19.0%	0.8	3
Allow a student to pay a fine for not returning by the due date	4	5	13	19.7%	18	26.5%	7	33.3%	0.5	4
Allow a librarian to register new students to the library	5	2	12	18.2%	8	11.8%	3	14.3%	1.0	2
Allow the librarian to exhibit the latest best-sellers on the portal	2	1	5	7.6%	15	22.1%	4	19.0%	0.2	5
Relative weight	2	1			1		0.5			
Total			66	100.0%	68	100.0%	21	100.0%		

Note that the computation is shown above for the sake of illustration and building of the concept, but it is not expected in the PMI-ACP® exam.

3.6.8 Requirements Prioritization Framework

The uniqueness of this framework[14] is that it gives different levels of precedence to different stakeholders based on their profile and importance from the project perspective. Thus the inputs or priority of the business goals from each stakeholder goes through a weighted comparison to arrive at the overall ranked list of priorities. The rating of the stakeholder helps to detect any overly influential close-knit group of stakeholders that could lead to a biasing impact on the priority of the requirements. The framework also helps to group requirements based on any identified dependencies among each other.

[14]Refer to https://resources.sei.cmu.edu/asset_files/WhitePaper/2013_019_001_299139.pdf

3.6.9 Balancing Risk and Value

So far we have seen how value and cost drives prioritization. What about risk?

High severity risk[15] needs to be given equal priority to high business value items as otherwise the risks can quickly erode value and render functionality needed by business unusable.

To prioritize between value and risk, Mike Cohn[16] has introduced a 2 × 2 risk-to-value matrix mapping both value and risk from high to low and recommends the most suitable strategy at dealing with them during prioritization. This is shown in Figure 3-10 below. In the top-right quadrant are the items that yield the highest value but carry the highest risk - these items should be of the highest priority and the recommended strategy is "Deliver first" The bottom-right quadrant is the items with high value, but low risks - these items have the second priority and should be looked at next. Items of low value and low risks appearing in the bottom-left quadrant should be attempted last. There is hardly any point in taking on the items in the top-left quadrant since they carry high risks, but yield low value. The best strategy to deal with such items is to simply avoid them.

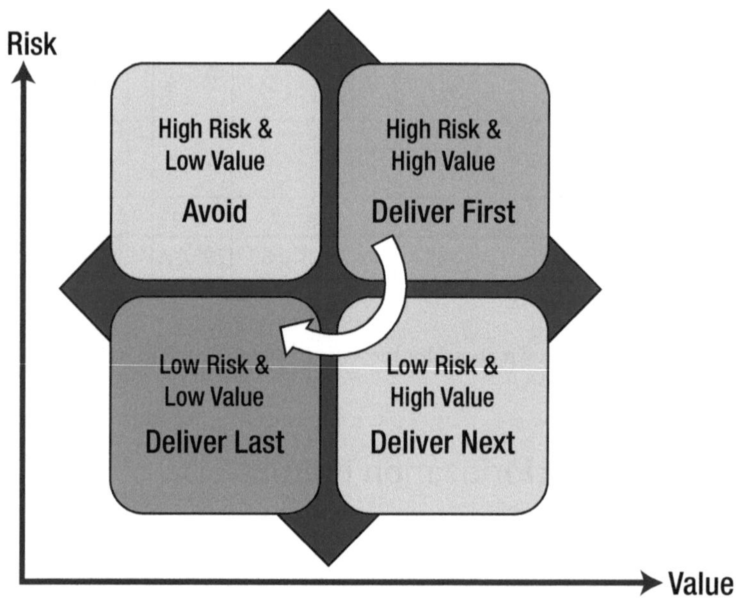

Figure 3-10. *Balancing between risk and value during prioritization*

[15]Remember the formula: Risk severity = Risk probability x Risk impact.

[16]Refer to *Agile Estimation and Planning* authored by Mike Cohn. (Upper Saddle River, NJ: Prentice Hall, 2005).

3.7 Product Backlog

As we have seen in Chapter 2 during discussion of Scrum artifacts, the product backlog is one of the key list of items that are yet to be implemented by the development team. It can contain business requirements expressed as epics,[17] features or stories, defects, risks, or technical tasks identified by the team. It is not necessary that all items in the product backlog will be implemented or necessary for shipping a working version of the product. Only the ones that yield value (or mitigates risks) are prioritized and delivered in the same priority order by the team. Some items from the backlog could even be simply discarded (so they never get implemented) based on very low priorities assigned to them. An example of such is a feature that is optionally required by a very small segment of users, but something that is very expensive to build and so will not yield a good return on investment.

The following sections present some of the key concepts related to the product backlog.

3.7.1 Backlog Grooming or Refinement

The Product Owner, as in the case of Scrum, continuously updates the backlog in response to one or more of the following events in the project environment:

- A new requirement emerges during review of the product at the sprint review meeting.
- A regulatory constraint was imposed.
- There are economic conditions at the market place (a share price for a commodity or a foreign exchange rate has changed) that might affect the business value of product. Consequently features could either be added, or deleted as a result of the same.
- A new customer segment has been discovered (or who have expressed desire to use the product).
- Dependencies with other internal products (in the same organization) or external interfaces (outside the organization boundary) are discovered.
- The team identifies a risk that needs to be mitigated.
- The product should seize competitive advantage because of similar offerings available from competitors.
- There are technical considerations that impact the architecture and design.

The set of activities that the Product Owner, in collaboration with the development team, undertakes to manage the product backlog items (also abbreviated as PBI's) is called *backlog grooming or backlog refinement.* The activities include:

- adding, modifying, or deleting requirements, features and enhancements;
- adding more details to existing PBI's based on enhanced understanding and incremental feedback obtained during examining previous versions of the working product;
- refining the business value of a given feature;
- changing of priorities in the PBI's;
- logging outstanding defects that need to be addressed;

[17] An epic is a complex or compound user story, which is disaggregated into user stories to help in estimation, planning and implementation. User stories and epics are described in details in Chapter 6: Adaptive Planning.

- disaggregating the PBI's into smaller and more manageable chunks of work items;[18] and
- refining and updating estimates on the PBI's.

3.7.2 DEEP Attributes of Product Backlog

The acronym "DEEP" is used to describe attributes of a product backlog as shown in Figure 3-11.

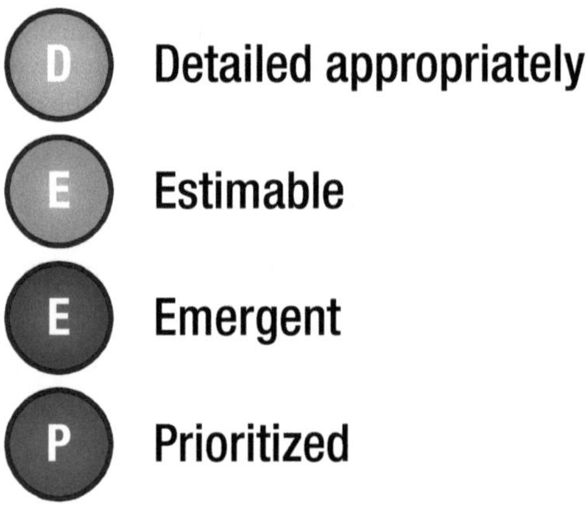

Figure 3-11. *DEEP acronym for product backlog*

Let us next look at each of these attributes one by one.

3.7.2.1 Detailed Appropriately

The Product Backlog Items (PBI's) should have enough detail that can be used to convey the necessary information to the project team. Note that during release planning and sprint planning exercises, conversations between the product owner and the development team ensue with an intent to hash out the details of the PBI's and user stories. PBI's that are of high business value are expected to have more details as they have a higher likelihood of being picked up for early implementation (e.g., the following iteration). It is recommended to (follow the principle of *progressive elaboration*[19] and) leave the PBI's of lower priority at a lesser level of details.

3.7.2.2 Estimable

Related to the previous attribute, PBI's should have enough details that makes it estimable. The items at the top of the backlog have the highest priority and are expected to have fine-grained estimates. As we shall see in Chapter 6, Agile estimations do not produce exact estimates, but ones with relative order of size and complexity, often expressed in units of ideal days or story points. Agile teams generally use techniques like Affinity Estimation to quickly produce a rough estimate for a very large list of items from the product backlog. Once estimated, the product owner is able to produce a release plan where the stakeholders can visualize how business value is realized over time.

[18]See Chapter 6: Adaptive Planning on how PBI's are prioritized, estimated and picked up during sprint planning.
[19]See Chapter 6: Adaptive Planning for a discussion on progressive elaboration.

3.7.2.3 Emergent

The word emergent signifies that the product backlog is a dynamic list. It is expected to grow, change and get reprioritized over the life cycle of the project. Items that are completed by the development team (i.e. met its *definition of done*) are removed from the backlog.

Note that anyone in the team has the right to add items to the product backlog. However, it is the product owner who has the final say on the value and priority of the items in the backlog.

3.7.2.4 Prioritized

It is the role of the product owner to ensure that the product backlog is prioritized with the PBI carrying the highest value featuring at the top of the backlog and the one with the lowest value at the bottom of the backlog. The following Figure 3-12 shows a prioritized product backlog.

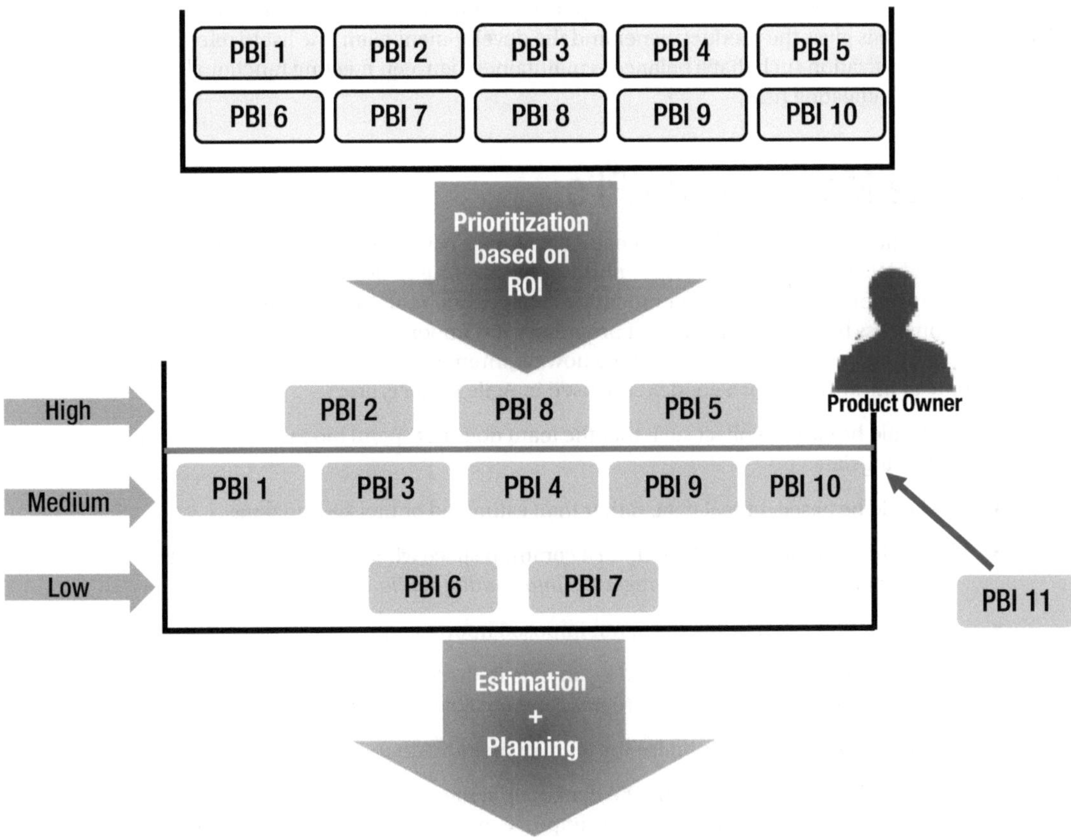

Figure 3-12. *A product backlog with items prioritized based on Return on Investment (ROI)*

Having a single prioritized list to track requirements, bugs, enhancements and change requests is extremely handy for one and all in the Agile team and acts a very handy tool for adaptive planning. Notice that in Figure 3-12, the item marked as PBI 11 is making an entry in the backlog (let's assume that it is a small change request obtained during the feedback of a previous iteration). In such a case the product owner determines the value and ROI of PBI 11 and chooses its relative priority order in the backlog. With constraints of a timeboxed iteration and the available budget, it is quite possible that an item with a lower priority will need to drop off to accommodate PBI 11. In some cases, the team might need a few extra iterations or releases (and hence more time) to complete the needed items from the backlog.

3.7.3 Risk Adjusted Backlog

The discussions around product backlog are not complete without considering risks, which is a very realistic aspect of project management. The theory on risk management practices in Agile is covered in details in Chapter 7: Problem Detection and Resolution. In simple terms, once risks are identified, they are analyzed for their impact, probability and frequency. Finally, appropriate responses are sought to mitigate them. These risk response strategies are then combined to the existing product backlog along with the functional requirements. This combined list containing the functional requirements as well as the risk responses in order of priority is called a *risk-adjusted backlog*. This gives the product owner and the development team one list to refer during planning and prioritization such that a balance is maintained between meeting functional requirements and mitigating risks.

3.8 Agile Metrics and KPI's

We have now reached the last section of this chapter. So far we have seen how value-driven delivery is embedded in the heart of the Agile philosophy covering all aspects of project initiation, planning, prioritization, execution, accommodating changes and mid-course corrections and realization of business benefits. As the project progresses it is important for the Agile team to track and monitor the progress of the team to see how requirements are transformed into working software. Some of the attributes of a good metric used in Agile projects are:

- It should be easy to collect such that the team does not spend too much time gathering data.
- It should be based on real data, rather than estimated or mocked-up data.
- It should be visualized and put up in a common space where anyone can view it. A commonly used term in this regard is *Information Radiator.*[20]
- It should be decided by the team, not imposed upon them.
- It should be dynamic and updated by anyone in the team, such that the team can feel that they contribute toward the progress and are able to observe trends.
- It should not be used to appraise the team or an individual.
- It should be used to understand the dynamics at the workplace and stimulate conversation on how to continuously improve the processes, tools and strategies.
- The team should be convinced that the effort and time spent in collecting metrics, analyzing it and acting upon it does indeed add value to the business.

Let us look at a few commonly used metrics.

[20]Information radiators are described in Chapter 4: Stakeholder Engagement.

3.8.1 Planned versus Actual Velocity

The concept of velocity is covered in Chapter 6: Adaptive Planning. However, for the scope of this chapter it will suffice to know that velocity is a measure of how much a team can accomplish during an iteration. It is computed as the sum of the story points (units of estimates) that a team can deliver in an iteration.

Consider Table 3-7. The first row shows the planned velocity of the team over iterations 1 through 6. This means that the team expects to deliver user stories or features that are worth 50 story points in each iteration 1-3. From iteration 4 onward, the velocity is expected to trend upward and reach the value of 50 per iteration.

Table 3-7. *Showing planned and actual velocities*

	Iteration 1	Iteration 2	Iteration 3	Iteration 4	Iteration 5	Iteration 6
Planned velocity	50	50	50	60	60	60
Actual velocity	30	45	55	35	70	55

However, reality is different. The second row reflects the actual velocity of the team over the 6 iterations. This is counted from the actual stories that are completed (met the *definition of done* criteria) at the end of each iteration. When the team comes together, its velocity is lower than expected during iteration 1, but it steadily increases and trends toward the planned velocity that the team strives to achieve. During Iteration 4, something unanticipated happens like unplanned absence of one or more team members or the team discovers further complexity in the tasks committed and so the velocity dips. However the team catches up during the next iteration where the actual velocity exceeds the planned value as the team realizes that they have overestimated a user story. This can be visualized in the graph showing planned and actual velocities of the team over the 6 iterations. Notice the dotted line showing an upward trend implying that the team's velocity increases over time as the team learns and synergizes better.

The velocity trend shown in the above Figure 3-13 is a valuable forecasting tool. Based on the actual performance observed, the team can tell whether they will finish the backlog of user stories by the planned number of iterations or not. If they are going slower, the customer should be aware than anticipated the customer should be made aware that a few more iterations (hence more time) will be required to complete the desired set of features.

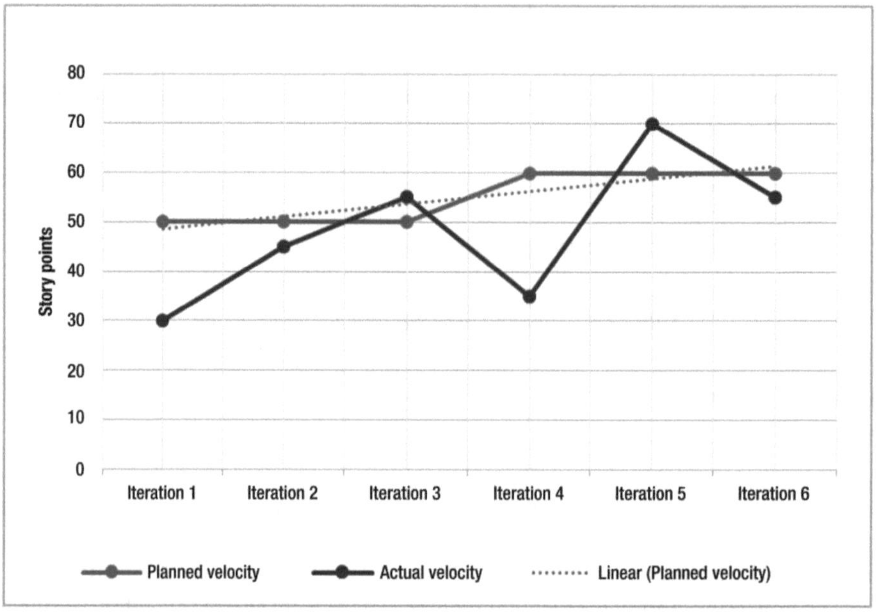

Figure 3-13. *Tracking planned vs. actual velocity*

Such velocity graphs should be publicly posted on the team wall, such that it is visible to one and all.

3.8.2 Release Burndown charts

A release burndown chart shows how much work is remaining at the beginning of each iteration and the likelihood that the project team will be able to achieve the iteration goal.

Continuing with the same example as in the previous Section 7.1, let us see how the team is progressing toward its goal, as reflected in Table 3-8. The team starts with a release backlog (iteration 1) comprising of features and user stories that have an estimated size of 330 story points. At the beginning of iteration 2, the team is planned to have achieved a velocity of 50 story points, which implies that the team has 330 - 50 = 280 story points remaining. Next, in iteration 2, the team has a planned velocity of 50 again. So at the end of iteration 2 or beginning of iteration 3, the release backlog size is 280 - 50 = 230 story points. This goes on, until all the stories in the backlog are done by the end of iteration 7.

Table 3-8. *Showing how the team is progressing toward its goal*

Story points remaining	Iteration 1	Iteration 2	Iteration 3	Iteration 4	Iteration 5	Iteration 6	Iteration 7
Planned	330	280	230	180	120	60	0
Actual	330	300	255	200	165	95	40

Let us now consider the actual velocity. The release starts with a backlog of 330 as before. But instead of the planned velocity of 50, the team achieves only 30 at the end of iteration 1. So the backlog at the end of iteration 1 (or at the beginning of iteration 2) is 330 - 30 = 300. Similarly for iteration 2, the team is able to complete only 45 story points instead of the planned value of 50. So the backlog at the end of iteration 2 (or at the beginning of iteration 3) is 300 - 45 = 255. This goes on until end of iteration 6, when it is observed that there are still 40 story points remaining. So the release cannot complete by iteration 6 as planned before. The team will need another iteration (iteration 7 is marked in amber) to complete the pending work items on the release backlog.

The progress of the team is displayed in the form of a graph called Release burndown chart in Figure 3-14. Notice that both the lines depicting the planned and actual values are shown here to help comparison.

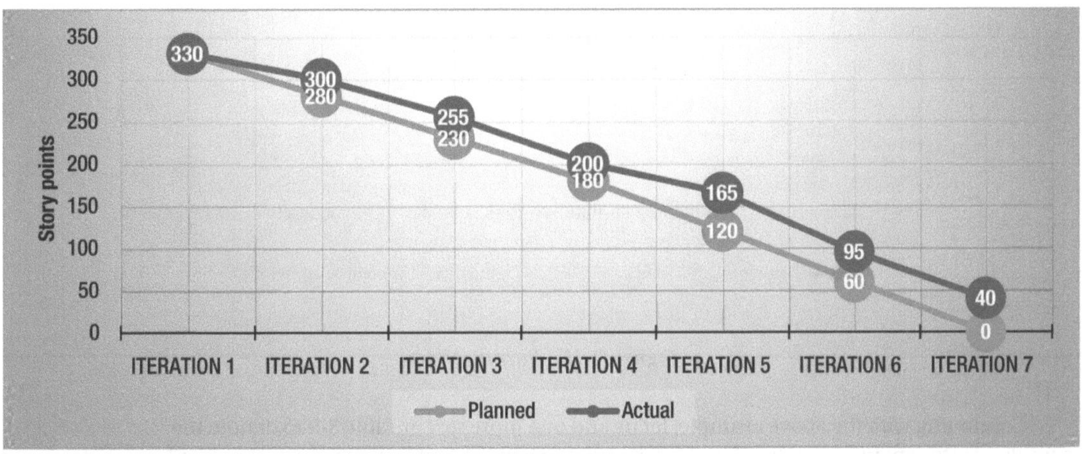

Figure 3-14. *A release burndown chart showing planned and actual progress*

The release burndown chart is a very powerful visual indicator and is very popularly used by the Agile community to track and communicate the progress of a team toward its goal. It is easy to collect the data that goes into a burndown chart as the estimates for the stories that are actually completed during an iteration are simply summed up and plotted on the chart. Tools like Jira[21] can be used to automatically create these burndown charts.

In this example, for simplicity, we have considered that no new scope is added to the backlog. In the above line graphs it will be very difficult to detect scope addition, removal, actual work done or change of estimation. For this reason, release burndown charts are also represented as bar graphs. This is explained in detail in Chapter 6: Adaptive planning.

Burndown charts can also be used to track the trend of risks (probability x impact) in a project. Risk graphs are expected to move in a downward direction as uncertainties tend to reduce[22] and risks get mitigated or closed as the project progresses over time.

---

[21]Refer to `https://confluence.atlassian.com/display/GH061/Viewing+the+Burndown+Chart`. The Greenhopper plug-in of Jira also allows one to configure both working and non-working days.

[22]Refer to the Cone of Uncertainty as discussed in Chapter 6: Adaptive Planning.

3.8.3 Burnup charts

Burnup charts are conceptually the opposite of a burndown chart displaying what has been done so far. While the burndown chart moves in the downward direction (as seen in Figure 3-15), burnup charts move in an upward direction as more and more stories are completed and delivered to the end user.

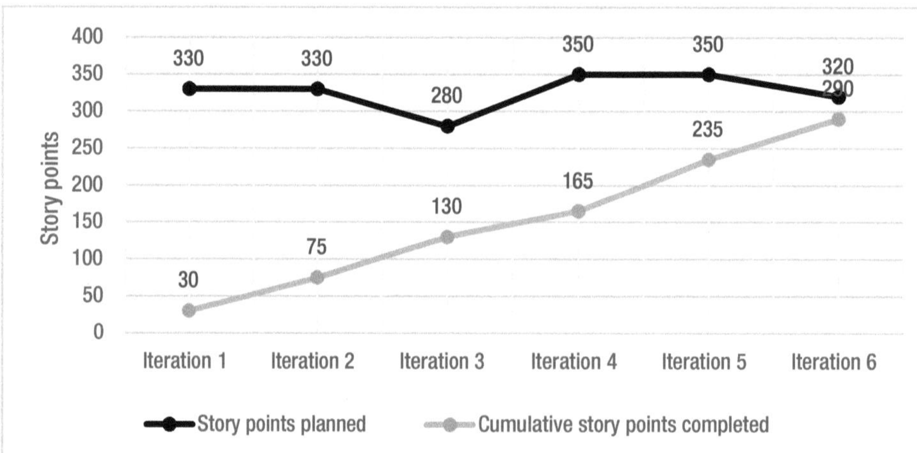

Figure 3-15. *Burnup charts*

Continuing with the above example, let us add one more row in Table 3-9 to denote the cumulative store points completed in every iteration. So in the first iteration the team completes 30 story points, 45 in the second and 55 in the third. Summing them up the team completes 30 + 45 = 75 story points and 75 + 55 = 130 story points by the second and third iterations respectively.

Table 3-9. *Showing the cumulative story points completed over 6 iterations*

	Iteration 1	Iteration 2	Iteration 3	Iteration 4	Iteration 5	Iteration 6
Story points planned	330	330	280	350	350	320
Story points completed	30	45	55	35	70	55
Cumulative story points completed	30	75	130	165	235	290

The one advantage of burnup charts over burndown charts is that it can depict change of scope very vividly. This is illustrated on the first row of the Table 3-9 that shows that although the project started with 330 story points to be completed, but during the second iteration the scope got reduced to 280 story points (for example, the product owner found out that some features would be unnecessary). However, in the very next iteration 4, scope got added to reflect a total of 350 story points on the backlog. At iteration 6, the total story points planned remains at 320.

If scope is added or remove from the backlog, that can be shown separately from the rate of progress of the project. Figure 3-15 shows the example of the resultant burnup chart.

With the plotting of two lines in the graph, it is easy to see how the gray line (i.e. work completed) is steadily inching up toward the blue line (i.e. the goal), although the blue line itself can move in either direction as scope changes during the project. It is expected that the gradient of the gray line should also be steady, otherwise it might manifest problems like a dip in velocity of the team.

3.8.4 Combined Burnup and Burndown Charts

Some teams also combine both burnup and burndown graphs on the same chart. Consider the data in Table 3-10 and Figure 3-16.

Table 3-10. *Showing both remaining and completed work*

	Iteration 1	Iteration 2	Iteration 3	Iteration 4	Iteration 5	Iteration 6
Actual story points remaining (before iteration)	330	300	255	200	165	95
Cumulative story points completed	30	75	130	165	235	290

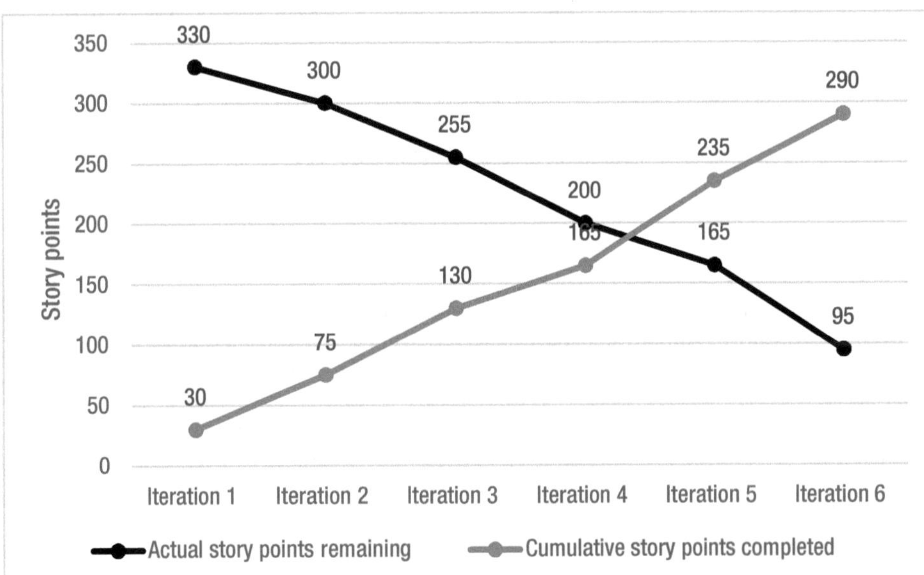

Figure 3-16. *Combined burndown and burnup charts*

3.8.5 Iteration Burndown Charts

Iteration burndown charts are very similar to the release burndown charts that have been described above, expect that the time scale on the X-axis is a day. So these daily burndown charts help to track the daily progress of the team toward achieving the sprint goal.

Figure 3-17 shows a daily burndown chart on how the team progresses on a committed goal to deliver 40 story points in an iteration of 10 days.

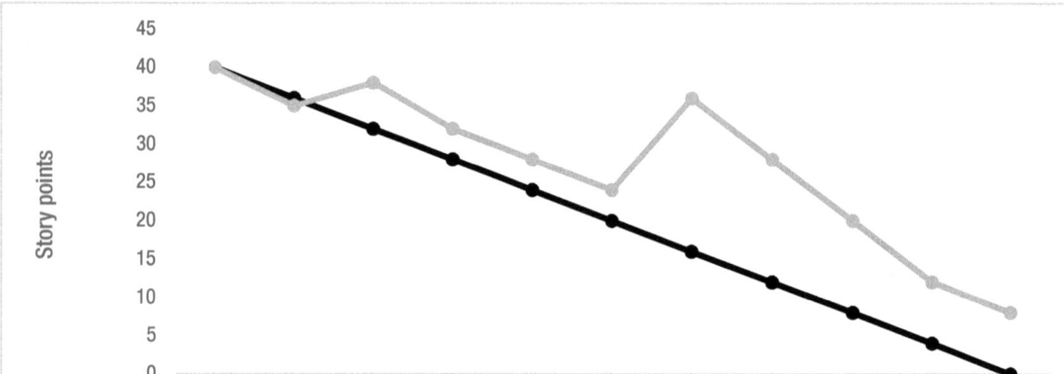

	Day1	Day2	Day3	Day4	Day5	Day6	Day7	Day8	Day9	Day10	Day11
Planned	40	36	32	28	24	20	16	12	8	4	0
Actual	40	35	38	32	28	24	36	28	20	12	8

Figure 3-17. *Daily burndown chart*

3.8.6 Parking Lot Chart

Parking lot charts have their origin from Feature-Driven Development[23] (FDD) methodology.

Apart from the burndown and burnup charts, Jeff DeLuca's Parking Lot chart is also a powerful method of visual representation of a team's progress toward completing the tasks for a release.

To begin with, the stories for each release are grouped in themes. These themes are represented in rectangular boxes (refer to Figure 3-18) containing information about:

- Theme Name (e.g., Payment handling).
- Number of stories related to the theme.
- Sum of the estimates for those stories expressed in story points.
- Percentage completion at the point of measuring, gives a fair idea whether the theme is on schedule or behind schedule needing more attention.

[23]Refer to Chapter 2: Agile Methodologies for a brief discussion on FDD.

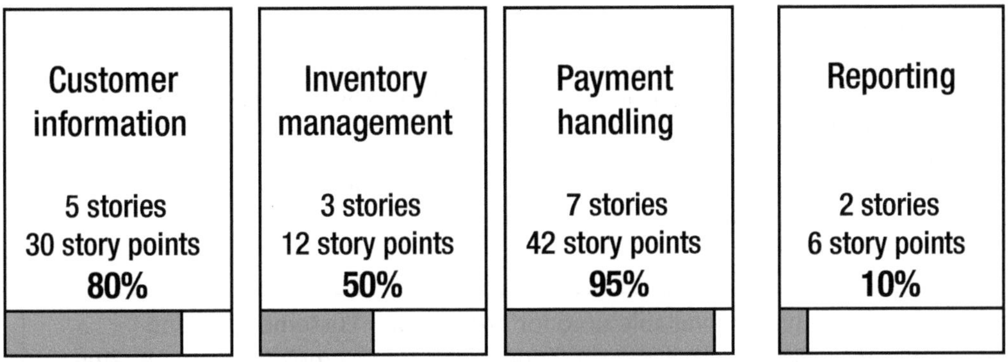

Figure 3-18. *Parking Lot Chart of an order handling application*

For example, from the above Figure 3-18, it can be concluded that for the theme on customer information, 24 out of 30 stories are completed and 6 are either in progress or not done. Note that even though information is not reported at the level of each of the stories that makes up the customer information theme, the summary information is very valuable for tracking and diagnostics.

3.8.7 Kanban board / Task Board

As we have seen in Chapter 2: Agile Methodologies, the Kanban board (refer to Figure 2-12) is a very powerful visual aid to track how the team is progressing toward completing its work. The Kanban board is a pull-driven system where the resources prevent work from piling up before a constrained process, so that the lead time to deliver value to the business does not get compromised. The team is disciplined to commit to work no more than its predefined WIP limit, thereby ensuring that the flow in the system is optimal. If a work item is blocked, the team swarms around and works together until the blocker is removed and the work item is completed.

3.8.8 Cycle Time and Lead time

As we have seen earlier in this chapter, cycle and lead times are some of the most important metrics that are used to track how soon value can be delivered to a customer. A lower lead time implies quicker time-to-market, which leads to customer satisfaction. In the example in Section 4.3, we showed how easily cycle time is captured and computed.

3.8.9 Throughput

This is another commonly used metric that tracks the number of completed work items in a week. A system with higher throughput is expected to respond to customer demand with more agility.

3.8.10 Takt Time

The metric of Takt time helps to gauge current productivity of the delivery process against customer demand. The word Takt is derived from the German word *Taktzeit*, which in English means clock cycle.[24] Takt Time is defined as the pace at which a team should release the software into production to match customer demand.

For example, if the customer expects 20 units of a product in a week, then the Takt time would be (40 working hours in a week) / 20 units = 2 hours per unit.

Expressed as a formula:

Takt time = Available time for production / customer demand
Where available time is the total number of hours employees are working minus any time for meetings, down times and breaks.

Note that the Takt time differs from the product delivery time or lead time, which could take several months or years from start to finish.

Once the Takt time is known, it can be compared with the cycle times for each of the stages in the value stream map and bring in improvements by identifying and removing bottlenecks, constraints and non-value added tasks in the system. With this the team can strive toward achieving a consistent, predictable, rhythmic and continuous flow of value to the customer.

3.8.11 Cumulative Flow Diagrams (CFD's)

As we have seen earlier in this chapter, CFD's are a very powerful tool that convey a lot of information about the cycle time of a process, total number of items in WIP state at a given time and most importantly identify any bottlenecks in the system. CFD's are more advanced than burndown and burnup charts because they not only depict to-do (what we called 'inbox' earlier) and completed (what we called 'done' earlier) items, but also items that are in a work in progress. Since CFD's track all types of items that comprise the total scope of the project, they can communicate a percentage completion at a given period of measurement. For example it is possible to derive information like - as on Day 5, 40% of the features are waiting to be picked up from the backlog, 15% of the features are undergoing analysis, 20% under development, 10% under testing, 10% are waiting to be deployed and 5% are delivered to production.

Agile Teams work hard to inspect the value stream map, eliminate all forms of non-valued added activities and continuously improve the way work gets done. The CFD provides a very handy visual to measure progress and check the effect of improvement practices on the overall value stream.

3.8.12 Nightly Builds Passed

As developers write code, it is imperative that the code is integrated many times during the day with the main version. Integration builds are a key step to prove that the code compiles, generates the needed libraries and executables, executes unit test cases that are kicked off as part of the build and prove that none of the dependent functionalities break. XP programmers, for example, practice 10-minute builds frequently (or whenever code is checked into the main branch) to ensure that the team never reworks or spend a great deal of effort fixing build and complex dependencies at a later period of time. Sophisticated build orchestration tools (like Teamcity, Hudson) nowadays, can run automated build, run code quality checkers,

[24]Referencing `http://www.linguee.com/german-english/translation/taktzeit.html` and `http://www.dict.cc/german-english/Taktzeit.html`

run test cases, notify programmers of the build status via a dashboard or through e-mail and provide enough information to diagnose reasons for builds to break, if any. Tracking history of builds might help the team to avoid any pitfalls, come up with best practices that improve code quality and enhance the success of a build.

3.8.13 Earned Value Management (EVM)

Traditional projects use a combination of S-graphs and Gantt charts to track costs and schedule respectively. With Earned Value Management (EVM) techniques, we have a very powerful visual depiction of a set of leading and lagging metrics in our hand to forecast the future based on past performances.

Figure 3-19 below shows the plotting of actual cost and earned value compared with the planned value of a project depicted in the form of an S-curve. All the values are measured on the day of reporting and are then extrapolated to forecast the end date and the estimated cost of completion of the project. On the right-hand side are the various pieces of information that can be deduced by reading from the graph. As observed, the project is expected to face schedule and cost overrun unless some serious actions are undertaken to bring it back on track.

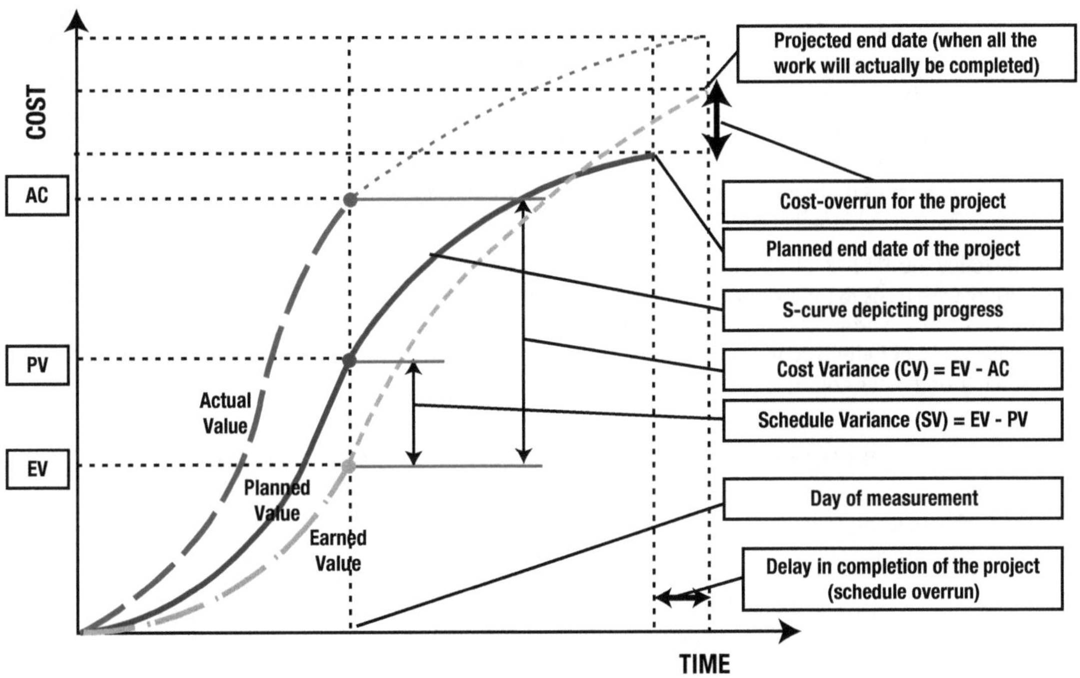

Figure 3-19. *S-curves showing EVM parameters for a project that is over budget and behind schedule*

EVM formulae and techniques could be applied to Agile projects, but with one word of caution. EVM techniques compare actual values measured against a planned or baselined value of cost or schedule. On Agile projects neither the scope nor the schedule is fixed up front and so the plans are subject to evolve over a period of time. It is not necessarily a bad thing if the team requires one or more iterations to accommodate a change or feedback or something as a result of imprecision in estimation or variability in velocities. Therefore the choice of the planned values has to be carefully made; otherwise the metrics will lose its significance and relevance.

Usually EVM techniques in Agile projects are applied at a release level. At a release level:

- Planned value = Sum of estimates (in story points) of all the stories planned for the release.
- Earned value = Sum of estimates (in story points) of all the stories actually completed as part of the release.
- Actual costs = actual money spent behind resource and non-resource costs to implement the stories in the release.

Based on the above, the two most common EVM metrics are as follows:

- **Schedule Performance Index (SPI)** = Earned Value (e.g., in story points) / Planned Value (in story points). A SPI less than 1 signifies that the project is behind schedule whereas a value greater than 1 means the project is ahead of schedule.
- **Cost Performance Index (CPI)** = Earned Value (e.g., in equivalent value of story points completed) / Actual costs incurred (money spent till date). A CPI less than 1 signifies that the project is over budget schedule whereas a value greater than 1 means the project is under budget.

The following Table 3-11 can be referenced to determine how the project release is progressing with basis to the two parameters of time and cost. The boxes colored green and white mean that the project is either ahead or on plan. The boxes colored as red indicates that the project is either behind schedule or is over budget and some imminent corrective actions are required to bring it back on track.

Table 3-11. *Project status lookup table based on CPI and SPI (EVM)*

Performance measures		Schedule		
		SPI > 1	SPI = 1	SPI < 1
Cost	CPI > 1	Ahead of schedule Under budget	On schedule Under budget	Behind schedule Under budget
	CPI = 1	Ahead of schedule On budget	On schedule On budget	Behind schedule On budget
	CPI < 1	Ahead of schedule Over budget	On schedule Over budget	Behind schedule Over budget

Note that the actual EVM formulae are rarely expected in the exam. The concept of EVM, the significance of the S-curve and the application of the concepts in Agile (e.g., in release planning) could appear in the exam.

3.8.14 Quality - Test Cases Written and Passed

As stories gets picked up and developed by the developers, the acceptance test cases (written at the back of the story cards) are executed to ensure that the code conforms to the requirements. The higher is the percentages of the tests getting passed, the greater is the chance of the features being accepted by the customer and avoiding any rework.

Another quality-related metric could be to track the amount of effort resourcing are spending fixing defects versus developing new stories and adding new features.

3.8.15 Escaped Defects

The term 'escaped defect' means the number of defects that is leaked to the next stage of the process, the next sprint, or in the worst case into the hands of the customer. The metrics of escaped defects is a good indicator of the quality of deliverables produced by the team and it can be correlated with the degree of satisfaction of the customer. By tracking it, the team can assess the effectiveness of their testing process (unit testing, automation testing, exploratory testing[25] etc) and hence the amount of confidence in it.

For Agile methodology, this metric could be measured as the number of defects that propagates to the next sprint. Over time the number of escaped defects should show a downward trend as the team stabilizes with its testing processes, brings in improvement and attains better understanding of the domain, platform and the related technologies. Figure 3-20 shows how escaped defects can be tracked and measured on the basis of each sprint or month by month.

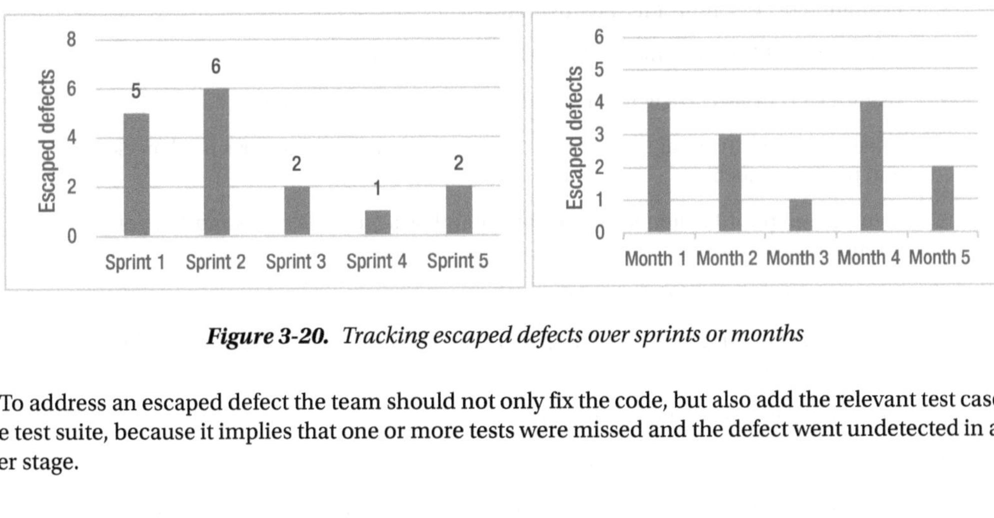

Figure 3-20. *Tracking escaped defects over sprints or months*

To address an escaped defect the team should not only fix the code, but also add the relevant test cases to the test suite, because it implies that one or more tests were missed and the defect went undetected in an earlier stage.

[25]These varieties of testing are described in detail in Chapter 7: Problem Detection and Resolution.

3.8.16 Compliance to Deadlines

Often Agile teams are required to work on items that are milestones and have a fixed due date. The due date could be to meet regulatory constraints or fulfill the dependencies with respect to another stakeholder or application that it interfaces with. Tracking how many times that the team meet its due-date performance goal is helpful. If a team meets it goal most of the time it builds trust, commitment and predictability. On the other hand, if the team misses its goal, then the business user may not be getting their value in a timely manner and so corrective actions are necessary.

3.9 Focus Areas for the Exam

- ✓ How value gets embedded in the different principles of Agile - starting from analysis, prioritization, execution and continuous improvements.
- ✓ Using economic models for to perform cost-benefit analysis - PV, NPV, payback, IRR and ROI. Note that the formulae are not required, but one should know higher or lower the better.
- ✓ Principal sections of a business case document.
- ✓ The importance of a project charter expressed in the form of the abbreviation W5H.
- ✓ The definition of an elevator pitch and its significance.
- ✓ Definition of cycle time and ways to reduce it.
- ✓ Little's law, which states that WIP = Lead time x Throughput.
- ✓ Using a CFD to visualize work in progress and identifying bottlenecks.
- ✓ What is a value stream map and how it is used to identify and remove bottlenecks and pursue perfection.
- ✓ Value-based prioritization technique with emphasis on MoSCoW, Kano, Wieger's method.
- ✓ Prioritization based on risk and value,
- ✓ Definition of backlog grooming and the product owner's role in maintaining the product backlog.
- ✓ DEEP attributes of the product backlog.
- ✓ Concept of risk-adjusted backlog,
- ✓ Agile metrics like velocity, burndown, burnup charts, parking lot chart, cycle, lead and Takt time.
- ✓ Visualization of flow and work-in-progress items using Kanban board, CFD's.

Quizzes

1. All of the following are part of an Agile charter, EXCEPT

   A. Project objective

   B. Precise estimates

   C. Who all will be involved or impacted on the project

   D. Project approach - how the project will be carried out

2. An executive wants help evaluating a proposed three-year project against two proposed one-year projects. Which economic model would be most helpful?

   A. NPV

   B. ROI

   C. MMF

   D. Velocity

3. In the Kano Model, features that provide great satisfaction are called differentiators or

   A. Threshold

   B. Linear

   C. Exciters or Delighters

   D. Neutral

4. A team member is looking at a chart that plots risk exposures over iterations. The graph is showing a downward trend. This chart is called ____________

   A. Risk Burnup Chart

   B. Risk Census

   C. Risk Burndown Chart

   D. Linear Chart

5. Calculate the Cost Performance Index when earned value and actual costs are respectively $5000 and actual costs are $4500?

   A. 1.11

   B. 0.9

   C. 500$

   D. -500$

6. What change do you observe on the release burndown chart once the team delivers 50 story points in an iteration?

   A. The top of the bar graph will move 50 points up

   B. The top of the bar graph will move 50 points down

   C. The bottom of the bar graph will move 50 points down (perhaps below the X-axis)

   D. The bottom of the bar graph will be raised by 50 points (perhaps above the X-axis)

7. What change do you observe on the release burndown chart once there is a reduction in scope by 50 story points in an iteration?

   A. The top of the bar graph will move 50 points up

   B. The top of the bar graph will move 50 points down

   C. The bottom of the bar graph will move 50 points down (perhaps below the X-axis)

   D. The bottom of the bar graph will be raised by 50 points (perhaps above the X-axis)

8. What change do you observe on the release burndown chart once the team realizes that they have underestimated and 50 story points should be added in an iteration?

   A. The top of the bar graph will move 50 points up

   B. The top of the bar graph will move 50 points down

   C. The bottom of the bar graph will move 50 points down (perhaps below the X-axis)

   D. The bottom of the bar graph will be raised by 50 points (perhaps above the X-axis)

9. Which of the following is the BEST estimation scale for use with estimating large units of work?

   A. Linear series like 1, 2, 3, 4, 5, 6, 7, 8

   B. Fibonacci series like 1, 2, 3, 5, 8, 13, 21

   C. Story points

   D. Boolean numbers 0 and 1

10. Which of the following is true about items in the Product Backlog?

    A. Higher-priority items are simply stated while lower-priority ones are detailed out

    B. Higher-priority items are described in more detail than lower-priority ones

    C. The lower the priority, the more the detail

    D. None of the above

11. What do we call the average time between deliveries of completed work items?

    A. Cycle Time

    B. Velocity

    C. Burndown charts

    D. Burnup charts

12. A schedule risk has a 20% probability and the impact could be a delay of 10 days. What is the EMV?

    A. 2

    B. 200

    C. 10

    D. 0.2

13. Which is the recommended project to choose?

    Project A has IRR: 2%, Project B has IRR -4%, Project C has IRR 2.2% and Project D has IRR 3%

    A. Project A

    B. Project B

    C. Project C

    D. Project D

14. Which is the recommended project to choose?

    Project A having NPV: $1200, Project B has NPV: $15000, Project C has NPV: $4000, Project D has NPV: $3000

    A. Project A

    B. Project B

    C. Project C

    D. Project D

15. In the context of project selection based on payback period computation, discounting means?

    A. Providing discounts on the price of the product

    B. Negotiation technique during contract management

    C. Either A or B

    D. Mapping future amounts back to their present value using a rate of interest

16. Which of the following has the highest precedence when choosing stories out of a product backlog?

    A. High Risk High Value stories

    B. High Risk Low Value stories

    C. Low Risk High Value stories

    D. Low Risk Low Value stories

17. Which of the following are NOT true about risk adjusted backlog?

    A. Both functional requirements and risks are enlisted in one backlog.

    B. It is only the product owner who needs to maintain and refer to the risk adjusted backlog during planning and prioritization.

    C. Like features and their priorities are subject to change, so are the probability and impacts of risks. New risks might also crop up and existing ones may become irrelevant. So the risk adjusted backlog must be constantly reviewed and kept up to date.

    D. The whole team needs to contribute to risk identification, analysis, mitigation actions for risks in the risk adjusted backlog.

18. Which tool do we use for tracking and forecasting Agile projects?

    A. Cumulative Flow Diagrams

    B. Burnup charts

    C. Burndown charts

    D. Graph Charts

19. The acronym DEEP is used to depict the characteristic of the product backlog. DEEP means:

    A. Demonstrable, estimable, emergent, prioritized.

    B. Detailed, estimable, emergent, primary.

    C. Detailed, estimable, emergent, prioritized.

    D. Done, estimable, emergent, primary.

20. Which of the following chart shows the total scope requested in a project?

    A. Burnup charts

    B. Burndown charts

    C. Task board

    D. Iteration Graph

21. Which of the following statements does not sound right?

   A. The metric of Takt time helps to gauge current productivity of the delivery process against customer demand.

   B. Parking Lot chart is also a powerful method of visual representation of a team's progress toward completing the tasks for a release.

   C. Earned value management technique can be applied to traditional projects, but not to Agile projects since there is no baseline to measure against.

   D. A Kanban board is used to visualize the work in progress for an Agile team.

22. In the MoSCoW model of prioritization, what does M and C stand for?

   A. Must-have, couldn't-have

   B. Mandatory, could-have

   C. Must-have, could-have

   D. None of the above

23. In Lean, the steps to use a value stream maps is as follows:

   A. Identify product to analyze, repeat and pursue perfection, identify steps and map value stream, eliminate waste, develop a plan to reach future state from current state.

   B. Eliminate waste, Identify product to analyze, identify steps and map value stream, develop a plan to reach future state from current state, repeat and pursue perfection.

   C. Identify steps and map value stream, identify product to analyze, eliminate waste, develop a plan to reach future state from current state, repeat and pursue perfection.

   D. Identify product to analyze, identify steps and map value stream, eliminate waste, develop a plan to reach future state from current state, repeat and pursue perfection.

24. A project manager is using Earned Value Analysis to inspect the health of a year-long project. At the middle of the project, she determines that PV is $25K, EV is $20K and AC is $30K. What can be determined from these figures?

   A. The project is behind schedule and over budget.

   B. The project is ahead of schedule and under budget.

   C. The project is ahead of schedule and over budget.

   D. The project is behind schedule and under budget.

Answers

1. B - Due to uncertainty in Agile projects, it is least likely to have a precise estimate in Agile charter.
2. A - Net present value, as it converts multiyear returns on investment to a value in today's terms.
3. B - Exciters (delighters) are those features that provide great satisfaction, often attracting a premium price to a product.
4. C
5. A - CPI = EV/AC = 5000/4000 = 1.11
6. B
7. D
8. A
9. B - Using nonlinear sequences is a better approach.
10. B - Higher-priority items are described in more detail than lower-priority ones.
11. A - Cycle Time is the average time between deliveries of completed work items.
12. A
13. D - Choose the Project D with the highest IRR.
14. B - Choose the Project B with the highest NPV.
15. D - Discounting is the process of mapping the future amounts back to their present values.
16. A
17. B
18. A - Cumulative Flow diagrams are a tool for tracking and forecasting Agile projects.
19. C
20. A - The Burnup chart shows both scope completed and total scope in the project.
21. C
22. C
23. D
24. A - The project is behind schedule and over budget as both SV (= EV - PV) and CV (= EV - AC) are negative.

CHAPTER 4

Domain III: Stakeholder Engagement

"Your customer does not care how much you know until they know how much you care"

—Damon Richards

We have spoken about stakeholders dozens of times since the beginning of this book and we will continue to do so in the following chapters. Such is the relevance and significance of stakeholders that this whole chapter is dedicated to aspects of stakeholder engagement as it pertains to Agile projects. Since projects are commissioned for the benefit of stakeholders, stakeholder satisfaction is a key objective for the project team. Irrespective of whether the other project constraints are met or not, stakeholder (e.g., customer) satisfaction or lack of it could translate into success or failure of a project. The most dominating stakeholder is the customer or the user of the software product being built by the Agile professionals, so a majority of the chapter is devoted to understanding how to engage them in project affairs from start to finish.

Engaging and managing stakeholders is not easy. To do this effectively, one needs a whole basket of soft skills and leadership attributes in varying ratios and proportions based on the situation at hand. This chapter dedicates a fair share of the content talking about these soft skills and leadership skills.

4.1 Understanding Stakeholder Needs

4.1.1 Identifying Stakeholders

Let us begin with the classic definition[1] of stakeholders that is applicable for any project situation. Stakeholders of a project are individuals, groups, or organizations that are affected or perceived to be affected either positively or negatively by a decision, activity, or outcome of a project.

Here are a few examples of project stakeholders:

- people who are working on the project;
- sponsoring it or supporting it (like senior leadership team);
- providing requirements or intending to use the final product, service, or result of the project;
- marketing and advertising the product or the service;

[1]This definition is derived from PMI®'s *A Guide to the Project Management Body of Knowledge* (PMBOK® Guide) – Fifth Edition.

S. Boral, *Ace the PMI-ACP® exam*, DOI 10.1007/978-1-4842-2526-4_4

- tracking financial health of the project;
- producing goods and services that are consumed by the project (like upstream applications who interface with an application);
- consuming the result of the project (like a reporting application who feeds the data produced by the software application).

There could be other stakeholders indirectly involved like those helping in recruitment activities, suppliers, shareholders, those performing administrative and logistic functions, property, security and janitorial services and so on.

It is of vital importance that the Agile project team begins with identification of right (and legitimate) stakeholders, understanding their needs, wants, wishes, dreams and priorities. Note that stakeholder identification is not a one-off activity that is done in the initial days of the project, but something that needs to be continuously monitored as the project moves along. Once the stakeholders are identified, they are depicted on a stakeholder map. An example of a stakeholder map for the library management system can be seen in Figure 6-10.

4.1.2 Analyzing Stakeholders Based on Power and Interest

Once the stakeholder map is created, the team should classify stakeholders based on their power and interest in the project and devise a strategy to deal with them appropriately. Figure 4-1 shows a 2x2 power-interest grid and the corresponding strategy in dealing with them.

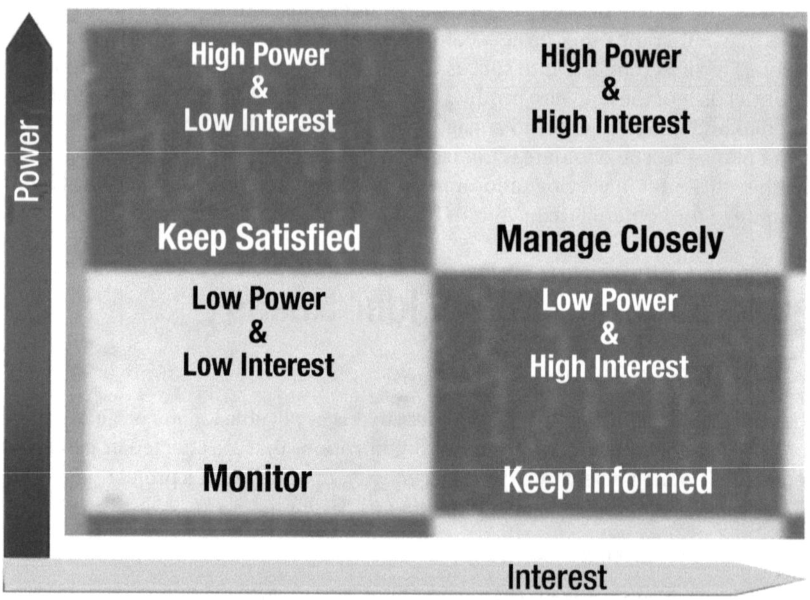

Figure 4-1. *Power-interest grid for stakeholder classification*

The top-right quadrant of the grid representing stakeholders having the highest power as well as interests in the project needs to be managed closely. Examples of such stakeholders are the sponsor and senior executives in the organization. The bottom-right quadrant is for stakeholders with low power, but high interest in the project. The examples of such stakeholders are team members who need to be kept well informed about the decisions of the project. On the top-left corner are stakeholders such as government, regulatory bodies and civic agencies who have high power, but low interest in the affairs of the project, but still need to be kept satisfied. The general community or the crowd occupies the bottom-left quadrant that denotes the set of stakeholders with low power and low interest in the project. Such stakeholders need minimal attention and at best need only to be monitored or communicated to passively.

The stakeholder classification matrix represents a very powerful tool for the team to do the following:

- decide where to devote their energy most and;
- devise the most appropriate strategy to communicate, satisfy, or involve the stakeholders in the affairs of the project.

It should be noted that during the life cycle of the project, it is quite likely that stakeholders could move from one quadrant to another; hence the analysis should be carefully updated periodically.

4.1.3 Analyzing Stakeholders Based on Engagement Levels

Another powerful tool is the stakeholder engagement matrix that is used to assess their current and desired engagement levels or outlook of the project. The engagement levels could vary as follows:

- Unaware - Stakeholders who are unaware of the project and potential impacts.
- Resistant - Aware of the project and resistant to change.
- Neutral - Neither supportive nor resistant.
- Supportive - Would like to see the change happen and has a positive outlook toward it.
- Leading - Actively engaged in ensuring the project is a success.

Based on this definition, the current and desired engagement level of each stakeholder could be depicted as in Figure 4-2.

Stakeholder	Unaware	Resistant	Neutral	Supportive	Leading
John	Current			Desired	
Mary			Current	Desired	
Richard				Current, Desired	
Anne		Current	Desired		
Chris			Current		Desired

Figure 4-2. *Stakeholder engagement assessment matrix*

The above tools are simplistic but form a foundation to understanding a complex anatomy of the stakeholders and their influence on the project. There are a lot more things that teams would ideally like to learn about their stakeholders. Following are a few of them:

- How passionate are the stakeholders about the project? Are they emotionally connected to its outcome?
- Do they have a financial stake in its success?
- Do they have a historical context? For example, have they experienced the past versions or releases of the products?
- What does success mean for them?
- What benefits do they perceive from the product?
- What kinds of communication requirements are appropriate for them? How about the content, timing frequency, choice of medium, of communication?
- Are there interrelationships and overlaps between segments of stakeholders? Are there conflicting needs and priorities?
- How is their outlook to change?
- How risk averse are they?
- Is it easy to move them from the current to the desired engagement levels? Is it easy to win over resistant stakeholders? If so, what are the strategies to follow? If not, can they be converted to neutral at least?

4.1.4 Stakeholder Modeling Using Personas, Prototypes and Wireframes

Understanding the stakeholders' needs and their priorities play a vital role while collecting requirements. Agile teams model user behavior by creating personas that depict different varieties of users that will be interacting or benefiting from the system. Each persona provides a realistic description of a typical user or a group of users in a segment exhibiting similarity in behavior or expectation from the system. Personas are created as an outcome of research of the demographics of the stakeholder base. Section 2.6.1 has a detailed description of the user personas, how they are created and an example of personas for our running example of the library management system.

Another set of tools that Agile teams use to 'read' stakeholder minds is prototypes, proof-of-concepts and wireframes. Prototypes and wireframes are quick and cheap to produce and used by teams to validate their understanding of the proposed system or its constituent features are aligned to the stakeholder's expectations. Often stakeholders are themselves not clear about how the end system will look like and often change their minds. Looking at a mock-up or a blueprint helps them converge to a decision and communicate to the team. Even if the prototype is completely wrong, it makes sense to 'fail-fast' and perform appropriate midcourse corrections at a fraction of the cost compared to what would have entailed in a traditional waterfall-based software development.

Section 2.6.5 and Figure 6-11 has a detailed description of prototypes, their significance and also a snapshot for one of the possible wireframes for the user interface of the library management system portal.

4.1.5 Agile Modeling

Agile modeling is a collection of values, principles and practices for modeling software development projects. Agile models are built with stakeholder consensus and the aim is to keep it intentionally lightweight so that they can serve the intended purpose without making it cumbersome to follow or adapt as required. In the following Figure 4-3, we see some elements where modeling is used in Agile projects.

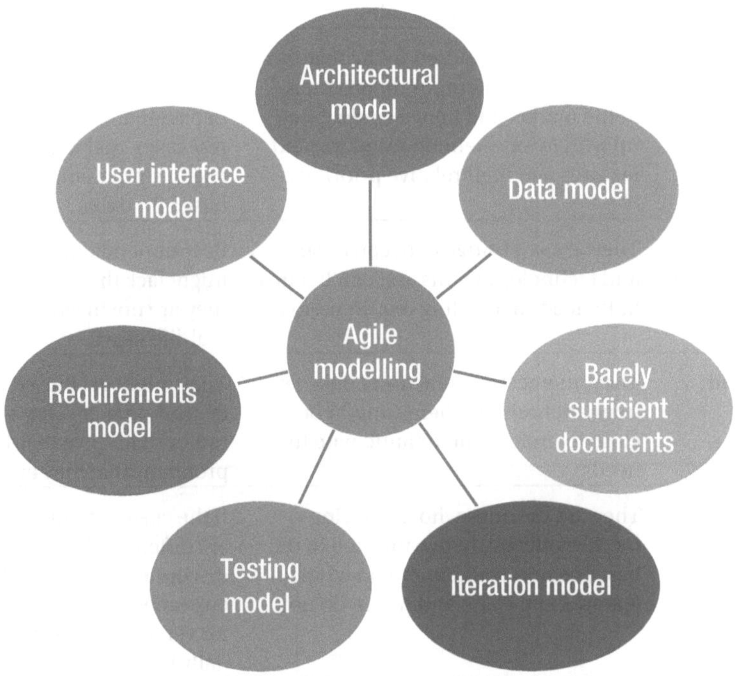

Figure 4-3. *Agile modeling*

4.1.6 Seek User Proxies Where Real Users Are Unavailable

We have seen above why the identification of the right stakeholders to elicit system requirements and provide feedback to product increments are very important in the life cycle of the Agile project. Unfortunately, there could be some times when the real users are unavailable because of location or time constraints. In such a case, the Agile project team reaches out to *proxy users* who may not be real users but substitute them when the real user is unavailable.

Mike Cohn[2] has given some guidelines on who could possibly play the role of proxy users with words of caution in dealing with them or depending on them. This is illustrated in Table 4-1.

[2]Refer to *User Stories Applied* by Mike Cohn. (Boston: Addison-Wesley, 2014).

Table 4-1. *User proxies*

User proxies	Their core competencies	Watch out for some drawback
Subject matter experts	SME's are well versed in the domain of the product and might have a fair overview of similar products already in the market. They could anticipate the different needs from the users and come up with business rules.	SME's could be far more seasoned about the domain compared to the real users. They may also be oblivious about the nuances of the workflow as experienced by a user.
Marketing team	They could be exposed to the features available in contemporary products in the market and hence could come up with recommendations of needed features and their relative priorities.	They are likely to lack detailed knowledge about product behavior and their acceptance test cases, making it hard to create useful stories and implementation based on them.
Business analysts	They act as a bridge between business and technology teams and can balance both needs in eliciting requirements.	Recommendations from BA's might lack the real-life touch if they are not in close contact with real-life users.
Technical support and Helpdesk	They interact with real users on a very frequent basis and hence might be close to understand or anticipate their needs.	They might get biased toward features that are easy to support rather than solve real-life complex problems that they encounter.
Customers	They are the ones who are paying for the software, hence they are in the best position to comment on which features add value and which do not.	If the customer and user roles are different, there might be disconnect between what the customer thinks they are paying for versus what the user uses on a daily basis.
Technical Lead	They have very good knowledge about the internal workings of the product and are aware of its capabilities, scope of improvement and can anticipate features that ought to add values to the users.	They might come up with features that might delight themselves technically, but not necessarily satisfy the user. For example, what is the benefit of a sophisticated user interface built on the latest technology that the end user feels as non-intuitive or causing discomfort?
User's supervisor	They are close to the operations performed by their teams so they might have some knowledge. Also they might be playing the role of users themselves currently or in the past.	As expected in case of supervisory roles, the focus could be on productivity and efficiency, rather than the core functionality of the software.

4.1.7 Soliciting Feedback

Stakeholder needs rarely remain static, more so in the case of long project or over a product life cycle. Needs evolve because of change of market conditions, a desire to keep up with the latest technology trends, to remain compliant to policies or retain revenue from customers and to keep competitors at bay. Agile teams, sensibly, realize that changes are inevitable and welcome it.

During the lengthy discussions on the values and principles around Agile Manifesto in Chapter 1, we have seen how Agile teams are short increments of a couple of weeks to a month or so. Baked into the process is a feedback mechanism by which stakeholders can view and inspect the software produced and can provide feedback reflecting their evolving needs. The cyclical mechanism of gathering feedback and incorporating the same and refining the system until it meets the needs of the stakeholders is the backbone for Agile delivery. For example, Scrum teams host a sprint review for 3-4 hours at the end of each sprint giving a demo of the working software and invite real-time user feedback. The captured feedback could be translated into work items that are entered into the product backlog and subject to prioritization, estimation, planning and development.

4.2 Ensuring Stakeholder Involvement

As we saw in Chapter 1, one of the 12 Agile principles states: "**Business people and developers must work together daily throughout the project.**" The principles promote a culture of participation and collaboration between stakeholders of a project - all working toward the same goal to benefit the customers by incremental delivery of valuable software increments.

Having so far identified stakeholders and collected their requirements, it is necessary to keep them involved and engaged as the project moves along. Following sections contain some recommended areas. Note that some of the sections have been described or cross-referenced in other sections of the book, but presented here for the sake of continuity of the topic and helping you to connect the dots on your learning journey.

4.2.1 Educating Stakeholders about Agile

Since Agile methodologies are relatively newer compared to waterfall or sequential model of software delivery, some stakeholders could be lacking familiarity with the subject. The basic idea of starting out without a detailed specification document that is not signed-off could cause a lot of anxiety. The idea of incremental delivery at the end of 2-3 weeks iteration could be a remote concept for such stakeholders to relate to. Also, the regular interaction and feedback loops required from the team and the business could appear to be an overhead and stakeholders might choose to stay at an arm's length. However, like we saw in section 1.3, such stakeholders could, albeit with a little effort and education, be converted to a supporting or over time, into a leading attitude toward Agile delivery methodologies. There is no secret sauce in it. Stakeholders, once they are immersed, get to see the benefits - they are happy that there are fewer disconnects between the project stakeholders, business gets to see some tangible outcome every few weeks or so, there is a conscious focus to quality and smart engineering practices, the feedback loops echo evolution of requirements and teams are eager to adopt to changes and reorganize between themselves and develop a greater camaraderie between stakeholders working collaboratively rather than in silos.

4.2.2 Establish a Shared Understanding of the Domain and the Product

As we have seen earlier, Agile principles promote cross-functional behavior. Knowledge of the domain and expertise of the product's behavior in the domain is no longer the solitary responsibility of the product owner, product manager, user (or a proxy-user) or a business analyst. Agile team members are essentially required to have a well-rounded knowledge of what it takes to deliver value end to end. If we take the example of estimation during a sprint planning session, we expect each of the team members to produce an estimate for end-to-end delivery of the piece of requirement and not in fragments like analysis, development, regression testing, build and user acceptance testing. We also observe the trend of collective ownership in XP teams, where, by virtue of pair programming or osmotic communication[3] that exists between co-located teams. Kanban teams *swarm* around to solve and remove a bottleneck in their workflow before they accept new work.

4.2.3 Release Planning

Release planning is also an area where stakeholder involvement is mandated. As Agile teams continue to maintain cadence of iterative and incremental development, it is important that they are able to ship working software into production as demanded by customers. Every release is an opportunity to get customers working on an incremental set of features freshly developed and realize value-added benefits.

A release plan is typically outlined by the product owner, who identifies the set of features that should constitute a meaningful and coherent release balancing with the team's capacity to deliver them. Stakeholders brainstorm, analyze options and come up with a release plan that is agreeable across themselves.

4.2.4 Co-Location

Imagine that a developer needed a piece of clarification while writing a piece of code related to validation for a business logic that processes inputs captured from the user. The developer attempts to reach out to the business user who knows about it the best. But the business user might be at a different time zone, so it is not easy to speak to him or her directly. The developer then has to resort to one of the slowest modes of communication, that is, e-mail. Even with e-mails, they could run into chains before the primary question is satisfactorily and unambiguously answered.

XP resolves this delay by having an onsite customer in the project who is available to assist the team in real time and keep the delivery shop running at all times. For rapid paced development, as in Agile, co-located stakeholders are a big enabler.

4.2.5 Choice of Iteration Length

Short timeboxed iterations in Agile help to cement stakeholder involvement and maintain a sense of urgency. If a delivery is too far away, stakeholders tend to go astray, leaving things until the deadline approaches (this is called student's syndrome[4]).

Stakeholders have a definite say in the choice of the length of an iteration.

---

[3]Osmotic communication is discussed in Chapter 5: Team Performance.

[4]Student's syndrome is discussed in Chapter 6: Adaptive Planning.

If an iteration is too long (say 6 weeks), it means that stakeholders will have to wait for that long to see any version of the developed software and any change midway will have to wait for a worst-case period of 6 weeks to be looked at. In a chaotic scenario of rapidly changing requirements and user priorities, longer iterations carry the disadvantages of delayed feedback and increased risk of going in the wrong direction and producing work that is no longer relevant.

Iterations that are too short (say 1 week) can be taxing for stakeholders as there is an overhead of iterating. Planning, development, testing, regression, demos all have to be squeezed in the timebox leading to team's going through the rigor rather than really churning out software increments that are of significant value and size. For example, if sprint planning takes a day and another day devoted to sprint reviews and retrospectives, then in a 1-week sprint, the team actually gets only 3 whole days to achieve any technical work to be accomplished. This could really turn out to be wasteful. Also expecting stakeholders to be captivated for half a day during the iteration demo could also be ambitious to achieve.

More factors on considering the length of an iteration is described in section 1.10 of Chapter 6: Adaptive Planning. The point to conclude in this section is that stakeholder involvement is required to trade off between several aspects that go into choosing how long an iteration should be.

4.2.6 Definition of Done

Like the choice of iteration, the 'definition of done' is another critical piece of understanding that needs to be shared and respected across stakeholders. As described in section 2.6.3 in Chapter 2: Agile Methodologies, teams should reach a consensus on what it takes to mark an item on the backlog as complete. Of course, one of the most important facets of doneness of a requirement is the passing of acceptance test cases, since that helps to bridge the customer's expectation and the actual behavior expected by the software.

4.2.7 Estimation

Involving relevant stakeholders in estimation and planning sessions are always recommended. While product owners and business representatives play a vital role in elucidating requirements and offering clarifications as sought, they are also privy to the estimates being arrived at by the development team. Although the granular estimates do not hold much significance to business representatives, however, they can call out if there are major deviations in understanding, or more importantly, see how the delivery for a particular release or an iteration is shaping up. When teams commit toward a sprint goal taking estimates of prioritized requirements into account, they also candidly share the capacity and capability of the team. Often it could be that a particular set of skills is lacking (e.g., a new technology) or a team member is on planned absence. Such a candid disclosure helps to foster a relation built on trust, collaboration and mutual appreciation and removes any perception of unwarranted over or underestimates.

4.2.8 Prioritization

Like in the case of estimation, involving stakeholders during prioritization and planning is essential to success. As we have seen in section 5 in Chapter 3: Value-Driven Delivery, considerations of business value, risk and costs go into the prioritizing of requirements, enhancements, features, defects and technical work items. By involving the relevant stakeholders, teams build transparency and help the product owner to maximize return on investment.

4.2.9 Information Radiators

Agile teams refrain from writing up weekly status reports to be e-mailed or saved on shared computers. Instead, Agile teams follow a tradition of communicating and visualizing progress very transparently using *information radiators.* They put up a variety of artifacts and metrics (as shown in Figure 4-4) on prominent public spaces like a large white board or a wall on the corridors or hallways so that they can be effortlessly viewed by anyone walking past them. Note that there is no recommendation or rule what the team should display on their walls.

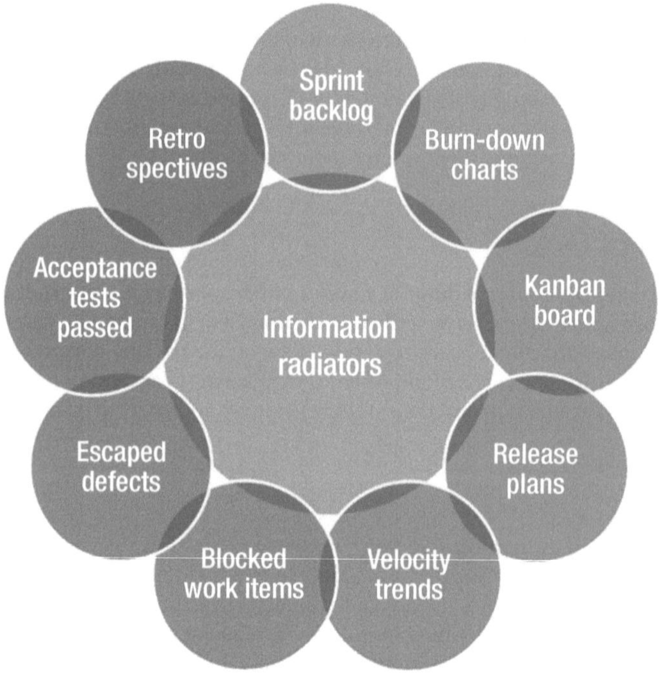

Figure 4-4. *Information Radiators*

Taking the analogy of the filament of an electric heater that radiates heat, these charts and artifacts radiate a lot of information to a passerby that is dynamic (updated by the team members frequently) and easily understood simply by observation (without asking questions). It is common to see teams assemble near the team boards during the daily stand-up meeting and reflect on their progress and impediments. Such a setup is also called *informative workspace.*

Anything that adds value to them, helps in a nonintrusive tracking, visualizing rate of progress can qualify to be worthy for putting up on the information radiator, as summarized below.

Example of information gathered from an information radiator are as follows:

What is the overall objective?
What has been completed so far?
What is currently in progress?
How much is still pending?
Is the rate of progress okay?
Are there any obstacles?
How good is the overall quality?

Note that the usage of a physical board and people writing on it using colored marker pens or pasting colored sticky notes appears to be old fashioned instead of using a sophisticated electronic system. Physical boards, from experience, tend to attract more attention and anyone in the team can simply walk up to it and post an update almost in real time. In contrast, a web page, a spreadsheet, or a document in the shared folder appears to be hidden - as if out-of-sight and out-of-mind. The opposite of information radiator is hence called *information refrigerator*, which hides information and because of the effort required to retrieve and post an update tends to make most people hesitant to use the same. Examples of such are password-protected weekly status reports that are accessible only to a few senior staff in the team. These reports are typically hard to access, detailed to a degree that is more than useful and takes considerable time and effort to maintain regularly.

4.3 Managing Stakeholders

We have seen so far how Agile teams identify stakeholders, analyze their power, influence, needs and involve them in various discussions and decisions that are made during the course of the project. In this section we are going to see a few aspects by which Agile teams and Agile leaders manage their stakeholders, beginning with communication, which occupies a center stage in an Agile project.

4.3.1 Managing Communication

The classic definition of communication management[5] is the process required to ensure timely and appropriate generation, planning, collection, creation, distribution, control, storage, retrieval and ultimate disposition of project information. It has been estimated that traditional project managers spend a majority (about 90%) of their time communicating. Successful communication to balance the stakeholder needs is a key to smooth operation of a project.

As we see in PMBOK, traditional project management follows a very a structured framework for communication consisting of the following processes:

1. **Plan Communication management** - A process in which the project communication is planned based on the stakeholder needs. This is documented in the project communication plan.
2. **Manage communication** - The process of making relevant information available to project stakeholders as planned.
3. **Control communication** - The process of monitoring and controlling communications throughout the entire life cycle of the project so that the information needs of the stakeholders are met.

[5]Refer to PMI®'s *A Guide to the Project Management Body of Knowledge* (PMBOK® Guide) – Fifth Edition.

Agile projects could also follow the above, however, communication is more free flow, frequent and continuous. With an emphasis of business and teams being co-located and a series of ceremonies (like planning, estimating, daily stand-ups, reviews and reflection workshops), Agile teams handle communication between stakeholders more effectively. In fact, with face-to-face communication, Agile teams can afford to do barely sufficient documentation.[6] Earlier we have seen the use of *information radiators* that are used to broadcast easy dissemination of information between internal and external stakeholders. In the next chapter, we will cover a few more aspects like osmotic communication[7] within a team. But before we finish this section, let us have a quick glance at Figure 4-5, which shows the different dimensions of communication (and their associated examples) that are at play while managing stakeholders.

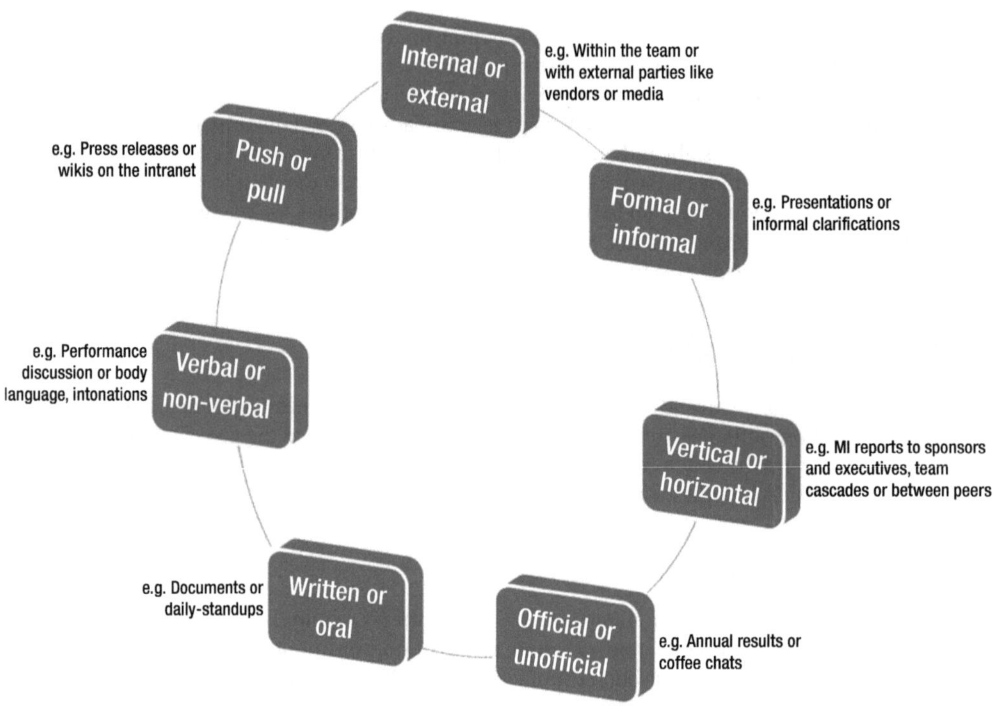

Figure 4-5. *Dimensions of communication*

[6]Remember the values in the Agile Manifesto where collaboration and interaction between individuals are valued more than plans, processes and documentation.
[7]Refer to Chapter 5: Team Performance.

4.3.2 Managing Vendors

Vendors are an example of external stakeholders. An Agile project team might have to involve third parties to deliver products or services that are needed in the project. In such a case, the project team is also required to manage the life cycle of the contract, which could include the following stages of involvement:

- Floating of requests for proposals (RFP's), tenders and organizing bidder conferences.
- Choosing the most appropriate vendor, negotiating and writing the contract (a legally binding document) that enlists elements of scope, milestones, quality and cost of the service or product.
- Administer the contract to make sure that the terms and conditions are being followed in delivering the product or services and any issues and conflicts are being resolved as per the same.

Traditionally contracts in software development projects are written where scope is well defined in advance (as in fixed-price contracts) or on a time-material basis (where the daily labor rate is fixed, but the duration varies). However, Agile contracts are written to accommodate incremental and iterative delivery models and where changes are accommodated without undergoing the overhead of change requests. We will cover further details on Agile contracting in Chapter 5: Team Performance.

It is also to be remembered the vendors may not necessarily have to follow Agile methodologies to produce their services or results, but if they are required to do so, a few things could be taken care of to maximize their engagement and solicit their enthusiastic support:

- Vendor teams operating in an Agile mode should be in sync with the Agile teams consuming their products or services. Like any other member of the team, vendors should also be treated as an augmented body of the same team.
- Vendors should be trained and made aware of the Agile principles, tools and conventions followed by the team. For example, they are recommended to have the same length of an iteration, shared definition of done and access to the same tools used by the project team.
- Vendors should whole-heartedly participate in planning, estimation, demos and retrospectives and have a say in the overarching release plan.

4.3.3 Managing Distributed Teams

Although Agile methods in their purest version advocate co-location for the richest form of communication, in these days it's quite prevalent to see teams that are geographically dispersed but working together on the same project. It is evident that distributed teams often miss out on the many perceivable benefits of real-time interactions. Some of the communication methods that we have seen in the past like physical walls displaying the task board or the burndown chart might get limited visibility in such cases.

4.3.3.1 Agile Tooling

Agile teams have a preference for a bunch of 'low-tech, but high-touch' tools. The low-tech tools include sticky notes, colored markers, writable walls, white boards and flipcharts where the teams can easily write or move things around without much effort. On top of that are few other tools to increase collaboration and coordination. These tools, techniques, practices and advanced communication technologies are collectively termed *Agile tooling* as explained below.

Note that distributed Agile teams do have to put in more energy and conscious efforts into mitigating communication barriers and overcome difficulties in remote collaboration. For example, they use communication technologies like audio and video conferences to bring together virtual teams frequently, as in planning, daily stand-up and retrospective meetings. It is common to see desktops fitted with web cameras and microphones through which real-time communication with a distant team member is possible.

Examples of some more collaboration tools and productivity software are as follows:

- Jira, Rally, VersionOne and online Kanban boards.[8] Jira is a very intuitive tool where one can have stories, issues and tasks on a planning board and track the progress with system generated burndown charts.
- Instant messaging or live-chat software (e.g., Lync[9] and Skype[10]),
- Desktop sharing and viewing (e.g., Webex,[11] Microsoft Netmeeting, or TeamViewer[12]),
- Continuous build and integration (e.g., Teamcity,[13] Cruisecontrol),
- Unit testing and regression testing framework (e.g., Junit,[14] Nunit),
- Document management (e.g., Sharepoint[15]),
- Wikis and collaboration sites (e.g., Confluence[16]),
- Multisite configuration management (e.g., Clearcase[17]),
- Version control software (e.g., SVN and Github[18]),
- Estimation tool using planning poker.[19]

4.3.3.2 Other Practices to Manage Distributed Teams

While dealing with distributed teams, there are a few more practices that Agile teams pursue. They are as follows:

- Conduct daily stand-up meetings location-wise and scrum-of-scrums[20] or meta-scrums to bring multiple teams together.
- Have team members adjust their work timings to an extent where some overlap between time zones are possible.

---

[8]Example of an electronic Kanban board : `https://kanbanflow.com/`
[9]Refer to `https://www.microsoft.com/en-in/download/details.aspx?id=35451`
[10]Refer to `https://www.skype.com/en/meetings/`
[11]Refer to `https://www.webex.co.in/`
[12]Refer to `https://www.microsoft.com/en-in/download/details.aspx?id=23745` and `https://www.teamviewer.com`
[13]Refer to `https://www.jetbrains.com/teamcity/`
[14]Refer to `http://junit.org/junit4/`
[15]Refer to `https://products.office.com/en-us/sharepoint/sharepoint-2013-overview-collaboration-software-features`
[16]Refer to `https://www.atlassian.com/software/confluence`
[17]Refer to `http://www-03.ibm.com/software/products/en/clearcase`
[18]Refer to `https://github.com/`
[19]Refer to `https://www.planningpoker.com/`
[20]Scrum of Scrums is discussed in Chapter 2: Agile Methodologies.

- Use a heavier process, documentation and methodology set - for example, coding rules, conventions, processes, best practices, etc.
- Simplify the system architecture such that decisions could be made more swiftly and the complexity of programming and adapting to inevitable changes are lowered.
- Teams could choose to organize themselves such that each location contains a relatively complete team that is experienced and competent to look after all parts of a system, which is perhaps loosely coupled (hence relatively independent) with other parts of the system.
- Bring team members together at least once, preferably at the beginning of the project and have them work together through one or 2 iterations or during critical events like release planning and deployments. Apart from the technical work, the social interaction and 'putting-a-face-to-the-name' helps in appreciating cultural differences, building trust, bonding and rapport among the team members.
- If travel budgets permit, take the opportunity to rotate team members across locations and encourage team members to undergo cross-cultural trainings.

4.4 Interpersonal Skills for Managing Stakeholders

It is now time to look at some of the soft skills that are required by Agile team members to manage stakeholders. Like all soft skills, these are also learned and perfected through experience and application in appropriate situations. This section is also important from the PMI-ACP® exam point of view.

4.4.1 Emotional Intelligence

Emotional intelligence is a soft skill required in the toolbox of the Agile leader or coach to acquire and apply knowledge from emotions of oneself and the team to effectively relate to them and lead them toward success. Coupled with negotiation and conflict management skills, this skill helps in a wide variety of situations.

In other words emotional intelligence means the ability to

- Identify and manage one's self,
- Understand one's feeling and emotions,
- Understand other's feelings and emotions,
- Respond to the situation appropriately.

In an article published by the science journalist Daniel Goleman,[21] he provided a brief overview of the five main components of Emotional Intelligence (EI). They are illustrated in Table 4-2 as follows.

[21]Refer to http://www.sonoma.edu/users/s/swijtink/teaching/philosophy_101/paper1/goleman.htm

Table 4-2. *Five components of Emotional Intelligence*

Component of EI	Characterized by the ability to	Hallmark or sure signs
Self-awareness	Recognize and understand personal moods and emotions and drives, as well as their effect on others.	Self-confidence, realistic self-assessment of one's emotion state, self-directed sense of humor.
Self-regulation	The ability to control or redirect disruptive impulses and moods, suspend judgment and to think before acting.	Comfortable with ambiguity, adaptable to change, taking responsibility for one's work and deeds, trustworthiness.
Internal motivation	A passion to work with energy and persistence for reasons that go beyond money or status. This is in pursuit of an inner vision of what one considers as important in life and a joy in doing something creative and full of learning.	Strong drive to achieve and optimism and perseverance even in the face of failure.
Empathy	The ability to understand another person's emotional condition and treating them based on it.	Expertise in building and retaining talent, cross-cultural sensitivity and service to clients and customers.
Social skills	Proficiency in managing relationships and building networks, equipped with an ability to find common ground and build rapport.	Effectiveness in leading and inspiring change, persuasiveness and demonstrated expertise in building and leading teams.

The aspects of emotional intelligence can be depicted in the form of a 2x2 matrix as given in Figure 4-6 below.[22]

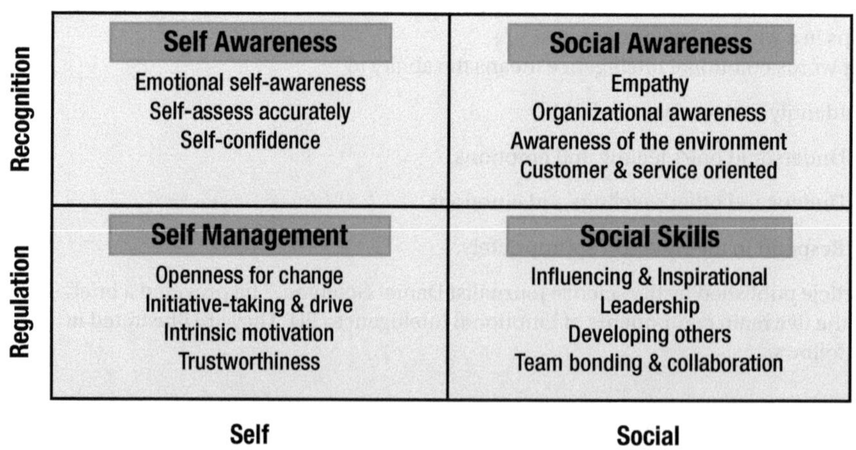

Figure 4-6. *Four elements of emotional intelligence*

[22]Refer to `http://www.sonoma.edu/users/s/swijtink/teaching/philosophy_101/paper1/goleman.htm`

Given this framework, Agile leaders can equip themselves to manage their conduct better in professional environments. Negative emotions at the workplace like frustrations, anger and unhappiness can be really toxic and spread fast. By being conscious of his own emotions and those of others, Agile leaders should be able to empathize with team members, develop them and inspire them toward success.

4.4.2 Collaboration

We have seen how collaboration plays a key role to bind an Agile team together. One of the values in the Agile Manifesto (as seen in Chapter 1: Agile Principles and Mindset) gives precedence to customer collaboration over contract negotiations. Agile leaders foster a collaborative environment where they facilitate interactions between the team members to plan, execute, track work and remove blockers on the way. The same collaborative culture exists between the business users and the team to progressively elaborate requirements over time and incorporate feedback incrementally.

4.4.3 Motivating

One of the 12 principles of Agile says, "Build projects around motivated individuals. Give them the environment and support they need and trust them to get the job done." Intrinsic motivation has a direct co-relation to the productivity or direction of travel for a team. Once the team member's personal goals are accomplished with the project's goals, they tend to stay more committed and contribute toward the success of the project.

Team members of an Agile project are self-organized. They are empowered to take their decisions and unlike traditional projects, they are not supervised and assigned work under a command-and-control regime. They share knowledge, take ownership of code and adopt processes and metrics that they feel add value. If there are impediments, team swarm around each other and look to collectively remove the blockers.

To keep people motivated in the team, Agile leaders have a significant role to play. Here are a few instances:

- They should conduct one-on-one meetings with each individual in the team and determine their personal needs, wants and desires.
- They should ensure that trust is built and team members never hesitate to be transparent about their statuses and take accountability for their achievements or failures.
- They should ensure that team members experience a variety of work that helps to nourish learning and cross-functional behavior.
- They should ensure that participation in estimation, planning, review and retrospective meetings are effective and the decisions are respected.
- They should align the personal motivators to the objectives of the project or the team.
- They should mentor and coach individually as well as a team.
- They should ensure that constructive feedback during performance appraisals is received and acted upon.
- They should maintain a sustainable pace of development such that stress levels are kept in control.
- They should handle escalations in good faith and manage interpersonal conflicts proactively and timely.

- They should encourage and handle diversity and cross-cultural interaction with sensitivity.
- They should create a rewarding atmosphere that team performance is encouraged and emphasized more than individual brilliance.

One of the ways in which teams can track motivation of team members is by using a *niko-niko calendar* or a *mood board.* The word 'niko' in Japanese means smile. A niko-niko calendar could easily be drawn on a flipchart with each row dedicated for a team member and the columns depicting the days of the month. During each daily stand-up meeting or at the end of the work day, all team members are asked to self-assess and indicate their mood with a relevant emoticon ranging from happy, neutral, sad, mad, etc. As shown in Figure 4-7 below, the niko-niko calendar is useful to trace the mood and feelings of the teams and each of its members over a period of time. It is an important opportunity for reflection with simple qualitative data.

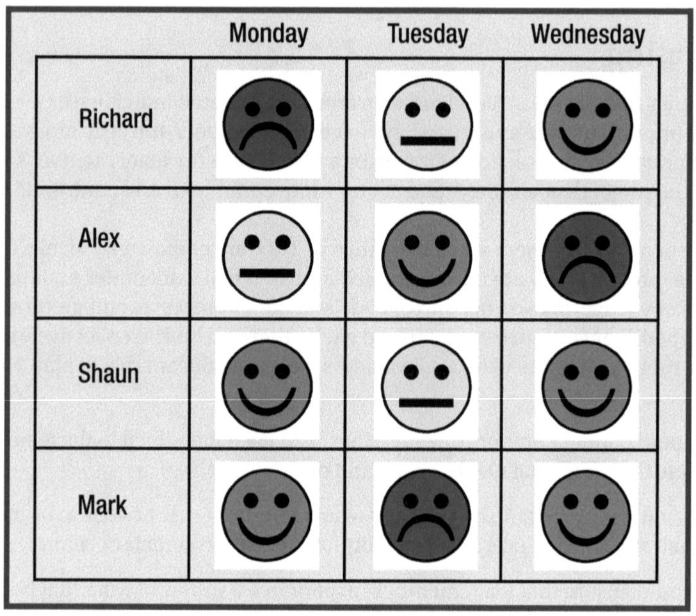

Figure 4-7. *Niko-Niko calendar to track moods of each team member*

4.4.4 Active Listening

One of the most important facets of good communication is *active listening.* Whether it is to learn, get trained, enjoy music, negotiate, resolve conflicts, or counsel, it is very important to be able to use all our senses to capture what one is trying to convey rather than just being limited to the words used to communicate. This technique requires the listener to submit feedback of what they hear to the speaker, by way of restating or paraphrasing what they have heard in their own words; to confirm what they have heard; and more importantly, to confirm the understanding of both parties.

With time and patience, the art of active listening skills can be developed. The key elements for active listening are illustrated in Figure 4-8 below and include the following:

1. Paying undivided attention and avoiding distraction or interruptions.
2. Using nonverbal signs (like eye contact, nods, facial expressions) to acknowledge what is being said. This, in turn, makes the speaker feel at home and communicate more easily, openly and honestly.
3. Providing feedback in the form of asking questions, paraphrasing what is being said, seeking clarifications, or summarization.
4. Deferring any temptation to interrupt the speaker with counterarguments, remaining neutral and nonjudgmental.
5. Responding in a respectful, transparent and candid manner.

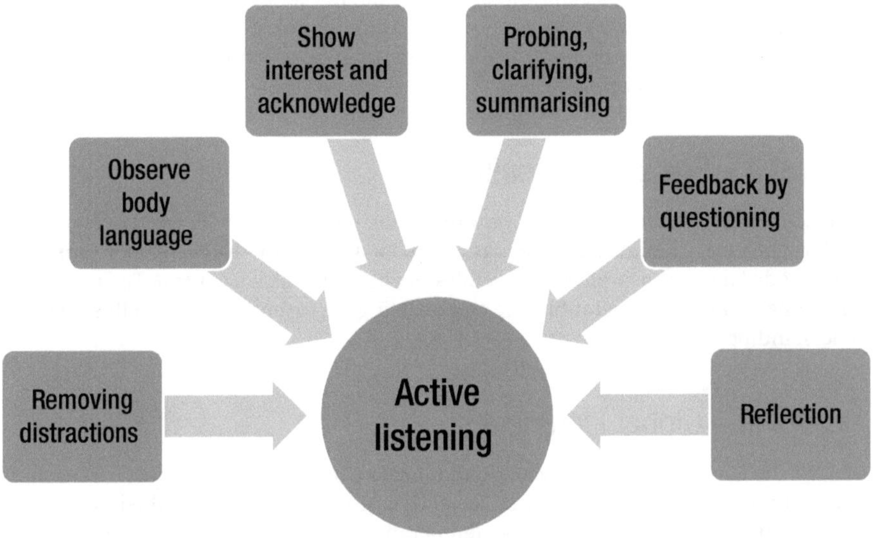

Figure 4-8. *Key elements of Active listening*

Laura Whitworth[23] illustrates the importance of active listening within a coaching context by describing the three levels of listening as shown in Figure 4-9.

[23]Refer to *Co-Active Coaching: New Skills for Coaching People toward Success in Work and Life* authored by Laura Whitworth. (London: Nicholas Brealey Publishing, 2011).

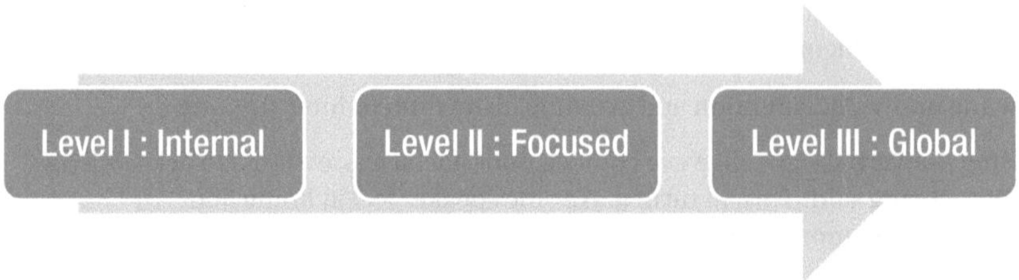

Figure 4-9. *Three levels of listening*

4.4.4.1 Level I – Internal Listening

At this level, although we hear what the speaker is saying and we focus on what it means to us. Rather than the speaker, it is actually listening to our own thoughts, judgment and conclusion. For example, when hearing a CEO of a product company at a seminar, we might actually be thinking, "Will I be able to afford the product?," rather than paying attention to the features of the product presented and the value it brings.

4.4.4.2 Level II – Focused Listening

In this level, we hear each individual word and how the speaker expresses them without allowing to be distracted by one's own thoughts and feelings. Sharp focus is put on the choice of words, tone of voice and body language as well as the overall story in the speaker's context. The core skills of summarizing, questioning, paraphrasing and restating are essentially used in this stage to deepen understanding and to build trust.

4.4.4.3 Level III – Global Listening

At the highest level the listener not only focuses on the speaker, his words and emotions, but also picks up everything available with all senses. Level III is also sometimes described as environmental listening because it helps to gauge temperature, energy levels, intent and the personal agenda of the speaker. In the previous example of the CEO's product demonstration, at this level the listener is also observing the speaker's gestures, pace of movement, usage of hands and the excitement or energy levels in his voice. Level III, hence, helps one to capture the fullest context of the shared information.

4.4.5 Negotiation

We now focus on the next interpersonal skill called negotiation, which is important and seen throughout the Agile context. The objective of negotiation is to obtain a fair and reasonable agreement and also build or maintain a good relationship between the two negotiating parties. The best outcome of a negotiation is a win-win situation and not where one party wins at the expense of the other. To achieve this, in most situations negotiating parties have to approach with a positive and optimistic viewpoint and be open to give or take based on the applicable situation.

4.4.5.1 Example of Negotiation

Let us now see the examples where negotiation prevails in Agile teams.

- Agile teams negotiate to obtain a healthy balance between the required functionality and the available budget required to sponsor its development.
- Users negotiate between themselves and internal stakeholders to shortlist the required features, functionalities and their respective priorities.[24]
- One of the properties of user stories[25] is that it is negotiable. User stories are subject to elaboration and change through conversations between the developers and the users. Over its lifetime, use stories could be rewritten, revised many times, or based on changing priorities; it could even be discarded.
- The Agile development team needs to negotiate on technical tasks and risk along with rest of the value-added features contained in the product backlog. All of the aspects of negotiations are centered on priorities, estimates and value.
- Agile teams negotiate on scope that can be accommodated based on their velocity to deliver during a timeboxed iteration.
- The Agile team can propose alternate solutions to solve business problems and negotiations could be based on pros and cons of each approach.
- Often the team needs to take build-vs.-buy decisions to procure products or services from vendors outside the organization. There is a good deal of negotiation that goes on between teams, vendors, suppliers. and contractors during the contract life cycle on aspects like vendor selection, scope, cost, schedules, financing, roles. and responsibilities.
- If the organization structure is a matrix organization, Agile team leaders have to negotiate with functional managers in securing resources with the appropriate skills and availability from the resource pools in the organization.

4.4.5.2 Negotiation Tactics

Figure 4-10 shows a few commonly used tactics in negotiations at various levels.

[24]Refer to prioritization techniques of Kano and MoSCoW introduced in Chapter 3: Value-Driven Delivery.

[25]Refer to the INVEST acronym used to describe attributes of good user stories. This is discussed in Chapter 6: Adaptive Planning.

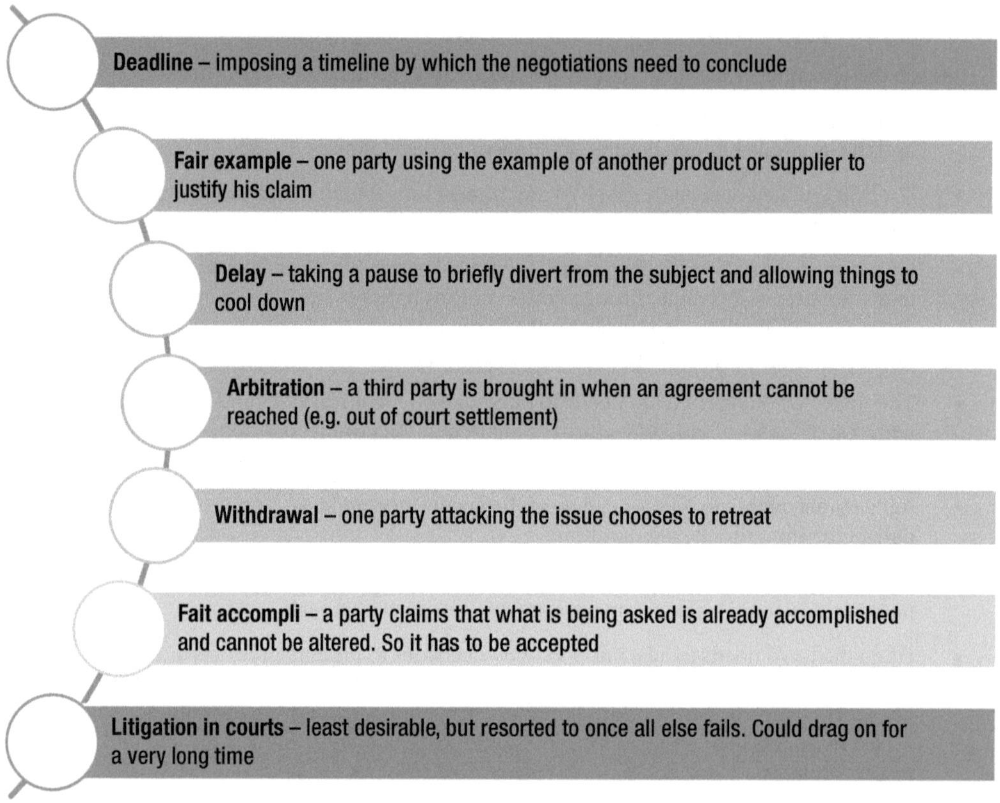

Figure 4-10. *Negotiation techniques*

4.4.5.3 Steps for Negotiation

In all the negotiation steps mentioned above, there needs to be a fair amount of preparation required before the actual negotiation happens. Such preparations help to be psychologically prepared on how to approach the negotiation and explore the possibilities that are expected. Some of the steps involved could be as follows:

- Determine the power, influence, legitimacy, history and background of the party that you are going to negotiate with.
- Determine what the stance you would need to adopt and the minimum that you would settle for.
- Do a SWOT (Strength, Weakness, Opportunity and Threat) analysis of the negotiating parties that will help to devise a strategy.
- Be objective and separate people from the problem (the negotiation topic).
- Anticipate issues and reactions from negotiating parties to help in arguments and counterarguments.
- Arm yourselves with data and facts to justify your stance (and weaken the one from the other side).

- Determine which of the negotiation tactics are most applicable to generate a win-win outcome or the most favorable one.
- Remain professional at all times and be diligent in your argument. But save some tactics up your sleeve for a last resort.
- Envision the worst-case result if a favorable decision is not arrived at the end of the negotiation. Have contingency plans in place.

4.4.6 Conflict Management

Any team is comprised of members having a variety of experiences, ages, cultures, competences, personalities and perceptions. Conflicts are an inevitable consequence of when such teams interaction in an organization. Not all conflicts are bad. Good constructive conflicts could expose a variety of options, innovative ideas, or opportunities that would remain explored if all were into unilateral way of thinking. But if conflicts that are harmful and destructive crop up, they need to be dealt with seriousness and in a timely manner.

4.4.6.1 Reasons for Conflict

Figure 4-11 below shows some of the top reasons for conflicts within a team.

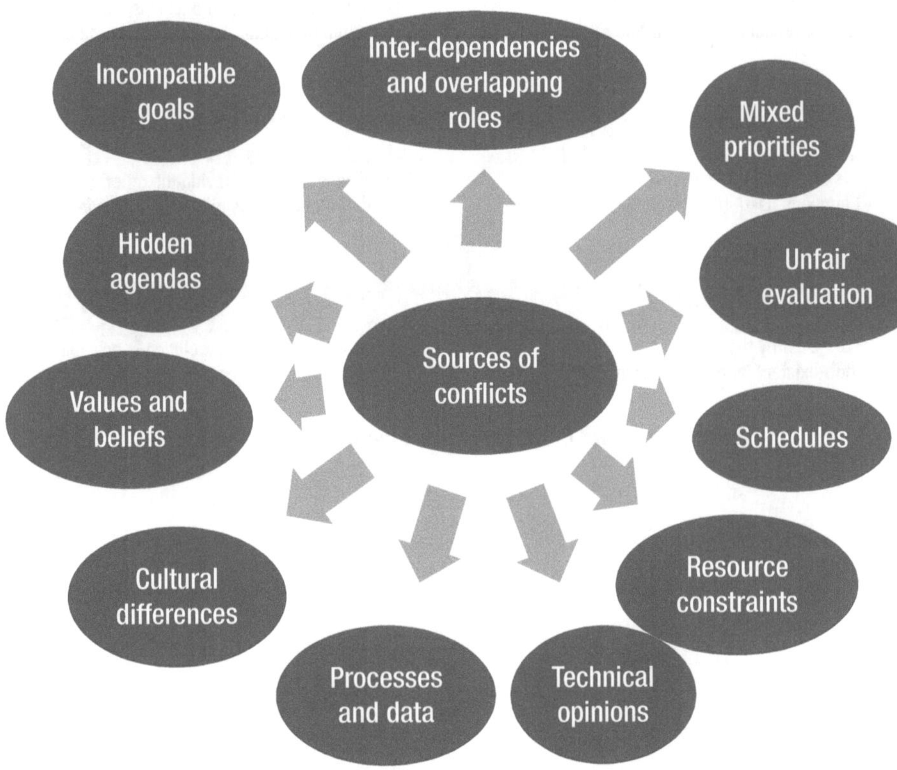

Figure 4-11. *Sources of conflicts*

4.4.6.2 Levels of Conflict

Once conflicts arise, one needs to observe the situation objectively, understand the level of intensity and determine the best way to resolve the same. Agile leaders, coaches, Scrum Masters and project managers frequently take the help of the framework offered by Speed B. Leas to assess and react to different levels of conflict. The levels of conflict range from Level 1: Problem to Solve and increases in intensity to Level 5: World War. This is shown in Figure 4-12 below.

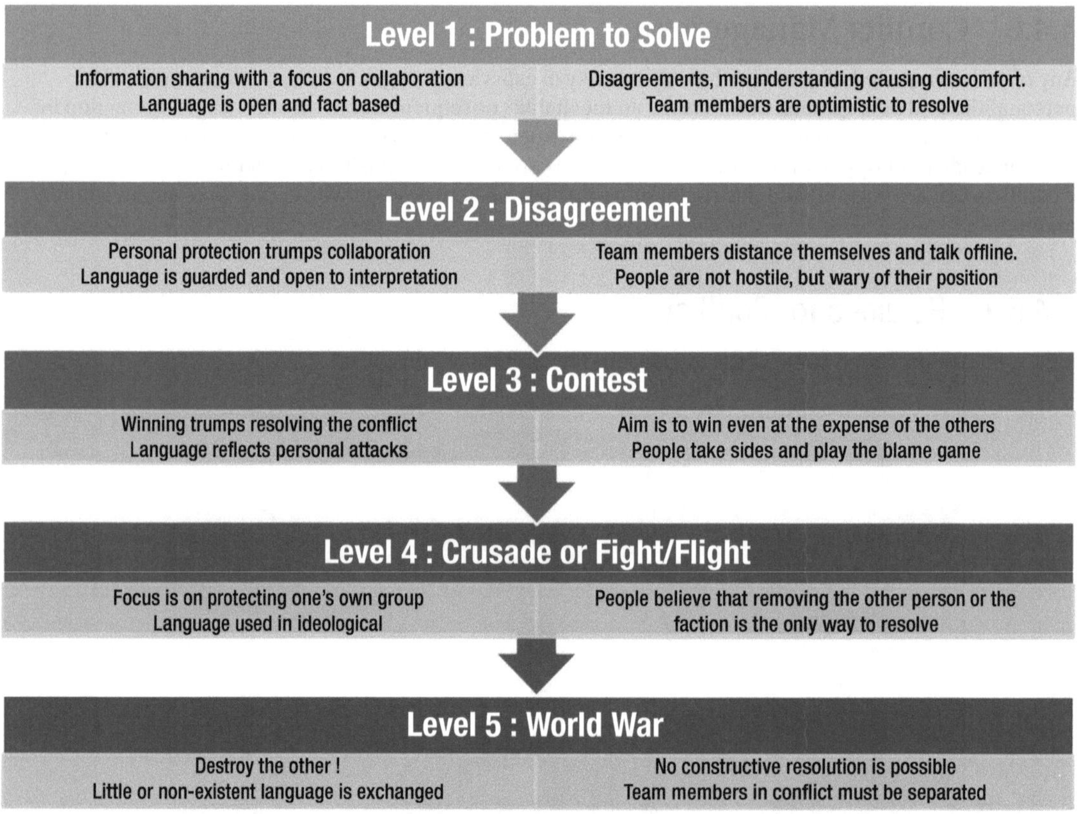

Figure 4-12. *Leas' Conflict Model showing levels of conflict*

The following Table 4-3 shows a few examples of languages used by people when they are in conflict. The intensity of the language can be translated into their corresponding levels.

***Table 4-3.** Examples of levels of conflict*

Levels of conflict	Language observed
Level 1	• Well, I see where you are coming from, but I have a different view. • Let's give it a try, but if we see it not happening we must go for plan B.
Level 2	• I think this appears to be a trust issue. • It's better let things carry on and fail and only then will all realize what I said.
Level 3	• His code is always full of bugs and that slows us down. • She doesn't even have the courtesy to let others take turns to speak.
Level 4	• He is always like that - egoistic and obstinate. • What's the point in even trying to convince them?
Level 5	• We must make sure we win. At all costs. • I don't care. It's do or die.

4.4.6.3 Conflict Resolution Techniques

Once conflicts surface they should be addressed directly. Generally it is recommended that the team members in a conflict resolve the conflict themselves as more often than not, it leads to a lasting resolution. In some cases, intervention of a third party might be necessary to hear about the sources of the conflicts, differences in opinions and act as a facilitator to convey messages between the two primary parties in the conflict. Although practically hard, it is advised to not let emotions and behavioral issues pollute the facts and the problem. Successful conflict analysis and an amicable resolution result in greater productivity, trust, empathy and positive working relationships within the team. Figure 4-13 below shows some of the commonly used conflict resolution techniques.

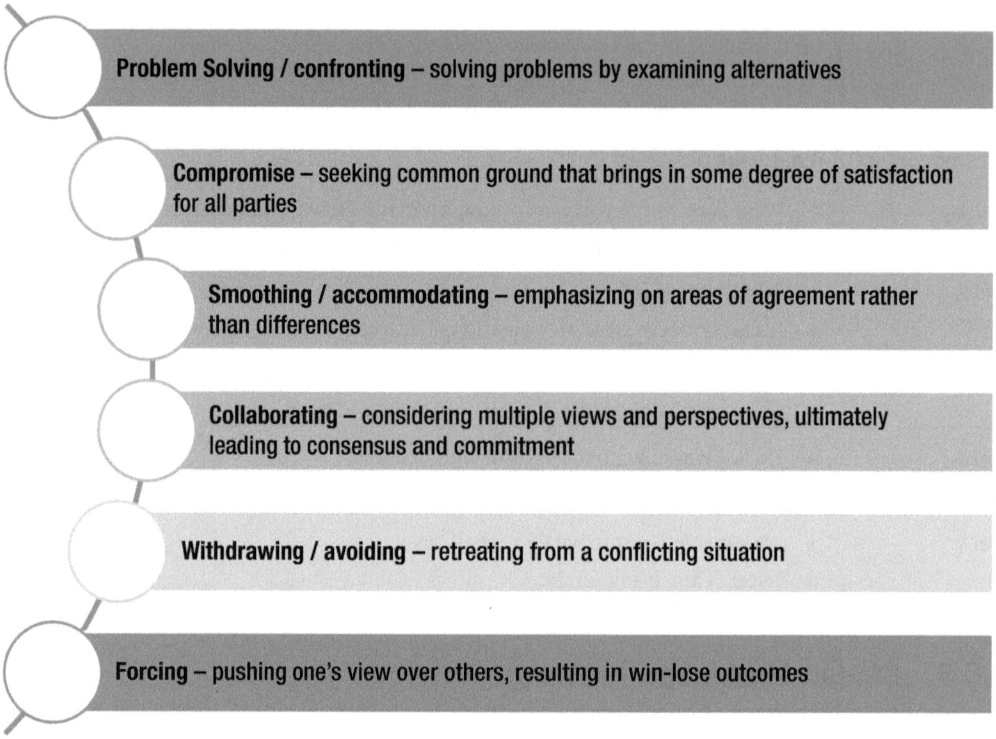

Figure 4-13. *Conflict resolution techniques*

Table 4-4 shows some applications of the techniques discussed above. Notice the tone of the language used to resolve the conflicts.

Table 4-4. *Examples of conflict resolution techniques*

Technique	Language observed
Problem Solving	• Well, this is neither an issue with intent or competence. Let's refer to the service manual and we can get the solution from it. • Applicable for level 1 and level 2 conflicts.
Compromise	• I agree to your first two points, but can you look at my suggestion as well? I suppose you will realize that it could work for both of us.
Smoothing	• I am sure both of you realize how important it is to fix the situation. I suggest we conduct a small experiment and then we can choose the best one. • Could be applied for level 3 conflicts.
Collaborating	• Let's see what the rest of the team has to say about it and then we can decide. • Applicable for level 1 conflicts.
Withdrawing	• I do not have time now. Let's talk next week.
Forcing	• Don't you remember what I told you so many times? Do it my way, that's it!

4.4.7 Group Decision-Making Techniques

One of the hallmarks of Agile teams is to arrive at a decision with full participation from relevant stakeholders like the business representatives and the respective teams. Agile leaders facilitate such a meeting where team members meet face to face and engage in transparent brainstorming on the possible options to arrive at a decision. Decisions reached in such a way helps to cement the agreement, commit and buy-in much better than decisions made by one authority and then imposed on a team. For example, during a planning poker session,[26] as the team estimates the size and complexity of a user story, they do it irrespective of who is going to work on it when the time comes. The estimate is arrived by the group and is respected by any developer who picks up the user story for implementation. Group decision-making techniques can be used during collection of requirements, prioritization, estimation, release planning, iteration planning and distilling action items out of retrospectives, etc.

This mechanism of involving multiple parties in arriving at a decision is also called *participatory decision models.* Let us now look at some of the styles and examples of making decisions in a group.

4.4.7.1 Styles of Group Decision-Making

There are three prevalent styles for arriving at a decision when a group is involved in generating ideas and opinions. They are shown in Table 4-5 as follows.

Table 4-5. *Styles of Group Decision-making*

Decision-making style	Characteristics	Advantages	Disadvantages
Command	An autocratic decision made by the leader with little or no input from the participants.	Takes less time. Applicable where there is not enough knowledgeable participants and the group perceives the leader to be an expert.	Participants feel that they didn't have a say, so they may not easily buy into the decision. They could feel alienated and disagree with the decision.
Consultative	Leader actively seeks inputs and advice from the participants.	Since participants are involved, there might be more buy-in.	Participants are consulted, but the decision still rests with the leader.
Consensus	A democratic decision is made where all participants provide input, vote and arrive at a final decision that the group commits to.	There is buy-in and the participants feel an obligation to meet their commitments as they have taken part in the decision-making process.	Takes long amount of time to gather the experts and participants. Could be time consuming if decisions do not converge quickly.

[26]See Estimation techniques in Chapter 6: Adaptive Planning.

4.4.7.2 Methods of Reaching a Decision

In most cases, the group decision is arrived by considering on of the four methods mentioned below in Figure 4-14.

Unanimity	Majority	Plurality	Dictatorship
Everyone agrees on a single course of action	Support from more than 50%	The largest block decides even if a majority is not achieved	One individual makes decision for the group

***Figure 4-14.** Making a decision in a group*

4.4.7.3 Thumbs Up/Down/Sideways

One of the simplest ways to ask participants in a group to vote and express consensus or agreement is through the thumbing technique. As seen in Figure 4-15, participants with thumbs-up or thumbs-down indicate agreement or disagreement respectively. The one in the middle, which shows thumbs-sideways, denotes the set of participants who need further clarification, has a conflict, are neutral or indifferent and are not able to vote either for or against the motion.

***Figure 4-15.** Thumbing technique for voting*

4.4.7.4 Fist-of-Five Voting

Another quick and popular consensus-based decision-making technique is fist-of-five voting. It can be viewed as an extension of the thumbs voting technique by allowing demonstration of a degree of support, rather than yes/no decision. As shown in Figure 4-6, fist-of-five involves raising of the hands when asked to vote with the number of fingers (0-5) indicating the level of agreement as illustrated below.

***Figure 4-16.** Fist-of-five voting*

- 0 fingers (closed fist) - means the voter has serious objections and will block the proposal.
- 1 finger - means the voter has strong reservations and wants to discuss issues and suggest changes that should be made.
- 2 fingers - means the voter is moderately comfortable but has minor issues that may not need discussion.
- 3 fingers - means the voter has a neutral standpoint because he likes some of it, but not all.
- 4 fingers - means that the voter is supportive of the proposal.
- All 5 fingers (show of the full palm) - means the voter is in complete agreement with the proposal and will also promote it.

Once the voting is done, the moderator inspects and makes a note of every person's hand. If a majority vote is obtained (let's say 3 or higher), it means consensus is reached and the moderator should move forward for voting on the next topic. If anyone is showing a closed fist, 1 or a 2, then the meeting needs to pause to hear that person's concerns and discuss them.

4.5 Agile Leadership Styles

In the context of stakeholder management, there are a few distinctive styles of leadership that are often seen. In this section, we will look at a few key terminologies that are used to describe leadership styles prevalent in Agile teams.

To begin the discussion let us contrast the focus of an Agile leader with that of a conventional project manager in traditional projects. Note that this comparison, as shown in Table 4-6 is role focused and an extension to Table 1-2 where we saw the differences between the two flavors of management.

Table 4-6. *How focus differs between an Agile leader and a traditional project manager*

Focus of an Agile leader	Focus of a project manager
People-oriented - individuals and interactions	Action-oriented - tasks and dependencies
Collaboration and communication	Plan driven, monitoring and control
Delegation to empowered people	Command-and-control
Participative style	Autocratic style
Consensus seeking	Commanding and consultative styles
Effectiveness, value-driven delivery	Efficiency, balance between scope-time-cost
Doing the right things (principle oriented)	Doing things right way (process oriented)
Reviews and retrospectives periodically	Lessons learned exercise at the end of the project
Direction and motivation	Speed and utilization
Adaptive	Predictive

4.5.1 Servant Leadership

Agile teams are self-organized. As seen in section 4.8 earlier, all Agile methods appreciate the fact that motivated and empowered individuals in a team have the best recipe to translate business requirements into working software. Given an environment and adequate support, Agile teams can be entrusted to get the job done on their own. They collaborate with business to trawl requirements and their priorities, estimate, plan incrementally and iteratively, track and measure progress, manage risks and issues, make midcourse corrections as necessary and inspect and adapt their tools and processes continuously to tailor the situation they are in. This leads to a distinct philosophy of leadership that Agile teams look out for.

In contrast to a plan-driven and command-and-control style of management, *servant leadership* is a commonly used term that describes Agile leadership roles like a Scrum Master and an Agile coach. The term *servant leadership* was coined by Robert K. Greenleaf[27] in 1970 and he went on to describe "*The servant-leader is servant first. It begins with the natural feeling that one wants to serve, to serve first. Then conscious choice brings one to aspire to lead.*" The primary focus of the servant leader is the well-being of the people and the community that they belong and so they channel all of their energy and power in serving their needs, developing them and propelling them toward high performance.

Servant leaders are also called humble stewards of an organization. The following list is adapted from Robert Greenleaf's 10 characteristics of servant leadership (this is not required for the PMI-ACP® exam):

- Listening to diverse opinions
- Empathy to issues related to work or well-being of the people
- Healing
- Awareness
- Persuasions instead of commanding
- Conceptualization
- Foresight and thinking long term
- Stewardship and humility
- Commitment to the growth of people and a trust-based culture
- Community building

As seen in Figure 4-17, a servant leader is expected to meet the following objectives:

1. **Communicate the project vision** – One of the key activities of the Agile leader is to reiterate the mission and vision of the project and the organization. This helps to bind the team, align the day-to-day decisions that are made, remove all dissipative forces and have all players in the team work toward the common goal. Using metaphors, references to the project charter and the project elevator statement are typical ways to keep reminding the team of the vision.

[27] Refer to `https://www.greenleaf.org/what-is-servant-leadership/`

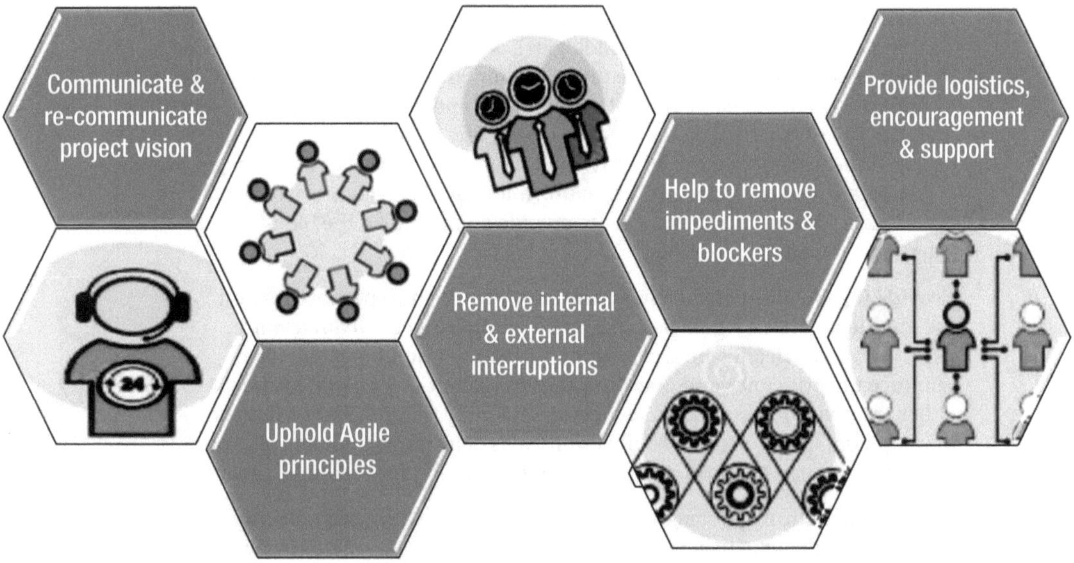

Figure 4-17. *Attributes of Servant leadership*

2. **Uphold the principles of Agile** - Agile leaders are expected to shepherd Agile principles, uphold them in all situations and maintain the rigor of roles, ceremonies and artifacts.

3. **Protect the team from internal interruptions** - The role of a Scrum Master is often compared to a sheepdog who does anything to protect the flock of sheep, keep it together and drive the wolves (read distractions and interruptions) away. An example of an internal interruption is the case where there is a temptation to introduce changes midway during a sprint. This can break the operating rhythm and jeopardize the committed plans for the project team. The Scrum Master needs to remind both requestors of the change (i.e. business representatives) and the acceptors of the change (i.e. the development team) that a fixed protocol exists to request changes via the product backlog maintained by the product owner. The Scrum Master reinforces the Scrum principles that state that while the development team commits to a sprint goal, the business representatives also commit toward resisting any temptation to make any changes while a sprint is underway.

4. **Protect the team from external interruptions** - Similarly, an example of an external interruption is in the case where resources are partially allocated to projects and get pulled away in multiple directions leading to a significant loss of productivity in context switching. Agile project teams are recommended to be dedicated and with their cross-functional skills they are expected to pick up and complete whatever tasks the team undertake. As much as possible, the Scrum Master shields the team members from distractions and helps them stay focused.

5. **Help to remove blockers** – As we have seen during the discussion on Scrum (in section 2 of Chapter 2: Agile Methodologies), one of the questions asked during the daily stand-up meeting is: "Are there any impediments?" The Scrum Master or the Agile Leader makes a note of the blockers reported by the team members and tries to resolve them on behalf of the team. The Agile leader is expected to use his or her management authority and influence to reach out to the respective stakeholders who could resolve a situation and help the team move forward. The Agile leader also owes it to the team to provide an update on the blocker as it progresses toward its resolution.

6. **Provide logistics, encouragement and support** – Being a part of the team, the Agile leader has a significant role to play supporting the team toward its objective. As a leader, he is expected to groom new joiners in the team, reinforce the principles and practices, act as a patient and trusted listener, help to resolve conflicts, facilitate meetings, identify training and professional development needs, provide feedback on areas of improvement and give positive encouragement in the form of rewards and recognition for accomplishments.

Using servant leadership, it appears that Agile leaders seem to have less control over teams. However, it reaps superior benefits in the long run. Servant leadership breeds trust, acts as catalysts for very high levels of engagement and performance in the team, boosts morale and results in an excellent and sustainable corporate culture.

4.5.2 Adaptive Leadership

In today's world, we observe the many simultaneously changing facets of an enterprise like the business domain, breakthrough technologies, demand for mobility, user behavior and expectations, social networking, economic conditions, competition in the market, compliance and regulatory constraints and many more. The key to survival and profitability in such a chaotic situation is agility in the enterprise – one that is flexible, adaptable to change, challenges status quo and fosters disruptive innovation. And Agile leaders play a very vital role as organizations try to transform an embrace agility.

Adaptive leadership is all about building and sustaining a culture of continuous learning, flexibility and collaboration in an organization framework. Jim Highsmith[28] differentiates between "Doing Agile" and "Being Agile." Doing Agile is mostly about processes, practices and tools that an Agile team needs. For example, iterative development is one of the basic practices that you expect out of a team "doing Agile." To "be Agile," enterprises and its leaders need to embrace the culture and behavior and deliver a continuous stream of solutions.

Continuing from the previous sections, here are a few attributes of adaptive leadership:

- Focus on value-added outcomes and not on tasks, plans.
- Proactively anticipate user expectations and opportunities in the market.

[28]Refer to `http://jimhighsmith.com/adaptive-leadership/`

- Break down silos and boundaries that are prohibiting within the organization and instead emphasizing and encouraging cooperation and collaboration.
- Encouraging generalization of skills over specialization, thereby fostering flexibility and nurturing multidisciplined teams.
- Breaking away from a hierarchical or a top-down management style and enabling free flow of information across all levels of the organization.
- Empowering people, sharing accountability, delegating effectively.
- Encouraging diversity and pursuing participative style of decision-making so as to enhance support and buy-in from the team.
- Taking risk-based decisions and mustering the courage to experiment, give room, make small incremental changes and solicit feedback.
- Being receptive to new ideas, champion creative and innovative ideas and encourage life-long learning.
- Upholding ethics and professional code of conduct like honesty, integrity, respects, fairness and responsibility.

4.5.3 Participative Leadership

As we have seen earlier in section 4.5, *Participatory leadership style*, also called democratic leadership is a management style that invites input from employees, team members and participants on a particular subject or decision pertaining to a project or an organization, but the leader finally retains the authority to make the final decision.

Every participant is given relevant information to decide on their own, their inputs and suggestions are synthesized, voted, analyzed and finally an outcome is arrived and communicated. Participatory decision-making could be applied in a variety of scenarios like organization strategy building, release planning, objective setting, making go no-go decisions, problem solving (as in a retrospective), or team building.

Depending on the type of involvement of the team and the leader, the variations of participation in decision-making could be illustrated as in Figure 4-18 below.

Figure 4-18. *Participative leadership style*

The advantages of participative leadership style are quite intuitive to understand:

- When relevant participants are involved, a fuller and well-rounded understanding of the core problem or the rationale behind the decision is better explored. This leads to the righteousness of the decision.
- With more people involved, collaborative culture dominates over competitive culture.
- Participants involved in the decision-making process are more likely to feel values and stay committed, as they do not need to enforce a decision made by someone else.
- In the long term it fosters trust, team spirit, high performance and sometimes this can work well even when the leader is absent.

However, participative leadership styles also carry a few disadvantages:

- Since decisions get delegated to team members, the quality of the decision made is a function of experience and competence of the participants and their intent (or lack thereof) to solve a problem.
- With a varied group, the opinions could be so divergent that it might take a lot of time to agree on a common stance. Related to time, costs could also be higher as more people need to be involved.

- Not all participants could be in a decisive state of mind. They might need clarifications, support, or have general concerns on exposing themselves by choosing one decision over another.
- If not done anonymously, there could also be the halo effect where one set of participants could have undue influence over the others and the divergent, yet valid, considerations might never get surfaced.

4.6 Focus Areas for the Exam

✓ Definition and identification of stakeholders.

✓ How to use the power-interest grid for stakeholder classification.

✓ Purpose of the stakeholder engagement assessment matrix.

✓ Use of personas, wireframes, proxy users.

✓ What are the choices of good user proxies?

✓ How to ensure stakeholder engagement in various decisions made around release planning, Agile delivery, definition of done, estimation, choice of iteration length.

✓ Concepts and examples of information radiators and how they help the team.

✓ Different types of communication involved in a project environment.

✓ How to manage distributed stakeholders by using communication technologies and bringing the team together.

✓ Concept of active listening and three levels of listening.

✓ Concept of conflict management with examples - sources of conflicts, levels of conflict and their resolution. techniques

✓ Use of negotiation skills, techniques.

✓ Concept of emotional intelligence and the four elements of emotional intelligence.

✓ Different styles of decision-making.

✓ Emphasis on group decision-making and participative style of leadership.

✓ Thumbing and fist-of-five voting techniques.

✓ Focus of an Agile leader versus a conventional project manager in managing stakeholders.

✓ Concept of servant leadership in Agile coaches and Scrum Masters. Expectations from servant leaders in evangelizing Agile principles, removing impediments and helping the team with encouragement, support and facilitation.

✓ Concept of adaptive leadership.

Quizzes

1. One of the critical activities in Stakeholder Management is to identify them. When should the team identify stakeholders?

   A. When the project begins

   B. At the time of release planning since their inputs are necessary

   C. During sprint execution

   D. Throughout the project

2. Which of these would you identify as a stakeholder?

   A. PMO

   B. Sponsor

   C. Architect

   D. All of the above

3. A Wireframe is

   A. A group-estimating technique.

   B. A frame where a Kanban board is displayed.

   C. A rough prototype of the final software.

   D. A technique for wiring the team with a common collaborative culture.

4. Which of the following communication methods have the highest 'temperature' and are preferred in Agile teams?

   A. E-mail

   B. Letter

   C. Face to face

   D. Memo

5. Referring to the graph on effectiveness and richness of communication mode, which of the following statements are true?

   A. E-mail communication has the highest efficiency and highest richness.

   B. Face-to-face communication has the highest efficiency and highest richness.

   C. Written documentation has the highest efficiency and highest richness.

   D. Audio conference has the highest efficiency and highest richness.

6. Richard and Ben seem to be in conflict. While sitting around with the team, you overhear statements like "the code is always full of defects and that slows down everybody." What level of conflict does the team have?

   A. Level 2 - Disagreement

   B. Level 3 - Contest

   C. Level 4 - Crusade

   D. Level 5 - World War

7. Display of the Kanban board, release plan and the cumulative burnup and burndown chart that is updated very frequently and situated at a central place is an example of:

   A. Information distribution or dissemination

   B. Daily status reporting

   C. Information refrigerators

   D. Information radiators

8. Wireframes and prototypes help teams to:

   A. Test high- and low-level design

   B. Confirm design

   C. Report design completion

   D. Estimate the project

9. Velocity is used for all except

   A. Team's work capacity

   B. Release plan validation

   C. Estimating work per iteration

   D. Maintaining list of features

10. On the project release plan a small change is requested, but the team members get into an endless debate. Which of the following techniques could prove to be helpful in this context?

    A. Wideband Delphi

    B. Fist-of-Five voting

    C. Pareto Analysis

    D. Retrospective

11. You are leading a distributed team spread across continents and different time zones. What is the best communication method to use?

    A. Set up a web page where all team members can post their photos to see each other.

    B. Set up kickoff meetings and let everyone to meet face to face.

    C. Set up common working hours, so everyone can work at the same time from their location and interact better.

    D. Set up a document repository where all team members need to upload hourly statuses at least once a day.

12. Leadership and management are related as:

    A. Leadership overrides management.

    B. Management overrides leadership.

    C. Management and leadership both work together.

    D. Management and leadership are mutually exclusive.

13. During a voting exercise, a participant shows thumbs-sideways. This means:

    A. They are for the motion.

    B. They are against the motion.

    C. They are neutral.

    D. They don't like this voting method and would like to leave soon.

14. The role of a servant leader is to

    A. Line manage the team members.

    B. Remove impediments to progress.

    C. Penalize anyone who violates the policies.

    D. Estimate and come up with the release plan.

15. Which of the following is a valid list of the quadrants of Emotional Intelligence?

    A. Self, others, recognize, optimize

    B. Self, team, recognize, optimize

    C. Self, team, regulate, recognize

    D. Self, others, regulate, recognize

16. Which of the following is not a decision-making style?

    A. Forcing

    B. Pleading

    C. Consensus

    D. Consultative

17. In Fist-of-five voting technique, showing 5 fingers or full palm means:

    A. Participant has a question or clarification.

    B. Participant is in full agreement.

    C. Participant is in disagreement and wants to discuss issues and suggest changes that should be made.

    D. Participant is in partial agreement and has minor issues that may or may not need discussion.

18. Which of the following is not an information radiator?

    A. Kanban board

    B. Burndown chart

    C. Status report

    D. Story Board

19. While listening to a speaker at a session, you start asking yourself whether the product will be useful to the business. What level of Active Listening is this?

    A. Level 1 Internal

    B. Level 2 Focused

    C. Level 3 Global

    D. None of the above

20. While listening to a speaker, you are not only focused on words and emotion but notice the energy level and intent of the speaker. This level of listening is:

    A. Global listening

    B. Focused listening

    C. Internal listening

    D. None of the above.

Answer

1. D
2. D
3. C
4. C
5. B
6. B
7. D
8. B
9. D
10. B
11. B
12. C
13. C
14. B
15. D
16. B
17. B
18. C
19. A
20. A

CHAPTER 5

Domain IV: Team Performance

If you want to build a ship, don't drum up people together to collect wood and don't assign them tasks and work, but rather teach them to long for the endless immensity of the sea.

—Antoine de Saint-Exupery, French Pilot, Writer and Author

This chapter is a continuation of the last chapter on stakeholder engagement. After all, team members and their leaders are very critical stakeholders for a project team. So almost all of the concepts, theories, practices, tools and techniques that were discussed are relevant to the content of this chapter, too. I recommend that you read this chapter after completing the previous one and then be at your liberty to flip back and forth between chapters to relate to interdependent concepts.

Earlier in this book we have encountered several adjectives and phrases to refer to Agile team - self-empowered, cross-functional, self-motivated, self-managed, self-organized, self-directed, self-correcting, participative and collaborative, etc. This chapter reveals what goes in forming such teams, keeping them together, empowering them and exploiting synergies to achieve success. Such important is the facet of communication within a team, there is a dedicated section on the different aspects of communication. Near the end of this chapter we briefly touch upon Agile PMO's and vendors that are also important stakeholders of a team.

5.1 Team Formation

Getting like-minded team players together is like laying a foundation on which future pillars will be erected. As Henry Ford, American industrialist and founder of the Ford Motor Company stated - "Coming together is a beginning. Keeping together is progress. Working together is success." Agile leaders recognize that individuals are the ultimate source of value,[1] and they strive hard to create an environment that boosts performance, productivity and stimulates positivity.

Let us now look at some of the key considerations at the time of team formation.

[1]Refer to the Declaration of Interdependence discussed in Chapter 1: Agile Principles and Mindset.

S. Boral, *Ace the PMI-ACP® exam*, DOI 10.1007/978-1-4842-2526-4_5

5.1.1 Team Selection - Cross-Functional and Generalizing Specialists

There are two key factors that need to be balanced while selecting team members for an Agile project - their technical skills and interpersonal skills.

5.1.1.1 Technical Skills

Team members are expected to be skilled to be able to transform business requirements into production-ready, working and usable software. The skills should be complementary, such that team members should be able to share the work among themselves. But at the same time there should be less of any key-man dependencies on any individual.

In order to promote collective ownership and accountability, Agile team members are expected to be cross-functional. By cross-functional, we mean team members that are specialists in their areas, but still have adequate competencies at one or more other skills required for the project. In other words they could be comfortable wearing multiple hats as required during different times of the project. For example,

- a business analyst, apart from his core duties of doing in-depth functional analysis and helping to write user stories, could also lend a helping hand in doing some exploratory testing,
- a developer, in addition to doing design, coding and integration, could write the scripts for an automated regression test suite that runs in an auto-pilot mode.
- a developer or tester could partake in conversing with the business to understand the domain and write down the user stories and related acceptance test cases,

Most organizations that operate in a projectized manner invest behind growing specialized technical skills in their people. People become expert architects, designers, Java developers, database modeler, UX designer, test manager. The whole organization could be structured into role families based on specialization and that's how career paths (and seniority, compensations, etc.) of individuals are chartered out as a function on their experience and demonstrated capabilities over long period of time. It is therefore not easy to find and hire cross-functional skills compared to certain specialized skills that are common. Even if a specialist is hired and willing to explore new technologies, tools, or techniques it takes time to go up the steep learning curve. Often this is dependent on the tacit knowledge, which as we will see below, takes time to build up.

Cross-functional skills are invaluable for Agile project teams, because of the following benefits:

- With cross-functional teams, it is easier to take shared ownership and group accountability for results. For example, if there is a problem on production related to a database deadlock issue, it is very easy for the Java programmer to shrug his shoulders and say, "it is not my problem!" But with a cross-functional skill, it is likely that the Java specialist knows a thing or two about the database calls made from the Java program and could lend a helping hand at scanning the logs and doing some basic diagnostics. This is effectively the same principle in which Kanban teams swarm around each other and try to solve problems before accepting new work.
- During the time of estimation, team members are forced to think what it will require to deliver the requirement to the customer. With a cross-functional hat on, developers, analysts and testers are not thinking only on their part and aggregating the estimation. They are thinking what it will take to meet the *definition of done.*

- When a story is picked from the product backlog, the team commits to deliver it. If each specialized roles is thinking of doing just their part and handover to the next team member, the likelihood of completing a story by the iteration deadline drops drastically. One of the positive side effects of cross-functional teams is that it also helps to keep the team size small and have minimal number of handovers and bottlenecks between specialized partitions in the team.

5.1.1.2 Interpersonal Skills

Following the discussion on technical skills, it is equally important to assess the interpersonal skills of a potential team member before inducting him or her in the team. Agile team members iterate and incrementally produce valuable software, but while doing this there are a range of soft skills that are required to succeed. We have seen some of them already and will continue to explore a few more in this chapter - collaboration, active listening, transparent and open communication, conflict management, negotiation, diversity, adaptability, flexibility, dealing with ambiguity, culture of continuous learning and improvement. It is advised that existing team members interview potential candidates and check for these skills and assess fitment into their team culture. Apart from technical and soft skills, past experience in working on Agile projects should also be an important factor to consider during the interview. All members of the team (including staff augmented from vendor teams) should be aligned to the purpose of the project and abide by the principles and practices defined, agreed and laid down by the team. Each member should be customer focused and take accountability of their tasks and the overall outcome of the project.

5.1.2 Optimal Team Size

As we saw earlier in Chapter 2: Agile Methodologies, optimal size of Scrum teams is 7 ± 2 cross-functional members.

This is the optimal team size that fits neatly into many facets of Agile projects:

- They can be co-located in the war room.
- They can limit duration of team meetings like daily stand-ups to 15 minutes and planning / review meetings to 4 hours.
- Smaller the group, more effectively is brainstorming, estimation, decisions making etc.
- Osmotic communication is most effective with such a team size. For larger teams, there could be more background noise that could distract team members.

Agile projects, can however, scale for larger projects. Scrum teams can scale with scrum-of-scrums and meta-scrum. The Crystal family of methodologies scale in size of teams and complexities from Crystal Clear to Crystal Clear and Crystal Orange. Another framework to achieve scalability at the enterprise level is the Scaled Agile Framework (SAFe®). All of these are introduced in Chapter 2: Agile Methodologies.

5.1.3 Bruce Tuckman's Stages of Team Building

When team members come together for the first time, they bring with themselves a lot of individualities - cultures, competencies, diverse experiences and background. In case of distributed teams, it is often suggested that teams in their formative stages gather for an offsite team building event at the start of the project. Although it might take a significant travel budget to accommodate team members from multiple locations to come together and met face to face, but the exposure to each other's culture, language, style and the opportunity to have light stress-free conversations have been found to be helpful at building rapport and making teams work together more effectively in the long run.

Bruce Tuckman, in his article published in 1965, identified the different stages of team building as illustrated in Figure 5-1.

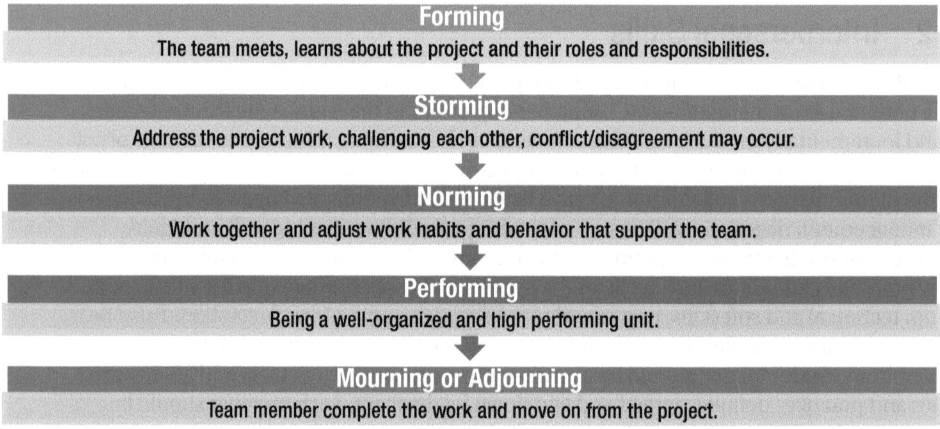

Figure 5-1. *Bruce Tuckman's theory on stages of team formation and development*

According to Tuckman's theory, teams move through the following stages progressively:

1. **Forming** - This is the stage where the team members come together at the first instance. They are mostly focused on themselves, their roles, responsibilities and goals rather than that of the team.

2. **Storming** - This is the stage where the team members begin to work on the projects, bring about their individualities, voice their opinions and at times, attempt to dominate. During this time, conflicts and disagreements are likely at play at various intensity levels. Some of these conflicts could be positive, but a few could be destructive and demotivating.

3. **Norming** - During this stage, the supervisor could intervene, set ground rules and emphasize what the professional behavior should be like. The team members attempt to resolve their conflicts, forgive and forget some nuances and get aligned to the shared goal of the project. Setting up of the norms and ground rules are particularly tough when the team members are distributed across multiple locations.

4. **Performing** - This is the highest ('nirvana') stage where teams are motivated to achieve the goals of the project. They are aware of each other's strengths and weaknesses and look to maintain a synergistic relationship between themselves. This is the stage for the highest performing teams and is difficult to reach. On most occasions, some teams never reach this stage, as the team composition or its leader is also subject to change during the life cycle of the project.

5. **Mourning or Adjourning** - This is the stage where the project is over and team members get released. They cherish the days of togetherness and collaboration and mourn the fact that they will no longer work together for the same assignment.

5.1.4 Shu-Ha-Ri Model

Another model that is often used to depict the maturity of learning and application in a team environment is the Shu-Ha-Ri model. The term Shu-Ha-Ri has its origin from a martial art called Aikodo in Japan and describes the stages in which a practitioner attains mastery over a subject. This progression is shown in Figure 5-2.

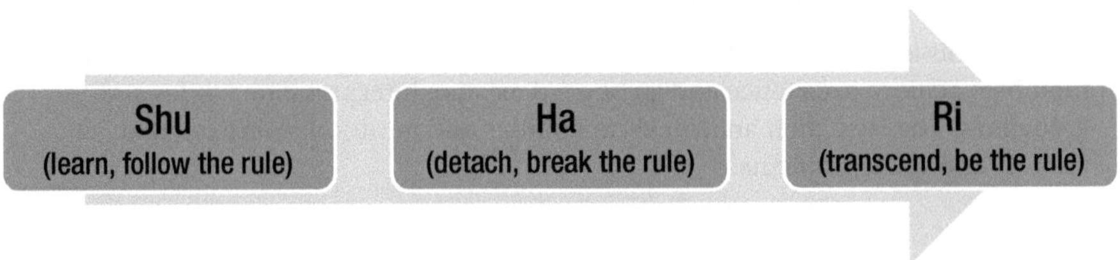

Figure 5-2. *Shu-Ha-Ri model*

The starting point is **Shu**, which means **learn**. At this level the team member obeys the rules laid down by the master or instructor precisely. He focuses on doing the task well, based on the practices and conventions.

The next level is **Ha**, which means **detach**. At this level the team member attains more maturity, gets deeper understanding, reflects on the rules that are at play, finds alternatives and exceptions and looks to "break" free from the rules.

The final level of mastery is **Ri**, which means **transcend**. At this stage the practitioner has attained mastery. He has learned from others and is now thinking originally, progressing at his creative best while not ignoring reality and demands of everyday life. For example, the authors of the Agile Manifesto were definitely in the Ri stage.

We realize that different members of the team could be in different maturity levels of learning and so in the Shu, Ha and Ri stages simultaneously. The same Shu-Ha-Ri concept can be applied to listening skills, learning a concept and coaching Agile teams (with stages teaching, directing, coaching, mentoring and advising).

5.1.5 Dreyfus Model

The last model mentioned on the course outline of the PMI-ACP® exam is the Dreyfus model of skill acquisition, although questions on it are not so much expected on the exam.

The Dreyfus model is used to assess the progress of skill development within the team. As seen in the previous models, while the team members move from Shu to Ha and from Ha to Ri stage or across the forming-storming-norming stages, they need to be supported on their learning journey. And this is how they can progress through the five skill levels as illustrated in Figure 5-3 below.

1. **Novice** - at this skill level, the team members have a very shallow understanding and need very close supervision. They need clear and unambiguous instructions that they follow almost mechanically.

2. **Advanced beginner** - at this skill level, the understanding of the steps involved such that they can apply the same steps in similar context. The team members are able to complete simple tasks without supervision, but struggle where complex troubleshooting is required.

3. **Competent** - at this skill level the team members have attained good understanding of the steps involved and are able to complete their tasks properly without supervision. They use conceptual models to solve and troubleshoot problems, make decisions and accept responsibility.

4. **Proficient** - at this skill level, team members have gathered sufficient practice, experience and deep understanding of the subject. They see actions holistically ('big picture') and routinely achieves high standards of performance.

5. **Expert** - this is the highest skill level. With lots of knowledge amassed, the team members achieve excellence and go beyond existing interpretations, rules and guidelines. They use their analytical capabilities and intuitions more often to identify and solve problems.

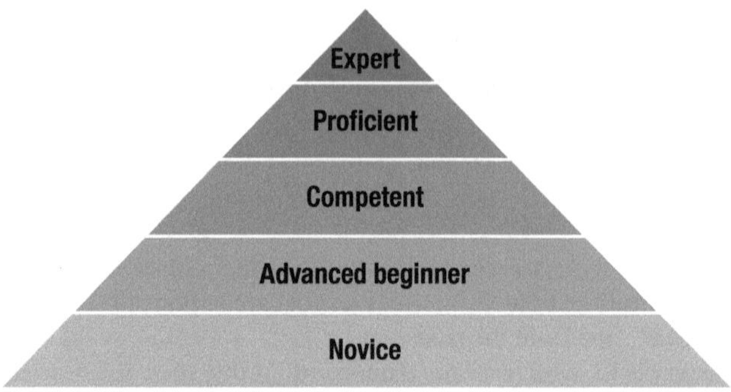

Figure 5-3. *Dreyfus model of skill acquisition*[2]

5.1.6 Situational Leadership Model

Extending from Bruce Tuckman's team formation and development theory, the situational leadership model created by Ken Blanchard and Paul Hersey depicts how an Agile leader needs to dynamically adjust his/her leadership style based on the competency and commitment levels of the team members being led. This is depicted in Figure 5-4 below that is adapted from the original one from Blanchard and Hersey.

[2]Refer to `http://devmts.org.uk/dreyfus.pdf`

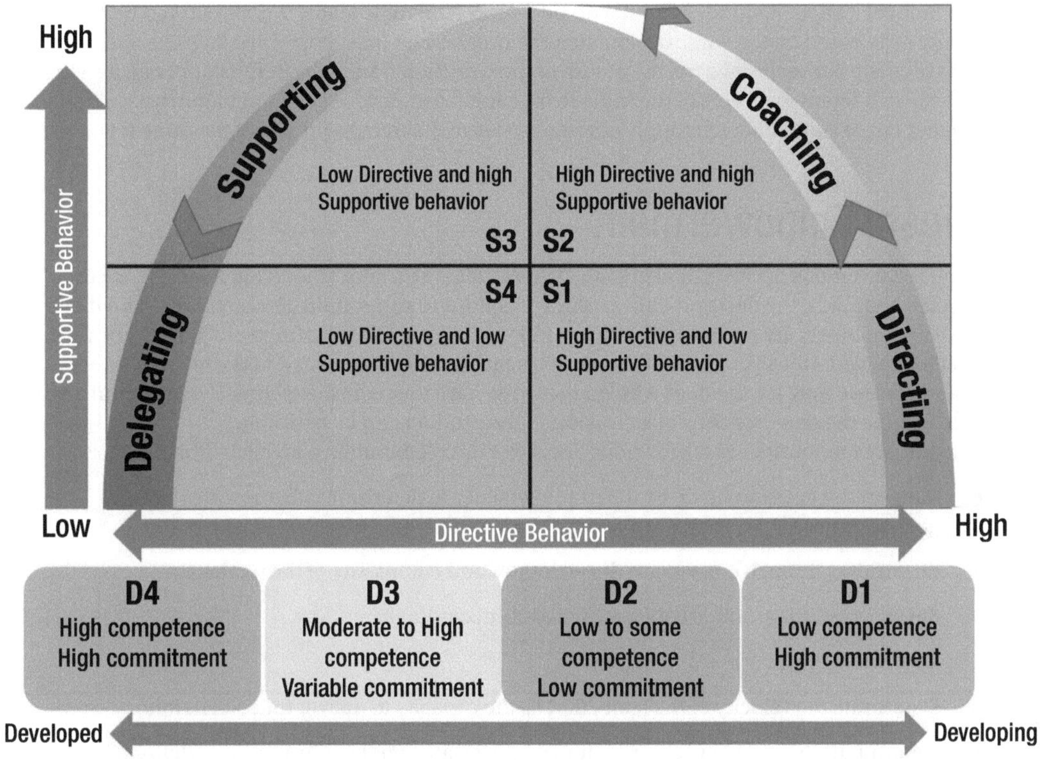

Figure 5-4. *Situational Leadership Model*

According to the model, there are four leadership styles:

1. **Telling style** - During stage 1, the Agile leader is working with a team having low competence and less experience. At this stage, the leader needs to exhibit a directing style giving clear instructions to accomplish the tasks and supervising the team closely.

2. **Selling style** - During stage 2, the team members are still novice, inexperienced and unable to take responsibility, but they are enthusiastic and willing to work. The Agile leaders in this situation should use a selling / coaching role to convince team members and follow the specific directions given by him/her.

3. **Participating style** - During stage 3, the team members are experienced and have the required skills, but lack the confidence to get the job done all on their own. In this case, the Agile leader plays a more participating role by blending with the team and supporting some of the decisions made by the team.

4. **Delegating style** - During the highest stage 4, the team members are mature enough, empowered and capable of handling a task confidently without the intervention of the leader. In this case, the Agile leader's role suffices to be of a delegating nature.

The situational leadership model says that to be a successful Agile leader, he/she should be able to adapt his / her style based on the context. Note that the progression from stage 1 to stage 4 is not linear, as teams might oscillate between stages as the nature of the work items and the circumstances also change. Also, realistically, different members of the same team could be at various stages of maturity levels and so the Agile leader has to simultaneously apply different styles to different members of the same team.

5.2 Team Empowerment

In traditional organizations decision-making mostly rests with the senior leadership teams. Once the strategic decision is made, the decision and the plan of actions to support the decision is cascaded to the teams. The team members are expected to comply, follow the plan and measure their progress or variances with respect to the plan. However, in Agile teams, decision-making is delegated to the team members, favoring them because they are the ones who do the work, have the requisite technical insight and are best placed to determine the repercussions of a decision to the product and its customers.

Agile teams are empowered to take various decisions by collaborating with each other:

- Support the decision made by the product owner to determine what features should go into a release.
- Determine, through consensus, the estimates and complexity of the work items.
- Set expectations around scope and schedule accordingly.
- Determine the length of an iteration.
- Determine the velocity of the team, that is, the capacity to deliver for each iteration.
- Determine what and how to report and inspect status on the information radiators.
- Own all aspects of quality and use problem solving techniques to resolve day-to-day issues and remove impediments.
- Determine what tools and processes add value to them and tailor them based on the situation at hand.
- Determine how to continuously improve themselves through self-introspection during reflection workshops.

To empower Agile teams, Agile leaders steer away from a command-and-control style into a servant leadership[3] style with the realization that empowerment breeds trust and individual commitment to the project. Agile leaders play an instrumental role in communicating (and recommunicating) the vision of the organization and project, create a collaborative environment that fosters productivity and creativity, remove blockers and impediments and encourage clear and transparent communication across stakeholders.

5.3 Team Collaboration and Commitment

Once the teams are formed, the success of the team depends on how people resolve their differences, be mindful of each other's strengths and weaknesses, exploit synergies and focus on a shared goal. In Chapter 4: Stakeholder Engagement, we saw several soft skills like active listening, negotiation techniques, conflict resolution techniques, emotional intelligence and servant leadership that Agile team members and leaders like coaches and Scrum Masters use for day-to-day interactions and coordination among each other. All

[3]Refer to Chapter 4: Stakeholder Engagement for a discussion on Servant Leadership style.

these are relevant for team members to build trust, commitment, work cohesively toward a shared goal and ultimately succeed. In this section, we will see some more of these team attributes.

5.3.1 Self-Organizing Teams

The self-organized clause has been used many times in the book. What it means is that Agile teams do not need to be directed and tracked on a plan by a manager in a supervisory role. As the team is competent and in an operating rhythm, they know how to approach a requirement or a problem and resolve it in a coordinated manner. This is exhibited in all of the ceremonies and practices in an Agile team. Almost all decisions around priorities, values, estimates, decision on a sprint goal, design, metrics and tools are taken in a group environment. Self-organized teams enjoy the freedom to plan and execute in a style that best works for them.

If there is a complex problem, they transparently raise it in daily stand-up meetings and work with each other to resolve it before committing to new piece of work. The team also periodically reflects upon and inspects its intrinsic processes and determines opportunities to make it better and better as time progresses. Agile teams are supported by Scrum Masters and Coaches who acts as in a more of a facilitation and advisory role, seeing that the principles are followed and impediments are removed on the way.

5.3.2 High-Performing Teams

Agile leaders invest a good deal of effort in building a high-performing team as that is critical success factor in achieving superior results. A high-performing team has a few attributes that we have seen:

- takes accountability and ownership,
- demonstrates commitment consistently,
- cross-functional,
- generates positivity in the team environment,
- adaptive to change,
- trust-worthy,
- self-organized,
- open, clear and transparent communication,
- focused on the customer needs,
- empowered to make decisions as individuals or through group consensus,
- has an eye for removing non-value added activities,
- values diversity and builds strong team bonds,
- works at a pace that is consistent and sustainable,
- regularly inspects and adapts processes and practices and
- takes pride from achievements.

5.3.3 Team Culture

As Agile teams build up, it is often necessary to be cognizant of the culture and diversity in the team. The differences could be more profound in the case where distributed teams work across different cities, countries and continents. Pair programming sessions, daily stand-up meetings, reflection workshops are forums where team come together and get exposed to a variety of styles of working and their cultures. It is really hard to change people's habits, so it is wise to be aware of the cultural differences as one learns to adopt and adapt.

It is generally recommended that at the beginning a project kick-off meeting is chaired by the Agile team leader to share the mission and vision of the project, solicit their commitment to the shared objective and allow the project team to self-introduce themselves to the team. As we have seen, during the formative stages of the team, resources coming from different cultures might have difficulty accepting and working together. So it is desirable that the team come together, share ice-breaking sessions, work together in a co-located style for a few weeks and experience the nuances of each other's cultural diversity. Face time immensely helps to build trust and rapport that goes a long way for a lasting relationship. Often, offline and distant communication is easier between two people if the underlying rapport is already built.

The cross-functional nature of Agile teams is engrained in their culture and is also a requirement on the job. Agile team members take the opportunity to train and cross-train each other on technologies and domain that are needed in the project. This in turn leads to a very enriching experience in their careers. Team members who are specialized in multiple disciplines also enjoy the respect from senior leadership.

As the Declaration of Interdependence[4] states: "We improve effectiveness and reliability through situationally specific strategies, processes and practices." This statement reminds us that there is no 'one-size-fits-all' approach. Teams need to work together and tailor their relationship management techniques based on the environment and circumstances.

5.3.4 Communication within the Team

Let us look at some of the ceremonies or events where Agile teams come together, communicate and collaborate.

- Release planning meetings - this meeting is chaired by the product owner and the team collaborates with each other to plan which feature could be delivered when. Release plans could either be feature-driven or date-driven.
- Iteration planning meetings - during this meeting the product owner brings along a prioritized list of features from the backlog and explains the requirements. The team estimates the requirements and based on its capacity to deliver commits to a handful of features for the timeboxed sprint. Estimates are arrived through a group consensus technique.
- Daily stand-up meetings - during this meeting each team member provides an update of their progress, plans for the current day and any impediments. The daily stand-up meeting is timeboxed for 15 minutes, where each team members gets a chance to speak and, in the spirit of transparency, reconfirms their commitment in front of their peers. It is to be noted that daily stand-up meetings are not for status updates to management or problem solving - so any lengthy discussions need to be conducted offline. Team members, however, can ask for short clarifications or volunteer to help each other to remove the impediments. In essence, this meeting can serve as a forum to see who needs help and who is available to help.

---

[4]Refer to Chapter 1: Agile Principles and Mindset.

- Iteration reviews - at the end of each iteration, the team demonstrates the work accomplished in the iteration and solicits feedback from the real users. This is another ceremony where business users and teams effectively collaborate and have rich conversations to continuously adapt and evolve the features in the system based on the requested changes.
- Retrospectives - during this meeting, the team reflects on what is going well for the team and what needs to improve. Based on the outcome of self-introspection, team members commit to implement the action items during the next iteration.

In a later section of this chapter, we shall see some further aspects of communication for the Agile team.

5.3.5 Systems Thinking

With the cross-functional and self-organized attributes of Agile teams, each team member is encouraged to see the big picture rather than stay bogged down on executing their particular tasks only. While planning for value-driven delivery, the holistic picture helps team members to think of the system as a whole, its complex assembly of closely integrated components and how each component interfaces with each other as one unit.

5.3.6 Ground Rules

Ground rules are unwritten rules that help to set clear expectations within the team - regarding what behavior is acceptable or not. Setting up of ground rules is mostly a collaborative effort by the Agile team. This ensures that all team members comply with it. Example of a few ground rules are:

- Daily scrum meeting starts at 9 a.m. at the same venue every day.
- Developers must check-in or undo-checkout of the code before they leave for the day, so that no part of the repository is locked out.
- Build errors, if any, should be resolved in less than 2 hours.
- All accesses to systems should be undergoing a user entitlement review every month.

5.3.7 Meeting Etiquette

Agile practices reduce the overhead of unnecessary meetings. Although it seems that there are fewer meetings, teams make up by using osmotic communication, information radiators, collaboration tools and use of technology to interact within distributed teams. To maximize the efficiency of meetings, here is some common etiquette that is recommended:

- **Agenda** - Meetings should have a clear agenda. For example, if a meeting is being held to arrive at a decision, set that expectation clearly to the participants. It is clear that in a daily scrum meeting, every member has to take turns to answer 3 key questions and nothing more detailed than that.
- **Advance preparations** - The meeting venues should be booked and availability of the required participants should be checked and confirmed in advance. The agenda on the meeting invitation also helps each team member to be prepared for the meeting - doing a background research or preparing a status update. So the host should be mindful of giving adequate time to the participants for preparation for the meeting. The meeting invitation should ideally include any materials or content that would be referenced during the meeting.

- **Punctuality** - Meeting should have strict timekeeping - they should start and finish on time. If a team member is late to a meeting, this amounts to disservice and disrespect to the other attendees.
- **Focus** - To maintain the focus the meeting has to be chaired and facilitated well. In some cases, like the daily stand-up meeting, participants stand up, so that they can be precise, stay focused and finish on time. A daily stand-up meeting should not be used to brainstorm and solve problems.
- **Representation** - Meetings should have the right audience. If a team member is invited to a meeting with no clear purpose, he or she should clarify ahead of time and if not required in the meeting, he or she should politely decline the meeting request. If a particular team member is absent, they should plan to send in a substitute who could represent them in the meeting. It is important that participants on an audio conference announce their names to indicate their presence in the meeting.
- **Fair and round-robin** - The facilitator should ensure that while a topic is being discussed, the relevant stakeholders get a fair chance to speak and express their thoughts. This could particularly be challenging because in a meeting there could be a mix of vocal and not-so-vocal participants. Also the facilitator should make sure that the participants got time to ask their questions and seek clarifications while respective of the constraints of time.
- **Distraction free** - Meetings should ensure that participants give their 100% attention to the topic. So it is very important to check that the meeting participants do not digress or stretch beyond the stipulated time. Otherwise participants may get distracted, engage in side talk, check their phones or watches and feel uneasy. On audio conference calls, it is highly desirable that participants are in an environment that is free from background noise. Also while they are not speaking, it is recommended that they should put themselves on mute so that background noise does not interfere with the ongoing conversations.
- **Use of Technology** - Meetings that need to use technology should have advance preparation. For example, in an audio or video meeting, participants should be sent the conference numbers, participant codes and instructions for joining well ahead of time. For the meeting to be effective, both the host and the participants should be comfortable to use the technologies used during the meeting.
- **Dress code** - Depending on the culture of the team, one should be professionally dressed for the meeting.
- **Recorded** - If the meeting ends with action items or decisions, it might be useful to keep a record of the meeting summary. The meeting host or facilitator could send out meeting minutes, take a picture of the flipcharts or whiteboards used, or make a a print of the content on the whiteboard.

5.3.8 Brainstorming

The above meeting techniques are applicable for brainstorming sessions that are used for risk management, planning, prioritization, estimation, retrospectives, or problem solving.

For an effective brainstorming meeting, a few best practices are listed below:

- **Send the invitation for the meeting early**, with a clear agenda so that participants can come in with adequate preparation.
- The **meeting venue should be well lit, well ventilated, comfortable and free from distractions.** The informative team space is best suited to have a brainstorming meeting. Whiteboards and flip charts should be available and the participants should be able to access information and data that they would like to reference during the meeting.
- Brainstorming works best with **small co-located teams of size 5 to 10 people**. The demographics of the participants should be diverse to make sure that stereotypes do not hinder creative thinking and different perspectives are presented and heard. The participants should welcome innovative and radical ideas.
- **The meeting should be facilitated** such that there is timekeeping, participants stick to the agenda and everyone feels empowered to generate ideas, listen to each other and thus participate actively. The facilitator should steer away from any attempts at personal criticism or group thinking, which can quickly degenerate the purpose of the meeting.
- **The meeting should end on a positive note** with a feeling that the time has been well spent. The action items and the decisions that were discussed should be collated, prioritized and circulated to the participants as meeting minutes for future reference.

Some of the commonly used techniques used in brainstorming are:

EXAM WATCH

- **Drawing a mind map** - here the participants are asked to adopt different mindsets for predefined periods of time while contributing their ideas to a central mind map drawn. This helps in uncovering many perspectives and generating ideas that would otherwise have been missed.
- **Quiet Writing** - here the team members work on generating a list of ideas individually, thereby limiting bias, peer influence, or 'herd mentality.'
- **Round-Robin** - here everyone gets a chance to suggest their idea in turn.
- **Free-for-all** - here the team members simply shout out their ideas.
- **Nominal group technique** - once ideas are generated anonymously, the group is asked to vote and rank each idea. The vote can be made by a show of hands or 'thumbing.'

5.3.9 BART Analysis of Team

Even with all the attributes mentioned above, there could still be dysfunction within a team environment. BART analysis is a tool used to identify problems and effectiveness of processes in Agile teams. The acronym BART stands for boundary, authority, role and task. With this tool, one can actually look under the hood to find out about ambiguity, lack of clarity, organizational issues, or other nuances of team dynamics by asking a few questions like this:

- Are the boundaries of the roles clearly specified and agreed within the team?
- Is authority formally defined and adhered to by all?
- Are there any informal roles in the team? If so, how does the team deal with them?

- Are all team members clear on their tasks?
- Are there any differences between the stated and actual ground rules in the team?

5.4 Communication in Agile Teams

As we have seen in the previous chapters, since there is less emphasis and dependence on detailed documentation, communication plays a vital role between Agile project teams. In this section we are going to begin with some generic discussions on a basic communication model and how complexity of communication and the channels of communication varies as the number of stakeholders or the size of the team increases. We will then look at specific communication practices that Agile teams adopt to ensure that there a is free flow of communication across the team.

5.4.1 Basic Communication Model

The basic communication model is derived from information theory. As shown in Figure 5-5, the model consists of the following components:

- A sender who is the originator and transmitter of the message.
- A receiver who receives, interprets the message and responds with an acknowledgment or feedback.
- A communication medium through which the message and its acknowledgment passes. The medium could be anything like a telephone line, a document, or a face-to-face conversation.
- Before the message is sent through the communication medium, it is encoded in a manner that the message is safely, securely received and interpreted at the receiver end.
- Once the message is received at the receiver end, it is decoded, interpreted and the feedback is formulated and transmitted. The same mechanism of encoding and decoding also follows when the acknowledgment is processed at the receiver end and sent back to the sender.
- On receiving the feedback, the sender is able to validate whether the receiver has been able to make sense of the original message that was communicated. Note that the responsibility of whether the receiver has understood the essence of the message lies with the sender.
- While the message is in transit through the communication media, it is subject to distortion because of noise. Such noise can be because of choppy phone lines, distance, physical distractions and use of language that cannot be comprehended or anything that acts as a barrier of communication or degrades the quality of the message in transit.

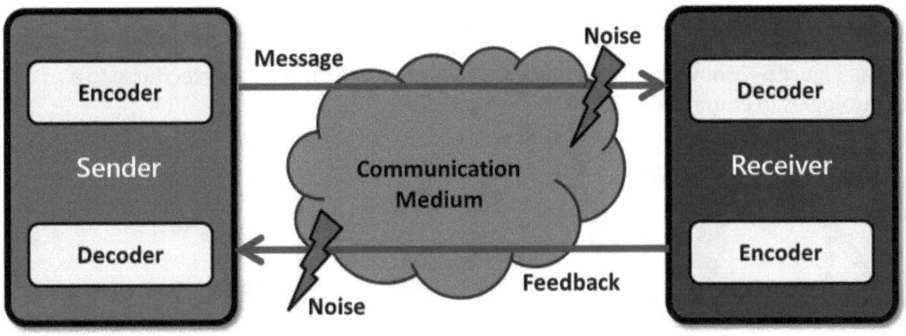

Figure 5-5. *Basic communication model*

5.4.2 Channels of Communication

Based on the above basic communication model, we observe that for an effective communication to take place, we need at least two entities - the sender and the receiver. However, as the number of entities (let's say number of stakeholders) increases, more and more channels of communication are opened up. Figure 5-6 shows a formula to compute the number of channels of communication between 'n' stakeholders. In the case of 4 team members, the number of communication channels (indicated by green arrows) is 6.

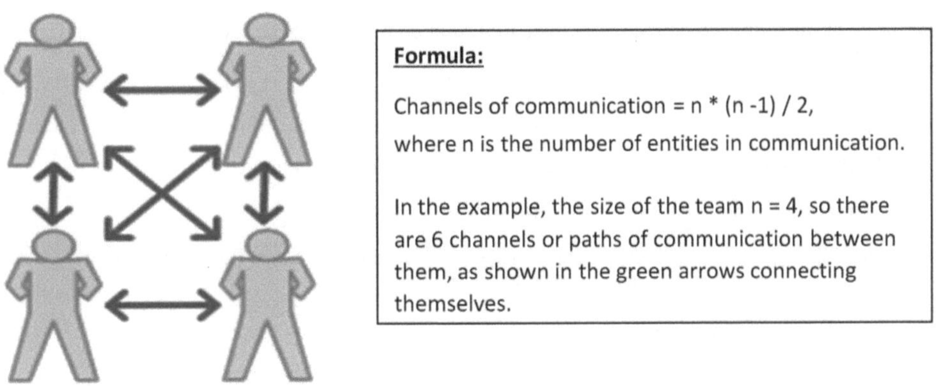

Figure 5-6. *Number of channels of communication*

The complexity of communication increases and the participating entities have to take care of a variety of aspects of communication - the need for communication as expressed or desired by different stakeholders, the appropriate type of communication verbal or written, the form of communication push or pull, the frequency, the content, the format, the choice of technology and many more aspects. This calls for a need for a mix of structured and unstructured communication methods between project teams.

5.4.3 Choice of Technology in Communication

As the following Figure 5-7 shows below, project teams and organizations have recourse to a variety of technologies in communication.

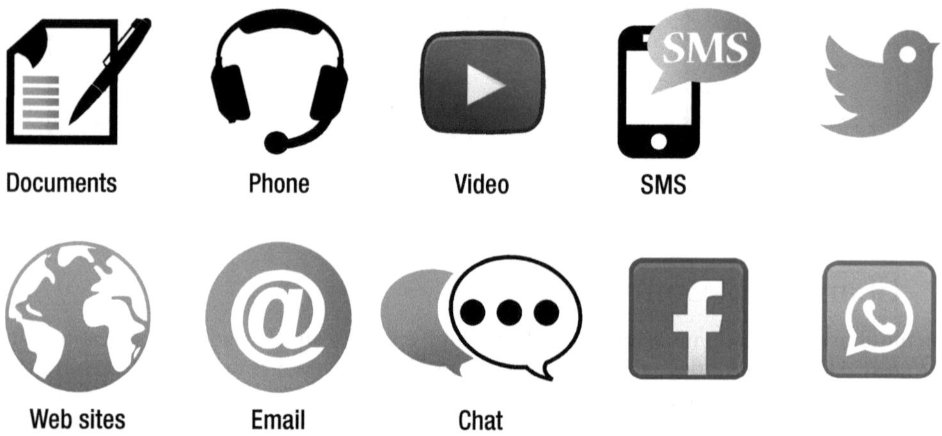

Figure 5-7. Technology used in communication

The choice of the technology used, however, depends on a variety of factors:

- Urgency, need and frequency of the information.
- Specific demand from the stakeholders.
- Number of stakeholders that needs to be simultaneously reached.
- Availability of technology for both the sender and receiver.
- Familiarity, accessibility and ease of use of technology, for example, social media and applications on hand-held devices.
- Sensitivity and confidentiality of the information.
- Specifics of the project environment - culture of the team, whether the team members are virtual or co-located.

5.4.4 Richness of Communication

Having seen quite a few varieties in the modes of communication, let us now have a look at Figure 5-8 below. This graph is an adaptation of the effectiveness vs. richness graph introduced by Alistair Cockburn.[5]

[5]Refer to *Agile Software Development – The Cooperative Game*, 2nd ed. authored by Alistair Cockburn. (Upper Saddle River, NJ: Pearson Education, 2006).

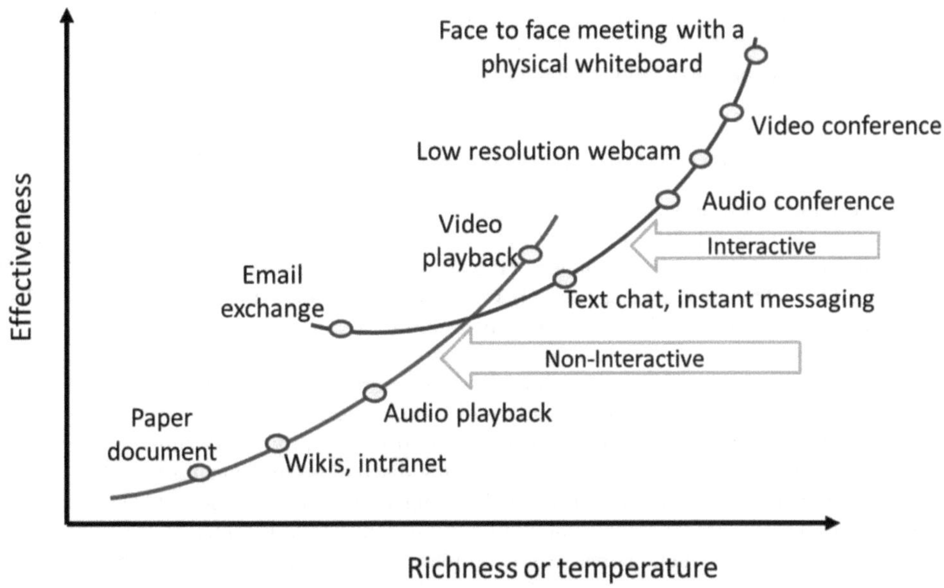

Figure 5-8. *Effectiveness of communication vs. Richness of mode of communication*

On the X-axis is the *richness or temperature* of communication. And on the Y-axis we see the effectiveness of communication. As we observe from the graph, as the mode of communication increases in richness, its effectiveness also increases. The richest and most effective mode of communication as per the graph is a face-to-face meeting between a few individuals equipped with a physical whiteboard. It is easy to understand such kind of communication conveys written, verbal and nonverbal (like body language, emotions, facial expressions, tone of voice and gestures) traits of communication very easily. With real-time feedback and active listening skills applied on top of it, this is the most recommended mode of communication wherever feasible. On the lowest portion of the graph are written documentations, which is the coolest mode of communication as it is left to interpretation of the reader and does not transmit emotional content. Other variations like audio recording, e-mail exchanges, audio and video conferences lie somewhere in between. Also notice that there are two lines in the graph - one that denotes interactivity between the parties in communication and there is capability to ask a question or answer it, while the other line denotes zero opportunity for any bidirectional interaction.

Note that while we just discussed the positives of face-to-face communication within the Agile team, there are times where a cooler communication channel is desired especially when there is a heated exchange of emotions between two parties whenever they confront each other. In such a case, emotion takes over and acts as a barrier for any exchange of messages.

5.4.5 Information Radiator

We have discussed in Chapter 4: Managing Stakeholders on the vital role that information radiators play in communicating up-to-date project status, metrics and other relevant information to casual and interested stakeholders in a nonintrusive way. Agile teams use anything like flip charts, large electronic displays, whiteboards, or boards with sticky notes or push pins to prominently display their progress in the project. If the team is not co-located, teams could also take the help of electronic boards, but the low-fidelity and high-usable manual boards are particularly more engaging and appealing.

In section 7 of Chapter 3: Value-Driven Delivery, we saw a range of metrics that Agile teams use to track their progress and self-organize and self-correct themselves. These metrics can easily qualify to be put up on information radiators.

5.4.6 Osmotic Communication for Co-Located Teams

Face-to-face communication, as we have seen in Figure 5-8 above is the richest form of communication and is a powerful tool to improve productivity and effectiveness in a team environment. In fact, we have also seen that one of the 12 Agile principles emphasizes face-to-face communication - **"The most efficient and effective method of conveying information to and within a development team is face-to-face conversation."**

The analogy is with the process of osmosis in Chemistry where molecules of a fluid passes through a semipermeable membrane from a less-concentrated solution into a more concentrated one, thus equalizing the concentrations of materials on either side of the membrane over time. When team members are working in close proximity of each other, they are exposed to a wide variety of sights, sounds, debates, discussions and conversations happening around them. Through their background listening mode, team members are likely to pick up essential cues and traces of information from these conversations even if they are not consciously paying attention to them. Sometimes if it is relevant, they might even join in these impromptu conversations. At other times, the information could be *drafty* or unwanted in nature and the team members could prefer to not pay attention to them or get distracted. This efficient method of information exchange is called *osmotic communication* and is considered one of the positive outcomes of co-location.

There are a few characteristics to observe in osmotic communication:

- Given the benefits of co-location and face-to-face communication, osmotic communication works best when following the *bus-length communication principle.* It says that effective communication happens when the walking distance between team members are less than the length of a school bus (so one can easily hear what the other person is saying). Anyone sitting or located at a farther distance spend more time and energy to communicate and thus experiences a radically lower effectiveness in communication.
- Information flow to all team members happen at the same time, so there is no lag.
- Since there is a real-time flavor, it has high *richness.* Team members can choose to join a background conversation and the interactivity also helps.
- The time, cost and energy for transmission of information through osmotic communication is low.
- Some questions simply don't get asked, if it's not easy to ask or retrieve a response. There is an inherent lost opportunity in such cases.
- Osmotic communication is difficult to achieve when people are working on several projects at the same time. Agile methods recommend full-time resources dedicated to the project.
- For a self-organized Agile project team, osmotic communication is a very effective means of collaboration on a frequent basis.
- Osmotic communication is effective when the morale of the team is good and there is healthy and amicable relationships between each other in the team. If team members get into clashes or try to avoid each other, then the communication can quickly degenerate.

- One of the drawbacks of osmotic communication is that team members can get sucked into irrelevant topics at times that might hamper productivity. Team members should selectively pick up the relevant information from the background or choose to ignore if it.
- At times, osmotic communication may not suffice as some conversations need to be recorded or documented for later use. An example is user stories and their associated acceptance test cases. While the specifics of the stories are uncovered through conversation, it is important that the acceptance test cases are written down at the back of the story cards to serve as a reminder for the team and act as a ready reference during implementation of the story.

5.4.7 Tacit Knowledge

One of the benefits of osmotic communication is retention of *tacit knowledge* in the team. *Tacit knowledge* is knowledge that cannot be adequately articulated by verbal means or documented. It is collective knowledge that an individual builds up over time through observation and practices, but difficult to communicate to others via words and symbols.

One simple example is learning to drive a car. While one can learn about traffic rules and signals by reading a book, it is almost impossible to pick up driving just by reading a driver's manual. One is required to persistently practice under the guidance of a driving instructor and experienced fellow drivers on how to use the brakes, accelerator, mirrors, signals. Once mastered, it comes naturally and then can be passed on to the next generation.

An example in the context of Agile teams, it may not be documented how to trigger on-demand builds. But a new team member can take guidance from experienced team members and study how a nightly build script is already configured. Even if he fails a few times in attempting the same, he can still consult with the fellow team members and retry with alternate options.

Much of the knowledge that binds a project is tacit knowledge that people have inside them, not on paper anywhere. Team members joining a project team gain this knowledge by pair programming with experienced people in rotation, learning to create simple flexible design choices and write clear and simple code accompanied by extensive unit tests. It is very hard to build tacit knowledge if the whole team is not co-located and this might influence the decision to keep team sizes small (10-12 members at the most).

5.4.8 Expert in Earshot

To exploit the benefits of osmotic communication and encourage building and retention of tactic knowledge in the team, another technique used is *expert in earshot,* which is putting junior team member in line of sight and within hearing distance of more experienced team members. This has been shown to improve the performance and learning journey of junior members even with no other forms of formal training.

5.4.9 Cone of Silence

While we have so far discussed the advantages of face-to-face communication, it is to be realized that there are times when team members want to seclude themselves from all forms of active and passive communication. Maybe they want to steer themselves away from drafts, irrelevant and unwanted communication, or simply get some quiet time when no one is allowed to talk in the zone. This time could be used to reflect on a design, a creative idea, ponder options, or go deep to troubleshoot a problem. In such cases, team members look for *a cone of silence*. If they would like to run an idea with a set of people who are not present at the same place at the same time, they can resort to cooler and asynchronous mediums of communication like e-mail, text messages and voicemail.

5.4.10 Caves and Commons

Osmotic communications, face-to-face meetings and information radiators all are communication tools used in the Agile team. Alistair Cockburn uses the term *Convection currents of Information*[6] to compare the movement of information to the dispersion of heat and gas.

In order to maintain a balance between the need for real-time osmotic communication and quiet times in cone of silence, teams could create two zones in the team space as follows:

- The *Commons* area is where the office furniture and logistics are arranged such that it maximizes information exchange and osmotic communication between people working in the same project. Such zones are typically well lit, ventilated, appear welcoming, display big and visible charts or information radiators and foster creativity. This could also be the place where the daily stand-up meetings, reviews and retrospectives are held.
- The *Caves* area is a private space where people can isolate themselves for short periods to make personal phone calls, check e-mails and cater to other personal needs.

5.4.11 Seating Arrangement

In order to determine the optimal seating arrangement, one has to balance the following:

- the need for increasing osmotic communication,
- but stop the flow of unwanted information that can disrupt or derail the project and
- give the team some privacy to cater for their personal needs.

Often team members arrange themselves around a circular table in the room where there is clear visibility of each other. The place where Agile teams work is called *team space or war room* characterized by big visible walls where teams could put up their task boards, backlogs, burndown charts and other meaningful information radiators. The war room setting is an example of a balance between the osmotic communication (since teams sit together, collaborate and engage in bus-length communication principle) and cone of silence (since teams are protected from external interference).

Another consideration is to have team members of different specializations sit together contrary to business representatives, developers, testers and analysts sitting in their communities. If the latter happens, each group starts to form their own factions, works in their own silos and ends up complaining or blaming the other group leading to dysfunctional team behavior. XP teams, for example, mandate that a business representation or a proxy user sit together with the development team such that there is rich collaboration in clarifying

[6]Refer to, *Agile Software Development – The Cooperative Game*, 2nd ed. authored by Alistair Cockburn, (Upper Saddle River, NJ: Pearson Education, 2006).

requirements, writing down acceptance test cases and transparency in sharing progress. Another advantage of such a seating arrangement is that, even if one of the specialists were to leave the team for some reason, the collective tacit knowledge of the group - built up over several months by osmotic communication and practices like pair programming, could possibly bridge the loss to some extent.

Also as people gather closer, they might indulge in less relevant conversations or feel uncomfortable with the volume of communication around them. Like most practices in Agile, arranging optimal seating in a team environment also evolves over time.

The following Figure 5-9 shows a sample floor plan for a couple of Agile teams. Notice the caves and common spaces in the figure.

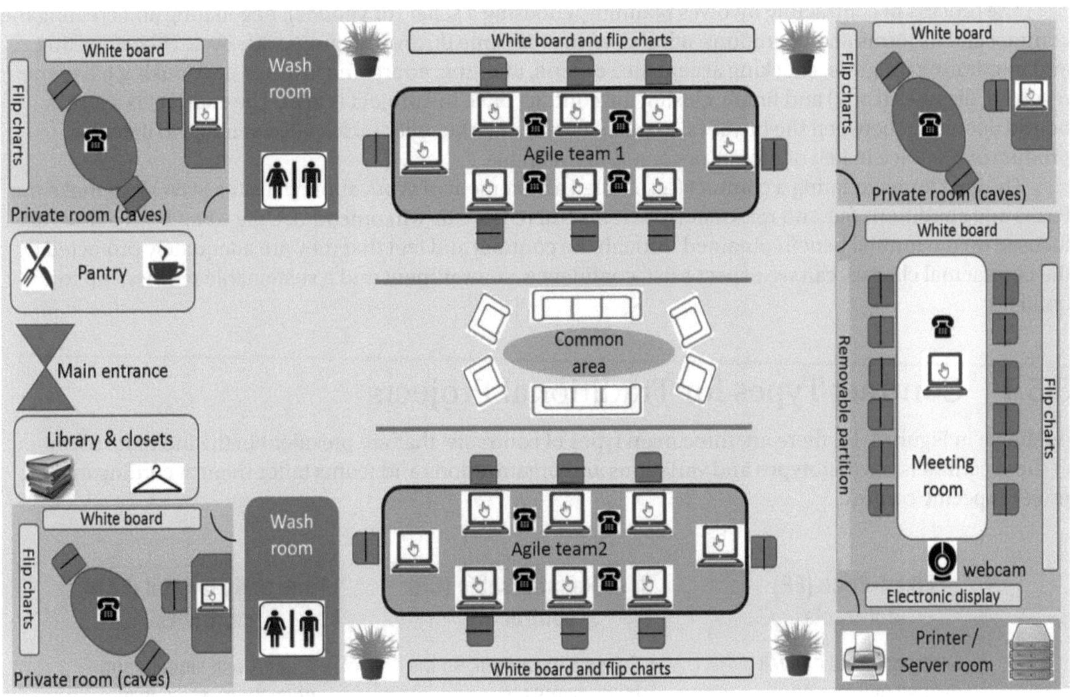

Figure 5-9. *Seating arrangement (floor plan) for Agile teams*

5.4.12 Virtual Teams

So far we have concentrated on co-located teams. In today's world virtual or distributed teams are the norm. In the case of distributed teams, osmotic communication could be a challenge. However, as we have seen in section 3, Agile teams use a variety of sophisticated tools and technologies to bring virtual teams together. Commonly used practices include audio conferences, video conferences, desktop or screen sharing tools, instant messaging tools, electronic dashboards, or other collaboration software. These tools do not provide the richness as face-to-face communication, but deliver some benefits of osmotic communication.

5.5 Agile Contracting

So far in this book, we have mostly concentrated on Agile teams that are within the organization boundary. As the complexity of projects increase, organizations and project realize the value of specialized software and services, some of which might be lacking within themselves. One option is to *build* the capability internally, especially if confidential and proprietary data and processes are involved. But that could take time and incur costs that may not be justifiable given the short-term needs required on the project. Often the chosen solution is to *buy* product and services from a vendor who specializes in them and use it only for the period that is required. Procuring services from the vendor could also help the organization transfer some risks in trying to build something on their own, especially in a domain where they have limited knowledge or capability.

The process of contracting involves planning, choosing a seller (or vendor), negotiating and creating the contract and its terms and conditions, administering the same during the project life cycle (like reporting and monitoring progress, checking acceptance criteria, auditing, approving invoices and making payments, resolving disputes if any) and finally closing the contract once the project is over. The contract is a legally bound document between the buyer (also called client) and the seller (also called vendor) to deliver a product or a service in lieu of money or something valuable.

The goal for negotiating a contract (also called a Statement of Work abbreviated as SOW) is to make the terms and conditions fair and reasonable such that there is a win-win outcome. Only when both parties are focused on the mutual benefit obtained through the contract and feel that they are adequately protected by the contractual clauses, can we expect trust, confidence, commitment and a sustainable partnership to build up.

5.5.1 Contract Types for Traditional Projects

As shown in Figure 5-10, there are three main types of contracts[7] that are prevalent in the industry. Some of these contracts have subtypes and variations and organizations and teams tailor them according to their project-specific context.

Fixed-Price (FP) contracts	Cost-Reimbursable (CR) contracts	Time and Material (T&M) contracts
• Contract based on well defined and agreed specifications from the buyer. • Seller plans for contigencies and charges a premium fee in lieu of the risk that it undertakes to complete the fixed scope in the contract.	• Scope is uncertain, so the buyer agrees to reimburse the seller for all legitimate costs incurred to complete the work, plus a fee for the seller's profit. • Considerable risk is involved on the buyer side as the costs are difficult to estimate at the outset.	• A quick and simple form of contract which is a hybrid between FP and CR in terms of risks shared between the buyer and seller. • Often used for staff augmentation where unit labour rate is fixed, but the duration of the contract is flexible.

Figure 5-10. *Types of contracts in traditional projects*

[7]Refer to Procurement Management knowledge area in PMI®'s *A Guide to the Project Management Body of Knowledge* (PMBOK® Guide) – Fifth Edition.

5.5.2 Contract Types in Agile Projects

On taking a close look at the contract types, it is evident that a fixed-price project would not suit Agile projects because scope is expected to change in Agile projects. Of course, changes can be made to fixed-price contracts, but that involves an onerous and time-consuming contract change control system. Secondly it is observed that fixed-price contracts are generally awarded to the vendors or suppliers that bid the least. While at the outset, this looks appealing, a low bid could be the result of the supplier underestimating or having limited understanding of the scope in hand. Keeping its own commercial interests in mind, suppliers more than often try to underbid in the face of competition, but tries to make up by penalizing the buyer by raising further demand through change control requests, by finding subtleties in the documented scope and taking undue advantage of it. This more than often could lead to friction and have undesirable repercussions on both the buyer and the seller. Given the value in the Agile Manifesto that values customer collaboration over contract negotiation, the vanilla flavor of fixed-price contracts are not favored in Agile projects.

It is, therefore apparent, that the Time and Material (T&M) contracts deals with changes better and are considered suitable for execution of Agile projects. The most popular flavor of T&M contracts are the staff augmentation model where the capacity and the skill demand of the team is kept fixed throughout the project duration, irrespective of the number and type of requirements that are to be delivered by the project - some of which are unknown upfront. As a result, internal Agile teams and contracted (human) resources can closely cooperate on a daily basis, continue with incremental and iterative delivery as long as the team adds value to the business (so there is a choice to stop as long as the project goal is achieved or terminate if the goal is no longer feasible or commercially viable) and adopt changes seamlessly. For example, if the project team and the business discovers more requirements or changes that must be delivered, they can choose to carry out a few more iterations by simply extending or renewing the contract and its resources. However, there is also a flip side with T&M contracts. Sellers have hardly any incentive to work efficiently - the longer the work stretches, the longer the contracts last and more the money they make out of it. If such things continue to happen, the trust between the buyer and the seller starts to break down, resulting in negative consequences.

Between these two contract types, Agile teams have creatively devised a few types of contracts that balance the need from the buyer and seller organization and at the same time being flexible enough to cope up with inevitable changes. Let us now look at some of the variations that are introduced in Agile contracts below.

5.5.2.1 Fixed Price, but with Provision for Change in Scope in Future Iterations

In this type of contract, the scope of the contract is reviewed before every iteration. Since Agile teams do not permit changes during the middle of the iteration, the scope can be considered fixed *during* an iteration making it suitable for a fixed-price, fixed-scope delivery in the timeboxed iteration. However, anticipating changes in requirements the contract should add provisions to introduce a feature of a higher priority for a future iteration (one which has not started) by agreeing to substitute lower priority items that have the same or higher effort estimate. In effect, what happens is that as a project nears its completion date, the lower priority items are starved of attention and never get done. This concept works well provided that the customer (buyer) works in close collaboration with the seller for every iteration.

5.5.2.2 Contract with Premature Closure Clause

Since Agile projects are value driven, it is quite possible that the customer or user realizes that there is no value or ROI in continuing further with the project as outlined in the contract initially. At that point, the choice might be made to discontinue the project and not carry out the rest of the iterations. Even if the project is discontinued, it is to be noted that since during every sprint that both parties collaborated together to build the features with the highest ROI. So at the end the business and the project team is left with tested and integrated code and a working product comprising the most valuable features. Any of the features that did not make it to the implementation stage yet are basically those that were considered unnecessary or of less priority.

Premature closure of a contract can cause hardships to the seller. In order to smoothen the effect, the Agile team should pay the seller at the end of every completed iteration, rather than a lump sum figure at the end of the project. Also, a clause could be included in the contract to pay a small fraction (say 15-20%) of the remaining contract in lieu of early termination to cover for its operational costs and maintaining healthy relationships for the longer term.

5.5.2.3 Fixed Fee and Not-to-Exceed Clauses

In case of premature closures of reduction in scope, the sellers may be adversely affected. To protect their interests, contracts could have a fixed-fee clause, which basically means that no matter what, the seller will get a fixed fee to cover their operational costs. Similarly, if the project goes slower than the estimated schedule, the actual payout from the buyer could shoot up. The not-to-exceed clause helps to protect the buyer by limiting the maximum amount that the buyer has to give to the seller.

5.5.2.4 Fixed Price per Story Point

Story points are unit of estimates for user stories. Once the definition of story points are formalized and agreed between the seller and the buyer, the seller could enter into a contract that uses a fixed rate per story point. So while the backlog of requirements could vary, the seller gets paid based on the number of story points it completes. As an example, consider that the seller considers all of its operational expenses and profit margins and comes up with a rate card of $200 per story point. For a given release, the seller delivers a set of features and stories whose estimates add up to 50 story points. So after the release is completed and accepted by the buyer, the seller expects to be paid $200 x 50 = $10,000.

5.5.2.5 Multi-Stage Contracts

In this variation, different types of contracts are chosen for different stages of the project, based on the intended outcome of the stage.[8] Let us consider an example of an Agile project that is developing a product from scratch.

- In the first stage the chosen vendor is asked to work on a T&M contract, collaborating with the buyer for a period of 3-4 weeks. The goal is to hash out an overall plan and gain enough knowledge to proceed with the next stage.

[8]Refer to *Lean Software Development: An Agile Toolkit* authored by Mary Poppendieck and Tom Poppendieck. (Salt Lake City, UT: Addison-Wesley Professional, 2003).

- In the second stage, the chosen vendor is asked work in a fixed-price contract to produce a proof of concept to establish their learning about the project. Based on the satisfaction of the buyer on the outcome of the proof of concept, the contract can either be terminated or proceed to the next stage.
- In the third stage the bulk of the Agile development happens. The buyer does not go beyond specifying a high-level objective of the project and anticipates rapid changes. The buyer and the seller enter into another T&M contract, with the buyer retaining authority to prioritize and deliver through a series of iterations closely collaborating with the vendor resource(s). The goal of this stage is to deliver the working software into production.
- In the fourth and final stage, the buyer could negotiate a fixed-price contract with the seller to provide warranty and fix any post-production defects, if any.

As we see here, over the life cycle of the project, the teams oscillate back and forth between the fixed price and T&M varieties of the contract.

5.5.2.6 Target Cost Contract

In this variation of the contract, the buyer and the seller mutually agree on a target cost and schedule of the project, which includes the profit margin of the seller. Note that since the cost is the main driver, the buyer protects the scope such that only the most important features that can be accommodated in the budget get worked upon. Two situations may arise:

1. If the project finishes off at a cost that is lower than the target cost, then the profit is shared between the buyer and the seller. The buyer has to pay less than what he expected initially and the seller not only gets its fee, but also a share of the profit incurred because of finishing early.
2. If the project finishes of at a cost higher than the target cost (like when the project is delayed), then both the buyer and seller would end up paying more.

Fixed-price contracts generally have a fixed-time flavor as well. A seller may be incentivized by getting paid at a higher daily rate for finishing early. On the other hand, in case of delays, the same seller might be paid on a lower daily rate.

5.5.2.7 Contract Extension and Payment Based on Delivery and Acceptance

Another variation of the contract is where, after each incremental delivery, the buyer pays out to the seller only when the acceptance test cases have been satisfactorily passed. If the delivery satisfies the buyer and the business value is obtained, the buyer (sponsor) can decide to renew or extend the contract for the next iteration. If the delivery does not deliver the desired result, they can choose to stop or modify the terms and conditions on the contract for the next iteration.

5.6 Agile PMO

In this last section of this chapter, let us take a quick look at the role of the Project Management Office (PMO), which supports Agile teams. In traditional projects the PMO is a department that centrally supports and guides project managers by introducing, training, maintaining and controlling a consistent and standard set of processes, practices, tools, techniques and templates relevant to project management.

In Agile projects, the functions of a classic project manager are distributed between the product owner, Scrum Master and the whole team. In doing so, it seems that the role of the PMO is either diminished or absent in an Agile team. However, in reality, the role of the PMO shifts from a controlling and policing style to that of a supporting, advisory and consultative function.

Here are some of the functions that the PMO can play in an Agile organization:

- **Agile transformation** - Help in the journey of Agile transformation in an organization, by working closely with top management, soliciting their support and reaching out to the entire organization hierarchy.
- **Agile adoption and training** - Help in adoption of Agile practices by spreading knowledge, making people aware of the benefits, showcasing success stories and providing comfort, as transitioning from a plan-driven mindset to an adaptive mindset could be disconcerting for a fair percentage of the population. For projects and teams to transition to the Agile way of working, PMO's can help in coordination of training and usage of the tools (like Jira, Rally, VersionOne, Cucumber, Greenhopper, Kanbanflow, Zephyr, Confluence, Sharepoint, webex, TeamViewer, etc.) and practices are important.
- **Agile coaching** - PMO's should also bring in experienced Agile coaches to train themselves and Agile team members. As we shall see later in this book, Agile coaches can coach teams (e.g., during ceremonies like planning, daily stand-ups, review and retrospectives) and mentor individuals (e.g., on the finer soft skills, communication, practices, etc.). If sufficient capability is built, PMO's could take up the role of coaching, advising and mentoring as well.
- **Agile governance and center of excellence** - With the product owners and Scrum Masters around them, PMO's can form a governing body or an Agile center of excellence for the organization where they uphold principles of Agile, maintain standard tooling, consistent best practices from the industry across teams (with, of course, variability allowed in choosing iteration length, type of contracts, velocity, definition of story points and definition of done).
- **Resource management** - Working together with the human resource and recruiting teams, PMO's can support project teams by maintaining a healthy balance of supply and demand. The supply consists of a pool of skilled resources that needs to be deployed across projects based on their respective needs. They can also work with facilities and property services to serve the needs of the team to sit together and arrange furniture to create a caves-and-commons environment.
- **Vendor management** - Assist Agile teams by following standard and consistent operational steps related to vendor management. For example, at an organization level they could orchestrate master service agreements (MSA's) with preferred vendors that have already been selected. At a project level, the Agile teams could strike up contracts with the same set of vendors that inherit the same terms and conditions from the MSA, but customized specific to the project needs. This saves a lot of time.

- **Reporting** - PMO's could also help in collating and reporting status to senior management, especially for large programs where there are multiple small Agile teams at play, often at distributed locations, each producing its own lightweight version of statuses.
- **Audits and compliance** - Help in performing and coordinating internal and external audits especially where compliance[9] to industry specific laws and regulations like SOX, HIPAA, Dodd-Frank, Basel, FDA and BS7799 are concerned. PMO's could track noncompliance, educate and help teams to adhere and take corrective actions.
- **Continuous improvement** - Keep track of non-value added activities that bothers a team (and cannot be addressed at a project level), help and influence the management to take decisions to eliminate them (e.g., chains of approvals and sign-offs) and encourage the team to continuously improve their practices. PMO's could also act as a channel for communicating best practices from one project team to another in the same organization.

The following Figure 5-11 summarizes the teams that the PMO's interact with and the functions that they serve.

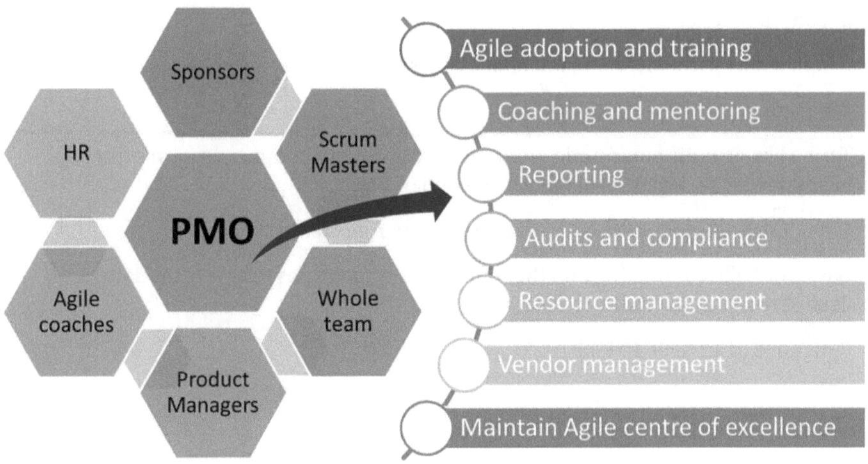

Figure 5-11. *Stakeholders and roles of Agile PMO*

[9]Refer to discussions around compliance in Chapter 3: Value-Driven Delivery.

5.7 Focus Areas for the Exam

- ✓ Bruce Tuckman's theory of team building - forming, storming, norming performing and adjourning.
- ✓ What are cross-functional skills and why are they important in an Agile team?
- ✓ What is the optimal size of ideal teams?
- ✓ Ground rules.
- ✓ What does Shu-Ha-Ri mean?
- ✓ What are the different leadership styles described in the situational leadership model created by Ken Blanchard and Paul Hersey?
- ✓ What is a self-organized team?
- ✓ What is systems thinking?
- ✓ Some common meeting etiquette.
- ✓ Basic communication model, channels of communication and choice of technology in communication.
- ✓ Graph showing the richness and effectiveness of communication by various modes.
- ✓ What are information radiators?
- ✓ Terms like osmotic communication, drafts, bus-length communication principle, tacit knowledge, expert in earshot and cone of silent.
- ✓ What is a caves-and-commons arrangement of Agile team spaces?
- ✓ Basics of Agile contracting and the different contract types to accommodate flexibility and adaptability to changes.
- ✓ Functions of an Agile PMO.

Quizzes

1. What is the optimal team size on Agile projects?

   A. 4 ± 3

   B. 7 ± 2

   C. 9 ± 1

   D. It could be any arbitrary number based on the duration of the project

2. In Shu-Ha-Ri, Shu means to:

   A. Detach

   B. Transcend

   C. Learn

   D. Attach

3. What are the correct stages for team building?

   A. Forming, Storming, Norming, Performing, Adjourning

   B. Forming, Norming, Storming, Performing, Mourning

   C. Forming, Mourning, Norming, Storming, Performing

   D. Forming, Storming, Adjourning, Performing, Norming

4. In ________ stage of formation and development, team members begin to work and most likely to have conflicts.

   A. Performing

   B. Storming

   C. Arguing

   D. Forming

5. In situational leadership models, at which stage do teams require high directive and high support:

   A. Forming

   B. Coaching

   C. Supporting

   D. Storming

6. All are characteristics of a self-organized team except:

   A. Constructive disagreement

   B. Empowered

   C. Trust

   D. Follow command-and-control regime

7. In a distributed team, which is the most effective tool to use for communication between team members?

   A. E-Mail

   B. Video conference

   C. Wiki / intranet

   D. Audio conference

8. In Agile, the PMO helps in ____________

   A. Status report collation

   B. Vendor management

   C. Facilitating training, coaching and maintaining a center of excellence

   D. All of the above

9. How many communication channels will be there when you have 10 team members on-board?

   A. 15

   B. 25

   C. 35

   D. 45

10. A developer is asking his peer whether it is okay to get his new code deployed at 4 p.m. on the system testing environment. Another developer overhears this and reminds him that another deployment is already planned at the same time in the same environment and there could be a potential conflict. This style of communication is named as ____________

    A. Effective communication

    B. Osmotic communication

    C. Interactive communication

    D. Conversation communication

11. Knowledge that is gained over the time through observation and experience but cannot be documented is named as:

    A. Internal knowledge

    B. Secret knowledge

    C. Tacit knowledge

    D. Company confidential information

12. A technique used to improve the performance and ramping up new and junior team members by seating them within hearing distance of more experienced and senior team members is called __________

    A. Expert in earshot

    B. Caves and commons

    C. Expert nearby

    D. Sitting together

13. A space where maximum information exchange takes place, displays whiteboard, well lit, well ventilated, with visible charts is called:

    A. Team space

    B. Public space

    C. Cave space

    D. Common space

14. A private space where a team member can isolate themselves for a short period either to make personal calls or check e-mails is called __________

    A. Private space

    B. Member space

    C. Caves

    D. Isolated space

15. Which of the following is not a valid example of an Agile contract?

    A. Time and Material contract

    B. Multi-stage contract

    C. Contract with premature closure clause

    D. Request for proposal

16. Which of the following technologies helps to improve collaboration in virtual teams?

    A. Common (and single) version control repository

    B. Common build environment

    C. Webcams on desktops

    D. All of the above

17. When team is not co-located, which tool is most effective to radiate information?

    A. Desktop sharing over the intranet

    B. PowerPoint presentation sharing over e-mail

    C. Spreadsheets in a document repository

    D. Project metrics report display on whiteboard

18. When it comes to team selection, which of the following should be ideal choices to work for an Agile project?

    A. Experts in niche domains

    B. Generalized specialists

    C. Highly skilled analysts who can write test cases and execute them

    D. All of the above

19. Which contract type allows early termination of a project?

    A. Fixed price

    B. Fixed price, but with a provision to scope change

    C. Time and material

    D. Cost reimbursable

20. How are contracts in Agile projects different from those in traditional (waterfall) projects?

    A. In Agile contract, scope changes are easy to make.

    B. In Agile contract, financial management is not required.

    C. In Agile contract, it works well when contracted as fixed price.

    D. In Agile contract, scope changes are hard to make.

Answer

1. B
2. C
3. A
4. B
5. B
6. D
7. B
8. D
9. D
10. B
11. C
12. A
13. D
14. C
15. D
16. D
17. A
18. B
19. C
20. A

CHAPTER 6

Domain V: Adaptive Planning

"It is better to be roughly right than precisely wrong."

—John Maynard Keynes

This is one of the most important chapters as far as the PMI-ACP® exam is concerned. The chapter is fairly exhaustive in terms of coverage of many terms and key concepts that are required for Agile projects. Also the position of this chapter is apt, almost in the middle of the book, which reflects that planning takes the center stage in Agile projects and other domains revolve around it.

6.1 Aspects of Agile Planning

We know that for any project, planning is an essential part that leads to better decision-making, trade-off between investment demand and revenue realization, communication across all stakeholders involved and setting of expectations across the organization or at the marketplace.

Some key facets of Agile planning that we shall see in this chapter are:

- Planning based on priority and business value realized;
- Deferring detailed planning until the last responsible moment;
- Planning for only value-added features that are pulled by the customer and no extras;
- Planning not in stages of SDLC, but such that all necessary activities are completed within the agreed timebox;
- Planning with the help of dedicated teams who are not multitasking;
- Planning as one whole team, so as to break the silos between role families like architects, designers, product management, developers and testers;
- Planning adaptively so as to cater for change and uncertainty on the fly;
- Religiously inspect and adapt the plan continuously based on feedback and retrospectives.

In the following sections we will look at some of these facets of Agile planning.

S. Boral, *Ace the PMI-ACP® exam*, DOI 10.1007/978-1-4842-2526-4_6

6.1.1 Deming's Plan-Do-Check-Act (PDCA) Cycle

The Plan-Do-Check-Act cycle, as shown in Figure 6-1, introduced by Walter Andrew Shewhart, but popularized by Edward Deming is the foundation of the principles of adaptive planning and continuous improvement in Agile.

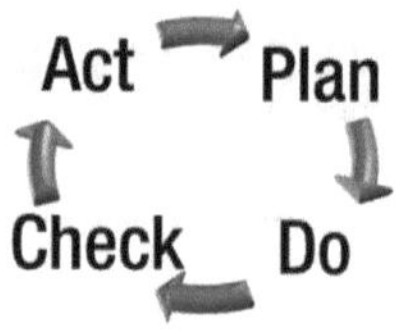

Figure 6-1. *Deming's Plan-Do-Check-Act Cycle*

Plan: Agile projects pursue a mix of both high-level long-term and detailed short-term planning approaches. There is not much up-front planning, but plans are detailed out just-in-time. This enables the plan to be flexible and adaptable to changes.

Do: This is the stage for projects to implement (designing, coding, testing, build, etc.) requirements or changes in the project. The ultimate outcome is a product increment that adds value to the customer.

Check: At periodic intervals, Agile teams pause to inspect the actual results and compare with the expected results. Users are provided an opportunity to review and provide feedback on the work produced. Also the team reflects on its way of working and looks to improve. Taking the example of Lean philosophy, this could translate into eliminating waste (any non-value-added activities) from the value stream.

Act: The outcome of the "check" stage is fed back into the project and the team plans to translate them into action. This includes taking corrective or preventive actions, incorporating the feedback received from the user, respond to change in requirements or priorities. This gives the flavor of *Kaizen* or continuous process improvement.

6.1.2 Bursting the Myth - "Agile teams don't need plans"

There is a prevalent misconception that Agile methods do not prescribe enough planning. As Alistair Cockburn rues in his book[1]- the Agile Manifesto, which states that Agile practitioners value "Responding to change over following a plan" has been subject to a lot of misinterpretation leading to negative results. People mistakenly suppose that Agile teams do not plan as they do not need them, or worse still, if they have plans then they are not sufficiently agile.

As we have seen in the PMBOK® Guide,[2] traditional project management consists of the phases (also called process groups) of Initiating, Planning, Executing and Closing. And during the Planning Phase, the project manager produces a (predictive) project management plan that contains all subsidiary plans for managing scope, time, cost, quality, integration, change, human resource, procurement, risk, communication and stakeholder. This plan is baselined at the end of the planning phase and is updated (and rebaselined) in response to an approved change request. The project is tracked against the baselined plan throughout the project.

---

[1]Refer to *Agile Software Development – The Cooperative Game*, 2nd ed. authored by Alistair Cockburn. (Upper Saddle River, NJ: Pearson Education, 2006).

[2]Refer to 5 Process Groups and 10 Knowledge Areas as defined in PMI®'s *A Guide to the Project Management Body of Knowledge* (PMBOK® Guide) – Fifth Edition.

In contrast, Agile project management does not have a dedicated planning phase upfront in the projects that produce a project plan. Instead there is a high-level release plan that echoes the customers need for features at specific times and a planning ceremony at the beginning of each iteration. The iteration plan factors in updated requirements and priorities and allows the team to react to changes far more smoothly. This is illustrated in Figure 6-2. Hence in reality, Agile indeed does a lot more planning and a lot more frequently than traditional processes.

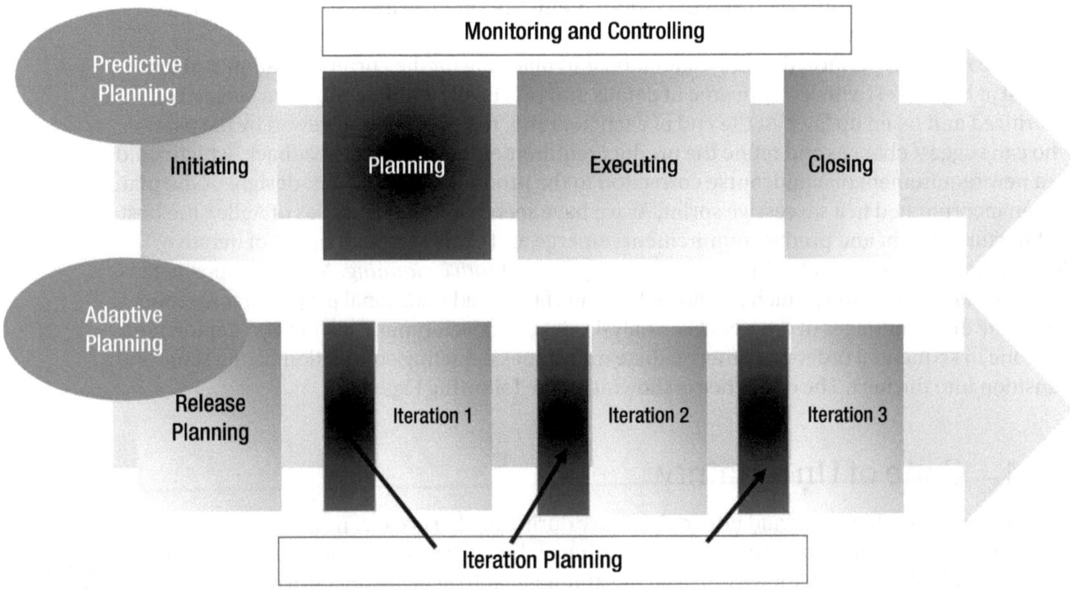

Figure 6-2. *Difference between predictive and adaptive planning*

Agile projects are good to start with coarse-grained long-term plans and time and cost estimates that are needed by the sponsors to justify the commercial value of doing the project. And from time to time the project team anticipates changes that are fed back into the project. However, for day-to-day needs the team needs a short-term fine-grained plan that is valid for a few days or weeks at a time. The short-term plan can be visualized as the sprint plan that delivers value-driven software increments at the end of each iteration. We look at the different levels of planning required when we discuss *Planning Onion* later in this chapter.

6.1.3 Progressive Elaboration/Rolling-wave Planning

Progressive elaboration is a technique where plans are detailed out as more detailed and specific information is available to the project team. So phases in the project that come later are only specified at high level, while the ones that are near (say for the next week or fortnight) are detailed at a more granular level so that it can be accurately estimated, assigned, tracked and monitored.

Rolling-wave planning is a form of iterative planning and progressive elaboration technique. The two words are often used interchangeably. The analogy is that waves seen at a very large distance from the sea coast appear to be small and blurred. But as the waves approach the coast, they become clearer and detailed.

In traditional plan-driven projects, changes undergo an expensive and thorough change management process that either admits the changes into the system or suppress for want of resources (time, cost, resources) leading to customer dissatisfaction. In contrast, Agile projects, during its lifecycle, anticipate change coming from business needs (e.g., market trends, economic factors, legal or regulatory requirements), technology evolution (new gadgets and technology products), constrained availability of resources, delays due to dependencies and so on. As we have seen during the discussion on Stacey's matrix,[3] Agile methods are best suited in the zone of complexity, which is uncertain and the requirements are yet to be agreed. Therefore it is a wasteful exercise to plan too far into the future.

Agile methods perform detailed estimation and planning for the current iteration and leave the rest at high level (with lesser degree of details and precision) in the product backlog to be prioritized and taken up later. At the end of each iteration, the product is reviewed by the users who can suggest changes and refine the product requirements further. The feedback, whichcould be a new requirement or a midcourse correction to the product specifications, design, or the plan, is then incorporated in a successive sprint. As we have seen in the 12 principles of Agile,[4] the best architecture, design and product requirements emerge and evolve through cycles of iterative development and frequent feedback. This is also called *adaptive planning.* And the opposite to that is *predictive planning,* which is followed in waterfall-based traditional project management where the different stages of progress like analysis, design, development, testing and deployment are done in sequential order with intermediate milestones depicting completion of one stage and transition into the next. The difference is showing in the following Figure 6-2.

6.1.4 Cone of Uncertainty

This theory depicts how risks and uncertainty vary during the life cycle of projects. Typically, it is seen that a lot of uncertainties exist at the beginning of the Agile project, when the definition of how the end looks like is unknown and also the approach and tasks are not clearly detailed out. At this stage, the range of estimate could be as high as +75% to -25%,also called an initial *Rough Order of Magnitude or ROM* estimate. This means that at an early stage a project estimated to take 6 months, could take anywhere between 3 to 9 months.

However, as the project proceeds, project teams get a better understanding of the needs of the customer and takes mitigation actions against the risks that have been discovered. So, for example, when the team is about to start implementation based on a detailed design, the estimates get more accurate and the range drops to ±20%, which is called *Budgetary estimate.* The same estimate of 6 months, could now take between 5 to 7 months. Then finally at later stages of development *definitive estimates* that are within a range of +10% to -5% can be produced.

So we observe thatthe uncertainties decrease over time and tapers to a minimum toward the end of the project and the accuracy of the estimates increases. This is depicted in the cone of uncertainty, also called Estimate Convergence Graph as shown in Figure 6-3.

---

[3]Refer to Chapter 1 : Agile Principles and Mindset.
[4]Refer to Chapter 1 : Agile Principles and Mindset.

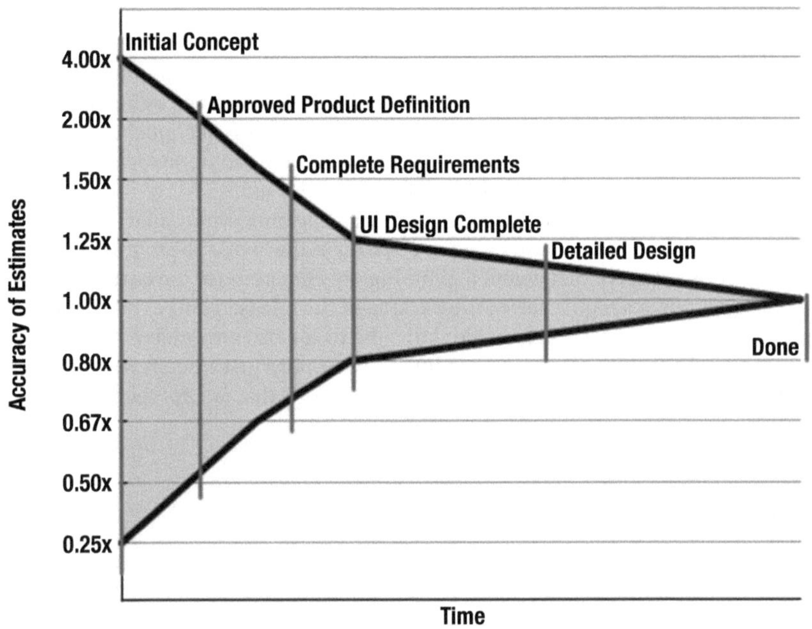

Figure 6-3. *Barry Boehm's Estimate Convergence graph*[5]

There are a few ways that Agile practitioners deal with the cone of uncertainty:

- Not trying to determine the absolute estimate, but expressing estimates as a range to cater for the unknowns.
- Pursuing incremental delivery instead of a big-bang approach that carries an inherent risk if the specifications are not clear and detailed at inception.
- Making progress transparent by giving the user opportunity to review product increments at frequent intervals. This fosters a collaborative mindset where the business and the technology teams are working together toward a shared goal.
- Running a couple of iterations to determine the velocity (capacity) of the team to deliver, instead of guessing upfront.
- Using relative sizing units like ideal time and story points, instead of hours, days, or months.
- Running short experiments called *spikes* to test out an approach or an idea. This leads to risk mitigation, increases confidence and decreases uncertainty.

[5]The Estimate Convergence Graph comes from Barry Boehm.

6.1.5 Just-in-time Planning

Agile methods follow a just-in-time (JIT) planning model. This concept originates from Lean manufacturing that eliminates all forms of wastes, prevents build-up of inventory and is pull-driven. Agile methods abstain from up-front planning, because the plans become brittle and cumbersome to maintain as the project proceeds. Also, all forms of planning-associated costs in the form of effort and time, are both valuable commodities for the team.

As we have seen before, Kanban pulls items from the backlog only when capacity becomes available, thereby reducing work items from being queued up in the 'work-in-progress' state. Coming to Scrum or XP, we observe that detailed planning only happens for the current iteration and anything outside it is left at a high level (in the backlog or the release plan) to be adapted based on change of requirements or priorities. Similarly, the user stories are elaborated and estimated just-in-time, architecture, design and coding also happens just when it is necessary. This prevents any elements of rework or aspects of design and code that are not required by the customer.

6.1.6 Timeboxing

A timebox, in the literal sense of the term, is a fixed duration of time within which a task must be accomplished. The duration is, generally, agreed by the team in advance and is given all due respect. The concept of timebox instills a sense of discipline where once the current timebox expires - the unfinished part of the work is stopped and moved to the next timebox. In no case is the timebox extended. It also implies that at the stage of iteration planning, only the work that can be accomplished in the timebox is committed. Anything that cannot be fit in the timebox (based on the team's capacity) will have to wait until the next iteration or timebox.

6.1.6.1 Examples of timeboxing

Here are some examples of indicative timeboxes that are commonly observed in Agile teams.

- Duration of iteration in XP - 2 weeks
- Sprint duration in Scrum - 2 to 4 weeks.
- Sprint of iteration planning - 8 Hours
- Daily stand-up meetings - 15 Minutes
- Duration of automated builds in XP - 10 minutes
- Sprint review - 4 Hours
- Sprint retrospective - 3 Hours

One of the ways in which timeboxing can be achieved is by using the *Pomodoro technique*,[6] which organizes personal work in 25-minute timeboxes. This proceeds along the following steps:

- Estimate how much time it will take to accomplish a specific task.
- While doing the work, protect it from distractions and interruptions (like emails, chats, phone calls, etc.), thereby giving it to get the complete focus required.

[6]Refer to the online video at `http://pomodorotechnique.com/`

- After the work is done, make sure that some time is allocated to review,
- Look at opportunities to improving the quality of the work or the approach followed.

6.1.6.2 Advantages of timeboxing

There are a few advantages of timeboxing:

- **Maintain a sense of urgency** and continuity of deliveries, so that the team is able to thwart any distractions (that is treated as waste) and give single-minded focus to the task in hand.
- Agile projects encounter complex situations where requirements are volatile and uncertain. Timeboxed iterations to do planning, development, testing, review and retrospective **bring in some much needed operating rhythm in the team**. The mechanism of real-time feedback at the end of the iteration ensures that the team is never off-track beyond the duration of the current iteration and a course correction in the event of change is not delayed. This also helps as a risk mitigation technique.
- **Avoid the effect of *Parkinson's Law*** - The law states that work tends to expand to fill all the time available for its completion. As an example, if a month is estimated for system design, the team will more than likely spend the entire duration in the same activity irrespective of whether all the activities are value-added or required or not. And in the process, it might even end up overcomplicating the task. By giving the team a short iteration of 2-3 weeks, Agile methods make certain that the team gets adequate time to complete the stories committed, nothing more than that.
- **Avoid the effect of *Student Syndrome*** - This is a form of procrastination and the analogy is with a student who will only start preparations for the exam when the deadline approaches, putting a lot of stress on himself. By adhering to deliveries in short timeboxed iterations, Agile teams maintain cadence and stay focused on the deadline (i.e. to achieve the sprint goal), which is never far beyond 2 or 3 weeks.

6.1.7 Iterative and incremental delivery

We have covered the essence of iterative planning as part of the discussion on timeboxing in the previous section.

Incremental delivery is all about developing the product in small increments, subjecting it to periodic review and feedback and adapting it to the evolving needs of business. At the end of each iteration, Agile teams look to deliver (to production) a working and integrated version of the product increment that is valuable and usable by the business. Based on the feedback obtained on the product and its features, their own ways of working and tools and techniques, the team looks to adapt and improve themselves.

Hence the advantage of using an incremental approach is to maximize ROI for every increment and also to reduce the cost of introducing change late in the product life cycle. The combination of iterative and incremental delivery therefore has become a critical success factors for projects that deal with uncertainty and a volatile scope.

6.1.8 Levels of Planning - The Planning Onion

Agile focuses on continuous planning and is illustrated in the six levels of the planning onion as in Figure 6-4 below - Strategy, Portfolio, Product, Release, Iteration and Daily planning.

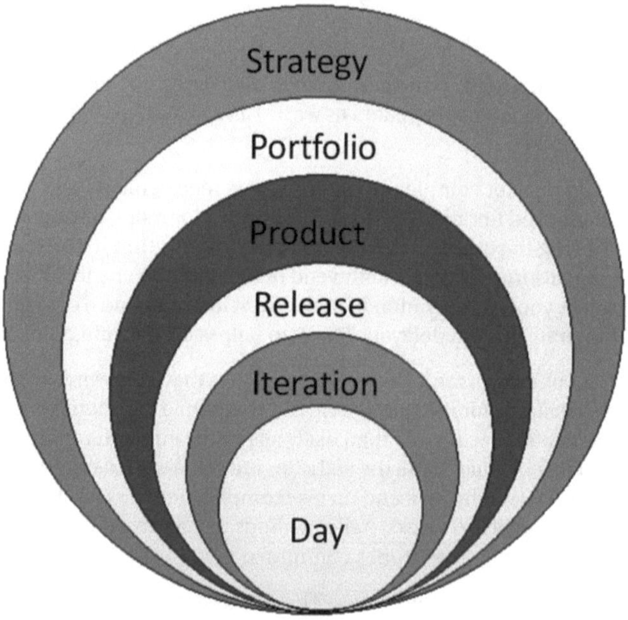

Figure 6-4. *Planning Onion*

The above-mentioned levels (or layers) are interrelated and span from the vision of the product or organization, into a roadmap and finally culminating into a daily delivery plan. Most Agile teams are concerned about the innermost three layers of the planning onion - namely, Release, Iteration and Daily planning. Let us briefly look into each of them.

6.1.8.1 Strategy Planning

This typically consists of a 3–5 year strategy that an organization charters out to serve its stakeholders. It consists of laying down a vision and overall direction that the company intends to follow.

6.1.8.2 Portfolio Planning

In order to fulfill the vision laid down in the strategy plan, the organization chooses a portfolio of products and services designed to reach a particular market or market segment. This plan could span up to 2–3 years.

6.1.8.3 Product Planning

The product vision is often expressed in the form of an *elevator statement*thatconsists of no more than 140 words and takes no more than 2 minutes to explain the same to another person.

With the product vision in hand, the next level of planning goes into creating the project charter and the *product roadmap*. The project charter[7] focuses on the business need and elements of time and costs to undertake the project. One or more projects impact the evolution of the product through its life cycle. The *product roadmap*, spanning between months to years is an overall view of the product's requirements and a valuable tool for planning and organizing the journey of product development. This is a point of reference not just for the product engineering team, but also other teams like sales, marketing, finance and senior leadership. The product roadmap can be organized in the form of planned releases and the features that are introduced or enhanced as a result of the planned releases.

The following Figure 6-5 shows a product roadmap for our library management portal.

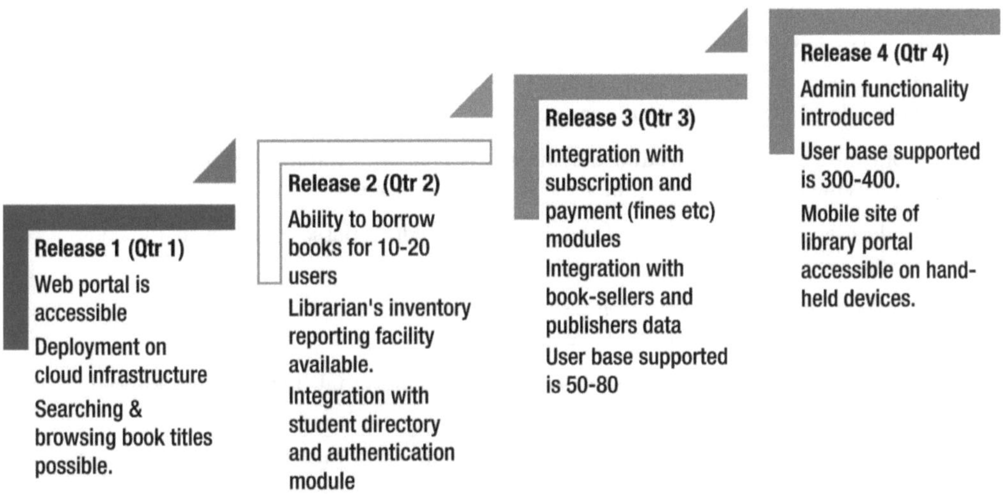

Figure 6-5. *Product roadmap for library management system*

6.1.8.4 Release Planning

During this step, the product roadmap is used to categorize requirements into themes by logically grouping them into usable set of features that can be released together. With a fair bit of prioritization and high-level estimation for the features happening at this stage, a tentative timetable is drawn for their release. Due consideration is given to the team's capacity to deliver and ensuring that the most valuable ones are done first.

Like most Agile artifacts, the release plan is frequently revisited to check on consistency and relevance as the project progresses.

6.1.8.5 Iteration planning

The release plans have no details other than a list of stories to be done by a date. Therefore as the name suggests, the iteration planning level focuses on the subset of the release plan stories that will be done in the very next iteration or sprint and nothing beyond. The time horizon for an iteration plan could be anywhere between 2 to 6 weeks depending on the choice made by the team and the urgency to deliver.

[7]Refer to Chapter 3: Value-driven Delivery for a discussion on project charter.

During the iteration planning meeting, the product owner[8] comes with a backlog of user stories prioritized based on business value. In the first half of the meeting, the team seeks to understandand get clarifications (from the Product Owner) on the stories in the backlog. During the second half of the iteration planning meeting they decide how the work will be built. The chosen collection of stories are decomposed into further granularity (development tasks), estimated to be built, tested and integrated. It is common to see that one of the developers will volunteer to own a particular task. The choice of the stories for a particular iteration is made based on the business value as articulated by the product owner, the cost of implementing the story as estimated by the team member, the team's capacity to deliver (taking velocity into account), consideration of defect logs from the previous iterations and any risks involved that need to be mitigated.

Let us look at the example of a story that reads, "As a borrower, I would like to search a book by its name." Such a story could be disaggregated into constituent tasks like the following:

- Design the user interface element that contains a text box to enter the name of the book and a button to trigger the search.
- Code the SQL stored procedure that takes the input as the name of the book and returns the matching result (null if the search is unsuccessful).
- Code a service that makes a call to the stored procedure, passes the name of the book as input and parses the output and formats it.
- Code the UI element that calls the service to execute the search and display the search results in the form of a HTML table.
- Perform integration testing to see that the different pieces talk to each other without any errors.
- Code such that up to 10 concurrent searches are possible from different user sessions (e.g., from different browsers on different computers).
- Perform testing to include scenarios like special characters in the name of the book and where the book is searchable but already reserved by another borrower.

The team commits to a set of stories based on its capacity to deliver (by accounting its velocity[9]), *definition of done* and any planned absence of the team members.

Apart from the periodic iterations, there are two prevalent practices of Sprint Zero and Hardening Sprint in some Agile teams that are sometimes argued as anti-patterns. Sprint zero is used for project setup, infrastructure provisioning, setting up of project document repository, standardizing tools and team building. So during sprint zero no stories that are valuable to the customer are delivered. At the time of final releases for complex pieces of software, a hardening sprint is required to pay down technical debt, ensure that stability tests are completed, aspects like license-to-operate are secured and user trainings are completed.

6.1.8.6 Daily Planning

Finally, the deepest level of Agile planning focuses on a single day, where the team meets for a daily 15-minute stand-up meeting to reflect on

> the previous day's accomplishment, the plans for the present day and any impediments faced on the way.

[8]Refer to the discussion on Scrum in Chapter 2: Agile Methodologies.

[9]The concept of velocity is described in detail later in this chapter.

It is said that the innermost layers of planning are where the strengths of the Agile approach lie, with the team getting an opportunity to respond dynamically to both the directions - from changes in the outer layers and the complexities encountered during something as basic as a break in the build process. The daily meeting is meant to foster a greater degree of collaboration in the self-empowered team.

In summary, Agile planning is designed to be flexible and responsive. This form of JIT planning can give anxious moments to a traditional project manager, who is used to looking for critical paths on the project schedule or milestones on the Gantt charts. But in fact the multilayered and iterative approach is actually more successful for developing complex software.

6.1.9 Choosing an Iteration Length

In the previous sections, we have listed the advantages of timeboxing and delivering in iterations. We have also seen how teams start off with release planning, then iteration planning and finally into daily planning. The choice of an iteration length is made based on consideration of the amount of time that the team needs to generate valuable increments of working software. Although the bias is for shorter iterations,[10] but for practical reasons, the team might choose to go for slightly longer iterations. Extreme programming teamscould have iterations as short as 1-2 weeks while 3-4 weeks are generally the norm in Scrum.

Let us know look at some of the factors that teams consider when they decide on the length of the iteration. This is also summarized in Figure 6-6:

1. **Overall length of the release** - ideally teams would like to have at least 4-5 iterations in a release. The higher the frequency of iteration means that more is the number of opportunities to seek feedback from the user and make course corrections. So if a release is 10 weeks away, iterations should be of 2 weeks' size.
2. **Risk and uncertainty in the requirement** - the more the amount of uncertainty, the higher is the benefit of shorter iterations as feedback is received sooner. There is an inherent risk of going too long (say 4 weeks) on an iteration, because at the end of the iteration the users might find the outcome worthless. Shorter iterations will also imply that teams can 'fail-fast' and discard an idea or an implementation that did not work or not aligned to the expectation of the end user.
3. **Unchanged priorities** - Agile methods do not allow change of scope or priorities in the middle of a running sprint. So the longer is the iteration, lesser is the team's ability to adapt to change in priorities. In the worst case, a high-priority iteration could have to wait two full length iterations before it is converted to working software.
4. **Overhead of iterating** - each iteration includes the ceremonies of planning, review and retrospective, all of which takes time. Reviews and demos can also be difficult to schedule at very short frequency if the users are not available to gather that frequently. Moreover all iterations need to perform round of regression testing, which if not automated can be quite taxing for the team.

[10]Refer to the third Agile principle (in Chapter 1: Agile Principles and Mindset) that states "Deliver working software frequently, from a couple of weeks to a couple of months, with a preference to the shorter timescale."

5. **Maintaining focus and sense of urgency** - A very small iteration (say 1 week) can be very stressful to the team and allows little recovery if one or more team members have unplanned leaves. On the other hand a very long iteration (say 4 weeks) can lead to a tendency called *Student's syndrome*[11] leading to lesser productivity at the beginning of the sprint, but rapid and stressful activities toward the end of the sprint. Most teams see optimal results from iteration lengths of 2–3 weeks.

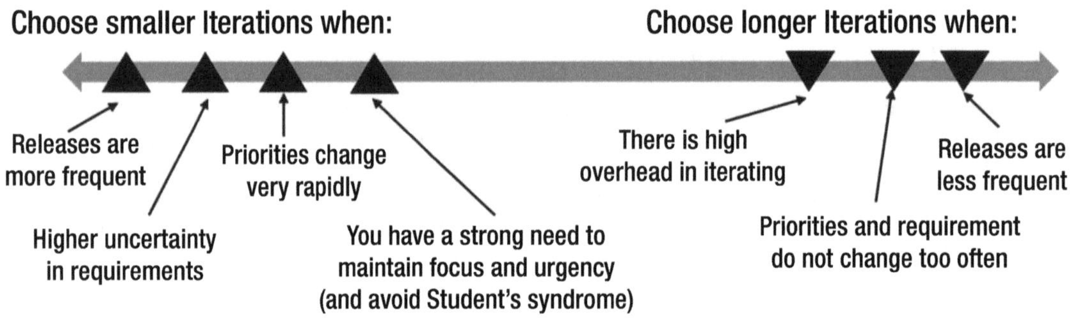

Figure 6-6. *Making the choice of an iteration length*

[11]Student's syndrome is discussed earlier in this chapter.

6.2 User stories

User stories are a fundamental concept in Agile methods. User stories describe requirements or functionalities of the software from a user's perspective. Such stories are written in a simple manner, free from technical details or jargons and captures the essence of who (the role), what (the feature description) and why (rationale / benefit) of the requirement. Agile practitioners write user stories on small cards or persist them on electronic systems (like Jira) and use them to trigger conversations to discover details of the business needs and how the software should be estimated, designed, developed and tested.

User stories can be used to represent a new feature, an enhancement to an existing feature, technical task (like a nonfunctional requirement), or a defect unearthed during testing. Once the stories are identified and prioritized in collaboration with the customers, developers estimate them and then slot them into one of the iterations for implementation. Once developed, the acceptance tests are executed to verify that the stories work exactly the way the customer expected it to be.

6.2.1 User Story Format

There are two popular formats in which user stories are expressed.

As a <user>, **I want** <some goal> **so that** <some action or benefit> happens

The first one is a very popular format. It uses the "role-feature-reason" template and the focus is on Who (the user), What (the desired goal) and Why (the end result).

Given <a pre-condition>, **when** the <user> does <some action>, **then** <the outcome> happens.

The latter is an approach developed by Dan North as part of *Behavior-Driven Development (BDD)* and *Acceptance Test-Driven Development (ATDD)*.[12] Tools like Cucumber[13] generate acceptance tests usingthe Given-When-Then approach (also called the Gherkin language).

Let us look at a few examples of user stories using this format:

- As a hotel seeker, I want to book a room for 2 nights at a hotel that is within 3 miles from my office, so that I save time on commute.
- As a library user, I want to check the availability of a novel and reserve it, so that I can read it during my leisure time.
- As an avid chess player, I want to keep track of my wins and losses, so that I can compete with my opponents with similar scores.

[12]Refer to discussion on ATDD in Chapter 7: Problem Detection and Resolution.

[13]Refer to `https://cucumber.io/`.

- Given the search window is open, when I enter the name of a student, I am able to see his attendance over the last 3 months.
- Given that I have sufficient balance in my bank account, when I attempt to withdraw an amount, the ATM dispenses cash and debits my account.

6.2.2 Card, Conversation and Confirmation

A user story is traditionally handwritten on a story card at the beginning of the project or any time throughout the project. Ron Jeffries, one of the authors of the Agile Manifesto and a cofounder of XP[14] described 3 critical aspects of user stories. The 3 C's are Card, Conversation and Confirmation. Figure 6-7 shows a sample story card.

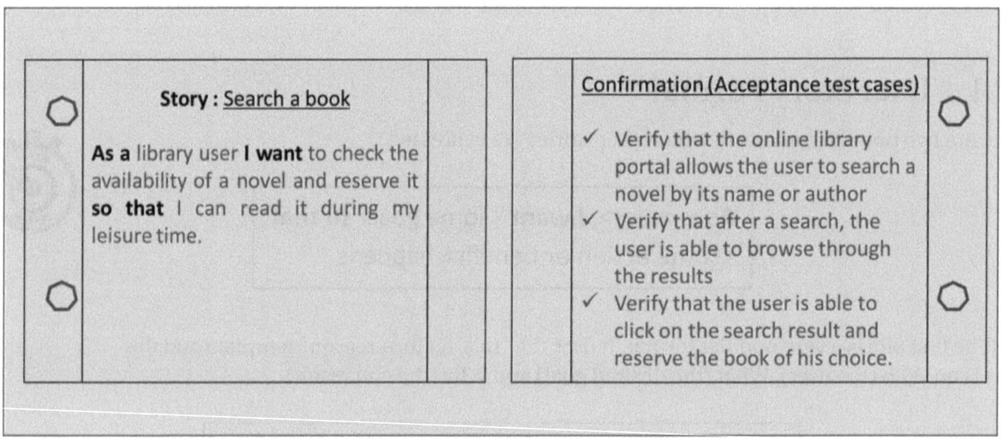

Figure 6-7. *Front and back of a sample story card*

The 4" X 6" **Card** has the description of the story written down. This description is not elaborate, but follows the principle of barely sufficient documentation that can be used by the team for planning, estimation and acceptance testing. In short, the sole purpose of the user story is to serve as a reminder to the team about the business requirement. This card generally has a shelf-life until the user story is complete (i.e. met its *definition of done*) and some teams even simply rip up the card after that.

Not all details are documented on the card (and it is not meant to be). It is the **Conversations** between the customer and the team that help to flesh out the details of the story. Such a conversation can happen anytime during the sprint, but most of it is initiated during sprint planning where the product owner explains the requirement on the card, based on which the design and estimates are decided.

Finally, at the back of the card contains the **Confirmation.** These are acceptance tests that are used to determine whether the implementation of the story is indeed correct and complete or not.During sprint reviews the team demonstrates that the software works as expected by showing that the acceptance test cases have passed.

[14]Extreme programming was founded and advocated by Kent Beck, Ward Cunningham. and Ron Jeffries.

6.2.3 Hierarchy of Epics, Features, Themes and User stories

In the context of user stories maintained on a backlog, it is usual to see a few words being used often and sometimes, interchangeably. Let us explore these in some details with the help of a running example of an online Library Management System.

6.2.3.1 Epic

An epic could simply be a large user story that can span several iterations. Such epics will have coarse-grained estimates (and hence with lower level of accuracy), but are useful for release planning. For the purpose of implementation and sprint planning, epics are disaggregated or broken down into stories.

For example, two such epics in the context of online Library Management system can be:

- Epic #1 - As a library user I should be able to search and borrow books.
- Epic #2 - As a library admin, I should be able to create reports of books, borrowers and pending requests.

Epics may either be compound (comprising of multiple short stories) or complex (one that is inherently large and cannot be easily decomposed easily into shorter stories).

6.2.3.2 Feature

A feature represents a high-level functionality required by the business. Similar to epics, features also need to be broken down into more manageable fragments like stories that can span several iterations to be delivered. Sometimes product based companies could look at features or a collection of such features that could be bundled, shipped and sold to customers separately.

For example, continuing with the above example, a few features could be:

- Feature #1 - Allow no more than two books to be borrowed by a user at a time and kept for a maximum time of 3 weeks.
- Feature #2 - Levy a fine if the book is not returned within the due date.

In terms of hierarchy, there is no prescription of whether the epic or the feature will be at the parent level and so both variations are commonly seen.

6.2.3.3 Themes

Themes are set of related user stories that are combined together to speeds up estimation, planning releases, or financial planning (at the sponsor level). The theme could be based on the persona (type of user) or some nonfunctional requirements like usability, mobility, performance and scalability.

One example of a theme could be the system uses a singlesign-on such that the user and its type (borrower or librarian) is identified throughout the browser session and there is no need of the user to login again and again to perform different actions.

One such depiction of the hierarchy is shown in Figure 6-8 below.

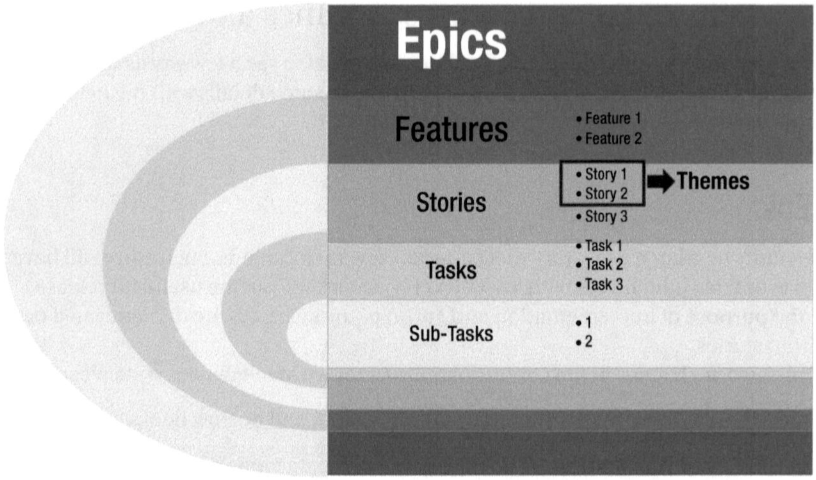

Figure 6-8. *Value-based decomposition and hierarchical relationships between Epics, Features, Themes, Stories and Tasks*

6.2.3.4 Stories

At the iteration level, it is the stories that are used as units for estimation, planning and implementation. Stories can belong to only one theme. Going by the above example, stories relevant to Epic #1 and Feature #1 could be

- Story #1 - As a library user I should be able to search books by the name of the book or its author.
- Story #2 - As a library user I should be able to browse through the list of books in the search result and be able to find more details by clicking on them.
- Story #3 - Given that I have fewer than 2 books reserved in my name, when I click on the "Borrow" button, then I should be able to reserve the book and get a confirmation over email.
- Story #4 - Given that 2 weeks have elapsed since I have borrowed a book, I expect to receive a reminder from the library 3 days before the due date so that I can return the book or request an extension.

6.2.3.5 Tasks and Subtasks

In order to implement the story, all the things that a developer has to do is called as a task. A task could be something that is technical in nature like creating a table on the database, building a widget or menu item, parsing an incoming XML file, adding business logic on the press of a button or connecting two systems via a message queue. In the context of the popular tool called Jira,[15] tasks can be further broken down into subtasks.

The process of breaking down epics into features, features into user stories and user stories into tasks is also called *value-based decomposition.*

---

[15]Refer to: `https://confluence.atlassian.com/jiraportfoliocloud/classic-plans-802170593.html`

6.2.4 Attributes of User Stories

Bill Wake, author of Extreme Programming Explored and Refactoring Workbook, has suggested the acronym INVEST for six attributes of a good user story. This is seen in Figure 6-9.

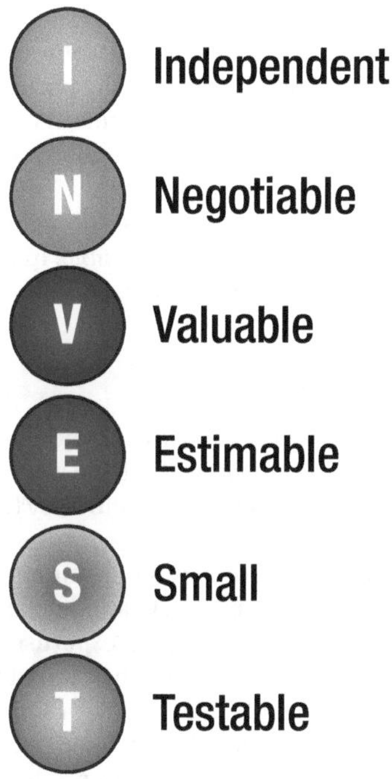

Figure 6-9. *INVEST acronym for user stories*

Let us now look at each of these attributes one by one.

6.2.4.1 Independent

The user story should be independent and not overlapping with each other; otherwise it might lead to problems in planning and prioritization. Self-contained stories are easier to move around between different sprints or iterations based on their priorities. In order to achieve independence, it might often be required to combine different parts of related stories or finding a certain way to split them.

6.2.4.2 Negotiable

A user story from the product backlog is not rigid or a written contract, hence subject to elaboration and change. A good story is meant to be a concise description of the desired requirement and an invitation for a conversation or collaborative discussion between the customer and the team members during planning and implementation. This is the reason that story cards leave out detailed specifications. As we have seen in Figure 6-7, while the front of the story card contains the essence of the requirement, the back of the card contains the acceptance criteria and rest of the details are intentionally left out to be hashed out between the team member and the customer. So that the team members do not forget the conversations, they could also jot down some notes on the story cards.In summary, a story in its lifetime in the product backlog is subject to negotiation; it can be rewritten and revised a number of time or even discarded based on the business priorities and other reasons as agreed by the team.

6.2.4.3 Valuable

In pursuant of the Agile principle to continuously deliver valuable software, a user story needs to add value to the customer. Since the user stories are prioritized from the backlog, it is this value that drives prioritization. Developers might be tempted to define value in terms of nonfunctional requirements (reusable modules or multithreaded software). But the team should be reminded that the value being talked about here is for the end users or customers.

One of the recommended ways to ensure this is having the customer or domain experts write the user stories themselves rather than the developers, wherever possible. In that way stories will have less of technical stuff and be possible for the product owner to prioritize it.

6.2.4.4 Estimable

The likelihood of a story being implemented in an iteration is a function of its prioritized business value and the estimateit will take to turn it into working software. It is to be noted that this estimate includes all the activities involved to meet the *definition-of-done* criteria for the story (for example analysis, build, unit testing, build, deployment and acceptance testing).

As we will see in the next section, during release or iteration planning,stories are estimated on the basis of relative size (e.g., whether one story is twice as complex than another)and not in terms of absolute figures. At times, estimation may be a challenge owing to lack of domain expertise or technical knowledge in the team. In that situation conversation with the customer or the subject-matterexperts might help.If the team unearths technical risk or uncertainty, they can decide to undertake a short and specific experiment calleda ***spike***. A spike is a brief research or a special type of story that are used to familiarize the team with a new technology or domain, prove their hypothesis, evaluate options, or produce estimates of greater certainty. Note that the spike itself should be small enough to timebox into an iteration. Once the purpose of the experiment has been achieved, the spike is discontinued.

6.2.4.5 Small

A story should neither be too small or too large for planning and implementation.Ideally a user story should be sized such that it can be planned, prioritized and slotted into an iteration.The thumb rule is to have user story sizes ranging from a few person-days to at most a few person-weeks. Stories that typically take less than half-a-day to implement (e.g., bugs, cosmetic changes) can easily be clubbed into one story, leading to lesser overhead of maintenance. In order to keep the user stories small, developers should resist the temptation for *goldplating*, which is addition to unnecessary features to impress the user.

Stories that are too large to fit in a single iteration can be split. The following could acts as guidance[16] for splitting user stories (this technique is also called *disaggregation*):

- **Split on the basis of the data handling or operations performed.** For example, different stories that cater to different behaviors of the system to do operations like lookup, insert, modify, or delete data could be split up accordingly.
- **Split based on mixed priorities of the smaller stories.** For example, validation of user inputs can be dealt separately from capturing and persisting user inputs.

---

[16]Refer to *Agile Estimation and Planning* authored by Mike Cohn. (Upper Saddle River, NJ: Prentice Hall, 2005).

- **Split on the basis of cross-cutting concerns** like application logging, exception handling, connection pooling and security. For example, if it's too complicated and time consuming, applications could build on these aspects as a separate story in a future iteration.
- **Split based on functional and nonfunctional characteristics**. For example, enhancements for singlesign-on features or higher performance could be catered as separate stories and kept independent of the functional stories.

6.2.4.6 Testable

Stories must be so written that they can be tested to confirm that they meet the user's expectation and satisfy the "doneness" criteria. User acceptance tests are often written at the back of the story card as shown in Figure 6-7 above.

Apart from the functional requirements, teams should also focus on nonfunctional aspects like usability, stability, performance and throughput. It is recommended that a majority of these tests be automated. As we have seen in Chapter 2 on Agile Methodologies, XP teams practice TDD (Test-Driven Development) where the acceptance test cases are written before coding and they pass to mark the completion of a story.

6.2.5 SMART Stories

Another acronym to denote attributes of user stories is SMART. See Figure 6-10.

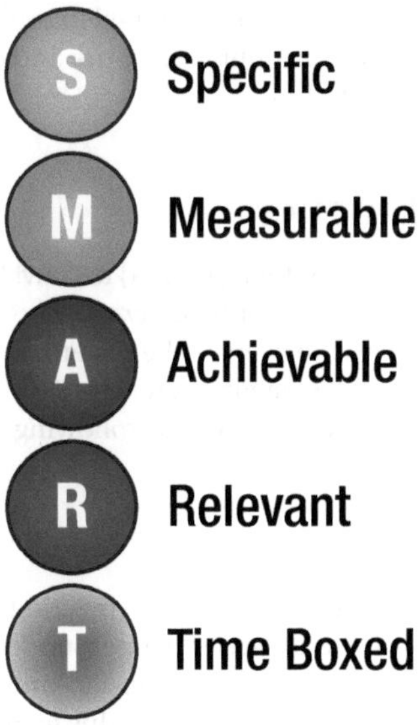

Figure 6-10. *SMART acronym for user stories*

6.2.5.1 Specific

User stories that are specific help to convey its purpose to the team and helps to keep it independent.

6.2.5.2 Measurable

User stories should be estimable (in terms of story points, for example) and measurable against the *definition of done.*[17]

6.2.5.3 Achievable

User stories should be unambiguous and the team should be able to achieve the *doneness criteria* within the timeboxed iteration. If the story is not clear, then the team can either split it into manageable parts or seek more clarification from the Product Owner to hash out the finer details of the stories.

6.2.5.4 Relevant

User stories should add relevant value to the customer and contribute, incrementally, to the overall objective or goal of the project. Since time and effort is expended, it is very essential that the ROI is maximized while implementing each story.

6.2.5.5 Timebound

Stories should be such that they can be reasonably accommodated in the timebox that the team mutually agrees. If the timebox expires, the team discards the unfinished work and does not count it toward the velocity attained by the team in that specific iteration.

6.2.6 Story-gathering Techniques

Agile teams engage with different types of users (or their proxies) to trawl functional and nonfunctional requirements. They look to reach out to a variety of user types, *create personas*[18] so as to get a complete understanding of the possible interactions with the users of the system. Requirement collection is not a one-time process, as it's expected to evolve as a result of feedback received during each iteration. Some of the commonly used techniques for collecting requirements are the following.

6.2.6.1 Interviews

In this technique, one or more team members schedule a formal meeting with a sponsor, customer representative, or a subject-matter expert, ask them a series of open-ended questions to identify their needs and desires of the system and document their responses. Face-to-face interview sessions are a very rich form of communication and, if the interviewees are carefully selected, this technique can be very useful to gather a lot of quality requirements.

[17]Refer to Chapter 2 for the discussion on Definition of Done.

[18]Refer to detailed discussion on personas in Chapter 4: Stakeholder Engagement.

6.2.6.2 Surveys and questionnaires

If one has a list of requirements, one if the easiest way to find out more information about them or their respective demand for a large user base set is via a survey or questionnaire. Surveys can be rolled out to a global audience too (e.g., online surveys). The audience is provided a set of questions to answer and the responses are analyzed. The analysis is meant to remove any outliers or detect a trend in the response, which helps to converge to a set of requirements. Note that contrary to interviews, surveys are one-way - as the audience of surveys has no means of asking back a question. Also they cannot be used to trawl new requirements.

6.2.6.3 Voice of Customer (VOC)

One of the varieties of surveys is the Voice of Customer, which is used to determine the customers' needs ranked in order of relative priorities and urgencies.

6.2.6.4 User role modeling and Persona

While trawling requirements for a system, it is important to identify and consider the variety of the users that will be interacting or benefitting from the system. The following Figure 6-11 shows some user types for the library management system.

- The student accesses the library because he can refer to a variety of reference books that is otherwise too expensive to buy during one semester.
- The research fellow would like to keep abreast to the latest happening in academia, so he/she wants to subscribe to journals, magazines and electronic content.
- The librarian looks at the overall organization of the library to make sure that the borrowers' needs are met and they are able to maximize the value of the inventory of books.
- The book sellers and publishers supply the books based on the demand placed by the readers. At times, they advertise some of the recently published books and best-selling ones to attract readers and increase their sales.
- The IT support team helps in 24x5 maintenance and upkeep of the web portal that is accessed by the variety of users. They also help in user management like registration, administration and access control.
- The Finance team maintains the ledger and performs accounting with respect to paying out invoices from book sellers, collecting fines and dues from the borrowers.
- The logistics and procurement team looks at the relationship and contract management with external stakeholders and looks after property services like lighting, furniture, equipment, networking and janitorial services.

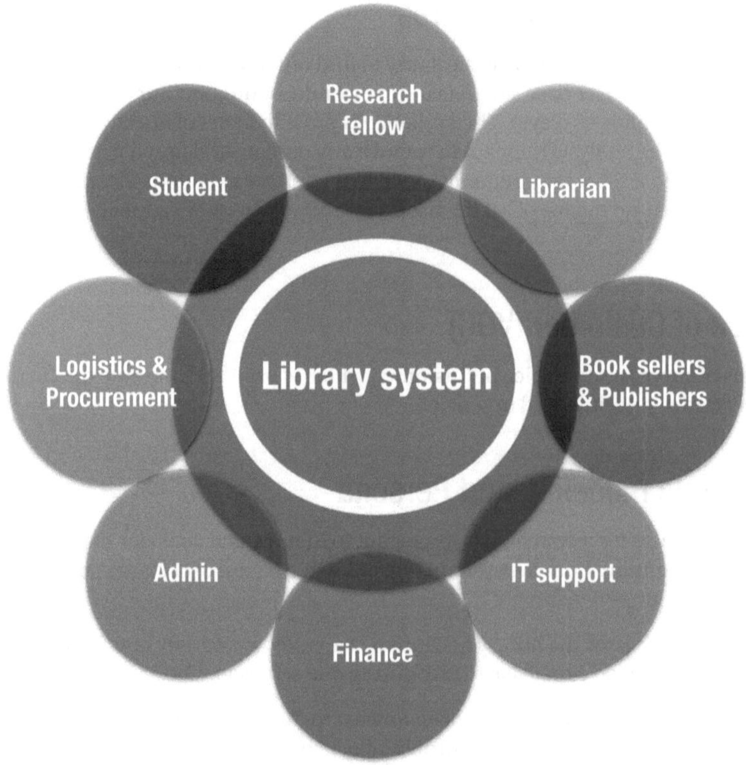

Figure 6-11. *User roles for the library management software system*

As you notice from the above each of the user roles have a varied backgrounds and have different needs from the systems, although some of the needs might also be overlapping (e.g., between the student and the research fellow) or related to each other (e.g., the book sellers submit their invoices to the finance department).

Mike Cohn[19] recommends the following steps to identify the different user roles in the system:

1. The team gets together to brainstorm and gather an initial segment of roles.
2. Organize and condense the roles in a way to place all the related or similar roles together (conceptually this is same as affinity mapping). This might lead to discussions, negotiations and option analysis.
3. Refine the roles based on attributes like proficiency, type of usage, frequency of usage, expected control and freedom, functional and nonfunctional needs (let's say some user type requires the system to be accessible via a mobile application).

[19]Refer to *User Stories Applied* by Mike Cohn. (Boston: Addison-Wesley, 2014).

4. Identify a ***persona***, which is an imaginary representation of a user role. The persona could have attributes like a name, address, age, a short description of his/her profile, his/her likes and dislikes, occupation, income level, a hypothetical photo and pretty much anything that is useful to represent the context and demographics (like color, race, religion, etc.) that the user is representative of. So for example instead of writing the story like "As a student I would like to search a book by its name," it is more appealing to write like "John Dever would search a book by its name" where John is introduced as a third-year student in the University of Austin, Texas,who is studying Chemistry as his major. Chemistry has been his favorite subject from high school where he scored very high marks. John comes from the state of Massachusetts and is a popular figure to spot in the college basketball club.

5. Consider ***extreme personas*** that are like extraordinary characters that might interact with the system. For example, consider Jeremy Parker who is so busy with extracurricular activities that he misses lectures often and would like to access video recordings of lectures offline from the library portal. Note that sometimes the needs from extreme personas may not be worth the ROI; however, it is still worth considering as some valuable stories might be discovered in the process that would have been missed otherwise.

6.2.6.5 Agile Prototyping and wireframes

Agile prototyping is a technique that is used by the development team to seek clarification on the requirements gathered. At the same time the endusers also get an opportunity to see a blueprint of the final product, as it is envisioned at that point in time. Giving the users a very early glimpse of what the product will look like at the end almost always invokes thoughts and helps to gather more requirements if they are relevant and related.

A prototype can be in the form of a proof-of-concept where the product development teams create a quick-and-dirty version of the desired product having similar look and feel but without much functionality. The intent is to

- actively engage customers, reconfirm what seems to be already understood and get doubts clarified.
- give customer an early view of what it could possibly look at the end, thereby minimizing some potential risks in design.
- allow them experiment by trying out some what-if scenarios and solicit feedback in the process.
- refine and converge to a narrower set of requirements, thereby speeding up delivery.
- create a closer bonding between the customer and the development team as both collaborate toward a shared goal.

The feedback obtained on the prototype could be on the design, size, special layout, color, contrast, spacing, alignment, usability, operability. and other visual aesthetics.

One of the prevalent forms of low-fidelity prototyping used in software is *wireframes*. Wireframes are used to mock up screens, user interfaces or web pages prior to development. A sample wireframe is shown in Figure 6-12 below.

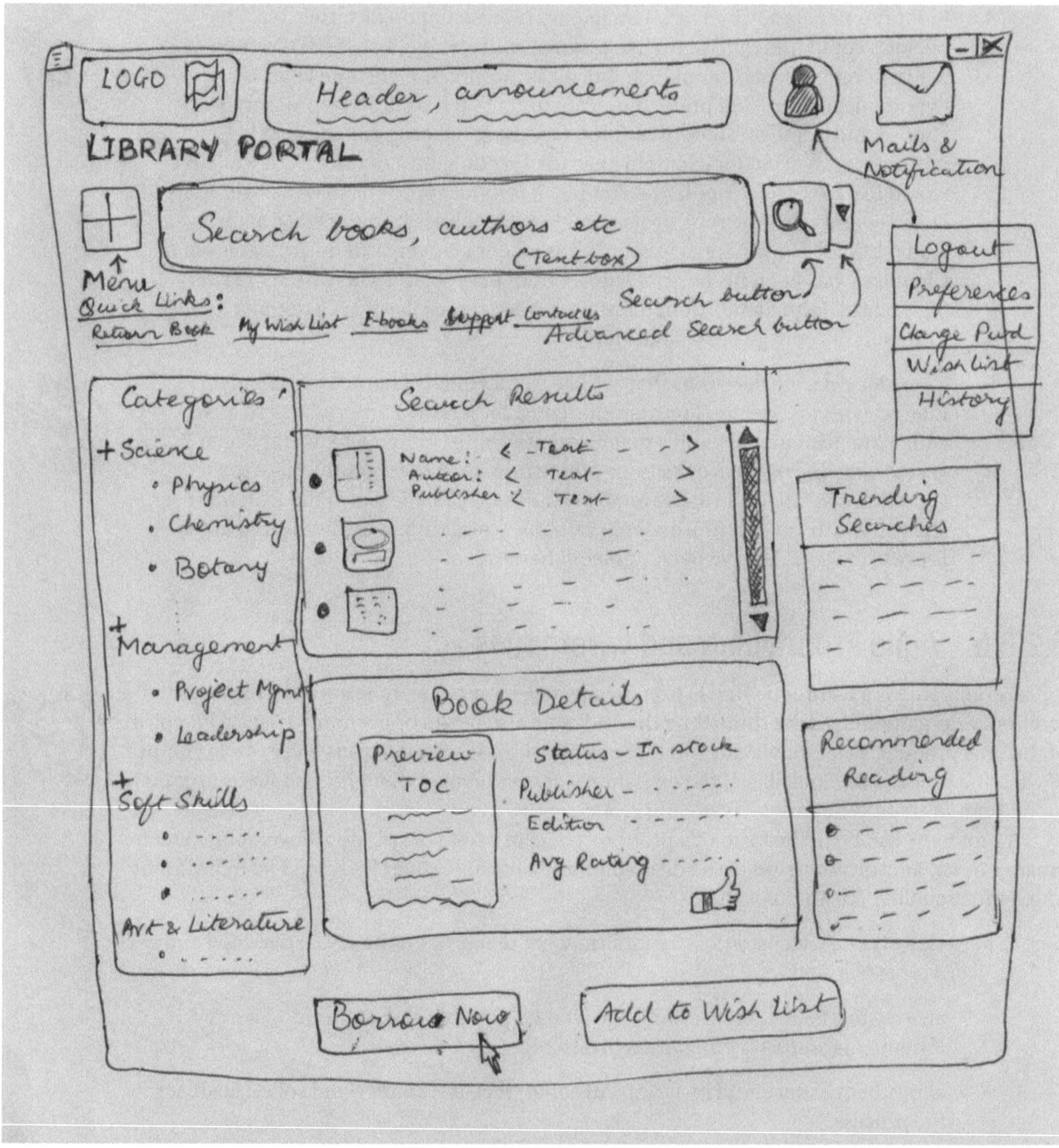

Figure 6-12. *A sample wireframe for the library management system*

6.2.6.6 Greenfield technique

In this technique the users are asked to imagine an environment where there are no constraints, boundaries, or existing structures. This stimulates original thinking about the product requirements, fosters creativity and frees the mind from unnecessary clutter.

6.2.6.7 Group creativity techniques

This set of techniques falls in the participatory decision model that Agile encourages. By involving the whole group, the techniques result in a greater buy-in within the team members who had a say in the decision. This is shown in Figure 6-13. Some of the examples follow:

- Brainstorming - technique to generate ideas about product requirements.Each person in the room gets turn to speak in a round-robin fashion and presents his ideas. Once all ideas are collated, they are evaluated and discussed.
- Nominal group technique - this is a form of enhanced brainstorming where the participants write down their ideas and shares them with the group. The ideas can be grouped together based on some affinity and are then voted and ranked to culminate in decision(s).
- Delphi Technique - collating anonymous feedback from experts, which removes any kind of biasing act.
- Idea/mind mapping - ideas are mapped out to determine commonality and differences.
- Affinity diagram - ideas generated are grouped into categories for further review and analysis.
- Multi-criteria decision analysis - using a decision matrix containing several criteria to determine the relative value, importance and uncertainties associated with the ideas.

Figure 6-13. *Brainstorming*

6.2.6.8 Focus groups and facilitated story-writing workshops

These are forums for interactive discussions heldbetween qualified, cross-functionalstakeholders and subject-matter experts. The experts are asked to come up with as many stories as they can think of. They put themselves in the shoes of different categories of the users interacting with the system and think what actions each of them would take to get their work done. The moderator of this workshop helps to steer the conversation in a direction that maximizes interaction, balances perspectives and builds trust and consensus.

6.2.6.9 Job shadowing

In this technique the team member 'shadows' and observes how a real-life user uses the system or interacts with the product and its environment. Such sessions are enlightening and often help the team to bridge the gap between what they state as requirements and needs versus what they actually do in the real and constrained environment. The shadowing session can also be photographed or video recorded so that it can be referred for future too. This technique helps to improve productivity and usability of the product.

6.2.6.10 Group decision-making techniques

Once the ideas are collected, decisions are made by following:[20]

- Unanimity - everyone agrees to a decision and a consensus is reached.
- Majority - more than 50% of the participants agree to a decision.
- Plurality - largest block decides even if majority is not reached.
- Dictatorship - one individual makes the decision on behalf of the group (e.g., when sufficient time is not available to reach consensus).

6.2.7 Innovation Games

Continuing from the above, in this section we cover some more exercises that engage real users and customers to elicit requirements that matter to them or converge on an idea to solve complex problems. The ultimate goal is to understand customer needs, foster a culture of participative decision-making, gain consensus on the right features and priorities and come up with a better strategy at delivering value. Innovation games, also called Collaborative games, are forms of group creativity techniques.

6.2.7.1 Buy a feature

The game starts with a list of features and their estimated cost to deliver them. Customers are provided with imaginary cash and ask the 'buy' the features that matter to them the most. The features are heavily priced compared to the cash with the customers and this leads to discussions and negotiations on the value of a feature. The outcome of this technique is a prioritized list of features that the customers are willing to pay for.

---

[20]Refer to PMI®'s *A Guide to the Project Management Body of Knowledge* (PMBOK® Guide) – Fifth Edition.

6.2.7.2 Product box

In this game the customer pretends that he is selling the product at the marketplace to another skeptical customer. He pulls features out of a product box and tries to impress the customer by telling him why it is worth buying it. The goal of this technique is to shortlist the most impressive and valuable features that the customer admires.

6.2.7.3 Prune the product tree

This game starts by drawing a large tree that represents the core functionality and branches of various widths to represent components and features. Users are asked to come up with new features, write them on 'leaf-like' cards and paste them on the tree or the branches, with the supporting features being closer to the trunk than others. As more and more cards get posted, the tree takes a shape that denotes where the majority of the functionality or improvement is desired. This results in an evolving version of the product vision.

6.2.7.4 20/20 vision

The aim of this game is to discover which feature is most important to which stakeholder. The analogy is with an optometrist who tries out lenses of different power to narrow down to the one that suits the eye most. Similarly the facilitator of this game writes the features on cards and shows them to the stakeholders one card at a time and asks them to rank them in order of importance. If the card has a lower importance it is placed lower in the pile and if the card denotes an important feature it is placed high up. The game ends when the pile of cards is exhausted and all cards have been arranged in order of importance.

6.2.7.5 Remember the future

In this game the project stakeholders are told to imagine a situation in future where the product has been delivered and it has been several months or years that they have been using the same. They are then asked to think of the product characteristics or features that caused the most meaningful difference to their lives or provided the maximum benefit to them. This helps to understand the stakeholder's definition of success.

6.2.7.6 Me and my shadow

In this exercise the team members literally sit next to the user and watches what they do and how. The sessions can often be recorded with a camera to watch how their eyes move and the actions they take to get their job done. At times the users areaskedopen-ended questions to justify their actions or read their minds. This technique helps to unearth hidden needs.

6.2.7.7 Sailboat

The game starts with drawing a sailboat on a whiteboard. The boat is expected to move real fast, but unfortunately there are a few anchors that hold it back. The users are explained that the boat represents the system and asked to identify the risks and bad features that act as anchors and impede the usability of the system or its performance. Similarly the users are also asked to identify positive opportunities or 'wind' that could propel the sailboat forward. These ideas could be scribbled on sticky notes and pasted on the whiteboard, as shown in Figure 6-14. With this in hand, the project team is able to put the risks, pain points and impediments on the watch list and proactively manage them better.

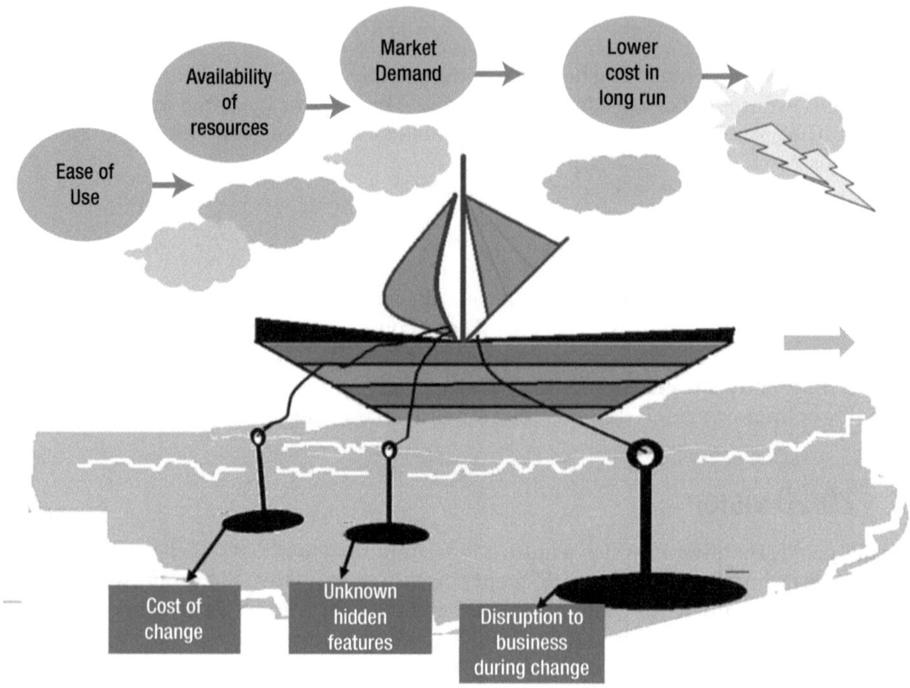

Figure 6-14. *Sailboat innovation game*

6.2.7.8 Bang-for the buck

This technique is used by the team and the customer together to rank the value and the estimated cost of a feature.

6.2.7.9 Start your day

In this game the participants are asked to describe their monthly, weekly and daily activities relative to the usage of the product.

6.2.7.10 The apprentice

In this game one of the team members uses the existing product in a way the actual user is expected to use it in real life. The real-life situation helps the team member create empathy with the customer and discover potential problems that need to be addressed to improve the usability of the product. An example could be a car mechanic driving a car to see what it feels like.

6.2.7.11 My worst nightmare

In this game the user is asked to imagine about the worst case scenarios that might be hidden and share with the group.

6.2.7.12 Force field analysis

The force field technique helps to analyze the forces that either drive or hinder a change in the system. The decision is taken in the direction of the desired change when the forces driving the change are stronger than the ones restraining it.

For example, consider the following Figure 6-15 where an organization is pondering whether they should replace the legacy software in their system with an opensource-based software. Using the Force field analysis technique, the organization can take a data-driven decision whether the outcome is favorable or not. Force field analysis technique is also commonly used during team retrospectives.

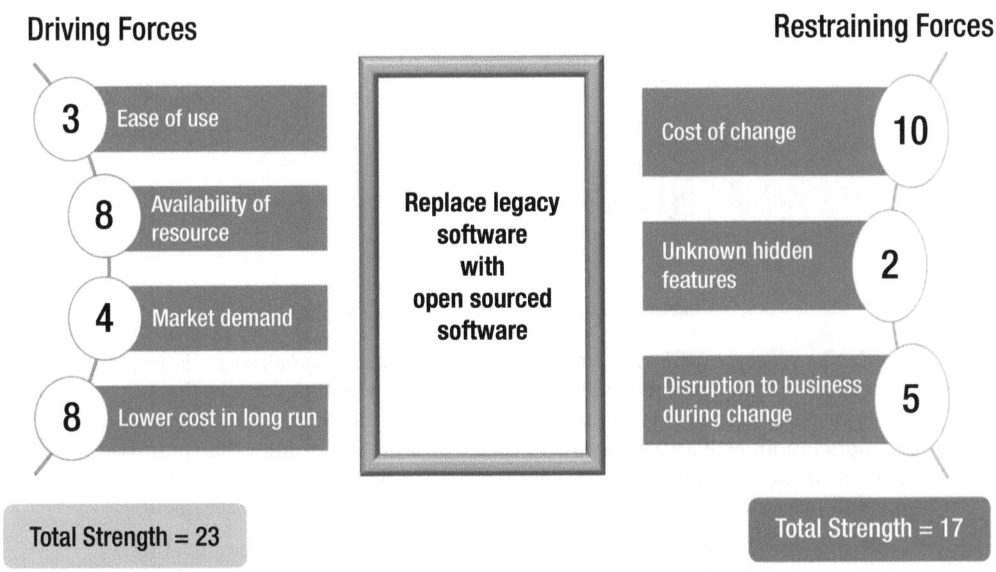

Figure 6-15. *Force Field Analysis - an example*

6.2.8 Few More Best Practices for User Stories

Apart from the ones mentioned above, there are a few other notable guidelines and characteristics for writing good user stories:

- If the customer is not available for writing the user stories, *consider user proxies*. They could be domain experts or former users. In some capacity a business analyst, trainers, technical support could also fill the role although with a word of caution as their role could be very focused in a single direction.
- *Slice the cake vertically* - Instead of splitting stories along technical components, consider one that includes end-to-end functionality and touches each layer. The term *Sashimi*[21] is used to describe this. To understand this better, let us take the analogy of a multilayered cake to denote a 3-tiered technology stack of software product. The layers in the "cake" from bottom to top consists of a database layer (for persistence), a middletier (having business logic encapsulated in exposed services and components) and a presentation layer (the user interface). If we split

[21]Sashimi is a Japanese dish of thin slices of fresh raw fish or meat, often served with dips like soy sauce and wasabi paste.

the story in layers, like just complete the database layer in one sprint, then it add little or no value to the customerif the presentation and business logic layer is not integrated. The recommended practice is to vertically slice the stack, as shown in Figure 6-16, such that customers experience an end-to-end flavor, albeit with limited functionality. This might be in contrast to the natural inclination of a developer to design and build one layer at a time.

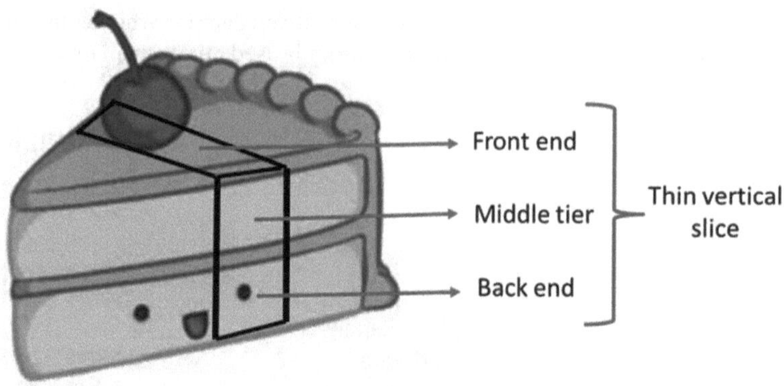

Figure 6-16. *Slicing the cake vertically*

- Splitting a user story vertically also aids in building a '*tracer bullet*', which is a very thin slice of functionality built to illustrate end-to-end functionality that passes through all layers of an application and helps to determine feasibility and appropriate connectivity between interfaces. An example is to allow the library user to enter a text in the search textbox and then call a lookup webservice that in turns connects to a database to retrieve a search result to be rendered on the browser.
- *Closed Stories* - Instead of being an ongoing activity, a story should be such that it achieves a specific and meaningful goal. For example 'The librarian can administer the content of the library portal' is not closed when compared against 'The borrower can read the ratings and reviews of book before reserving it on the library portal.'
- Write for one user (and not a group of users of different categories) and in Active Voice so that it is easy to understand and relate to it.
- *Use the simplest tool* - While some sophisticated electronic tools like Jira and VersionOne are available, user stories are often written on index cards, a paper with a feature number, priority number and story points. Index cards are very easy to work with and are therefore an inclusive modeling technique.
- *Write it in simple language* - Stories need to be described using simple and understandable language rather than using complex business and technical terms. For example, the user story 'Students can track the research paper status online' does not contain any technical or business term and is easily understood by any stakeholders.
- *Defer user interface details as long as possible* - Since it is subject to adaptation many times.
- User stories are distinct from use cases, which are descriptions of the set of interactions between a user and the system. User stories are much smaller in scope and detail, shortlived and generally devoid of any user interface specifications.
- Once user stories or epics are identified they are inserted into the product backlog. Each of these items are also generally called Product Backlog Items or PBI's and represent work that is not yet implemented. The product owner prioritizes the backlog and ensures that the stories with the highest priorities get delivered first.

As the project progresses, newer stories might be discovered, which will also need to be prioritized with respect to the rest of the stories in the backlog. The following Figure 6-17 shows a product owner at work - prioritizing the product backlog.

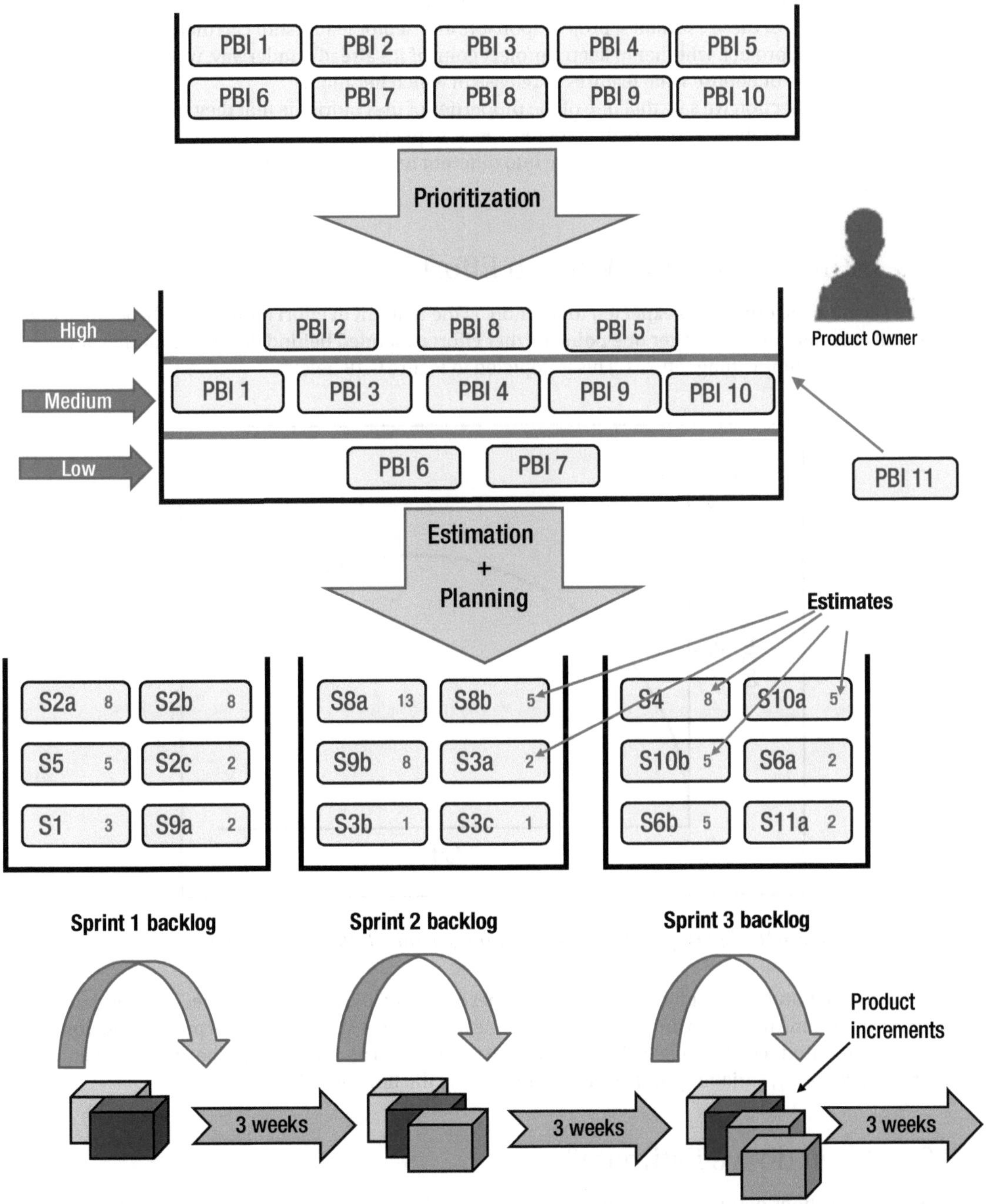

Figure 6-17. *Relation between the product backlog and the sprint backlog*

6.3 Agile Estimation

Like traditional projects, estimation in an Agile project is a valuable aspect that is used to gauge the commercial value (financially, in terms of return on investment) and feasibility (e.g., in terms of schedule, when and how much of a benefit that can be realized, competition or regulatory time constraints) of a project. With the help of these estimates, project sponsors and senior leadership can make a decision whether to approve a project, whether to keep a project going if it's already underway, whether to perform any course correction or choose what features to release in which iteration.

In the previous section we saw that one of the properties of user stories is that they should be estimable. These estimates form an integral part of the different levels of planning that the Agile team commits to deliver. In this section, we are going to deep dive into different units of estimation and estimation techniques adopted by Agile teams.

6.3.1 Estimation Comes With an Effort

The more accurate the estimate is expected to be, more is the amount of effort required by the team to come up with that estimate. However, after one point, further effort expended behind detailed planning and estimation leads to diminishing returns. This is depicted in Figure 6-18 below.

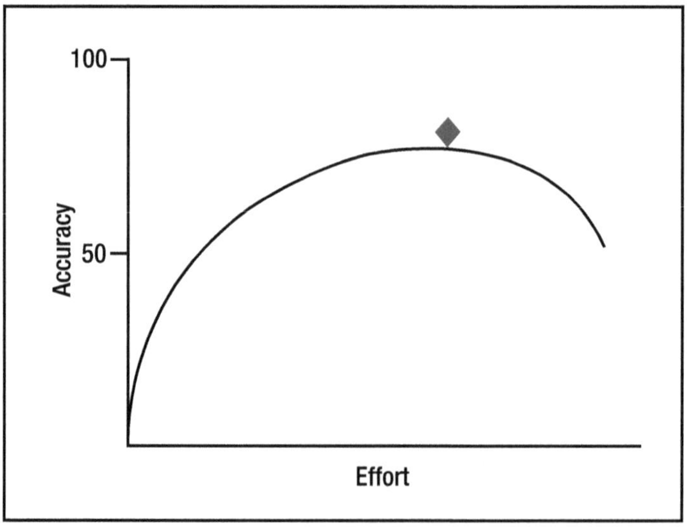

Figure 6-18. *Effort spent behind estimation generates little value beyond a point*

We have seen how brittle a plan detailed upfront becomes. Agile uses a variety of techniques that are sufficient to determine the approximate size and complexity of a user story. Instead of precise and absolute figures, estimates produced by Agile techniques are often expressed as a range in proportion to the amount of inherent uncertainty, variability and level of confidence at the time of estimation.

6.3.2 When do we Estimate?

In the previous sections of this chapter, we have seen how Agile follows the rolling-wave planning and how the *'cone of uncertainty'* depicts the level of understanding and uncertainties in a project as time progresses. When an Agile team does release planning, it primarily deals with the epics and at that time estimation is done on a rough order of magnitude. The estimation technique that can be used at that stage is Affinity estimation, which is discussed later in this chapter. However, at the level of an iteration, the epics are further broken down features and those into stories and tasks. At that time estimates produced by the team are more definitive than before and arrived at by techniques like Planning Poker.

As we have seen in Scrum and XP, each iteration is preceded by a planning ceremony. It is during this time, that the first set of estimates is produced by the team based on the conversations between themselves and the business (product owner in Scrum). The estimates cover every task that the team needs to accomplish to meet the *definition of done*, that is,convert a user story into a piece of working software increment. So it encompasses analysis, architecture, design, coding, testing, build and deployment. However, as the user story gets worked on, it is quite possible that the team members unearth some aspects which had been missed or not considered earlier. So the team member is at liberty to indicate the remaining time estimate on the user story. In the scenario where the remaining estimate is beyond the duration of the iteration, then the story is marked as incomplete and is put back to the product backlog for reprioritization and reestimation.

Finally, since estimation is done at different planning levels in Agile, it has to be kept in mind that totals need not match while disaggregating. For example, when epics are broken down into stories, the sum of estimates of the stories does not need to match the exact estimate of the epic. And similarly once stories are broken down to tasks, the sum of estimates of the tasks need not match the estimate of the story. This is illustrated in Figure 6-19 going back to our Library Management system. Notice that the epic to create the landing page of the portal is denoted by a big boulder that has an approximate effort of 120 days. This is broken down further during the planning phase into stories denoted by rocks, stones and pebbles of sizes proportionate to the complexities of their implementation. Note that, what is important for the Agile team from an estimation point of view is the stories that make up the epic and the capability of the system and their relative sizes. The sum of the estimates of the stories does not necessarily need to add up to the estimate of the epic.

Figure 6-19. *Breaking an epic into stories and relative sizing*

6.3.3 Units of Estimation

6.3.3.1 Relative sizing

One of the notable differences between estimation in traditional versus Agile is that Agile projects do not care about the absolute estimate of a user story or a task, but rather considers relative sizing as sufficient for all practical purposes. To understand this concept, let us look at an analogy as follows.

The distance[22] between Boston and New York is 216.1 miles and it takes 4 hours 8 minutes while driving by the fastest route available. Also the distance between Boston and Washington is 439.4 miles and takes 7 hours 34 minutes to drive. Now, while this static data denotes precision, in realistic terms while driving from the source to the destination a driver is likely to encounter traffic, diversions because of road closures and repairs, or need to take a few breaks en route. So, in most cases, the precise estimated data is not useful. However, if one is a frequent driver between Boston and New York and someone tell him that Washington, DC, is roughly twice the distance from Boston and will take double the time, he can relate to it far more easily. And it is also likely that more people would be able to remember that in relative terms, Washington, DC, is *double* the distance from Boston compared to New York.

Similarly in software development, it is fairly straightforward to realize that estimating work relative to a known baseline or something that has been completed in the past is easier than coming up with an absolute value, which of course, widely varies with relevant experience and competence.

Also, as we shall see in the next section the value of estimates are numbers from a no-linear sequence (as in Fibonacci series). This emphasizes the fact that the absolute estimate is less of a bother for an Agile team, as long as they are able to gauge the relative complexity of a work item. Agile teams will not spend too much effort differentiating between 12 or 14 days of an estimate, since they know that estimates are fickle as changes are inevitable.

6.3.3.2 T-shirt Sizes

One of the applications of relative sizing is to use T-shirt sizes like XXS, XS, S, M, L, XL and XXL as estimates for user sizes. Refer to Figure 6-20. The concept is that the team chooses a convention what a "Small" story would look like. And based on that, if the other stories are slightly smaller or larger it will be estimated as XS or M or L. If there is a considerable difference, then the team chooses the extreme values of XS, XXS or XL and XXL.

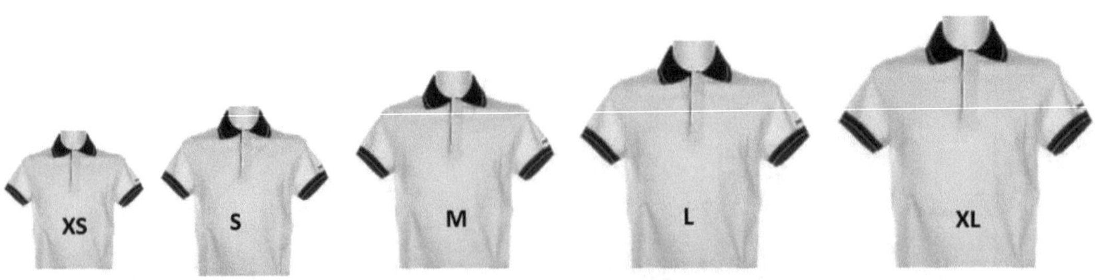

Figure 6-20. *T-shirt sizing*

The goal of using T-shirt sizing is that the estimation process takes less of a time, since the team is not considered about precision, but about relative sizing. Also the team can estimate without having all the finer details in hand, which is necessary in case of an absolute estimate

[22]Data based on Google Maps.

(in man-days for example). A sample mapping of what the T-shirt sizes could denote in terms of duration, size of team and cost is shown in the following Table 6-1.

Table 6-1. *Visualizing the relative estimates in absolute terms*

Size	Estimated duration	Team size	Cost (in thousand $)
XS	1 - 3 weeks	1 - 2	0.5
S	1 - 2 months	2 - 5	1 - 2
M	3 - 5 months	5 - 10	10 - 30
L	6 - 12 months	10 - 20	25 - 100
XL	1 year or more	20 or more	More than 100

6.3.3.3 Ideal time

Another prevalent unit of estimation in Agile projects is Ideal days. Ideal time is the number of days or hours a task will take if you focus entirely on it and work on it without any interruptions.

Let's take an example.

A developer is asked to estimate building a web page. He responds with "10 days." At this point the developer's manager takes this as a commitment and expects the screen to be done in 10 days. However, as time goes, the manager notices that the work is falling behind schedule. He either doubts the developer's estimation techniques or pushes him to burn the midnight oil and complete the task by the "deadline."The obvious fallacy over here that the developer, when he was asked to estimate, meant *actual*days' worth of work. But in reality, he was pulled to do production support work as well as attend a mandatory technical training. Worse still, he was out sick for a day. It is understood that the confusion stemmed from the fact of ideal days and elapsed days are different and both the developer and his manager should have had a common understanding in the first place.

Generalizing for software projects, team members are often distracted by one or more of the following:

- Training and workshops
- Team Meetings, consultations and phone calls
- Emails
- Performance appraisals
- Application support, addressing production issues
- Context switching between multiple projects or tasks
- Sick leaves and planned absences
- Interviews and recruitment activities
- Voluntary or philanthropic activities

As most of these distractions are uncertain events, accounting for them in the time estimate will not produce an efficient estimate. It, therefore, makes sense to produce estimates in units of ideal time rather than elapsed time by discounting some of the natural overheads that one encounters while working on software projects.

Now in spite of taking all the overheads into consideration, surprises do happen. So how do Agile teams handle that? Agile teams continuously keep track of the remaining time and tasks in the timeboxed iteration. If they find that the remaining capacity is less than that required for remaining tasks, then they drop some user stories (scope) from the iteration. In other words, these stories will not meet the definition of done and will be put back into the product backlog.

When estimating in ideal time it is assumed that:

- The story or feature is the only piece that is being worked upon (no multitasking here).
- All dependencies and things needed will be available before start and no idle time is spent.
- There will be no interruptions. If there are, the clock would need to be adjusted accordingly.

Ideal times are a popular unit of estimation simply because they are easier to estimate and also explain them to someone outside the team. However, the main drawback is that the measure of ideal time varies from one person to another based on their own skills and competencies and hence difficult to use as a baseline.

6.3.3.4 Story points

Similar to T-shirt sizing, a story point is actually a relative measure of size of a piece of work like a user story or a feature. Story points are, perhaps, one of the most popular units of Agile project estimation. It is important to realize that a story point does not directly correlate to actual hours. However, it depicts the amount of complexity, effort to build, or the risk involved in a story as compared to another one.

Similar to the concept of ideal time, the Agile team will have to agree on a baseline story thatis say, is of 1 story point estimate. A story that is twice as complex than this baseline will have an estimate of 2 story points. And the one that is four times as complex than the baseline will be estimated at 4 story points and so on.

Let us consider an example of a simple web page consisting of one text box to capture user input and a button to submit or save the input in the database. The team agrees that this is a baseline story with an estimate of 1 story point.

The next enhancement of this screen will be to turn it into a login screen with two inputs, namely, user id and a password, which is validated and an error prompt is seen if the credentials are not valid. The extra user input and the validation logic turns this into a story having 2-story point estimate.

The business then requests the team to have more sophisticated user login validation by using a dynamic captcha-based validation, making sure that only humans are interacting with the system and also providing an option for the user to retrieve or reset his password using his email address, if he has forgotten it. The team could very well treat this as a complex requirement compared to the baseline story and decide on an estimate of 8 or 10 story points to deliver the same.

In the above example, we observed a chosen baseline story of estimate 1 story point. However, teams frequently choose a collection of stories of varied sizes are reference. For example, the collection could have a story of sizes 1, 5 and 13. Given a story that is estimated to be bigger than the one sized 5, but smaller than the one estimated at 13, the team could settle down to somewhere middle like 8 story points. This technique of comparing to more than one reference is called *triangulation*.

It is worthwhile to add here that the choice of story points as a unit of estimation, although common, is arbitrary. It is not unusual to see teams using exotic estimating methods like

- Basic numeric sizing (1 through 10),
- Fibonacci sequence (1, 2, 3, 5, 8, 13, 21 and so on ...),
- Starbucks coffee cup sizes (Tall, Grande, Venti and Trenta),
- Dog breeds (ranging from a Chihuahua, Dachshund, poodle, bulldog, Labrador, St. Bernard to a Great Dane).

The important thing is that the team shares a common understanding of the scale it is uses, so that everyone in the team is comfortable with the scale's values across multiple iterations of the project. At this point, it is to be remembered that story points and the baseline story are specific to a particular project. Story points of one project may not mean the same size or complexity when applied to another project.

Story points are an important concept. We will continue to discuss more about it in latter sections like burndown charts and velocity.

6.3.3.5 Advantages of story points over ideal days

Ideal hours are easier to explain and understand compared to story points as unit of estimates. However there are a few notable advantages of estimating in terms of story points rather than ideal days.

- Story points are not affected by increasing proficiency and experience of the team. Since it is a **"pure" measure of relative size**, the estimate of a story in not related to the proficiency of the person developing it. Therefore an experienced team member will complete the story in quicker time, as reflected in the iteration velocity, but the estimate will still remain the same. However, in case of ideal days, the estimate will change based on the person working on it.
- It is **faster to estimate** in terms of story points, because one need not be concerned on the availability or competence of the person working on it. It is only the relative size of the story that matters in arriving at the estimate.
- Story points also **encourage the Agile philosophy of cross-functional behavior** where one has to think of all facets of analysis, design, implementation, testing, administration and risk mitigation to arrive at an estimate. In case of ideal hours, one tends to partition work based on specialized roles of analysis, development, testing and then summing up individual estimates. The former behavior is certainly encouraged in a self-organized team as it helps to meet the *definition of done*for the story rather than get satisfied at merely completing one's part of the work.

6.3.4 Estimation techniques

In this section we look at a few techniques that Agile teams use to estimate the size, complexity and risk associated with their work items.

6.3.4.1 Affinity estimation

The dictionary meaning of the word 'affinity' is similarity. In the Affinity estimation technique the Agile team groups user stories or product backlog items (abbreviated as PBI's) based on their similarities in complexity and size. This technique works well when 40 or more stories need to be estimated quickly.

In its simplest form affinity estimation proceeds in the following steps (refer to Figure 6-21):

1. The team uses large white wall and divides it into columns. The team agrees to label each column header with some measure of size (let's say XS, S, M, L, XL) or story points with values increasing from left to right.
2. The product owner brings along with him a list of prioritized stories from the backlog that needs to be estimated by the team. The entire estimation exercise is set up and facilitated by the Scrum Master.
3. Each story is shared with the team, who then slots it into the corresponding column based on size and complexity. This could physically be done with sticking the card (on which the story is written) using thumbtacks or push-pins or pasting post-its (colored sticky notes) on the wall. Most of this exercise is done silently by each individual.
4. In the next round, the estimates are checked against those of existing stories in the same column and if agreed, they are moved across in either direction to the most appropriate column. This goes on until the backlog of user stories are all estimated and the team is comfortable with their positions on the columns.
5. The product owner participates in the exercise in order to clarify requirements or where there are wide disagreements regarding the relative size of the story. The team could also respond to challenges from the product owner and, if required, change estimates on the fly.
6. As the exercise ends, it is essential that the estimates agreed are persisted into an electronic tool (like Jira[23]) for future reference. Any stories in the backlog that could not be estimated are taken away by the Product owner for further clarifications.

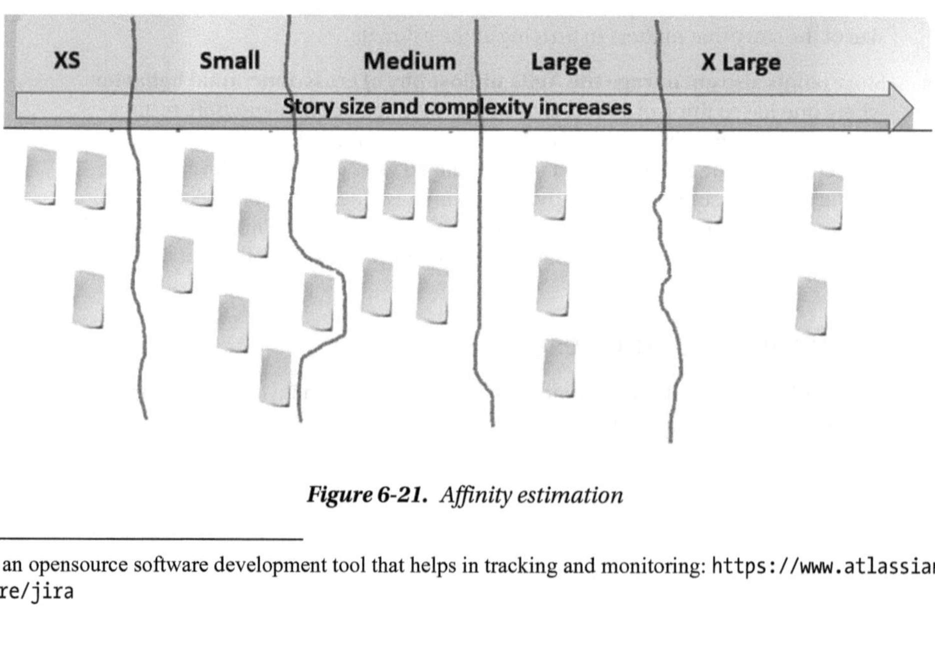

Figure 6-21. *Affinity estimation*

[23]Jira is an opensource software development tool that helps in tracking and monitoring: `https://www.atlassian.com/software/jira`

This technique lacks precision in the estimated values, but is particularly attractive since it is very easy and fast at grouping and estimating a fairly large backlog of stories. It is commonly used at release planning stages where it is okay to have lesser precision in estimates. As an example, it has been found that this technique can estimate a backlog of about 100–150 stories in less than 2 hours, which is great.

6.3.4.2 Wideband Delphi

The Wideband Delphi technique is a group-consensus technique popularized in the 1980's by Barry Boehm.[24] In this technique a group of experts come together and anonymously provides estimates that are collated with an aim that a consensus will be reached. Derived from the forecasting tool called Delphi that has been in use for several decades, the Wideband variant puts an added emphasis on interaction and communication between the participating experts.

The steps involved are as follows:

1. The moderator carefully selects a set of experts (4-6 of them) in the relevant field to do the estimation. This is done in a way to exploit the '*wisdom of crowds,*' with each expert bringing along with them their individuality, experience and diversity of opinions.
2. The moderator then presents the user story to the expert group and asks them to vote / submit estimates (and assumptions) anonymously. Since the estimates (often expressed in units of story points) are done independently, there is less of a chance of *'halo effect,'* peer pressure, bias,or '*herd mentality*'.
3. The moderator collates the submitted estimates and looks for a convergence in the numbers. If there are outliers (i.e. widely varying numbers), the moderator provides a summary of the estimates and the assumptions made. This is done so that participants come on the same page and can review their previous submissions.
4. In the next round, this exercise is repeated with each expert resubmitting their estimates and assumptions based on the revised understanding gathered from the previous round.
5. As the moderator now collates the revised forecasts, the expectation is that the range of estimates will become narrower and consensus will emerge. This game can be repeated a few more times, with an ultimate goal that the estimates converge into a figure that is agreeable by most, if not all.

The power of Wideband Delphi technique comes from:

- It is estimated by a group of individuals who are cross-functional, specialized in their domains and carries a well-rounded perspective from all disciplines in the project. Hence estimates are found to be more accurate compared to those done by individuals.
- Since estimates are submitted anonymously, there is less bias.
- With healthy debates and discussions that happen between the participants, transparency, trust and bonding develop. Over time, each participant respects and appreciates each other's thought process.

---

[24]Refer to *Software Engineering Economics* authored by Barry Boehm. Prentice Hall (October 22, 1981).

- An estimate emerging out of a team-based consensus is more likely to be acceptable.
- Also since the estimation is a teamgame, it is immaterial whether the person who estimated it is actually going to implement it or someone else who is available.
- In contrast to Affinity estimation, Wideband Delphi produces more precise estimates and hence is used during iteration planning.

6.3.4.3 Planning Poker

The Planning Poker technique is a variation of the Wideband Delphi estimation technique discussed above. This technique is used in XP and Scrum sprint planning meetings to determine estimates of user stories and so is also called Scrum Poker. The method was first defined and named by James Greening in 2002, but was popularized by Mike Cohn in his book called *Agile Estimating and Planning.*[25]

The setup for Planning Poker is very much like that of Wideband Delphi with a few differences:

- The team members are provided with a deck of playing cards.[26] These cards are numbered in Fibonacci sequence (0, 1, 2, 3, 5, 8, 13, 21, 34, 55...) or a modified Fibonacci sequence like 0, ½, 1, 2, 3, 5, 8, 13, 20, 40, 100, ?, α. The last 2 symbols denote 'not sure' or 'too complicated to estimate'. The beauty of using the Fibonacci sequence is that the ratio between two successive numbers in sequence is constant at 1.6 (8/5 = 1.6, 34/21 = 1.6, 55/34=1.6 and so on) and so naturally represents an increasing difficulty at estimating the size of a work item as it grows larger and larger. Refer to Figures 6-22 and 6-23 below.

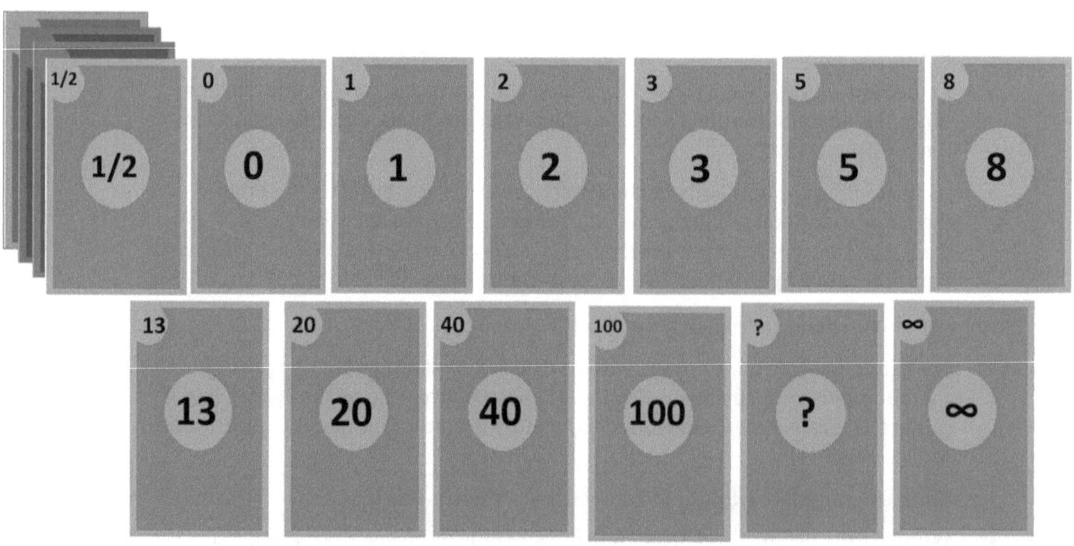

Figure 6-22. *Planning Poker cards for Agile estimation*

[25]Refer to *Agile Estimating and Planning* authored by Mike Cohn. Prentice Hall (November 1, 2005). Mike Cohn, founder of Mountain Goat Software, LLC has also trademarked the term Planning Poker.

[26]A pack of Planning Poker cards can also be purchased online at `http://store.mountaingoatsoftware.com/products/planning-poker-cards`

$$F(n) := \begin{cases} 0 & \text{if } n = 0; \\ 1 & \text{if } n = 1; \\ F(n-1) + F(n-2) & \text{if } n > 1. \end{cases}$$

Applying the formula :
F(2) = 1, F(3) = 2, F(4) = 3,
F(5) = 5, F(6) = 8, F(7) = 13 .....

Figure 6-23. *Fibonacci series*

- The Scrum Master acts as the moderator and chairs the meeting. The Product Owner picks prioritized items from the backlog and clarifies requirements, assumptions and risks and then asks the team to estimate them.
- When the time comes, the team member estimates the story in unit of story points,[27] choosesthe corresponding card and places it face-down on the table. For example if the estimates size of a user story is 5 story points, the team member will pick the card with 5 written on it and puts it face-down on the table. This means that the estimates are so long independent, secret and unknown to others. The assumption is that a baseline story has been agreed by the team in advance and all estimates are relative to the same baseline.
- When everyone is done voting, the moderator asks the cards to be revealed simultaneously.
- If the estimates are same, it means that agreement is already reached and they can move over to the next story to estimate.
- But, if there are team members who have produced outliers (i.e. estimates that are too low or too high compared to the median), they are asked to offer justification and any assumptions that they made. This could lead to a discussion, but it is timeboxed (let's say 2-3 minutes) by the moderator.
- Once the discussion is over or timed out, the moderator asks everyone to vote again and repeat the steps.
- After playing 2 or 3 rounds, the estimates are expected to converge or be within an acceptable range. If it does not, then the moderator could go with the majority, mean or a weighted average of the estimates.

The following Table 6-2 shows how the estimates converge as the team works through a couple of user stories from the backlog.

[27]You could potentially use other units of estimates like Ideal Days instead.

Table 6-2. *Rounds of planning poker for 2 user stories and 6 team members*

User story	Round #	Jack	Mary	Joe	Henry	Bill	Emily	Decision
As a user I want the feature to reset my login password	1	8	5	21	8	3	5	Estimates vary, let Joe and Richard explain, replay
	2	13	8	13	8	3	5	Estimates vary, discuss, replay
	3	8	8	13	8	5	8	Go with the majority vote, select 8 as the estimate.
As a user I want to update my contact information	1	5	8	5	3	3	3	Estimates vary, discuss, replay
	2	5	5	5	3	5	5	Go with the majority vote, select 5 as the estimate.

The Planning Poker tool has become very popular in the Agile community. There are applications that can be installed and used on smartphones. Also there are sites on the public domain that allows team members to estimate without a physical setup that is particularly attractive for virtual teams. You may explore further at `https://www.planningpoker.com/`

6.4 Velocity

Velocity is a very important metric in determining the progress of an Agile project. Originating from the time and distance theory in physics, it is used to measure how much the team accomplished during a particular interval. The interval is generally chosen as the sprint or iteration duration and the progress as the amount of stories accomplished.

6.4.1 Computation of Velocity

In simple terms velocity is the sum of the story points that a team can deliver in an iteration.

So, if we say that the velocity of the team is 24, it means that the team has capacity to deliver stories (meet the *definition of done*) whose estimates aggregate to 24 story points in one iteration. The length of the iteration itself could be anything between 2 to 4 weeks as we have seen.

Let us look at the following illustration in Figure 6-24.

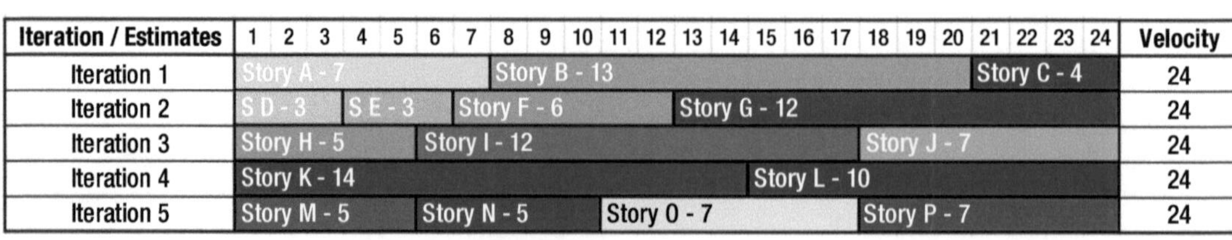

Figure 6-24. *Iteration plans*

In Iteration 1, the team completes 3 stories A, B and C having estimates of 7, 13 and 4 story points respectively. Hence the velocity of the team is 7 + 13 + 4 = 24.

In Iteration 2, the team completes 4 stories D, E, F and G having estimates of 3, 3, 6 and 12 story points respectively, achieving the velocity of 3 + 3 + 6 + 12 = 24.

Similar cases can be seen for the iterations 3, 4 and 5. The point to be noted here is that velocity does not depend on the actual number of stories done or on the duration of the iteration.

The above illustration is simplistic in the sense that velocity of the team does change over iterations. So the team should compute its velocity at the end of every iteration. Note that only stories that are *done* qualify to be counted as part of the team's velocity.

For example the following graph (Figure 6-25) plots the velocity of the team as it varies between 24, 30, 15, 35 and 24 during iterations 1 through 5.

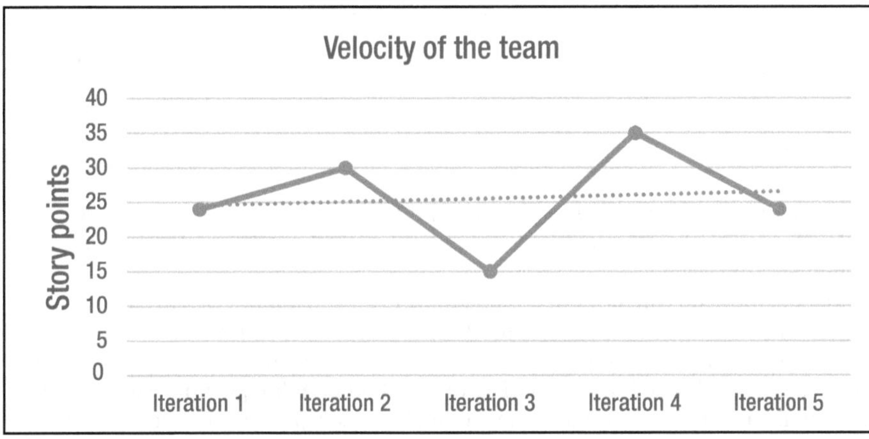

Figure 6-25. *Actual velocities of the team measured during iterations*

6.4.2 Computing Initial Velocity of the Team

Generally the most recent 3 iterations are considered to calculate the average velocity of a team.

However, let us consider the case of the first iteration, where the project team comes together for the very first time. The choice of velocity in such a case could be done in one of the following 3 ways:

1. **Based on historical data** - if the project is similar to a previous one based on technology, domain, environment and team composition, historical data could be used to forecast the velocity of the current team. However, to be on the safe side it is better to express the velocity in terms of a range rather than an absolute figure.

2. **By running a few iterations** - if it's possible to initiate a project, its best to run 2-3 iterations and predict the velocity based on the observed velocity of the team in motion.

3. **Deduce based on expert judgment or hypothesis** - in cases where historical data is absent or it is not feasible to run a few iterations, one has to resort to deducing velocity estimates based on expert judgment. This is often done by randomly selecting stories, splitting them into tasks, estimating them and slotting them into iterations. By summing up the story points that fit into this hypothetical iteration, it is possible to make a forecast for the team's velocity. And finally, as mentioned earlier, such estimates should be expressed in a range to cater for uncertainty in the figures.

6.4.3 Deciding Sprint Backlog based on Velocity

In a sprint planning meeting, the Product Owner brings in a list of product backlog items (called PBI's), which are prioritized based on business value. During the meeting the team and the product owner jointly work together to see that the most valuable items are implemented first, such that the team maximizes the return on investment (ROI) for the amount of effort spent.

Let us now look at an example how the team comes up with a sprint goal based on a target velocity of the team (say 24) and the sum of the story point estimates.

Scenario 1

Table 6-3. *User stories – their priorities and estimates*

Items from the backlog	PBI 1	PBI 2	PBI 3	PBI 4	PBI 5	PBI 6	PBI 7
Priority ranking	1	2	3	4	5	6	7
Story point estimate	13	8	3	2	1	5	8

The above Table 6-3 shows the *product backlog items* PBI 1 - PBI 7 arranged in order of priority based on business value. The team has also come up with the estimates for the relevant items as mentioned in the last row.

In this situation, the team will pick PBI 1, followed by PBI 2 and finally PBI 3 to be included in the sprint goal. The sum of the estimates for the 3 items are 24, which equals to the velocity of the team and means that the team has no further capacity to work on any other PBI. Note that in this case, the team did not choose PBI 4 and PBI 5 over PBI 3, since although more work items (in terms of count) could have been done, but the team simply stuck to priority order as specified by the product owner.

Scenario 2

Table 6-4. *User stories – their priorities and estimates*

Items from the backlog	PBI 1	PBI 2	PBI 3	PBI 4	PBI 5	PBI 6	PBI 7
Priority ranking	1	2	3	4	5	6	7
Story point estimate	13	8	8	2	1	5	8

In this scenario (Table 6-4), after choosing PBI 1 and PBI 2, team has a spare capacity of 3 (24 - 13 - 8). However, the highest priority item left PBI 3 is too large to be accommodated in the current sprint. In this case, the team could choose between two options:

- Explore if it's possible to further split PBI 3 into smaller chunks so that it could be accommodated.
- Skip PBI 3 and choose PBI 4, which is the item with the next highest priority. PBI 3 could be subject to reprioritization and chosen in a successive sprint.

Scenario 3

Table 6-5. *User stories – their priorities and estimates*

Items from the backlog	PBI 1	PBI 2	PBI 3	PBI 4	PBI 5	PBI 6	PBI 7
Priority ranking	1	2	3	4	5	6	7
Story point estimate	13	8	8	2	1	5	8

In this scenario (Table 6-5), let us ascertain how many sprints would be required to complete all the 7 PBI's.

The velocity of the team is 24 and the sum of the estimates for PBI 1 - PBI 7 is 13 + 8 + 8 + 2 + 1 + 5 + 8 = 45. So the number of sprints required = 45 / 24, which when rounded to the next highest integer is 2. The second sprint in this case will have some spare or unutilized capacity.

6.4.4 Ways to Improve Velocity

There are a few suggested ways by which teams can look to improve their velocity.

- Continuously focus on refactoring code, so as to remove all traces of technical debt. Any code that is not used has to be removed. A simple and flexible design and code is always easy to estimate and be worked upon.
- Motivate the people to give in their best, allow people to think instinctively and creatively. Allows teams to take credit and maintain a sense of accomplishment.
- Ensure team members are fully focused and they can keep distractions at bay.
- Engage with the customer and solicit his presence so as to clarify requirements, bounce ideas, or seek feedback often.
- Bring in more people to share the work, although that will have an increase in cost. There might be a short period to train and get the new joiner on-boarded, but over a period of time, his/her productivity will increase.

6.4.5 Schedule and Budget Estimation (Agile accounting) with the Help of Velocity

As we have seen before teams spend time estimating a project so that its duration and schedule can be planned. And often, projects are sanctioned by a sponsor on these parameters.

In traditional plan-driven projects, the high-level scope is decomposed into manageable parts in the form of a Work breakdown structure (WBS). On the basis of the WBS, resources (and skillsets required) are planned, duration estimates are prepared and task dependencies are chalked out. This helps to determine the overall schedule of the project, intermediate milestones and tasks on the critical path. Using the same estimation techniques, the project manager prepares a budget for the project accounting for the fixed and discretionary costs, as well as apportioning a fraction of the budget for mitigating risks and having a contingency plan in place.

In case of Agile projects it is done differently, as the entire project is implemented as a series of iterations. The steps involved are illustrated with the help of numbers:

Inputs

1. The project team starts off with a project backlog. The backlog is estimated using one of the techniques like Affinity estimation or Planning Poker (described in the earlier sections of this chapter). Let us assume that the aggregate estimate of all stories in the backlog at the beginning of the project comes to 240 story points.
2. The team agrees to a *definition of done*,which includes analysis, design, implementation, testing, build and deployment to the live environment.
3. The project team plans to deliver incremental value to business in iterations that are of 3-week duration.

4. The project team also computes its velocity as 24 story points per iteration (using one of the techniques described above).

5. The project team consists of 5 team members. Each member has a daily (labor) rate of$400. Let us assume that the team follows a 5-day work week, so the weekly expense behind labor will be $400 * 5 *5 = $10,000.

6. Also the project will incur a fixed cost of $15,000 to procure hardware, software and licenses for this project and another $5,000 for training and travel.

Computation steps

1. Since the backlog is of 240 story points and the velocity of the team is 24 story points per iteration, the team will take 240 / 24 = **10 iterations to complete the project**. The simplistic assumptions over here are that the backlog remains static, estimates are perfect, infrastructure is provisioned just-in-time and there are no dependencies on other projects or other teams and the team's velocity remains constant at 24. Neither of these assumptions may remain true in a real-world situation, but, again, this is an oversimplified scenario.

2. Given that each iteration is of 3-week length, the **total time to complete the project** (deliver all stories to production) is 10 * 3 = **30 weeks = 7 months (approx.).**

3. Now let us look at the cost aspect. The weekly spend behind labor is $10,000. Since an iteration is of 3 weeks, during each iteration, the team spends $10,000 *3 = $30,000. This is also called the *iteration burn rate.*

4. As we have derived that it will take 10 iterations to complete the project, **the total expense behind labor will be $30,000$ * 10 = $300,000**.

5. Now taking the fixed and travel costs into account, the **budget of the project** will come to labor costs + (fixed costs + other costs), that is, $300,000 + $15,000 + $5,000 = **$320,000$.**

6. Finally if the team might want to include an additional levy of 10% on the budget to factor in contingency amounts (to cover known risks), the total budget of the project will be **$320,000 * 1.1 = $352,000.**

One more observation from the above computation is that 240 story points are estimated to a total cost of $352,000. Hence the cost of each story point will be 352,000/240 = **$1467.** This can be used as a parameter to determine the ROI of a user story. For example the cost of a 15-point epic is $22,000 and it makes sense to implement only when the realized value exceeds this amount.

The above computation is fairly straightforward, but an important topic for the PMI-ACP® exam. So it is advised that you spend some time to reflect and absorb the key concepts and the computation. In real-world situations, there could be some variations that will impact the duration and budget estimates:

- Addition or removal of stories to the backlog in the middle of the project.
- Addition of *spike* tasks to mitigate risks when the team would like to experiment with an idea or approach.
- Replacing story points with ideal time as the unit of estimates. And expressing ideal day as a fraction (say 80%) of the person day.
- Depreciation of infrastructure costs.

6.4.6 Some Important notes about velocity

1. Velocity of 2 teams cannot be compared to each other. In other words, if Velocity of Team A is 20 and that of Team B is 30, it does not imply that Team B works harder or is more efficient than Team A. This is because velocity is based on story points and 2 teams do not share the common definition of a story point (the baseline story also varies from team to team).
2. Incomplete stories (i.e. the ones that have not met the *definition of done*) should not be considered when reporting progress on the basis of attained velocity. So, if in a sprint the team completes user stories worth 5, 7 and 2 points and partially completes 2 user stories worth 6 and 2 points respectively, the total velocity at the end of the iteration will be 5 + 7 + 2 = 14. Unfinished work represents sunk costs, with no tangible value to the customer as it could be pretty hard to deduce the amount of work or rework required to complete the story in a successive sprint. In such cases, one could split the story into smaller and more manageable chunks and allow the team to take partial credit or not take any credit at all (by making the unfinished part available for further reestimation and prioritization).
3. Velocity helps to iron out inaccuracies in the estimates. Even if the estimates are not accurate, by tracking the trend of actual velocity achieved over several iterations, the team gets better at their projections.
4. Velocity is not a measure of productivity. It should never be used as a yardstick to perform performance appraisals of the team members.
5. Since knowledge of velocity of a team is used for forecasting (e.g., how many iterations are required to complete a backlog of 'n' stories), the team should consider optimistic or best case (when velocity is fastest) and pessimistic or worst cases (when the team is at the lowest velocity). Distinction should be made between the projected velocity and the actual velocity achieved to evaluate the estimate to complete the project.
6. Velocity of teams are expected to increase over a period of time as the team matures, acquires more experience and control over the domain, technology and the customer needs. An experienced team gets used to work cohesively with each other, exploiting synergies and improving its way of working continually.

6.4.7 Significance of the velocity trend

Plotting of the actual velocity of the team gives a very powerful insight into the capacity and performance of the team.

- Ideally the trend line (shown as dotted line) should have an upward gradient, indicating that the team is working more efficiently over time. However, sharp increases might indicate problems in estimation of stories, the team is overachieving because of overtime, or the tracking of progress is not uniform.
- A dip in the velocity trend might indicate some problems like:
  - The team unearthed some complexity that was not anticipated during estimation.
  - There was attrition in the team or a new replacement has joined.
  - One or more team members were absent due to leaves or non-project activities like trainings and the planned work could not be accomplished.

- By looking at the velocity trend, the team can do a more realistic release planning. For example, the team in the above scenario can commit to a sprint backlog of
  - 24 story points for Iteration 6 in the most likely case by taking an average of last 3 sprints ((15 + 35 + 24)/3 = 24.67).
  - 21 story points in the pessimistic case by taking average of the last 3 worst sprints (15 + 24 + 24)/3 = 21).

6.5 Release Planning

We have seen earlier in the chapter that with each release the project team delivers working software to the customer that add values and brings benefits. Each release consists of an incremental and meaningful set of interrelated features that are developed over one or more iterations. While iterations are smaller in duration (like 1 to 4 weeks), releases typically have a longer horizon spanning 3 to 9 months.

The release plan is generally outlined by the product owner. He uses the release plan to provide visibility to all stakeholders by giving them what to be expected when. At a high level the product owner could base the release plan on a few circumstances prevailing in the project and its environment, like:

- Regulatory constraints that the product and the organization needs to comply with,
- Gaining competitive advantage in the market place,
- Contractual obligations to meet a particular milestone,
- Passing on benefits to the customer,
- Exploiting opportunities to test incremental versions of the product (e.g., beta testing of some features),
- Avoid losses or penalties for not delivering a predetermined scope at a particular time.

Let us take a close look at Figure 6-26 below that depicts a sample release plan. Conceptually a project can comprise of one or more releases (three in this case) and each release can have multiple iterations[28] (the number could vary for every release). The project starts off with a *Sprint zero* where most of the setup is done and before every release there is a hardening sprint where the software stability is ensured before being released to production. Every release ends with a review of the working software and a retrospective. It is also to be remembered that during iteration planning, the team maintains a close vigil on the overarching release plan and see that all items required in the release are completed during the iterations that go into a release.

[28]We are using the words sprints and iterations interchangeably here.

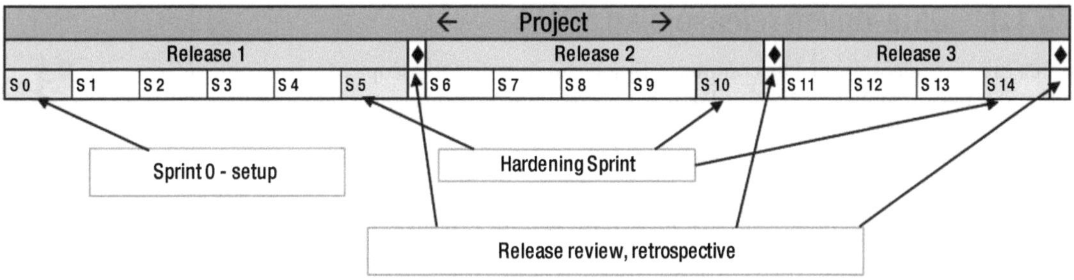

Figure 6-26. *Release planning*

As an example, let us consider the library management system.

In the first release the library user is expected to search a book by its name, author, or publisher and reserve it in his name. Also there are constraints on the number of books he can borrow at a time or the duration after which he must return the book or renew it further. The library user therefore expects to view his account and the current status by logging into the online portal with a registered user id and password.

In the second release, the library user expects to add himself to the waiting list, if the book he wishes to borrow is already in circulation. He should also be able to place a request for a book that is not there in the library so that the librarian can purchase it or borrow it from another library thathas it. He should also be able to access other types of media like electronic books, CD's, DVD's and other learning materials.

In the third and final release, the library user should be able to renew his membership by paying the fees online and also be able to pay fines, if any by the same way. The librarian also gets a few features to keep a tab of inventory and books in circulation.

The project progresses by working in iterations of 2 weeks during which multiple stories are prioritized, estimated, coded, tested and completed by the team. By the 12th week, the first release is ready with the committed scope and is delivered to production. In another 10 weeks, the second release is delivered and so on.

6.5.1 Types of release Planning

One of the common principles of Agile delivery is "Develop on Cadence, Release on Demand."This means that the project team continues to maintain a sustainable pace at converting user stories and themes into working software during every iteration, but delivers to the customer based on pull or demand. Release planning, as an activity, is driven by the product owner (as in Scrum) or onsite customer (as in XP) and mostly done at the start of the project. The outcome of this exercise is a release plan that helps to set expectations of what can technically be achieved by what time frame. The release plan, as we have seen in the earlier section, dovetails into the overall product roadmap and the strategic vision of the organization. Since a release also acts as a logical milestone, the sponsor can also apportion a budget for that particular release. It can be thought as buying a set of valuable feature and functionalities at a price.

The release plan is frequently updated throughout the lifetime of the project to keep it up to date with change in requirements, priority and velocity of the team.

There are two common approaches followed for creating a release plan.

6.5.1.1 Date-driven release plan

In this case the releases must be completed by a given date, but the scope of features included in that release is negotiable. The fixed date may be coming from project commitments or regulatory constraints.

The following are the steps by which the team arrives at the release scope:

1. The team starts off with a prioritized[29] backlog of stories and estimates them. At a release planning level a technique like Affinity estimation (described above) is well suited.
2. The team determines an estimated velocity (through one of the techniques mentioned in previous sections) and an iteration length.
3. Based on the release date, they determine the number of iterations that can be completed by the release date. So, if the release is 12 weeks away and the iteration length is 3 weeks, then only 12/3 = 4 iterations can be delivered.
4. The team finally computes the total estimate of the stories that can be delivered in that release by multiplying the estimated velocity with the number of iteration. For example if the projected velocity of the team is 100 story points in each iterations, the team commits to deliver 100 * 4 = 400 story points in 4 iterations.
5. So the team will choose the stories of highest priority from the backlog whose estimates add up to no more than 400 story points.

6.5.1.2 Functionality-driven release plan

In this case, the aggregate of features are predetermined to be delivered together, but the team progresses to deliver them as soon as possible. The set of features are chosen by the product owner based on user requirements or marketplace conditions.

The following are the steps by which the team arrives at the date for the release.

1. Like in the above case, the team starts off with a prioritized backlog of stories and estimates them.
2. The team determines an estimated velocity (let's say 100) and an iteration length (let's say 3 weeks).
3. The team aggregates the sum of estimates of all the stories that are to be included in a particular release. Let's say the sum comes to 600 story points.
4. Dividing the total estimate by the planned velocity, the team computes the number of iterations that the team will need to deliver the agreed scope. In this case the number of iterations will be 600 / 100 = 6.
5. With each iteration being 3 weeks in duration, the total time to complete the release will be 3 * 6 = 18 weeks.

Note that in both varieties, velocity is an important input to determine the scope of a date-driven release plan or date of a feature-driven release plan. As we have seen in the section on velocity, teams can have variable velocity over several iterations. So they should consider optimistic, pessimistic, or the most likely velocities to refine their release plan.

---

[29]Prioritization could be done by using MoSCoW technique as described in Chapter 3: Value-Driven Delivery. Prioritization could be done based on value, risk, or cost of doing it.

6.5.2 Story Maps, walking skeleton and minimally marketable features (MMF)

One of the ways to depict a release plan is through *story maps* as illustrated in the Figure 6-27 below. The figure consists of time in the X-axis and the criticality or optionality of a feature in the Y-axis. Reading this diagram row-wise, the first row depicts the *backbone* that is the group of stories that are must-have and have the highest priority. The next row is the '*walking skeleton*' that depicts a tiny implementation (bare bones) of the system that performs a small end-to-end functionality. The third row onward represents more 'flesh' or more sophisticated functionality that is optional and could be added to the future releases.

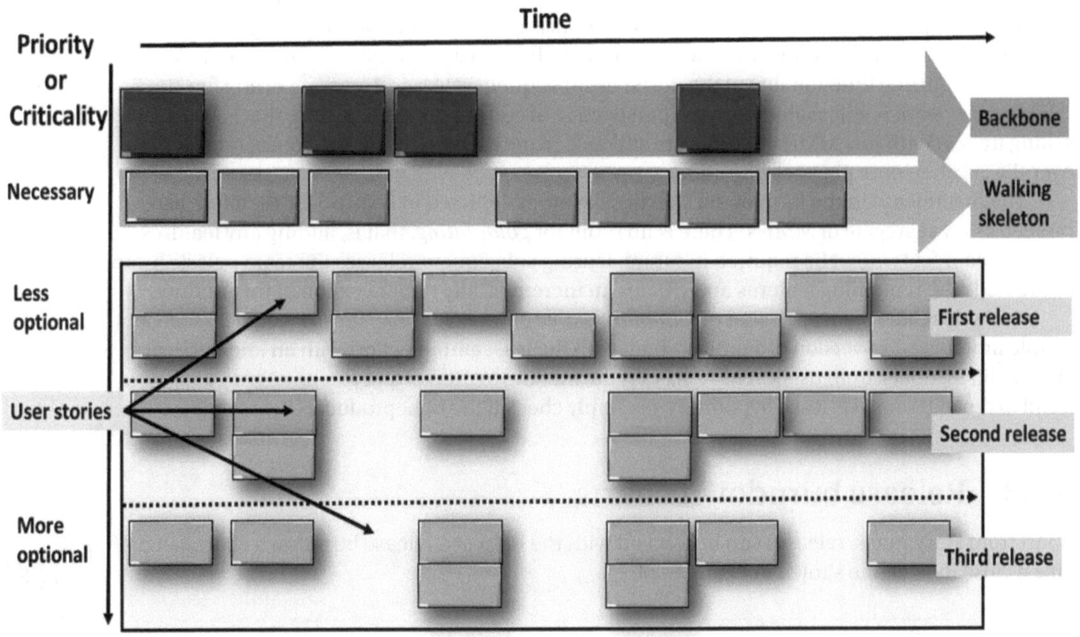

Figure 6-27. *Story maps and walking skeleton*

Each of these rows could conceptually represent a release that consists of a group of related stories to be implemented in priority order. The amount of time required is based on the story estimates, iteration length and the velocity of the team.

Let us look at the example of the library management system again. The walking skeleton could consist of a basic text box that captures user inputs and then on the press of a button triggers an action that performs a search and retrieve a count of search hits (not even the search results).

In later versions, the search results, their formatting, user authentication, search categories and a more sophisticated web page could be rendered. Note that even in the walking skeleton, the team should still use their agreed standards and best practices like checking in code into version control, build and integration and regression testing.

The advantage of the walking skeleton is that it proves that the design and architecture is working properly by linking the components together. The architecture can further evolve along with required functionality from future releases, so it is opened up for adaptation. By doing an early release, the team also experiences a winning moment, by getting something working very early in the project, albeit with minimal functionality.

In the above example, we saw how the walking skeleton represented a very simple, yet usable version of the sophisticated library management portal. This set of the smallest piece of functionality that is delivered and usable by the users is also called *Minimum Marketable Feature,* abbreviated as MMF. The word minimum signifies that a small fraction of effort and cost are spent to achieve the desired outcome. Often the minimal version of the product acts as a risk reduction technique by giving the user some idea about how the end product will look like or be used. The second word marketable refers to the fact that the customer does perceive value in the early version and be able to get some early return on investment of effort spent on building the same.

Let us look at another example to understand a MMF for a web portal to accept trades from a stock broker. The system is meant to replace paper-based transactions, which are difficult to maintain and prone to manual errors. In its initial release, the portal might give the user the ability to list the different trades and buy or sell them at a chosen price point. However, the site may not yet have the capability to produce management reports out of his /her portfolio, trigger email alerts when the prices moveor store user preferences. In this case, we can assume that the team defers the reporting functionality of the portal to subsequent releases. However, even after the first release the system is still usable from the perspective of conducting transaction, that is,buying or selling trades. With this MMF, the users are still able to derive benefits of electronics transactions over the cumbersome paper applications.

The first release in the form of the walking skeleton, depicted in Figure 6-27 therefore can be seen as an aggregate of MMF's. There is no room for *goldplating,* that is, adding any features that the team feels *might* be required in future. During subsequent releases the team invests more effort, adds the remaining features and creates an incrementally richer version of the product.

A closely related concept is that of *minimum viable product (MVP).*[30] A MVP could be seen as a simple prototype-like version of a product built with the least amount effort with an intent to learn and obtain feedback from users. A MVP has a reduced time to market and can be used to analyze a trend in the marketplace, test a hypothesis, or simply check if the right product is being built.

6.5.3 Release burndown charts

Apart from story maps, releases can be tracked with the help of a release burndown chart. Let us take a close look at one shown in Figure 6-28.

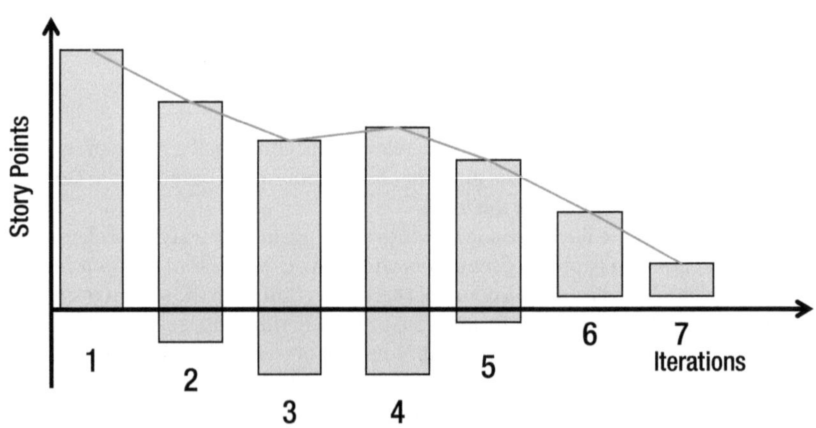

Figure 6-28. *Release burndown chart*

[30]The term MVP was coined by Frank Robinson and popularized by Steve Blank and Eric Ries.

Iteration 1: The development team starts the work for the release at a predefined velocity. The height of the bar graph indicates the total estimate (in units of story points) of the features and stories that are planned for the release.

Iteration 2: As work gets completed in iteration 2, we observe that top of the bar gets lowered. However, during the same timeframe, some work has got added to the release backlog and is depicted as the portion that is lowered below the X-axis. This could be as an effect of the product owner realizing that additional amount of work needs to be accommodated during the release as it will lead to significant business value.

Iteration 3: During iteration 3, the top of the bar is lowered again showing work continues to get done, but the gradient is lesser than the one in the previous iteration. This indicates that the velocity of the team has slowed down during this iteration. A reduction in the actual velocity is a perfectly acceptable scenario and could have happened naturally as a consequence of one or more of the possible reason as below:

- Some stories might have been underestimated and as the team understands the scenarios better, have increased the estimates of the pending work items.
- One or more team members were away because of illness or leaves and the planned amount of work could not be accomplished.

During the same iteration, the Product Owner again added some work to the backlog, resulting in further lowering of the bottom of the bar below the X-axis. Please note that at this time, it is quite possible that the amount of work pending for this release could even exceed the total amount planned at the beginning of Iteration 1.

Iteration 4: Work continued to get done in iteration 4, but visually we observe that some reestimates raised the top of the bar. No work was added, hence the bottom of the bar remained intact.

Iteration 5: During this iteration the team accomplished more work, resulting in lowering of the top of the bar. However, the Product Owner also removed some work (e.g., deprioritized from the release or deemed unnecessary), as depicted in the raised bottom of the bar. The point to note here is that the above diagram doesn't care or tells us which work was removed - the one that was initially planned or the one that was added later.

Iteration 6: During iteration 6, the top is lowered again implying that more work was completed. We also observe that the bottom of the bar is raised above the X-axis, which depicts a further amount of work that was removed by the Product Owner.

Iteration 7: No further work was added or removed, but the work remaining decreased consistently toward the end.

As the above illustration shows, the release burndown chart is a very powerful, yet simple means of tracking the progress of the project, demonstrating concepts of variations in velocity and dynamic addition, subtraction or reprioritization of work in the backlog.

For the purpose of the PMI-ACP® exam, one needs to remember the following four principles how the bar graph moves in the release burndown chart:

- When work is completed by the development team, the top of the bar is lowered.
- When work is reestimated, the top of the bar moves up or down based on whether the estimate is increased or decreased respectively.
- When new work is added by the product owner, the bottom is lowered below the X-axis.
- When work is removed by the product owner, the bottom is raised and can even be raised above the X-axis.

6.6 Focus areas for the exam

- ✓ Differences between concepts of predictive and adaptive planning.
- ✓ Concepts around Deming's PDCA cycle, progressive elaboration, rolling-wave planning.
- ✓ Levels of planning as depicted on the planning onion and how each levels are related.
- ✓ Concepts on just-in-time (JIT) planning, cone of uncertainty and estimate convergence graph.
- ✓ Concept of Timeboxing and how it avoids effects of Parkinson's Law and student syndrome.
- ✓ Considerations for choosing an iteration length and the initial velocity of a team.
- ✓ 3C's of User stories and best practices of user stories.
- ✓ Relation between Epics, Themes, features, stories and tasks.
- ✓ INVEST and SMART acronyms related to user stories.
- ✓ Innovation games in Agile.
- ✓ Units of Agile estimation like ideal time and story points.
- ✓ Agile estimation techniques using relative sizing, Affinity diagrams, Wideband Delphi and Planning Poker.
- ✓ Definition of velocity, how it is computed and how sprint planning is done with the knowledge of velocity.
- ✓ Scheduling, budgeting and Agile accounting with the help of velocity.
- ✓ Release planning in a date-driven or feature-driven manner.
- ✓ Concept of story maps, backbone, walking skeleton and MMF.

Quizzes

1. Your team committed to delivering 20story points this iteration, but it looks like you will only complete 14. You should:

   A. extend the iteration

   B. add more resources to the team

   C. complete 14 points and put rest back in the backlog

   D. adjust the iteration plan from 20 points down to 14

2. Which of the following collections of planning units is most typical for agile projects?

   A. a release plan containing multiple projects, each with multiple iterations

   B. a project plan containing multiple releases, each with multiple iterations

   C. a project plan containing multiple iterations, each with multiple releases

   D. a release plan containing multiple iterations, each with multiple releases

3. When converting size estimates to duration, remember to:

   A. ignore distractions and use ideal time

   B. divide the timebox capacity by the number of stories

   C. factor in distractions and use available time

   D. calculate the payback period for the estimated duration

4. While auditing your project, the PMO notices that project planning is incomplete as only the next couple of iterations have a plan. They raise a flag calling it a problem that needs to be addressed as soon as possible. As a Scrum Master of the team what would you do?

   A. explain the principles of progressive elaboration.

   B. create detailed iteration plans for the remainder of the project as instructed by the PMO.

   C. ignore them, since they clearly have no rights to be reviewing your project.

   D. ask the team what needs to be done to solve the problem.

5. Which of the following statements correctly describes Agile planning?

   A. plan at multiple levels and have managers create iteration plans.

   B. use appropriate estimate ranges and exclude diversions/outside work.

   C. plan at multiple levels and have team members create iteration plans.

   D. use fixed point estimates and base projections on completion rates.

6. Which of the following is NOT a characteristic of Agile estimation?

   A. team-based

   B. collaborative

   C. iterative

   D. fixed-point

7. When conducting an iteration planning meeting using a Scrum approach, which of the following statement is NOT true?

   A. the product owner is responsible for the priorities in the backlog items

   B. the team is responsible for the estimates

   C. the team breaks down user stories into tasks

   D. the Scrum Master selects the topic items off the backlog

8. You are leading a team with an average velocity of 85 points per iteration. Another team of the same size in your organization is working on a different project with similar complexity. The other team's velocity is averaging 125 points per month. Your team should:

   A. undertake affinity estimating to check their estimates

   B. work longer hours

   C. ignore the difference

   D. hire additional resources to increase the velocity

9. Estimates should be presented as ranges to

   A. allow for change requests

   B. keep the sponsors flexible

   C. allow for scope creep

   D. represent uncertainty in estimates

10. A team has an estimated velocity of 25 story points. There are stories with estimates 13, 5, 8, 5, 2, 3 and 21 present in the backlog. Which one should be picked for the iteration?

    A. Choose the largest story, that is, one with estimate 21 first to have the largest piece done upfront.

    B. Choose the smallest ones with estimates 2, 3, 5 and 5 first as there is a chance of getting more stories done quicker.

    C. Choose the ones that the Scrum Master recommends.

    D. Cannot say based on the given information as the business values of the stories and their priorities should be known first.

11. A team has an estimated velocity of 25 story points. The stories A,B,C,D,E,F,G,H has been sequenced in priority order and have estimates 13, 5, 8, 5, 2, 3 and 21. Which should be an appropriate strategy to pick stories for the iteration?

    A. Select stories A, B, D and E, skipping over C because it is too large.

    B. Select stories A, B and split C appropriately so as to fit in the iteration (along with any others if there is room).

    C. Estimates are not accurate. So start with stories A and B and then assess how much of the rest can be picked up.

    D. None of the above.

12. Your team is averaging 40story points per two-week iteration. They have 200 points worth of functionality left in user story backlog. How many weeks do you expect it will take until development is completed?

    A. 2.5

    B. 5

    C. 10

    D. 20

13. When using story points to estimate a project, which of the following statement is most accurate?

    A. the team owns the definition of what constitutes a story point

    B. there should be a company-wide standard definition of a story point

    C. the definition of a story point is refactored every iteration

    D. story points can be used for iteration planning but not release planning

14. On Agile projects, generally midcourse adjustments are:

    A. not necessary

    B. the exception

    C. the norm

    D. mandatory

15. When calculating final project costs, which of the following expressions best outlines the basic concept?

    A. Time + (Rate X other project costs)

    B. (Time X Rate) - other project costs

    C. Time X Rate X project duration

    D. (Time X Rate) + other project costs

16. Affinity estimating is the process of

    A. averaging the over and under-estimations

    B. checking the stories given the same size estimate are of equivalent magnitude

    C. checking that stories in the same functional areas are of equivalent magnitude

    D. estimating your favorite stories first

17. The term "progressive elaboration" means

    A. scope always keep growing

    B. plans are refined as more details emerge

    C. the development team progresses steadily

    D. the iteration size increases over time.

18. You are a full-time Scrum Master on an Agile team. A team member becomes ill in the middle of an iteration in which the team committed to deliver 25 story points. Which action is most appropriate?

    A. ask the remaining team members to work overtime to make up

    B. send the work home to the sick team member

    C. start development yourself

    D. deliver what you can within the sprint

19. A team consists of 5 members each with a weekly rate of $200. The team has a projected velocity of 40 story points in an iteration of 2 weeks. What is the cost of completing a story having size of 8 story points?

    A. $1000

    B. $400

    C. Cannot be computed as the availability of the team members (part time/full time or plannedleaves) are not specified

    D. None of the above

20. During a planning poker session, participants come up with estimates of 5, 8, 13, 38, 5 and 5 respectively during the first round for a particular story. What should the facilitator advise?

    A. Choose 5 as it has majority voting.

    B. Choose 8 as it came from the lead developer and he has profound experience.

    C. Understand the rationale behind the outlier (38) and then ask the team to play another round.

    D. Give up since the team is not able to make up their mind and reach consensus.

21. During estimation and sprint planning sessions, the team should bear in mind:

    A. Relative sizing of the stories

    B. Velocity of the team

    C. Definition of done for each story

    D. All of the above

22. The letter V in the INVEST acronym used to depict attributes of user stories stands for:

    A. Verifiable

    B. Viewable

    C. Valuable

    D. None of the above

23. A story that is too complex could be split. While splitting user stories, some broad guidelines include:

    A. Split based on cross-cutting concerns like logging, exception handling and security.

    B. Split based on 'slicing-the-cake' concept so that the user gets a slice of end-to-end functionality.

    C. Split based on mixed priorities within the complex story.

    D. All of the above.

24. Which of the following is NOT an innovation game?

    A. Prune the product tree

    B. Wideband Delphi

    C. Speedboat

    D. Remember the future

25. What does the Cone of Uncertainty depict?

    A. It is difficult to estimate at the beginning of the project and the estimate contains a high range of uncertainty.

    B. The estimate converges to a ±10% confidence level following detailed design.

    C. Both A and B.

    D. Neither A or B.

26. The 3C's for a story card stands for:

    A. Card, characteristics and conclusion

    B. Card, conversation and confirmation

    C. Card, concept and consumption

    D. Card, contact numbers and conversation

27. A Minimally Marketable feature (MMF) is:

    A. A feature that is valuable, essential and relatively small.

    B. A feature that can be sold and marketed.

    C. A feature that has a fairly high ROI.

    D. All of the above.

28. When doing triangulation, team members choose a reference point. This can be

    A. A story that is small and another one that is medium in size, such that a story can be compared to them.

    B. A story that is exactly 1 story point.

    C. A set of stories that has already been implemented in the previous project.

    D. A set of stories that has already been implemented in another department of the same organization.

29. Agile recommends Just-in-time (JIT) planning because:

    A. JIT planning eliminates waste incurred in up-front detailed project planning and keeps the plan up to date as change requests get approved.

    B. JIT planning means lesser amount of effort in planning.

    C. There is no role of a Project Manager to create a project plan in Agile.

    D. Agile coaches advise that JIT planning is helpful.

30. As far as hierarchy goes, list the below items from smallest to biggest:

    A. Theme, task, story, epic

    B. Task, story, epic

    C. Story, task, epic, feature

    D. Story, theme, epic

Answers

1. C - An iteration is timeboxed. Unfinished work is returned back to the backlog.
2. B - A project can have one or more releases and in each release there can be one or more iterations.
3. C - When converting size estimates to duration, we need to consider the availability of the resources. If a resource is available 50 percent, then task duration must be twice as long as if a resource is available full time.
4. A
5. C
6. D
7. D - Scrum Master's job is to facilitate the team and not to make plans or tell what items to be added in sprint/iteration. The rest all are correct statements.
8. C - Velocity is a team-specific metric.
9. D
10. D - The product owner and the team should choose the stories that give the highest ROI.
11. B
12. C - There is no indication of a team's availability or any distractions, therefore assuming straight calculation. Total iterations = estimates / velocity = 200/40 = 5. Total duration = 5 iterations X 2 weeks per iteration = 10 weeks.
13. A
14. C
15. D
16. B
17. B
18. D
19. B - In 2 weeks the total spent is $200 X 5 members X 2 = $2,000. Cost of 1 story point = 2000/40 = $50. Cost of 8 story points = $50X8 = $400.
20. C - It is common to see variability in estimates at the beginning of the estimation session, so it's advisable to play a few rounds for consensus to emerge.
21. D
22. C
23. D
24. B - Delphi is a group-consensus technique used for planning and estimation.
25. C
26. B
27. D
28. A
29. A
30. B

CHAPTER 7

Domain VI: Problem Detection and Resolution

"One thing is sure. We have to do something. We have to do the best we know how at the moment... If it doesn't turn out right, we can modify it as we go along."

— Franklin D. Roosevelt

Agile teams are self-organized. At the beginning of every iteration, they collectively commit to deliver a certain scope within the timebox based on their capacity. However, even with the best of intentions, surprises do crop up in projects. A characteristics of self-organization involves dealing with problems, identifying them proactively and responding appropriately by taking either preventive or corrective actions. In the two main sections of this chapter we look at two dimensions of problems - first, which are uncertain and called risks. The other one is about the methods that Agile teams use to assure quality of their incremental deliverables. For the latter, Agile teams use a bunch of metrics[1] to assess their progress, reflect periodically and adapt themselves according to the demands of the situation.

7.1 Risk management

In traditional project management, risk management is dealt separately in conjunction with the project plan. As per PMBOK®, risk management is a separate knowledge area that is pursued by project managers to protect the value of the project and maintain the balance between scope, time, cost, quality and customer satisfaction. Risks are traditionally identified, logged and tracked on a risk register and reported at periodic intervals.

While the theory of risk management is mostly the same in Agile projects, the important point is that risk management is a continuous activity in Agile project execution and receives a significant amount of focus during each of the ceremonies or events. Instead of a separate knowledge area, in Agile projects, the risk management aspects is well integrated with planning, prioritization and execution cycles. Agile projects, as we have seen in Chapter 3: Value-Driven Delivery, balances both value and risks. The culture of iterative delivery and frequent reflections in Agile projects not only help in identifying or detecting risks early, but also plan potential responses in the event of the risks happening well in advance. This is extremely helpful, as otherwise, the risks and issues get carried over to the later phases of the project (e.g., during a cumbersome integration or end-to-end testing stages) where the cost of change escalates exponentially.

[1]We will frequently refer to the section on Agile metrics in Chapter 3: Value-Driven Delivery.

S. Boral, *Ace the PMI-ACP® exam*, DOI 10.1007/978-1-4842-2526-4_7

So an Agile project not only maximizes value by implementing business functionality, but also looks to minimize risk to achieve the same outcome.

7.1.1 Risk definition

We begin with a very basic definition of risk. A **risk**[2] is defined as an uncertain event or condition that, if occurs, has an effect on at least one project objective (e.g., on scope, cost, duration, quality, or customer satisfaction). Although the definition encompasses both positive risks (that are called opportunities) and negative risks (that are called threats), let us for the current discussion concentrate on risks that have a negative outcome. If the functional features in the product backlog are expected to add value, risks do just the opposite, that is,they erode value. To prevent this from happening, teams spend a considerable amount of time identifying potential threats and their causes, analyze their impact, timing, frequency and probability and come up with actions to mitigate them or plan contingencies. All these actions do come up with a cost that needs to be factored as part of project planning.

Let us look at our running example on the library management system to see how risks are managed. As the system computerizes most of the workflows and eliminates paperwork, it is important for the system to invest behind backups for disaster recovery. The library stores electronic research papers on niche subjects and also processes financial transactions like collecting subscription fees and fines from borrowers and payment of invoices from the book sellers and publishers - all of which are subject to audit and hence should be retained for records for several months to years. From an initial investigation the project team determines that the probability of failure of the primary system could be around 15% and could cost the team about $20,000 to perform a recovery of critical data. As a risk mitigating action, while building the portal, the development team sets aside a portion of the project budget to procure infrastructure (redundant hardware like storage disks) and writes code that automates daily backup of transactional data to a safe archive from where future retrievals will be easily possible.

7.1.2 Risk identification

It is to be remembered that the **whole team** is accountable and responsible for risk identification and its management. This includes the development team, the Scrum Master, the sponsor, the onsite customer, the product owner, the subject-matter experts (like those who have historical context, relevant experience and domain expertise), the end users and so on. It is understandable that the product owner will be in a better position to identify the business risks, while the developers will look at technical risks. In the end all identified risks need to be collated, analyzed, tracked and managed.

There are a few dedicated ceremonies where risks are discussed explicitly:

1. **Iteration planning** - During iteration planning, estimation and prioritization, due consideration is given to risks. Items with high risk and high value are prioritized for early implementation. Those items that need proactive risk mitigation (e.g. by conducting a proof-of-concept or a spike) are prioritized along with the business features to be developed.Items thatare highrisk, but of low value are eliminated.

2. **Daily Scrum meeting** - Agile teams are self-empowered and in a spirit of transparency, they share their obstacles or potential issues in front of their peers. The Scrum Master who acts as a facilitator looks to resolve the impediments and helps the team to move on.

---

[2]This definition of risk comes from PMI®'s A Guide to the Project Management Body of Knowledge (PMBOK® Guide) – Fifth Edition.

3. **Iteration retrospective** - Retrospectives are used to perform risk audits. Seeing in the lens of risk management, the questions addressed by the team could be as follows:
   - What went well? ➤ Which risks were mitigated or closed?
   - What did not go well? ➤ Which risk recurred, or their severities were increased?
   - What could have been done differently? ➤ What are the risk responses (like mitigation, transfer or contingency actions) to be taken?

The following Table 7-1 shows some of the identified risks for the library management system. Observe that there are some additional data captured in the table - namely, the name of the risk raiser, a date, current status and a potential response to address the risk.

Table 7-1. *Identified risks and their potential responses (risk register)*

Risk id	Risk description	Raised on	Raised by	Status	Potential responses
1	UX designer not available to design the front end of the portal	June 10, 2016	Bill	Open	Look for a contracting option.
2	Dependency on vendor software to perform user authentication and authorization	June 10, 2016	Barry	Open	Consider open sourced version that does not require any vendor lock-in.
3	Library users are not accustomed to using a computer	June 11, 2016	Bill	Open	Plan for some training and awareness sessions.
4	Web portal registration is time consuming	June 18, 2016	Tom	Open	Reuse an existing domain if one exists.
5	License cost and lifetime maintenance cost of Websphere server is high	June 20, 2016	Barry	Open	Consider cheaper application server software.
6	Booksellers and publishers have their own systems to which interfacing is very complex	June 28, 2016	Tom	Open	Perform some due diligence on the technical requirements.
7	Existing hardware has reached end of life	July 5, 2016	Barry	Open	1) Consider an upgrade, need cost estimate. 2) Check feasibility of cloud-based solution (AWS / Azure).

(*continued*)

Table 7-1. *(continued)*

Risk id	Risk description	Raised on	Raised by	Status	Potential responses
8	Javascript and CSS skills are not available	July 15, 2016	Mary	Open	Conduct technical trainings and hire an experienced contractor. Do a couple of POC's to gain experience and confidence.
9	Integration challenges with student database on active directory	July 25, 2016	Mary	Open	Perform some due diligence on the technical requirements.
10	Attrition of a senior developer who looked after the software configuration	August 18, 2016	Barry	Open	Continue with the cross-training plan and look out for a replacement.

7.1.3 Risk analysis

Once the risks are identified, the Agile team goes about determining their characteristics. The main parameters that are of interest are the probability, impact, frequency and timing of the risk as mentioned above. But other factors like the source of the risk, any historical context attached to it and any trends are also equally relevant. In the following section, a couple of risk analysis techniques are described.

Attributes of risk

- ✓ Impact
- ✓ Probability
- ✓ Urgency
- ✓ Timing
- ✓ Frequency

7.1.3.1 Risk categorization

The team could choose to group risks based on their categories so that they can be owned by a dedicated entity or handled with a common set of routines. For example, a risk could be internal within the remit of the project team, or at an organization level (e.g., operational and systemic issues that involve multiple departments in a matrix) or completely external, which could have arisen out of macroeconomic, political, regulatory,or environmental conditions.

The acronym PESTLE is used to categorize risks as shown in Figure 7-1.

Figure 7-1. *PESTLE categorization of risk*

Another example of risk categorization is observed in banks and financial institutions. Commercial and investment banks have separate dedicated departments that are accountable to handle day-to-day operational risks (like manual errors in processing, security, or equipment malfunctioning), market risks (like movement of stock prices and foreign exchange rates that impact assets and liabilities) and credit default risks (like those for loans and mortgages).

7.1.3.2 Risk simulation

In order to understand the behavior of risks and their impact on the outcome of the project, Agile teams also use mathematical techniques like Monte Carlo simulations. This takes the application through a series of 'what-if-scenarios' to obtain a statistical view of the results. Details of this technique are not relevant from the PMI-ACP® exam point of view.

7.1.3.3 Probability impact matrix

As we begin to analyze the risks, the next important question is how do we quantify the risks and compare one with another? Without risk quantification, it is difficult to gauge the seriousness and urgency of the risk or what should be the course of remedial actions to address it.

Let us again refer to the two critical dimensions of risks:

1. **Probability** (likelihood of occurrence) - this is expressed as a fraction between 0 and 1, with 0 denoting not a possibility and 1 meaning absolute certainty.
2. **Impact** - which could be on several aspects of the project like schedule, budget, quality, complexity, motivation and customer satisfaction. Impact of a risk, for the ease of understanding, is often expressed in qualitative terms like very low, low, moderate, high and very high. In order to translate the actual measure of the impact to these qualitative terms, one can use a simple lookup table as follows:

Table 7-2. *Risk Impact assessment matrix*

Impact / Risk type	Very low	Low	Moderate	High	Very high
	0.05	0.1	0.25	0.5	0.75
Schedule risk	Negligible schedule deviation	1-5% schedule deviation	6-10% schedule deviation	10-20% schedule deviation	More than 20% schedule deviation
Cost risk	Negligible cost deviation	1-10% cost deviation	10-15% cost deviation	15-25% cost deviation	More than 25% cost deviation
Customer dissatisfaction	CSAT score of 9/10 or 10/10	CSAT score of 7/10 or 8/10	CSAT score of 5/10 or 6/10	CSAT score of 4/10	CSAT score below 4/10
Motivation level and team bonding	Minor disagreements that are self-resolved	Level 1, 2 conflicts that needs some intervention	Repeated escalations, level 3 conflicts that need periodic interventions	Level 4 conflicts and discord within the team	High levels of attrition, significant loss of productivity

In this lookup table (Table 7-2), based on project metrics on schedule, cost, customer dissatisfaction and employee motivation, risk impact is translated into a scale ranging from 0 to 1. So for example, if the cost deviation of a project is measured at 12%, (highlighted cell in the table above),it is considered a moderate risk to the project and assigned an impact score of 0.25. If the customer is dissatisfied and reflected in a customer satisfaction (CSAT) score of less than 4 out of 10, it is considered as a very high impact risk (resulting in loss of revenue, reputation etc.) and assigned animpact score of 0.75.

We will now go back to our list of risks related to our online library management system. The risks in Table 7-1 are analyzed to determine the probability and impact of each risk as shown in Table 7-3. Referring to the table we observe that Risk id #4, which refers to the time-consuming process of web portal registration, is analyzed to have a 25% probability and a high (0.5) impact.

Table 7-3. *Risk assessment or risk census - showing probability and impact for each risk*

Risk id	Risk description	Risk probability (0 - 1)	Risk impact (0 - 1)	Risk severity = probability x impact
1	UX designer not available to design the front end of the portal	0.8	0.5	0.4
2	Dependency on vendor software to perform user authentication and authorization	0.5	0.25	0.125
3	Library users are not accustomed to using a computer	0.8	0.75	0.6
4	Web portal registration is time consuming	0.25	0.5	0.125
5	License cost and lifetime maintenance cost of Websphere server is high	0.9	0.75	0.675
6	Booksellers and publishers have their own systems to which interfacing is very complex	0.25	0.1	0.025
7	Existing hardware has reached end of life	0.9	0.5	0.45
8	JavaScript and CSS skills are not available	0.8	0.5	0.4
9	Integration challenges with student database on active directory	0.6	0.25	0.15
10	Attrition of a senior developer who looked after the software configuration	0.5	0.25	0.125

Notice that the values in the last 3 columns of the table are measured at a particular date and time. As the project moves on, these values are subject to change. The optimistic expectation is that the cumulative risks will go down over time. We will come back to this shortly.

7.1.3.4 Risk quantification using EMV

Another related question is - how do we compare the risk to the business value of the features in the product backlog? The latter, as we know, is easier to compute from the expected revenuegenerated or the penalty if not implemented.

Agile teams use the concept of *Expected Monetary Value (EMV)* to obtain the value of the risk using the formula:

Risk severity or risk exposure or EMV = Risk Impact x Risk Probability

So in the above example of library management in section 1.1, the EMV or severity of the risk in losing data and requiring an expensive retrieval mechanism is \$20,000 X 15% = \$3000.

We can do the same computation for each and every risk that the team identifies. The one with the highest EMV is the most severe risk and could lead to serious consequences if not dealt with proactively and appropriately. The ones with the lowest EMV in the list are noncritical and could be simply put on the watch-list until they can be marked as closed. The ones in the middle of the list need to be tracked persistently by the team. Spend a bit of time reviewing how the EMV or risk severity (last column) is computed for each risk and entered in Table 7-3 above.

One pertinent remark - it is hard to determine the exact probability and impact of a risk. The data available about a risk needs to be reliable and accurate as the EMV calculation is based on it. Otherwise subjectivity could creep in. What is important, however, is a relative estimate and a dialogue within the team that justifies the numbers chosen. The ultimate goal is to obtain a consensus between participating stakeholders and being able to prioritize business requirements and risks consistently and uniformly.

7.1.4 Risk responses

The ultimate goal of risk management is to take proactive action to decrease the probability or impact of a risk. This is called a risk response strategy. The point to note here is that the risk response is highly dependent on the risk tolerance of the project team, stakeholders and the organization.

There are four prevalent risk response strategies, as seen in Figure 7-2.

Figure 7-2. *Risk response strategies*

7.1.4.1 Avoid

In this strategy the project is driven in a direction that deviates it from the risk and its impact. This removes the risk in its entirety. For example, for a project that is on the verge of missing its deadline, could follow a avoidstrategy by either extending the deadline or reducing the scope of the project.

7.1.4.2 Transfer

In this strategy the impact of the risk is shifted to a third party, often in lieu of a premium or fee charged by the third party in owning the liability of the risk. For example, outsourcing of work to a third-party service provider using a fixed price contract is a risk transference strategy. The delivery risks are shifted to the vendor, who in turn, retains a profit margin to cover for its risks and uncertainties.

7.1.4.3 Mitigate

In this strategy, the aim is to decrease the impact and / or the probability of the risk. As described in section 1.1, investment behind redundant storage disks and backup infrastructure is an example of risk mitigation strategy.

7.1.4.4 Accept

There could be cases where it is not possible to proactively respond to the risk in a feasible manner. In such a case, the risk is accepted - letting it happen, if it happens. However, the team can choose to allocate a contingency amount to it to cover the impact of the risk. In the extreme case where the contingency is not effective, the team could come up with a fallback plan.

7.1.5 Risk monitoring

As we alluded earlier, risk management is a continuous process. The whole team is continuously involved in risk identification, analysis, mitigation, contingency planning and monitoring. In the following section, we shall see a few ways in which Agile teams monitor the risks in their projects.

7.1.5.1 Spikes

One example of a risk mitigation strategy prevalent in XP is the use of ***spike*** tasks during an iteration. As we saw in Chapter 6: Adaptive Planning, spikes are used by Agile teams to conduct a brief experiment, test a hypothesis, perform option analysis and come to a conclusion. After the experiment, the learnings and findings remain, but the spike code itself could be useless and in most casesis thrown away.

As Figure 7-3 shows, the outcome of the spike helps the team to:

- mitigate risks with uncertain technologies or domain
- make better quality of estimates that can stand ground amid uncertainties
- check feasibility of architecture or design options
- help the team fail-fast. If the experiment is unsuccessful, it implies that the project that would have been based on the same assumption or solution would have failed as well, incurring wastage of time, effort and money. Based on the outcome of the risk-based spike, the project team thus becomes wise in choosing alternative options to invest resources.
- ascertain worthiness of the investment

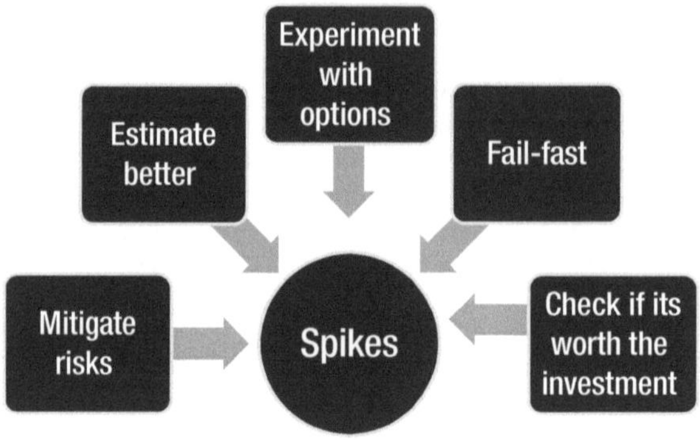

Figure 7-3. *Purpose of Spikes*

One of the special types of spikes is the architectural spike. They are generally conducted a few weeks before release planning (or maybe as part of sprint zero) to come up with solutions with the help of modeling and prototyping to analyze architectural options and their feasibilities. At the end of the spike, the team comes up with a reference architecture that encapsulates some rough knowledge about the system boundaries, its internal and external components, interfaces between them, constraints, dependencies, infrastructure, performance and capacity. Based on the architectural decision, the design decisions follow. If a design spike is required, they are conducted during the iterations themselves.

7.1.5.2 Checkpoints for frequent feedback

As Agile teams progress with iterative delivery, they conduct reviews during periodic checkpoints to keep a tab on risks, issues, problems, seek feedback from stakeholders and adapt accordingly. The checkpoints help the team to make decisions at the *last responsible moment.* This follows the inspect-and-adapt style of Agile and Deming's Plan-Do-Check-Act cycle that we have discussed earlier in Chapter 6: Adaptive Planning.

Let us take a quick look at some Agile ceremonies and how they are used as checkpoints.

- **Iteration planning meeting** - During this meeting the Product Owner initially takes the lead, brings in the risk-adjusted product backlog and tells the development team which are the most valuable features that should be implemented during that iteration. The team not only estimates the cost of implementation, but also shares any technical risks that need to be addressed during the sprint. By having a very open and transparent conversation between the team and the customer, the outcome of this meeting is a sprint goal that is a fair balance between value and risk.

- **Daily stand-up meeting** - Not only does this meeting provide a forum to do a dipstick check on what the team members are currently working on, but it helps to discover about their blockers. The Scrum Master, as in Scrum, makes a note of these impediments and helps the whole team to collectively resolve them and move ahead.

- **Iteration review meeting** - Remember that Agile teams follow the *fail-fast principle* - where if they have an idea, they perform a small experiment and either go with it or trash it if found to be infeasible, expensive, or lacking value. Rapid iterative development and short feedback loops helps to achieve this purpose. Iteration reviews are one of the most important checkpoints where the customers get to see what the team has achieved during the iteration and provide feedback. Since the customer is always close to the team, they have been involved in planning and clarifying requirements and their relative priorities on the way there are fewer chances that the team goes astray. Also, since the elapsed duration between commitment to a plan and delivery are never more than a few weeks (duration of the iteration), chances of a gross mismatch between the customers and the team are very low. During the review meeting, the team not only demonstrates what got done, but also what could not be accomplished because of problems on the way. The unfinished work is discarded and is moved back into the backlog for future prioritization. Any feedback, problems, technical risks, or issues encountered are registered at the end of the meeting.

- **Iteration retrospective meeting** - In this checkpoint meeting, the team reflects on the effectiveness of its processes and takes actions to improve them.
- **Backlog grooming** - Throughout the project the product owner grooms the backlog by maintaining the list of features, requirements and the risks in one prioritized list. During backlog grooming the product owner makes several decisions regarding change of scope or priorities. In some cases, the product owner may also think of removing features altogether or even scrapping the project because it is found to be of no value to the customer. Backlog grooming is, thus, a very important risk management checkpoint for Agile teams.

Referring back to the Agile Planning Onion that we saw in Chapter 6: Adaptive Planning, the following Figure 7-4 shows the different lengths of the frequent feedback cycles that Agile teams have. As we see, the feedback cycles ranges from monthly releases all the way down to continuous interaction between developers if they are following pair programming or working in a co-located manner.

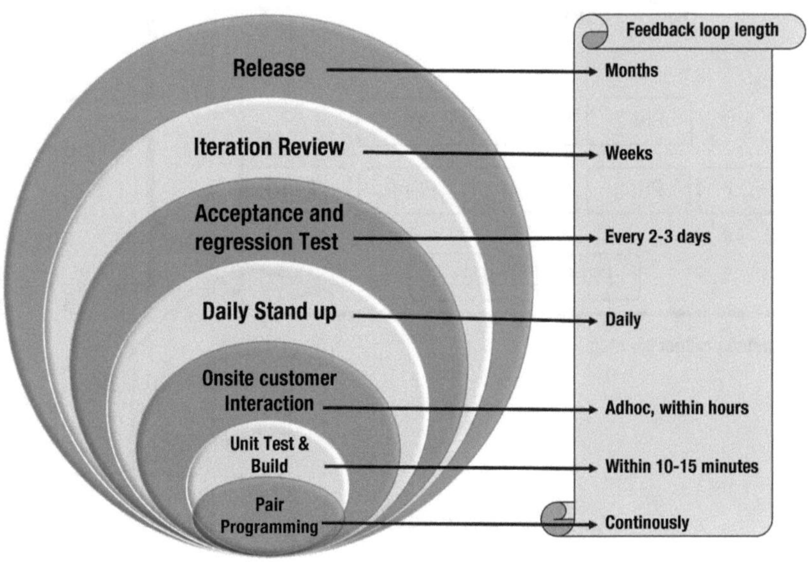

Figure 7-4. *Feedback loops and their durations in Agile teams*

7.1.5.3 Risk-adjusted backlog

Now how do the product owner and the team look at requirements and risks together?

In the last section, we saw the four risk response strategies. Implementation of these strategies could have varied degrees of complexities and could also give rise to secondary risks. All risk responses come with their own cost of implementation and that needs to be factored by the team. So just like features and requirements, addressing risks in a project also has to go through the same prioritization and planning process by considering its severity (EMV) and its cost of implementation. For this reason, the risk responses, sorted in order of their relative severities, are combined with the existing functional requirements on the product backlog. This combined list is called a *risk-adjusted backlog*. This artifact helps the Agile team to balance value and risk.

Let us look at an illustration in Figure 7-5.

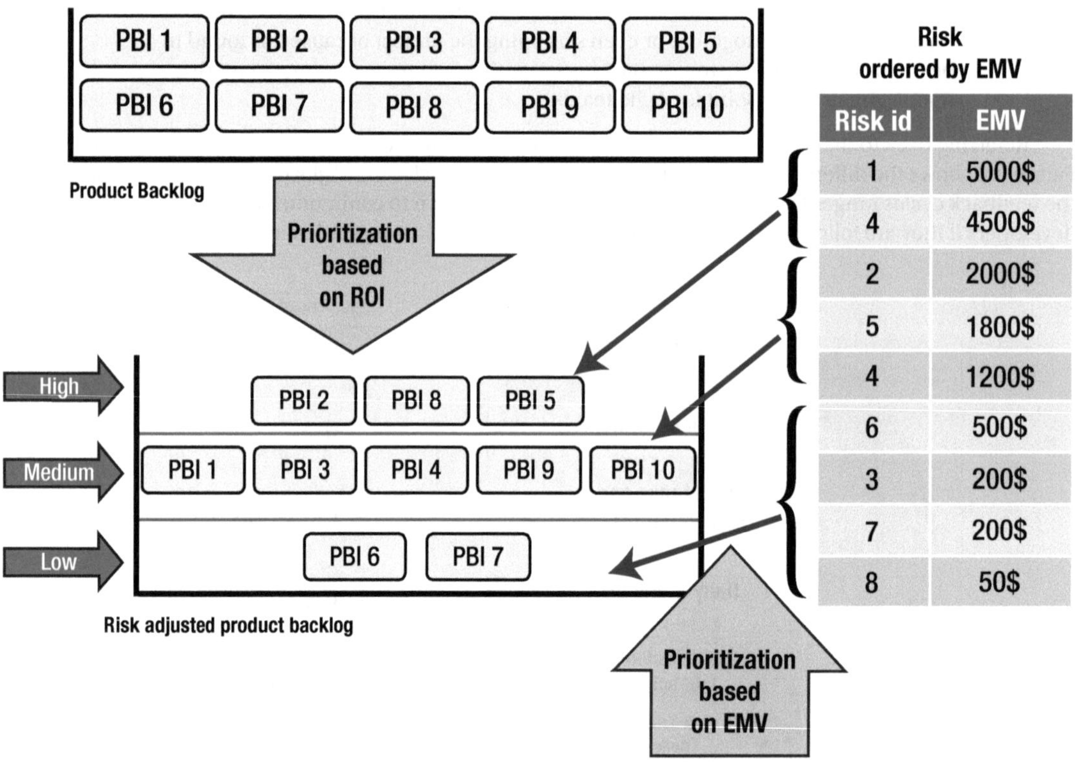

Figure 7-5. *A risk-adjusted product backlog*

A careful inspection of Figure 7-5 shows how risks have been factored during prioritization of a backlog. Let us see how this happens sequentially.

1. On the right hand side is the list of known risks that the team has identified.
2. The team has also qualitatively analyzed the risks to determine the probability and impact of each risk and multiplied them together to come up with the EMV (using the formula mentioned above).
3. The risks are then sorted with the one having the highest EMV appearing at the top of the list and the lowest one at the bottom.
4. They are then combined with the product backlog with the risks with the highest EMV appearing in the same bucket as the features or stories with the highest business value. This ensures that the risks with the highest severity are treated at far with the high-value features and are addressed early in the project.
5. The *risk-adjusted backlog* thus created gives the product owner and the development team one list to refer during planning such that a balance is maintained between meeting functional requirements and mitigating risks.

7.1.5.4 Risk burndown graphs

In Table 7-3, we saw how risk severity is calculated. However, this is based on values measured at a particular time. Probability and impact of a risk do not remain static. Also, new risks might crop up or an existing risk might be closed as it is deemed no longer relevant. During the lifecycle of the project, the parameter of risks is subject to change based on a number of factors. Accordingly, the EMV or severity of a risk is likely to change several times during the project. The general observation is that uncertainty and risks are highest in a project at the beginning and are expected to show a downward trend as the project progresses.

Let us refer to Table 7-4 and study the variation of probability, impact (and hence the severity) of the risksthrough iterations as encountered by the project team working on the Library Management System.

Table 7-4. *Progress of risk severity figures through 5 iterations*[3]

		Iteration 1			Iteration 2			Iteration 3			Iteration 4			Iteration 5		
Risk id	Risk description	P1	I1	S1= P1xI1	P2	I2	S2 = P2xI2	P3	I3	S3 = P3xI3	P4	I4	S4 = P4xI4	P5	I5	S5 = P5xI5
1	UX designer not available to design the front end of the portal	0.80	0.50	0.40	0.80	0.30	0.24	0.80	0.30	0.24	0.60	0.30	0.18	0.60	0.10	0.06
2	Dependency on vendor software to perform user authentication and authorization	0.50	0.25	0.13	0.25	0.25	0.06	0.25	0.00	0.00	0.25	0.00	0.00	0.25	0.00	0.00
3	Library users are not accustomed to using a computer	0.80	0.75	0.60	0.60	0.75	0.45	0.50	0.50	0.25	0.50	0.25	0.13	0.20	0.25	0.05
4	Web portal registration is time consuming	0.25	0.50	0.13	0.25	0.40	0.10	0.10	0.40	0.04	0.00	0.40	0.00	0.00	0.40	0.00
5	License cost and lifetime maintenance cost of Websphere server is high	0.90	0.75	0.68	0.90	0.60	0.54	0.50	0.40	0.20	0.50	0.40	0.20	0.20	0.40	0.08
6	Booksellers and publishers have their own systems to which interfacing is very complex	0.25	0.10	0.03	0.25	0.10	0.03	0.25	0.10	0.03	0.25	0.10	0.03	0.25	0.10	0.03
7	Existing hardware has reached end of life	0.00	0.00	0.00	0.90	0.25	0.23	0.50	0.25	0.13	0.25	0.25	0.06	0.00	0.25	0.00
8	Javascript and CSS skills are not available	0.00	0.00	0.00	0.50	0.20	0.10	0.40	0.20	0.08	0.20	0.20	0.04	0.10	0.10	0.01
9	Integration challenges with student database on active directory	0.00	0.00	0.00	0.50	0.20	0.10	0.50	0.20	0.10	0.40	0.20	0.08	0.20	0.20	0.04
10	Attrition of a senior developer who looked after the software configuration	0.00	0.00	0.00	0.00	0.00	0.00	1.00	0.60	0.60	1.00	0.30	0.30	1.00	0.10	0.10
	Cumulative risk severity			**1.95**			**1.84**			**1.66**			**1.01**			**0.37**

Let us concentrate on a few rows of the above table.

Risk #7 is about existing hardware reaching end of life. To address the risk, the team chose an *avoid* response strategy by migrating the software of the library management system to a cloud-based solution, which uses a pay-as-you-go model and the infrastructure components are maintained by the cloud service provider. The risk was identified in the second iteration, but with the provisioning of the cloud and the migration to it, the team was able to close out the risk completely during the fifth iteration.

In the second iteration, the team realized that they were lacking the necessary skills to develop the front end of the library management portal. To *mitigate* the risk #8, from then onward, the team members invested behind JavaScript and Cascading Style Sheet (CSS) training and capability building. Training, without hands-on application, is ineffective. So the team also conducted a *spike* where they developed a proof-of-concept and a small prototype of the front end (in an iteration). The outcome of the spike helped the team members gain confidence and also ascertain their level of knowledge on a technology that was once unfamiliar to them. By the end of the fourth iteration, the team members built enough expertise to complete the front-end tasks of the project and the risk was fully mitigated.

In the third iteration of the project, the team encountered the issue of losing capability of managing the software configuration as a resource had resigned and was on the verge of leaving. The team reacted to the risk #10 with a *transfer* strategy where they outsourced the work to a vendor. The vendor completed the transition before the resource left and carried on with the specialized work in the project.

---

[3]P1, P2, P3, etc., are the probabilities of a risk for Iteration 1, 2 and 3 respectively. I1, I2, I3, etc., are the quantified impact of the risks for Iteration 1, 2 and 3 respectively. And S1, S2, S3 etc., are the corresponding severities, which is computed as the product of the probability and impact.

The observation from Table 7-4 is that the cumulative risk of the project (depicted in the last row) shows a gradual declining trend from the first to the fifth iteration. This is a positive sign for the project health. In order to visualize the overall situation of the cumulative risks in a project, Agile teams use a *risk burndown graph*.

A *risk burndown graph* can be constructed easily using the stacked area graph feature of Microsoft Excel®. To do that, let us first transpose the risk data shown in Table 7-4 into the format shown in Table 7-5.

Table 7-5. *Iteration-wise progress of risk (data for the risk breakdown graph)*

Date	Severity of Risk 1	Severity of Risk 2	Severity of Risk 3	Severity of Risk 4	Severity of Risk 5	Severity of Risk 6	Severity of Risk 7	Severity of Risk 8	Severity of Risk 9	Severity of Risk 10	Total
Iteration 1	0.40	0.13	0.60	0.13	0.68	0.03	0.00	0.00	0.00	0.00	**1.95**
Iteration 2	0.24	0.06	0.45	0.10	0.54	0.03	0.23	0.10	0.10	0.00	**1.84**
Iteration 3	0.24	0.00	0.25	0.04	0.20	0.03	0.13	0.08	0.10	0.60	**1.66**
Iteration 4	0.18	0.00	0.13	0.00	0.20	0.03	0.06	0.04	0.08	0.30	**1.01**
Iteration 5	0.06	0.00	0.05	0.00	0.08	0.03	0.00	0.01	0.04	0.10	**0.37**

On converting this data to a stacked area graph, it looks like Figure 7-6 as follows.

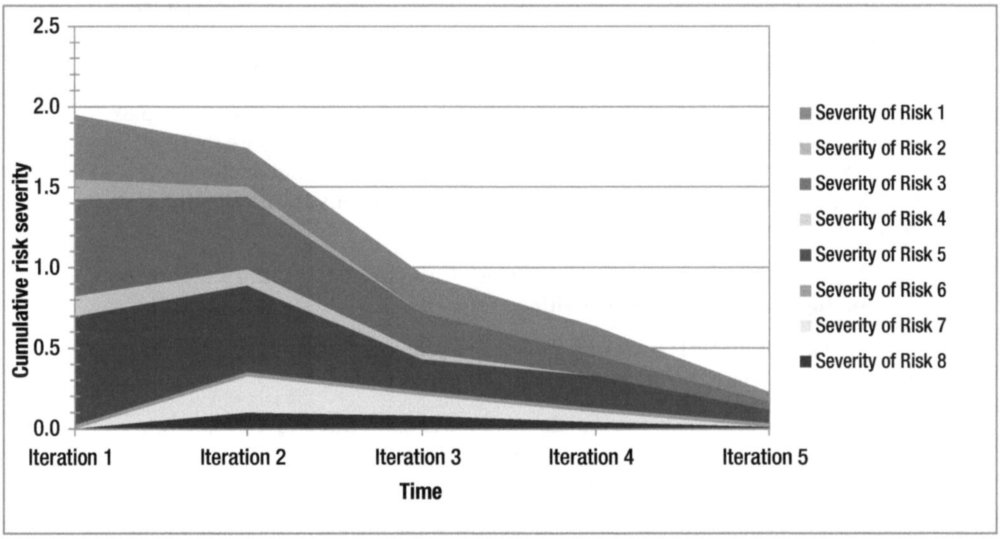

Figure 7-6. *Risk burndown graph*

Similar to a release burndown chart, the risk burndown chart shows how the cumulative risk severities of the project are progressing over time. Ideally the graph should show a downward trend as it is presumed that the amount of uncertainty or risk is maximum at the beginning of the project and starts to decrease as the project progresses over time. The reduction of the risk could be because of the risk response strategies undertaken by the team or the increased level of confidence they accumulate by performing several experiments or spikes. On the other hand, a rising graph should be worrisome and requires serious intervention and corrective measures.

The visualization of the current risk trend also serves as a pertinent information radiator and could be displayed on the team's walls.

7.2 Quality control practices in Agile

Throughout this book, we have seen how quality is embedded in all disciplines of Agile. It is well understood how the cost of defect removal increases exponentially if they happen to be detected late in the life cycle of the project. Not only does complexity increase because more and more code is built on top of the bug, but also fixing a defect needs a prolonged and complex regression cycle because the change impacts many systems, modules, components and data as well as stakeholders who are already using them. Agile teams are attentive to quality upfront and within their practices they embed the principles of prevention, early detection, containment and early resolution of problems and defects. Let us see how this happens in the following sections.

7.2.1 Embedding quality principles

Although we have seen some of these quality control measures scattered throughout the book, it makes sense to do a quick recap and summarization of the concepts centered on quality. Later on in rest of the section, we will cover some additional topics on TDD, BDD and ATDD.[4] Here are the following:

- **Incremental delivery**, as in Scrum or XP, is an opportunity to develop, test and deploy in small chunks. This exposes latent bugs early and avoids most of the onerous integration and testing requirements at the end of the project. One of the characteristics of incremental delivery is **simple emergent design.**
- **Iterative delivery,** as in Scrum or XP makes sure that teams frequently get their software tested and reviewed by the users, so that it can be iteratively modified based on the feedback. This is called **frequent validation and verification.**
- XP uses **small releases** that eliminate prolonged development cycle and complex testing cycles. By decreasing the sizes of the releases, XP teams ensure that working software is coded, version controlled, tested, built, integrated and deployed. With small timeboxed releases, it is important that the teams **automate their test regression suite.**
- Lean has a continuous focus on quality by using a **value stream map** and ruthlessly **eliminating non-value added activities.**
- Kanban teams **limit WIP and swarm** to resolve problems collectively, before they accept any new items of work.
- Agile teams, not only look after functional requirements, but they are equally mindful about **nonfunctional requirements** that contribute to performance, stability, resilience, scalability and usability of the system.
- Scrum teams collaborate with the product owner and the users to determine the **acceptance test cases** that validate whether the implementation conforms to the requirements. These test cases are documented at the back of story cards.
- Scrum teams come up with a **Definition of done** to determine when a story could be marked as completed. This includes all the aspects of quality to prove the product conforms to requirements and its fitness for use.
- Scrum teams have daily **stand-up meetings** during which they openly share their progress and the impediments. Some of these impediments could be related to quality practices.

[4]Hold on, we will come back to what these abbreviations mean later in this chapter.

- Feature-driven development (FDD) uses **code reviews** to ensure good quality of the code and prevent defects even before the code is executed.
- For distributed teams, it is generally a good practice to document **coding conventions** such that the whole team can comply with the same.
- XP teams perform **pair programming**, which is also a quality control measure. While one person is writing code, the other person reviews the code instantly, looks at the bigger picture and provides overall directions.
- Agile teams, especially in XP, has a strong emphasis on **test-driven development (TDD),** where the teams write test cases first and then write enough code to pass the tests. Details of TDD are described later in this chapter.
- XP teams continuously **refactor code** to remove technical debt. There are sophisticated software engineering tools and practices like SONAR® that can assess code quality (using SQALE®), detect technical debt, as well as provide indicative effort estimates to remove the violations from code.
- Agile teams use a variety of tools and smart engineering practices to maintain **version control repository** and perform **continuous build and integration** - most of which are in use continuously throughout the working day. We will see more on continuous integration in a later section of this chapter.
- Scrum teams have **retrospectives**, while XP teams have **reflection workshops** where they look to continuously improve their way of working at the end of every iteration. We will see more about this topic in Chapter 8.
- As seen in Chapter 3: Value-Driven Delivery, Agile teams could choose to use a bunch of **metrics** to track their delivery and focus on aspects of quality. Some examples of these metrics are cycle time and lead time (which helps to uncover some wasteful activities that do not add value to the customer and ought to be eliminated), escaped defects (which depicts the defects that leaked and propagated to the customer), number of test cases written vs. passed, number of failed builds, etc.
- **Team involvement and participation** in all ceremonies, events, or checkpoints like release planning, iteration planning, prioritization, estimation, review, risk identification, risk analysis and mitigation and problem solving helps to get diverse and well-rounded views and greater buy-in from the participants.

7.2.2 Test automation

The end-to-end integration testing activity that happens at the end of the development phase in traditional waterfall-based projects, often encounters plenty of problems. Either code does not integrate properly or expectations mismatch between the development team and the testing team or there are constraints around the availability of test data, environments and participating systems at the same time. This results in a lot of heartburn, rework and missed deliveries.

For quite some time, even before Agile practices actually demanded it, automation testing has been adopted, especially where the final integration or regression testing is required. An example of a popular automation tool is Quick Test Professional, more popularly known by its abbreviation QTP. But still there are some well-known challenges with testing late in the development cycle:

- It's quite difficult to trace the origin of the defects since lot of code is now built on top of it.
- The defect could have propagated from one lifecycle stage to another, compounding the complexity and the cost of removal.
- The defect might be hard to simulate in lower environments, if the environment (code + data + configuration) is not identical or the problem surfaces in a sporadic nature.
- Environments may not be available for the lengthy process of testing + defect fixing + retesting. In some extreme cases where project teams share infrastructure on which test environments are built, one project might be starved (and get delayed) because the environment might be blocked or reserved by another project, which itself might be delayed. This creates a domino effect, often impacting the end customer.
- Since the duration to complete testing and defect fixing is often constrained by the project schedule, the project team members might have to make short-term decisions to provide a tactical fix or workaround. More than often, these tactical decisions lead to technical debt in the software produced.
- Often the defect needs to be triaged, simulated, located and fixed only by the developer who coded it and he or she might be busy elsewhere.
- Although serving the same project, development and test teams could still be working in silos and contesting with each other.
- The testing team always have to 'catch-up' with maintaining the automation test suite, otherwise it will become very brittle and of little value.

7.2.2.1 Why automate?

Because of the nature of iterative and incremental delivery, Agile and devops practices necessitate a fairly high level of automation in testing, build and integration practices. Without this, the team will not be able to produce a working piece of software at the end of every iteration. Agile teams contain the defect propagation by making sure that sufficient testing is conducted during every sprint, such that, not only the cost of addressing the defect is low, but the user also accepts the software increment at the end of the sprint. Also, with a cross-functional team, there are really no silos between the development and test teams. The tester would have to learn to write scripts and stubs to test, the developer would need to write unit test cases before they write code (as in TDD). This calls for enhancing of competencies within the team. Of course, even with the best intentions, some elements of testing like that of legacy code or code encapsulated within vendor products may not be effectively automated.

7.2.2.2 Where to automate?

As Agile teams look for automating test cases, here are broad guidelines that take precedencewhile deciding where to target efforts to automate:

- Automate the red routes[5] viz. modules or components that are going to be heavily used or encounters heavy volumes (e.g., month-end processing).
- Automate the ones that need to be concurrently tested (e.g., simulating multiple users concurrently).
- Automate the scenarios or cases that are very critical to the business and have low tolerance to failure (e.g., if a particular component goes down, the whole application will become unavailable and maybe there are financial repercussions).
- Automate the 'high-touch' areas, which need to be coded and tested repeatedly, often with the same test cases and same input test data.
- Automate the areas that would need to be tested under multiple (and almost similar) environments (e.g., testing the same UI on multiple browsers, testing the same UI on different hand-held devices, testing the mobile application on multiple operating systems like Android, iOS, etc.)
- Automate nonfunctional testing that typically deals with heavy volumes (as in endurance and performance tests) and long testing cycles (as in longevity testing).
- Automate the areas that are expected to have a long shelflife, if that information can be gathered.
- Automate creation, use and destruction of test environments that use virtualized environments or the cloud.

7.2.2.3 What levels to automate?

Automation testing can be done at various levels, as shown in Figure 7-7.

[5]Analogy with the routes marked in red in London to alleviate congestion problems. Refer to `https://tfl.gov.uk/modes/driving/red-routes` if you are interested in knowing more.

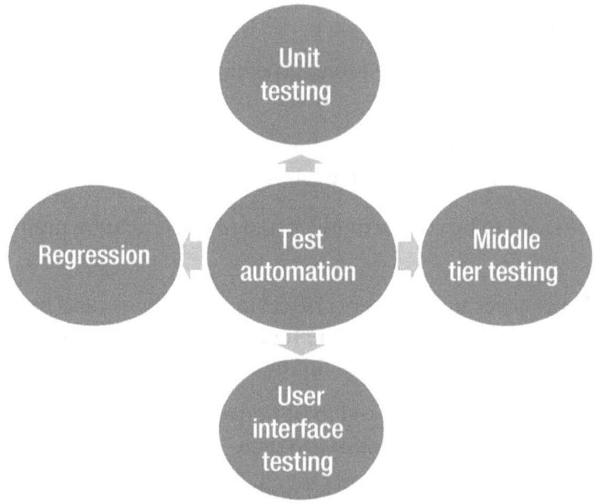

***Figure** 7-7. Automation testing at different levels*

- **Unit testing** - this is the foundation level, where most of the test cases should reside and act as a base for the rest. Developers can write automated unit test cases using frameworks like Junit (for Java) and Nunit (for C# and .NET). Automated unit tests appeal to the developer since they are written in the same programming language and almost pinpoints the location of the defect in the code. Often these unit tests can be integrated with the build agent, such that whenever code is checked in, the automated build is triggered and after compilation and generation of the runtime executable these test cases are automatically executed. If the test cases fail (e.g., failure of the assert statements in the junits), the developers are notified.
- **Middle tier testing** - developer can test business logic and middle tier code like components, web services (as in Service Oriented Architecture) using tools like Cucumber and Fitnesse.[6]
- **Front end or user interface testing** - this is supposedly the hardest part to automate (and not encouraged, especially early in the project), as the user interface is subject to frequent changes. Keeping the UI automation test suite up to date could pose as a considerable challenge to the testing team, irrespective of the tool used. Developers can use tools which record and playback user interaction with an UI. The test scripts binds with uniquely identifiable user interface elements and are able to take actions like data entry, button clicks, scrolling, etc., just like a real user. Examples of popular tools that are in use include Jasmine,[7]Selenium, Loadrunner and JMeter.
- **Regression testing** - the aim of a regression suite is to make sure that not only the features added in the current iteration work, but also the existing ones continue to function as expected. Note that some aspects of programming (like database testing) cannot be effectively regressed and there is not enough tooling for the same. So, if not 100%, then we should automate regression testing as much as practically possible. The lesser is the manual intervention in regression testing lesser is the overhead of iterating.

[6]Refer to `http://www.fitnesse.org/`

[7]Refer to `http://jasmine.github.io/` and `http://www.seleniumhq.org/`

7.2.3 Exploratory testing

Given that iterations are timeboxed for 2–4 weeks, Agile teams hardly get sufficient time to perform elaborate test strategy, planning, design, scripting and execution beyond what they achieve during test automation (as we saw in the previous section). To compensate, they use a combination of automation testing and *exploratory testing*. *Exploratory testing* is an approach in which testers perform minimum test planning and maximum test execution simultaneously while they also continuously learn the domain and the evolving product characteristics. Instead of following a rigid and predefined test plan or test script, exploratory testers leverage their tacit knowledge, imagination and freedom to focus on high risk areas, new and existing features to discover latent issues that could possibly impact the product adversely.

Exploratory testers start with a test charter that contains a short declaration of the scope that will be under test for an hour or so and the approaches to be used during the same. Although exploratory testing can be done at any time during the development lifecycle, the assumption here is that the system is functioning and stable in the test environment on which the testing will be done. Otherwise the team might end up spending too much time to bring up the application to test (with the latest version of the code).

Going back to our library management system example, exploratory testers could probe the system behavior with a set of leading questions. These may not be explicitly states as functional requirements or user stories, but are sort of implicit and unstated expectation from the user. Some sample questions are:

- What would happen if the book borrower accidentally presses the 'backspace' button when she is just about to reserve the book?
- Will the search results showing the list of books disappear if the refresh button is pressed on the browser?
- What will happen if the borrower logs in from the computer as well as from a hand-held device simultaneously?
- How will the portal behave if the (noncritical) component that interfaces with the service returning the best-selling books (that are advertised by the publishers) do not work?
- How will the librarian be able to report lost and damaged books?

As these tests are executed, the results - at least the failures are noted and reported. Often a failed scenario could actually instigate the exploratory testers to probe further and run some variations of the test previously conducted by tweaking the input data, input conditions, scenarios and test steps. This happens in realtime and could, in turn, lead to discovery of related problems very quickly.

As described above, exploratory testing does not really replace 'scripted' testing, which is valuable. The real application of exploratory testing is in complex situations where a black-box approach is required or it is targeted to a product that is relatively unknown and it is quite difficult to identify and document a whole suite of test cases in advance. With very little advance preparations, the results could indeed be quite rewarding.

7.2.4 Usability testing

Usability testing is a type of exploratory testing and is generally applied to testing the user interface of the software. This testing could be orchestrated by a group of UX designers who want to obtain insights into how the users will be interacting with the system on a regularbasis, although with a conscious emphasis on features and functions that are accessed most of the times or considered valuable. A usability testing session could typically be conducted by inviting one or more of the user representatives in the room and asking them to 'play'with the system. The session could be recorded by the team member who is hosting the session. He / she could probe the user with leading questions and capture the areas where the user appears to be struggling to do their tasks.

The following is an indicative list of what could be checked out during usability testing:

- Whether the design is simple, aesthetic and intuitive.
- Whether the system is responsive and providing feedback of its status when applicable (like an hourglass showing that processing in going on).
- Whether the system is helping the user with tooltips, prompts, contextual help (prefilled textboxes) and online documentation.
- Whether the system maintains parity and consistency in the usage of language in the real world and that in the system.
- Whether the system gives freedom to the user - like following different paths to do the job, pausing and remembering or backtracking.
- Whether the system prevents errors by highlighting and detecting errorsthrough diagnostic messages and recoverywithout a lot of rework.
- Whether the system in flexible and usable by a wide user community who can vary in experience or sophistication.

7.2.5 Shift-left testing

We are now living in an era of rapid volatility in the marketplace that requires software to keep pace with disruptive trends in social media, cloud computing, big data technologies and mobile computing. In this environment the traditional approach of testing, which focuses on processes, methodologies, specialized testing skills and rigid infrastructure are fast becoming a thing of the past. Organizations and teams that are adopting Agile have now shifted their focus to early and regular delivery of value to the customer with the help of tools and practices that give a combination of speed and flexibility. As a result we see that industry-wide best practices are getting rewritten, the status quo is getting challenged and people are harnessing novel ways to deliver value.

One such radical thinking is *shift-left testing*. In traditional projects, end-to-end and integration testing mostly consists of testing scenarios by providing inputs from the GUI. This is shown as an ice-cream cone[8] in the left-hand side of Figure 7-8. There is very little focus on unit testing, as the bulk of the testing action was deferred to the later phase of the project. Consider

[8]The phrase ice-cream cone in this context was used by Martin Fowler. Refer to `http://martinfowler.com/bliki/TestPyramid.html`

an example of a defect that has its origin in the design phase, but does not get detected and addressed until at the end of coding or during the middle of the testing cycle. In contrast, in shift-left testing, which is a *devops* practice, the emphasis is more towardcontinuous unit testing.

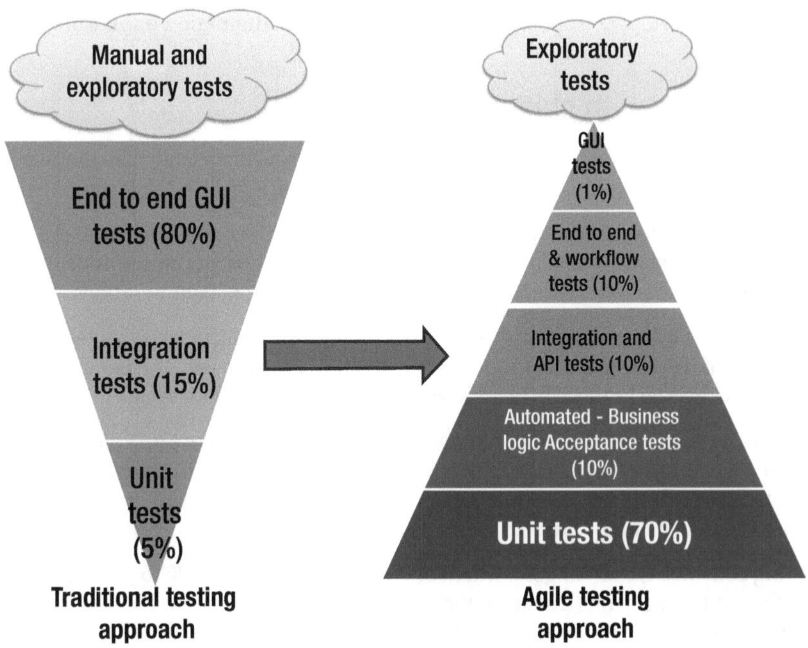

Figure 7-8. *Shift-left testing and comparison between traditional and Agile approaches*

7.2.5.1 What changes with shift-left testing?

Here is a brief synopsis of what happens during shift-left testing:

- A lot more emphasis goes into unit testing and component testing. Notice in Figure 7-8 that unit testing now occupies 70% of the effort compared to 5% earlier in a traditional approach.
- Notice that since unit test cases have such a wide coverage, the higher level tests can afford to be lighter as the different scenarios have already been covered at the base level. If an integration test case failed, it might be because a unit test case was missed. So to address the failed case, the code has to be fixed *and* one or more unit test cases need to be added.
- Testing activities are performed in parallel to development activities. Testers who were otherwise idle and waiting for the developers to deploy code, are more engaged upfront in the project.
- The focus changes from detecting defect to preventing defects.

- With developers and testing teams working together to plan, prioritize, estimate and execute together a lot more convergence of ideas is achieved. Shift-left testing concept is effectively augmented by other concepts of test automation and test-driven development (TDD) that we discuss later.
- Testers and developers work together to create the test automation framework.

7.2.5.2 Advantages with shift-left testing

Shift-left testing is becoming increasing popular, not just among Agile teams, but also the rest of the software industry is catching up to it. Let us look at some of the several benefits of shift-left testing:

- Developers tend to get periodic feedback of their code faster with respect to the customer expectations. This in turn reduces risk and the cost of change as defects are identified earlier and they are prevented from propagating to later iterations.
- As production release dates approach, fewer integration defects are expected. With reduction of risk, the stability of code on production is improved. The benefits continue to accrue as this can be used over the entire product lifecycle.
- The silos between the development team and the testing team break. Roles are no longer specialized - they become cross-functional. Developers are expected to write Junit test cases during the iteration, testers are expected to write test scripts and code, technical business analysts can take part in business or acceptance testing.
- Testing activities are no longer bottlenecks to deliver finished code to production. Neither are testing teams under undue pressure to somehow complete testing haphazardly as the deadline approaches. With the product being under testing oversight for a longer time, the overall quality of the product is expected to be better.
- Test environments are utilized better and continuously.
- Just like continuous build and integration, shift-left testing acts as an enabler for continuous delivery and helps Agile teams scale.
- Openness, transparency, trust and cohesion within the team build up. In fact with developers joining hands with testers, the total available capacity of the team to conduct testing activities is also enhanced.

7.2.6 Test-Driven Development (TDD)

Test-Driven Development, abbreviated as TDD, is a technique where developers write tests before they write code for new features. The code is changed to make the tests pass and subsequently is refactored to meet the functional and nonfunctional requirements. This sequence of steps is repeated until all test cases for all features pass and can be marked as successfully completed.

7.2.6.1 Steps in TDD

In Figure 7-9, we get to see the steps involved in TDD. The steps are also known as 'Red, Green, Refactor' or 'Red, Green, Clean' as shown above.

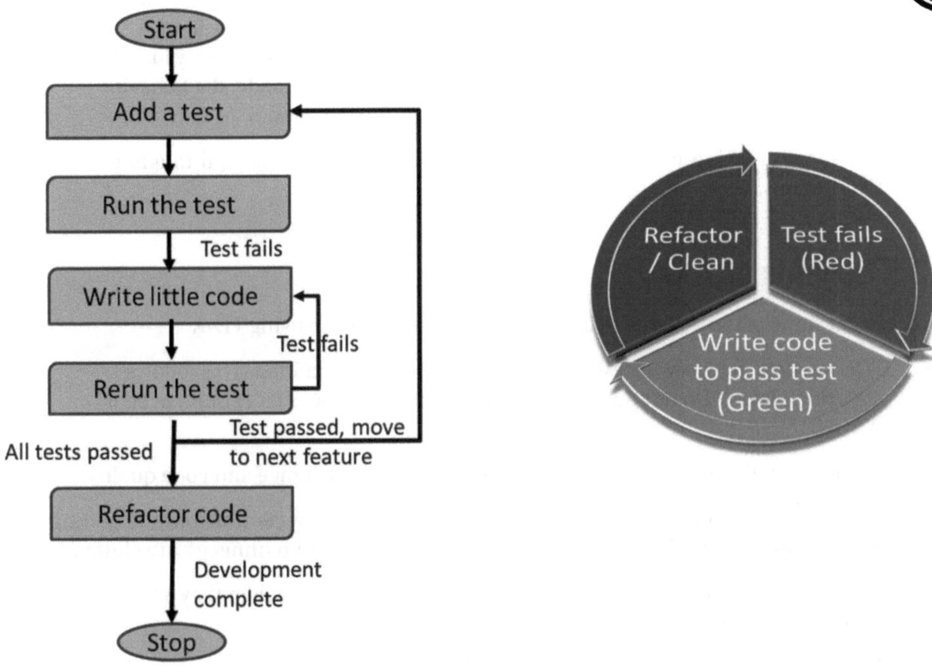

Figure 7-9. *Steps in Test-Driven Development*[9]

The steps are as follows:

1. The first step is to understand the requirements, feature, or the user story and write a corresponding test for it. The test case could be like a Junit or Nunit depending on the programming language used.
2. The second step is to run the test case, which will obviously fail, because there is no valid code to execute. This is the *red* step.[10]
3. In the next step, stubs of code are written that successfully compiles and can be invoked by the test case. At this stage if the test is run, it should call the code stub, but still fail because it lacks of functionality.
4. In this stage, sufficient code is now written that makes the test case pass. One can hard-code return values, use constants, mocked-up objects and any other means to satisfy the test condition. This is the beginning of the *green* step.

---

[9]This figure is adapted from the original one by Scott Ambler.
[10]The analogy is the red-colored alert that shows up on failed Junits. Ditto for the green color when Junits pass.

5. During the next stage, the developer keeps adding code to address the functional and nonfunctional requirements, making sure that the linked tests continue to pass. If there are more features to be added, new test cases have to be written first and the process repeats itself.

6. In the *refactor or clean* stage, the code is updated to address any code quality issues, simplification of design, eliminate technical debt, removeany hard-coding, duplication, unused parameters, methods, classes, unnecessary log statements, etc. Note that while these technical changes are made, the behavior of the code is kept intact and the tests should continue to pass.

7. The above cycle is repeated for each story, feature and functionality throughout all iterations.

7.2.6.2 Benefits of TDD

Let us now look at some of the benefits that Agile developers reap from using TDD.

- TDD ensures that only necessary and sufficient code gets added. This follows the principles of "Do not Repeat yourself" (DRY) and "You aren't gonna need it" (YAGNI).[11]
- If followed religiously, TDD could result in better code coverage and code quality.
- Since the success criteria aredefined upfront, developers concentrate only on getting the test case to pass. This keeps the code simple and free from unnecessary clutter.
- A team following TDD naturally makes sure that user stories, when they are created, are testable (T in the INVEST acronym).
- The unit test cases are written in the same programming language and stored on the same version control repository where code is checked in - so the developers are not only familiar with it, but also own it. There is no need to maintain separate test case documentation elsewhere.
- With refactoring, there is a continuous focus to contain and remove technical debt, thereby making the code easier to maintain, make changes and understandable by the team.
- The suite of tests can be run over and over again (many times a day) to prove that the software continues to work irrespective of adding newer functionalities.
- The use of TDD shortens the feedback cycle, as once the code is written, built and executed, the test results are immediately ready in a matter of minutes. This supports the concept of frequent validation and verification.

[11]Refer to the discussion about the core value of Simplicity in XP in Chapter 2: Agile Methodologies.

- The successful outcome of TDD contributes to the 'definition of done'.

  While we have discussed the benefits of TDD, there are a few words of caution. First, if the same developer who writes the tests also writes the code to pass it, it is pretty much left to the imagination and level of interpretation of thatdeveloper. So if the understanding is not aligned properly, a passed test case could give rise to a false sense of security and there could be far-reaching negative consequences. Second, not all code like that behind user interfaces can be reliably and efficiently unit tested. Teams will have to complement TDD with other forms of testing like exploratory testing to achieve the end purpose. Third, maintaining a test suite over the life cycle of the project is essential and should be a key consideration that the team will have to factor during their planning and estimation exercises.

Finally, before finishing this topic, we should introduce another closely related term called *Test First Development (TFD)*. This is basically the same as TDD, but minus the refactoring step.

7.2.7 Acceptance-driven development (ATDD)

ATDD is similar to TDD as it is based on the same concept of producing tests before code. However, the focus now widens from the code to the business requirements. The ultimate goal of ATDD is to write better stories, come up with the acceptance criteria before coding starts and deliver functionality that passes the criteria.ATDD, which happens at the business level, is well integrated with TDD, which is at a developer level.

The following Figure 7-10 shows the 4 stages of ATDD.[12]

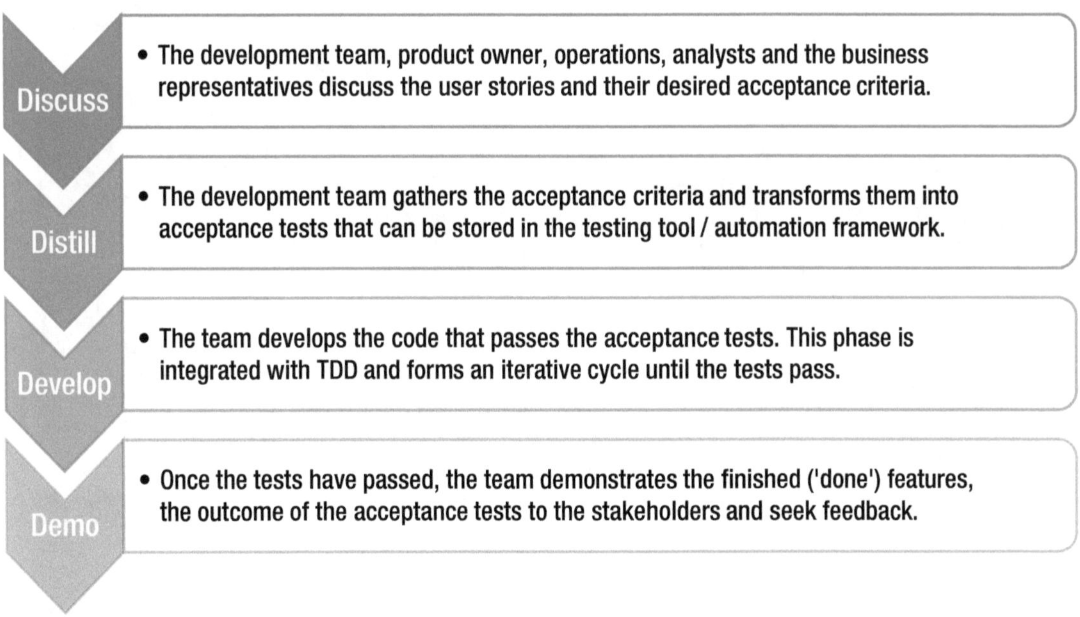

Figure 7-10. *Stages of Acceptance Test-Driven development (ATDD)*

[12]Refer to *Lean-Agile Software Development: Achieving Enterprise Agility* by Alan Shalloway, Guy Beaver and James R. Trott. Addison Wesley; 1 edition (22 October 2009).

7.2.7.1 Behavior driven development (BDD)

Another variation of the concept of TDD is BDD. BDD is more customeroriented as the focus is on the behavioral aspects of the system rather than the technical details. While tests in TDD are written in programming languages, tests in BDD are written in a more English-like language to describe desired system behavior. For example, one of the BDD tools called Cucumber uses a language called Gherkin that uses the format of 'given-when-then'[13] to describe acceptance tests.

7.2.8 Continuous Integration (CI)

CI is a core practice that has its origin in XP. As developers collaborate and churn out code, it is important that the code is checked into a version control repository (maybe several times in a day) and integrated with the existing code base. The frequent merging of the code helps to prevent or quickly address any issues of code conflicts.

Once the code is checked in, it needs to be compiled (e.g., into bytecode), built (to produce the executable), deployed (manually or automatically) and then tested (by smoke testing, automation testing, or regression testing) to prove that the changes are compatible with each other and nothing has been broken as a result.

This is neatly summarized in the illustration below (Figure 7-11).

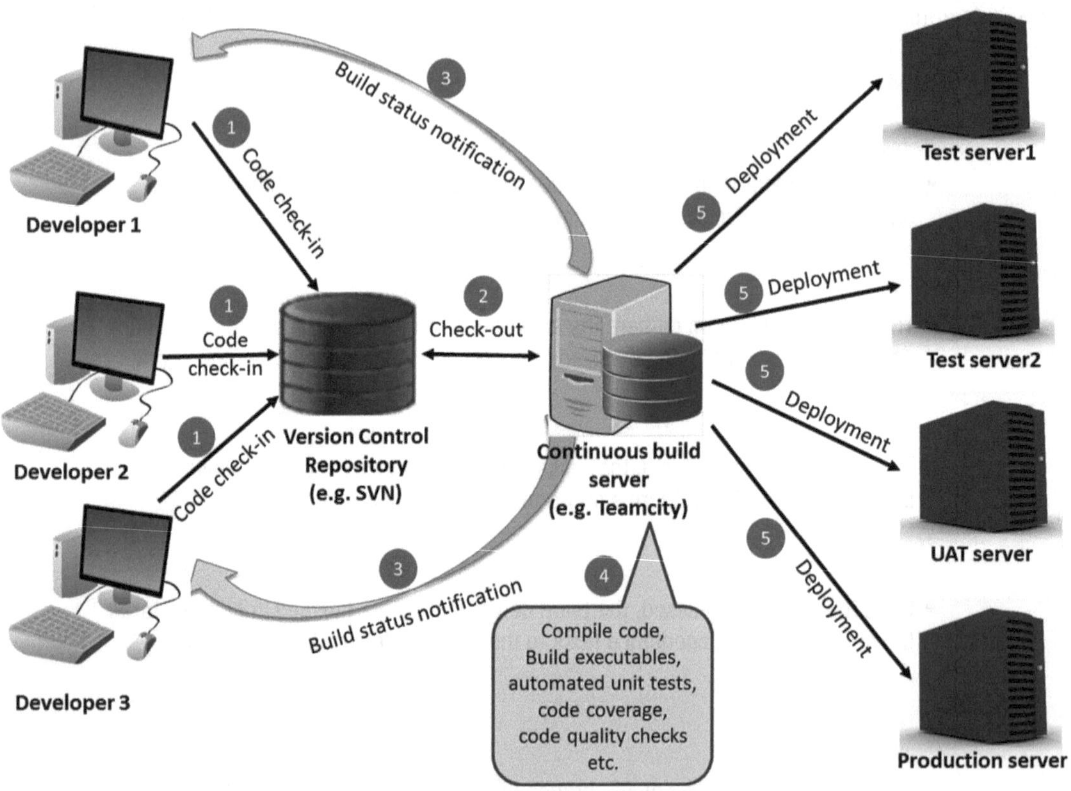

Figure 7-11. Steps in continuous build and integration

[13]Refer to user story formats in Chapter 6: Adaptive Planning for examples.

7.2.8.1 Goal of CI

The goal of CI is to

- obtain quick feedback on their implementation.
- detect and resolve problems quickly saving time and effort.
- mitigates risks in the one-time big-bang integration that happens in traditional waterfall-based projects and is plagued with lots of problems and issues.
- support continuous delivery of valuable software increments into production.
- increase the amount of collaboration as all team members adhere to a uniform set of tools and disciplines.

Most of these tasks become complex where team members are distributed across multiple locations or time zones. In order to manage this situation, CI concepts are extended to Distributed Continuous Integration (DCI). This mostly is based on common principles, disciplines and tooling that is collectively agreed by the team members and religiously followed irrespective of what they are working on and when. For example, team members could agree that only compile-ready code can be checked into the integration branch, or only the code that has passed all the automated unit test cases could be tagged and picked up during the integration build. Commercial tools like Jenkins, Cruisecontrol, Teamcity and Bamboo deal with these action and prove to be quite handy for Agile developers.

Note that for an effective use of CI and its associated tools, there is an up-front investment behind procuring the tools, provisioning a dedicated build server (and build agents) to run several builds in a day (including concurrent builds) and training the team members on how to use them. All of these should be done at the beginning of the project before active development starts, perhaps during iteration zero. The whole concept of CI sticks together as long as every team member abides by the principles, otherwise its effectiveness could fast degenerate.

Having said that, the benefits of continuous integration are so much that most teams absorb the concepts like a sponge because value and efficiency are realized from day one. Let us take a look at some of the best practices in CI now.

7.2.8.2 Some best practices in CI

As each Agile team is free to choose what best works for them, there are a set of best practices[14] in continuous integration that have proven to yield positive results when adopted.

- **Use a consistent IDE or integrated development environment** - although there are many IDE's in the market, it is convenient that the development team uses one consistently across. The IDE should be smart to highlight compilation errors, be able to easily integrate with source control repositories, run builds and be extended as per the requirements of the team. Otherwise there could be subtle differences in configuration, behavior, rendition of code and integration with other toolsets and plugins.
- **Check code quality (technical debt)** - the team should agree with a set of coding conventions and rules that should be automatically checked before the code is submitted. Also technical debt should be removed during refactoring of code. One example of a good open source platformused for checking code quality is SQALE.[15]

[14]This is an adapted version from the articles of Martin Fowler.
[15]Refer to `http://www.sonarqube.org/tag/sqale/`

- **Perform peer code reviews** - developers should have the capability to perform smart peer code review (aside from pair programming) using tools like Fisheye and Crucible.
- **Use a version control strategy** - teams could use tools like Subversion, GIT, Stash and Artifactory[16] for their configuration management and version control needs. While doing that they should agree to abide by a few conventions. Some of these could look like:
  - Allow only tested code to be checked in.
  - Store everything that is to be version controlled at one place, recommended in subfolders - code, unit test cases, third-party libraries, database scripts, configuration and documentation.
  - Enforce that at all times the code in the version control (tools like GIT, SVN) should be ready to deploy without additional dependencies (like third-party libraries) by simply importing it into the developer's workspace or the test environment.
  - Team members should commit their changes regularly such that they do not keep an exclusive lock for more than a day.
  - Developers should label or tag the code belonging to an iteration or a release so that it can be referenced together as one unit. If a particular build breaks, team members should be able to revert back to the last working version using this label or tag.
  - Teams should agree on a branching and merging strategy. For example, they could keep the trunk (main branch) in sync with the production version, while work on each iteration in a separate branch. The branch could be merged with the trunk when the code is released to production.
- **Automate the build and deployment** - using a tool like Cruisecontrol, Teamcity. or Hudson, the team should be able to build executables and deploy them with a click of a button. The team should be able to monitor the status of the current and previous build reports on a dashboard, or get notified by an email alert if there is a break. The build should also trigger code quality checking and running of the test regression suite to determine the sanctity of the software.
- **Speed up the build** - the build should be fast (consuming less than 10 minutes for example), such that it can be easily run over and over again, without any long wait in between.

[16]Refer to `https://www.jfrog.com/open-source/`

- **Invest behind production quality test data** - such that the testing cycles are representative of what would happen in production. Test data population could be integrated with the tasks of deployment. Some data could be copied from production (and sanitized by removing sensitive information like customer details) and uploaded to the test environment. Interfaces with other systems and external applications, if not available, could be virtualized as a service as required.
- **Demo what is built** - for the purpose of the demo, do not prepare a separate build as it will defeat the very purpose of the review. The runtime environment used for the demo should, ideally, always be up to allow exploratory testing to happen anytime.

7.3 Problem resolution

Problems are best tackled by the team members themselves, as they are the ones who are closest to the ground level and have the maximum amount of information required to diagnose the root cause of the problem and come up with options to resolve them. Agile leaders like coaches and Scrum Masters have an important role to play. They should not try to intervene and mediate;instead they should empower the Agile team, remind them of the values, principles and the vision; and encourage them to take ownership and solve the problems on their own. Of course, if there are impediments that are raised beyond their remit, it will need the Agile leaders to step in directly and resolve it through facilitation, influencing, conflict management and negotiation skills.

Daily stand-up meetings are an important forum for the team members to come forward and share their problems openly. However, the meeting itself should not be used for problem solving, as most problems will need a good amount of thinking and evaluation that should be taken offline.

7.3.1 Process of problem solving

Problem solving should be done with the end in mind. Tactical solutions could often be brittle and the problem could likely come back and haunt them again. Teams should also remember that there is an element of timing to diagnosing and resolving problems as well. If the critical period has passed, the problem might be hard to detect or simulate or find an effective solution. Often the cost of addressing the change escalates because of the delay.

The process of problem solving has these steps as shown below in Figure 7-12.

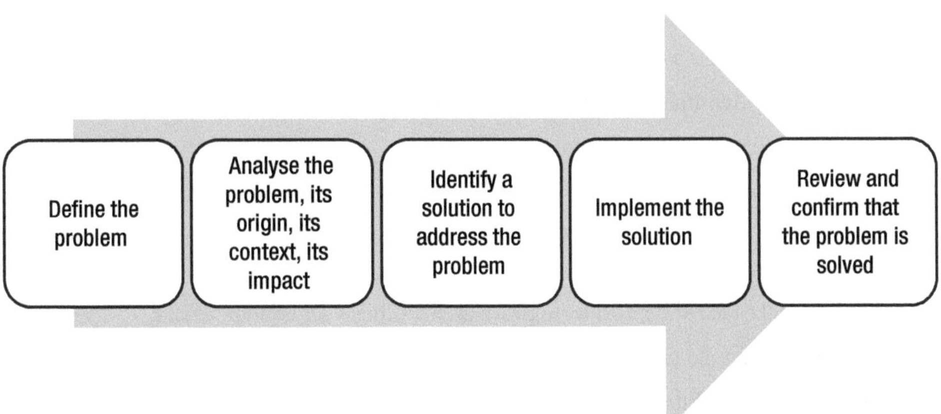

Figure 7-12. *Steps for problem solving*

7.3.2 Techniques for problem solving

Let us take a quick look at some of the techniques used for problem solving.

- **Divide and conquer** - breaking down complex problems into simpler and more manageable problems that are easier to resolve.
- **Expert judgement** - consulting with a subject-matter expert who has 'been-there, done-that before'.
- **Simulation** - scaling down the complexity of the problem into a simpler model that is easier to control and trying out multiple permutations and combinations of scenarios.
- **Brainstorming / war room** - gathering all experts together in one place to come up with ideas, logical reasoning, debate, discuss. and plan action items.
- **Metaphors** - using analogy of the solution for a previous problem to resolve the current problem.
- **Trial and error** - trying different alternatives repeatedly until the resolution is obtained.
- **Spikes** - experimenting with alternate options to check out viability and feasibility of the solution.
- **Trend analysis** - trying to figure out a pattern in the system behavior.
- **Probing** - asking a series of questions to get to the bottom of the problem, rather than treating it based on symptoms.
- **Sandboxing** - solving the problem in a smaller and controlled environment, before applying the fix on the live system.

7.4 Focus areas for the exam

✓ Definition of risk and its characteristics.

✓ How risk management is a continuous activity in Agile projects.

✓ Risk identification is a collective responsibility of the whole team.

✓ How risks are identified and analyzed using the probability and impact matrix tool.

✓ Risk categorization - PESTLE analysis.

✓ Formula of risk severity, risk exposure, or expected monetary value (EMV).

✓ 4 strategies or risk responses to deal with negative risks - avoid, transfer, mitigate and accept.

✓ What is a spike task and its utility to prove an hypothesis and mitigate risks.

✓ Checkpoints in Agile for monitoring and identifying risks and problems.

✓ Feedback loops at different levels.

- ✓ Concept of risk-adjusted backlog and risk burndown graphs to maintain visibility of risks.
- ✓ How quality principles are embedded in day-to-day activities in the Agile team.
- ✓ Necessity of test automation, where to automate and at what level.
- ✓ Concept of exploratory testing in XP and how it complements automation testing.
- ✓ The recent devops trend of shift-left testing and its benefits.
- ✓ Steps in test-driven development (TDD) and its benefits.
- ✓ Concept of ATDD and BDD.
- ✓ Goals and best practices of continuous integration - bringing together practices of version control, build, deployment and automation testing.
- ✓ Steps for problem solving.

Quizzes

1. The formula for risk severity is as follows:

   A. Risk severity = Risk probability x Risk impact

   B. Risk severity = Risk probability / Risk impact

   C. Risk severity = Risk probability + Risk impact

   D. Risk severity = Risk probability - Risk impact

2. At which phase of the project is Risk planning done?

   A. Iteration planning

   B. Sprint planning

   C. Release planning

   D. During the entire project lifecycle

3. Product parts are often subject to damage during shipment,which causes a high level of impact to the customer. To manage the risk, the project team insures all shipments. This risk response is a good example of:

   A. Avoid Risk

   B. Mitigate Risk

   C. Transfer Risk

   D. Accept Risk

4. Errors missed by quality assurance and control process and released to the end user are:

   A. Cost of change

   B. Undocumented features

   C. Escaped defects

   D. Change request

5. An experiment performed to address the risk identified for a user story is called:

   A. Risk response

   B. Risk-based spike

   C. Risk mitigation

   D. All of the above

6. An approach where testers perform minimum test planning and maximum test execution is known as:

   A. exploratory testing

   B. automation testing

   C. test-driven development

   D. acceptance-driven development

7. Frequently integrating new and changed code is known as

   A. Integrating continuously

   B. Continuous integration

   C. Integration control

   D. Constant integration

8. Test-Driven Development (TDD) technique is performed as:

   A. Red, green, black

   B. Green, red, refactor

   C. Green, red, register

   D. Red, green, refactor

9. All are frequent verification and validation techniques, except:

   A. Pair programming

   B. Iteration planning

   C. Unit testing

   D. Iteration demos

10. Steps to perform while using TDD technique:

    A. write test, write code, refactor

    B. write code, write test, refactor

    C. write code, refactor, write test

    D. write test, refactor, write code

11. Continuous integration provides:

    A. Slow feedback

    B. No early detection of code issues

    C. Frequent feedback

    D. Delivers software only at the end

12. TDD focuses on Code whereas ATTD focuseson:

    A. Development tools and practices

    B. Business or customer

    C. Release plan

    D. Process tailoring

13. Spikes helps to

    A. Increase velocity

    B. Mitigate risk with uncertain technology/domain

    C. Freeze estimates

    D. Continuously build and integrate

14. During a problem detection session, you ask WHY five times because

    A. People feel frustrated if asked a sixth time

    B. Truth comes out only when asked why five times.

    C. Gather data around the issue

    D. To get to the root cause of an issue

15. When performing Risk analysis, which of the following is NOT a risk parameter:

    A. Probability

    B. Impact

    C. Timing

    D. Risk burndown chart

16. Which of the following changes are observed when a team adopts the shift-left testing approach?

    A. Focus changes from detecting to preventing defects

    B. Break the silos between the development and testing teams

    C. Development and testing activities progress in parallel

    D. All of the above

17. Choose the correct stages of ATTD process:

    A. discuss, distill, develop, demo

    B. discuss, develop, distill, demo

    C. discuss, develop, demo, distill

    D. distill, develop, demo, discuss

18. Which of the following testing is recommended to be automated on top priority?

    A. User interface

    B. Database stored procedures and triggers

    C. Back-end code that deals with formulae and algorithms

    D. Build scripts

19. All are Shift-left testing benefits, except:

    A. Resolving testing bottlenecksduring the end of the project

    B. Getting quick customer feedback

    C. Decrease the utilization of shared test environments

    D. Fewer integration defects

20. Select the correct sequence of steps for problem resolution:

    A. Identify solution, analyze, define, implement, review and confirm

    B. Define, analyze, identify solution, implement, review and confirm

    C. Identify solution, define, analyze, implement, review and confirm

    D. Analyze, define, identify solution, implement, review and confirm

Answers

1. A
2. D
3. C
4. C
5. B
6. A
7. B
8. D
9. B
10. A
11. C
12. B
13. B
14. D
15. D
16. D
17. A
18. C
19. C
20. B

CHAPTER 8

Domain VII: Continuous Improvement (Product, Process, People)

"Learn from yesterday, live for today, hope for tomorrow. The important thing is not to stop questioning."

—Albert Einstein

From the name of this chapter, it appears that this is a repetition of what has already been covered so far in the book. In fact, that is indeed right. Almost everywhere we have seen how feedback and continuous improvement is an integral part of all Agile practices. This is the seventh and last domain from the PMI-ACP® course outline.

In this chapter, we discuss about the three legs of continuous improvement in Agile teams - product, process and people. These three are intricately related to each other and address the 'what', 'how' and 'who' or 'by whom' part of the Agile project.

Before we get down into the details, let us spend few moments reflecting on the project framework as illustrated in Figure 8-1. Projects are conceived as a result of a variety of needs - requirements from stakeholders, demands from environment, competition from the market, pursue innovation and thought leadership, to maintain operational hygiene, or remain compliant to laws and regulations. These requirements need to be incorporated into products. *Products* are meant for customers who use them to get some tangible benefit out of it. *People* develop *products*. They apply their intellect, technical and soft skills to transform requirements into the *product*. In doing so, they follow *processes*, which in turn are laid down by the people themselves.

Now, each of these aspects - product, process and people needs a continuous evolution to stay relevant, competitive and fit for purpose. Products need to evolve based on needs and feedback. Processes need to adapt to evolving needs. People need to continuously improve through training, coaching and mentoring. In other words, the software ecosystem is in a forever loop for learn - inspect - adapt.

S. Boral, *Ace the PMI-ACP® exam*, DOI 10.1007/978-1-4842-2526-4_8

Let us cover them in sequence in this chapter.

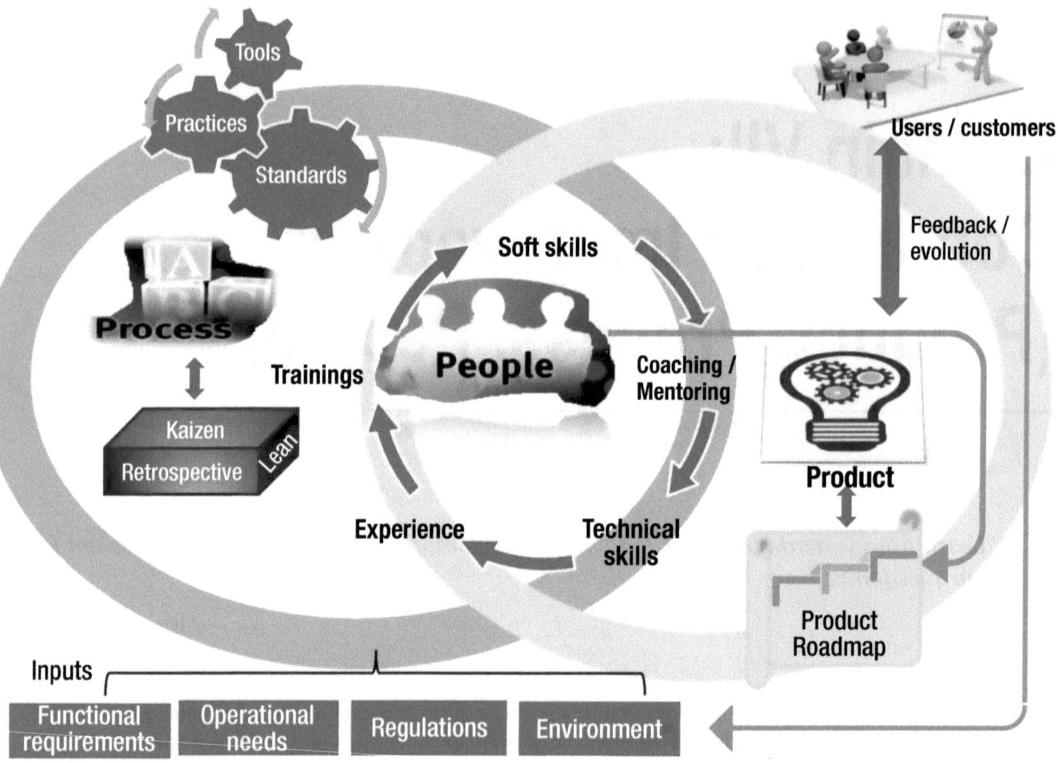

Figure 8-1. Interplay between product, processes and people

8.1 Product improvement

The ultimate goal of any software product is to meet the needs of the business and yet remain commercially viable to maintain. Over a length of time we expect to see customers' needs evolve and that should be reflected in features of the product. In this context, it is relevant to refer back to our discussion on the Agile Planning Onion that we introduced in Chapter 6: Adaptive Planning. In the third ring from the outside, we saw product planning. One of the most important artifacts is the product roadmap that captures the journey of evolution of the software product through its life as it keeps pace with customer needs and technology advancements.

8.1.1 Continuous improvement of product quality and effectiveness

The goal of Agile teams is to create a sustainable operating rhythm that delivers quality software in the hands of the customer at periodic intervals. And the most critical aspect is that, with the iterative delivery model, customers get an opportunity to view intermediate versions of the product as it gets built, provide feedback and request change of direction if required.

In Chapter 7: Problem Detection and Resolution, we saw how quality principles are embedded in all Agile practices. There is a persistent focus on defect prevention over defect detection as prevalent in traditional waterfall-based projects.

We also saw how Agile teams perform frequent validation and verification at different stages to obtain feedback and incorporate them as soon as possible.

> **Verification** - Are we building the right product for the customer?
>
> **Validation** - Are we building the product right?

8.1.2 Dissemination of knowledge

As products grow in complexity, it is important for organizations to ensure that knowledge is sticky within the project team. As team members keep working on iterations, they gather and retain knowledge that is vital not only for the current and future iterations in the project, but also from a future maintainability of the product. Agile projects, as we have seen earlier, do not invest in comprehensive documentation, but maintains barely sufficient documentation that is needed to support the product and also provide reporting to meet organizational and regulatory obligations. So there is a variety of ways in which Agile teams invest behind dissemination of knowledge among each other. We have seen these before, but let us do a quick recap:

- Osmotic communication between co-located team members and the onsite customer.
- Tacit knowledge build-up as team members sit together.
- Advanced communication tools and technologies to connect distributed teams.
- Using forums for collaboration like brainstorming, group decision-making for planning, estimation, problem solving. and risk mitigation.
- Iteration demos to share knowledge between stakeholders on what the team achieved during an iteration.
- Wireframes, personas and prototypes to arrive at a blueprint of what the system should look like at the end.
- Retrospectives to determine ways to improve the way of working.
- Information radiators to share project metrics and progress with stakeholders.
- Daily stand-up meetings where team members share their progress and impediments so that everyone is aware what everyone is doing.
- Swarming around a problem by gathering around it, diagnosing. and resolving it as a team.
- Expert in earshot where junior and new team members gather knowledge about the project and the product by sitting close to more senior and experienced team members.
- Pair programming and pair rotation so that knowledge of the system implementation is shared between multiple team members, leading to collective ownership of code.
- Continuous build, integration, automated and exploratory testing to provide real-time feedback on the code.
- Investing behind training and upskilling the team (refer to the Dreyfus Model discussed in Chapter 5: Team Performance).
- Conducting spikes to gain knowledge on unfamiliar technologies.

8.2 Process improvement

A lot of focus in Agile projects goes into visualizing progress (through Kanban boards, burndown charts, CFD's and other information radiators) that exposes opportunities for the team to improve their way of working.

Note that a process-compliant team may not guarantee success of a product, but a structured process helps maintain consistency, predictability and align to organizational requirements. However, none of the Agile practices are rigid as far as process-compliance goes. In fact, Agile teams choose what best suits their unique situation and context and ensure that consistency, efficiency and effectiveness is maintained. Like products, processes also go through their evolution and maturity cycles. This follows Deming's Plan-Do-Check-Act cycle that we saw in Chapter 6: Adaptive Planning.

Let us now explore a few ways in which Agile teams look to improve their processes.

8.2.1 Kaizen

Kaizen is the practice of continuous improvement. This is a word that is commonly found in books and literature on Lean philosophy. The Japanese word Kaizen is a combination of two words Kai and Zen, which means to change for the better.

Kaizen = Kai (change) + Zen (for better)

Kaizen is characterized by many small and continuous changes that cumulatively result in big improvements over time. Similar to Deming's Plan-Do-Check-Act cycle,[1] team members following Kaizen look for opportunities to eliminate wasteful activities and incrementally improve their day-to-day processes. The important point to note is that Kaizen activities are typically originated within the team and not enforced by management. The concept of Kaizen is mostly related to Lean manufacturing that has its origin in Toyota, but has now gained popularity in other domains.

8.2.2 Process analysis

Agile teams look to improving the efficiency and effectiveness of their processes by identifying and removing overheads, constraints, or anything that does not add value. Some of this analysis could be proactive or reactive or as an outcome from a team retrospective. Process analysis steps begins with identifying system and process flow - so are conceptually similar to the value stream analysis and mapping that we saw in Chapter 3: Value-Driven Delivery.

One of the examples of process improvement could be how code changes are deployed to the test environments. Team members could feel that manual build and deployments are time consuming and hence a bottleneck as team members attempt to deploy incremental builds (code changes for requirements, enhancements, or bug fixes) many times during a release. The natural reaction would be to use and configure a build-and-deployment tool that does most of the plumbing work in a fraction of the time.

[1]Refer to Chapter 6: Adaptive Planning for the discussion on Deming's PDCA cycle.

8.2.3 Lean 5S technique

Another improvement technique that we have seen earlier in this book[2] is the 5S tool as used in Lean. The acronym 5S stands for sort, set in order, shine, standardize and sustain. The goal of this technique is to remove waste materials from the workspace, keep it clean periodically and follow standardized processes to facilitate a smooth flow.

8.2.4 Kanban Kata

The word Kata has its origin from martial arts, which requires one to practice a set of predefined movements over and over again until perfection is achieved. Applied in the context of Agile, Kanban Kata is another continuous improvement strategy that uses a series of questions to help improve in small steps such that day-to-day work and improvements happen simultaneously.

A set of Kata questions could look like as follows:

- What is the target state that we are trying to achieve?
- What is the current state?
- What are the impediments or blockers on the way?
- What is the next step to resolve the impediment?
- When can we see what we learned from taking that step?

8.2.5 5 Why's technique

The 5 Why's technique is used by teams to identify the root cause of a particular problem by asking a series of 'why' questions. The questions explore the cause-and-effect relationships between observations. There is nothing magic about the number 5, but it is observed that by the fifth 'why' question, the team has gathered enough information about the process that can be helpful to address the problem or prevent a future recurrence. Note that problems can have more than one root cause, in which case, the technique has to be repeated for each branch.

Let us see an example how a team attempts to resolve a problem by using the 5 why's technique. The library management system had an incident on production and the system was unavailable to borrowers and other users for a period of 2 days, causing a lot of inconvenience. On interrogation, the team found out the following response as shown in Table 8-1. Notice how a question is framed based on the response received for the previous question.

[2]Refer to the section on Lean described in Chapter 2: Agile Methodologies.

Table 8-1. *Application of the 5 Why's technique*

#	Question	Response
1.	Why did the incident happen?	Our application database went down.
2.	Why did the database go down?	The file system became full and there was no disk space left.
3.	Why did the support team not monitor the disk usage levels proactively?	They are new to the team and do not have enough knowledge of the diagnostic tools and how to deal with the system-generated alerts.
4.	Why did the new support team members not have enough knowledge?	The knowledge transition has not fully happened. Our team memberslack the experience in using the diagnostic tools.
5.	Why has the knowledge transition not happened?	We have been so busy with issues daily, that we couldn't prioritize the training sessions. But we should do that as soon as possible, otherwise we will have more issues like this.

8.2.6 Fishbone diagram

The fishbone diagram, also called the Ishikawa diagram, is an extension of the 5 why's technique to determine the root cause of a problem. It asks a series of questions to explore cause-effect relationshipsuntil the addressable root cause is determined. Fishbone analysis technique happens in a facilitated environment with the relevant participants. It is popularly used for defect prevention and process improvement.

Let us look at an example of the fishbone diagram as illustrated in Figure 8-2. The root cause analysis technique using the Fishbone diagram comprises of the following steps:

1. Starts with writing down the problem statement at the head of the fish denoted by the arrow head.
2. Determine the main factors that could have contributed to the problem. They can be categorized commonly into different buckets like machines, people, materials and measurements. These are denoted by the respective arrows (like bones) that are directed toward the backbone.
3. For each category, the respective root causes are determined and written down on arrows (pointing to the bones).
4. This process repeats itself until an addressable set of root causes isdetermined.
5. The fishbone diagram is analyzed and the corrective actionsare determined and agreed upon.

As seen in Figure 8-2, the library management portal went down because of issues related to materials, measurements, people and infrastructure. On probing the infrastructure category further, it is identified out that the server has reached its end-of-life and is out of support because there has been no funding allocated to renew its operating license. Similarly, under the people category, it is found that the team members lack the competencies to perform the support role. When probed further, it was determined that their training needs were not prioritized in the past (highlighted in red on the figure). Now that the impact is well understood, the team should undertake adequate training so that they are well versed with the support process and the tools to prevent future recurrence of the problem.

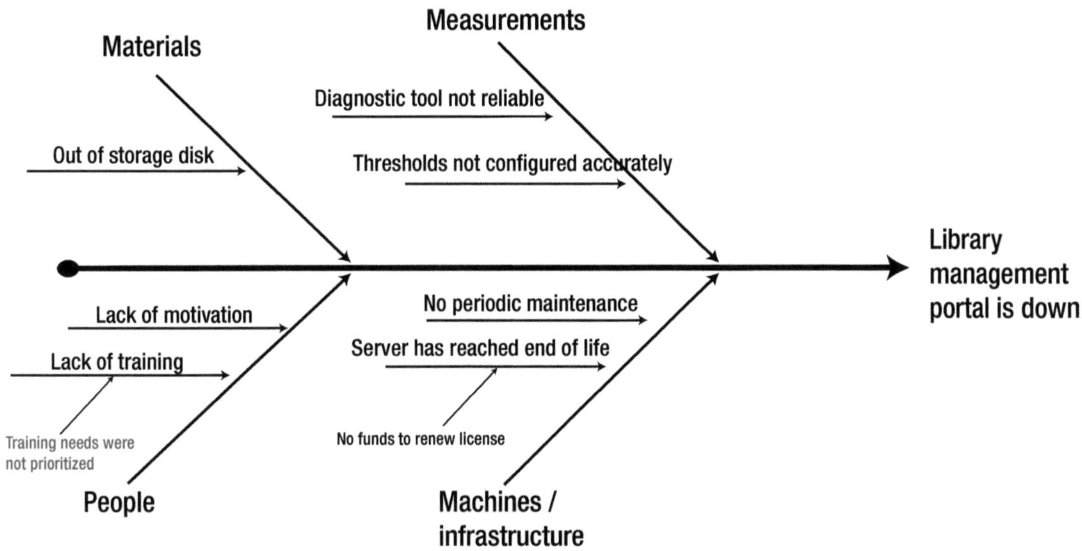

Figure 8-2. *Fishbone diagram*

8.2.7 Pareto Diagrams (80-20 rule)

The Pareto principle, also called the 80-20 rule is based on measuring the frequencies or occurrences that cause the most of the problems. The rules state that 80% of the problems are due to 20% of the causes. Alternatively stated, 80% of the system errors can be removed by resolving 20% of the defects.

The Pareto chart can be conveniently created as a histogram of an event against the number of occurrences in descending order. Figure 8-3 is the Pareto chart corresponding to the data in Table 8-2.

Table 8-2. *Tabulating the count of incidents for each cause*

Root cause of incident	Count of incidents	Cumulative count	Cumulative %
Lack of training of support staff	48	48	43.6%
Software support not available	33	81	73.6%
Hardware is unstable	12	93	84.5%
Bugs in code	7	100	90.9%
Bad data	6	106	96.4%
Others	4	110	100.0%

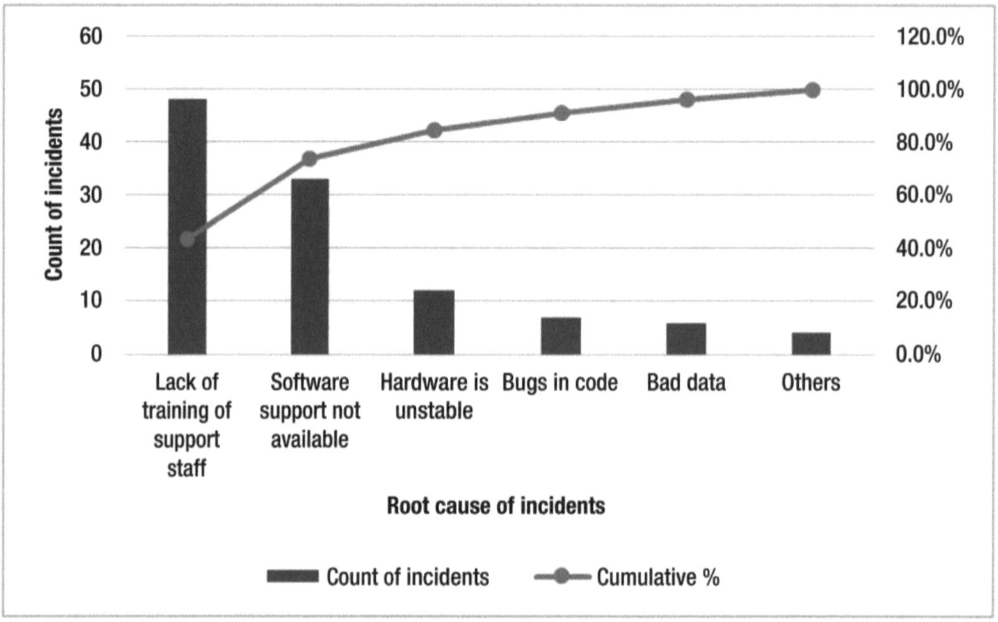

Figure 8-3. *Pareto chart*

As the Pareto diagram shows, almost 75% of the production incidents are caused because of two fundamental issues related to lack of training of support staff and software support not being available. If the team focuses on addressing these two causes, most of the problems will get resolved.

8.2.8 Control charts

The next tool used for process diagnosis and quality improvement is the statistical process control chart or Shewhart chart. This is used to determine whether the performance of a process is within the expected range demarcated by upper and lower limits. Usually the upper and lower limits are specified at a three-sigma value (sigma is standard deviation) on either side of the mean. If the measured parameter has a value within this range it is said to be stable or under control. If the process is out of control, then adequate actions like process updates are necessary to bring it back into control.

Figure 8-4 shows a control chart with points plotted based on the value measured of a system parameter. In the middle of the chart is the statistical mean, denoted by μ. Following the normal distribution curve (also popularly called the Bell curve), the upper and lower control limits are defined at 3 sigma values. Also, indicated in the control chart are the upper and lower specification limits from the customer as part of the acceptance criteria of the product. Observe that the control limits are within a conservative range that it has a narrower band than the specification limits.

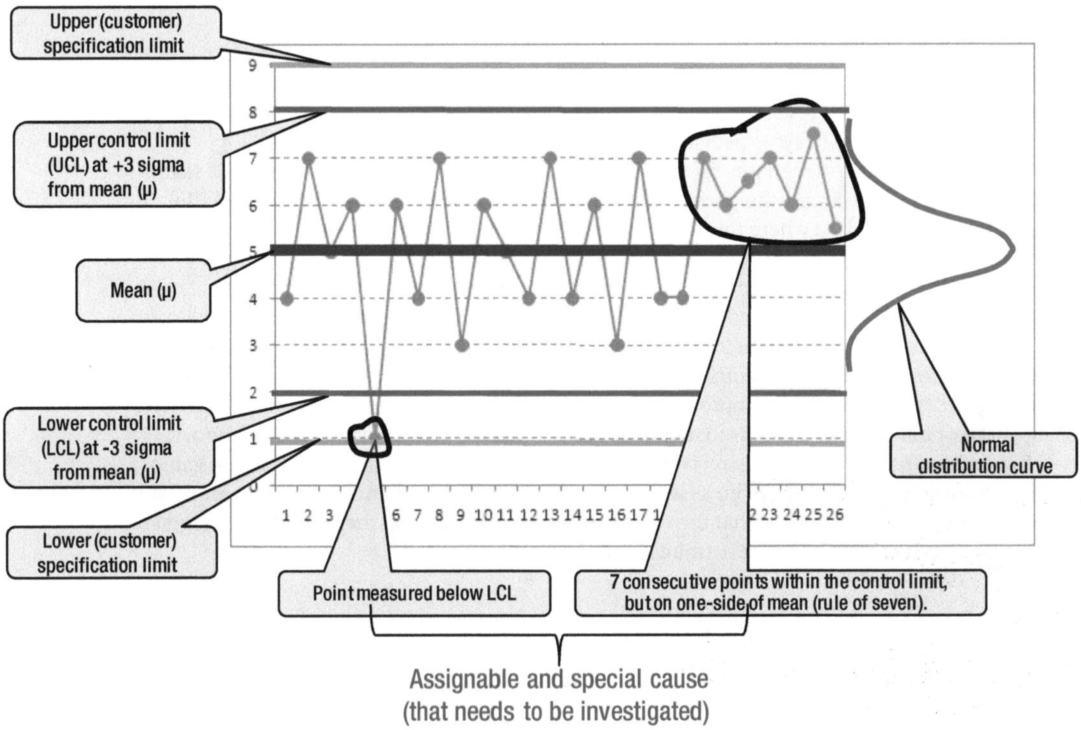

Figure 8-4. *Control charts*

While measuring the behavior and stability of the process, we see that the process fluctuates on either side of the expected mean value. If the observed fluctuations are within the control limits, this is said to be because of *common cause,* which is not of concern as it is attributed to normal day-to-day variations. However, there are three conditions under which the process is said to be out of control because of a *special cause variation*:

1. A point is plotted in the control chart that resides below the lower control limit (even if it is within the specification limit).
2. A point is plotted in the control chart that resides above the upper control limit.
3. From among the points plotted, seven consecutive points, even though within the control limits, lie on one side of the mean. This is depicted by a black circle in the figure above.

Special causes need to be further investigated and addressed by the team. Control charts can be used by Agile teams to diagnose the performance of their processes with respect to a tolerance range and take corrective actions as appropriate. Examples of usage are limiting defect propagation from one stage to another, limiting work in progress on Kanban boards, observing the trend of committed but unfinished work in sprints, trend of average velocities over iterations and trends of failed builds.

8.3 Retrospectives

Retrospectives, arguably, are one of the most powerful techniques in the toolbox of the Agile professional. From the PMI-ACP® exam perspective, too, this is the most important section of this chapter. You can almost always expect a bunch of questions around retrospectives.

Retrospectives, also sometimes referred as *reflection workshops,*are forums for Agile teams to look back, reflect and evaluate the performance of their processes at the end of each iteration. In Agile methods like Kanban where there are no iterations, teams could be running retrospectives at predefined intervals like once in 2 weeks or so, timeboxing it to an hour or two.

During a retrospective, the team members collectively reflect on what went well and what needs to change. Based on this,adaptive actions are committed and implemented from the next iteration itself. The goal of a retrospective is to improve efficiency, eliminate wasteful activities and bad practices (also called *Agilesmells*), increase productivity, quality and team learning. This is a hallmark of the philosophy of continuous process improvement. The outcomes of retrospectives are often displayed on flipcharts or information radiators to remind team members of their commitment to improve.

It is important that the discussion is healthy and constructive and there is no blame game or finger-pointing if things did not go as well as expected. The participants in the retrospective should acknowledge and believe that the team honestly achieved what they could do best given the information in hand and the constraints in the environment.

8.3.1 Styles of retrospectives

As the following Figure 8-5 shows, there are three prevalent styles in which the actions out of retrospectives are determined.

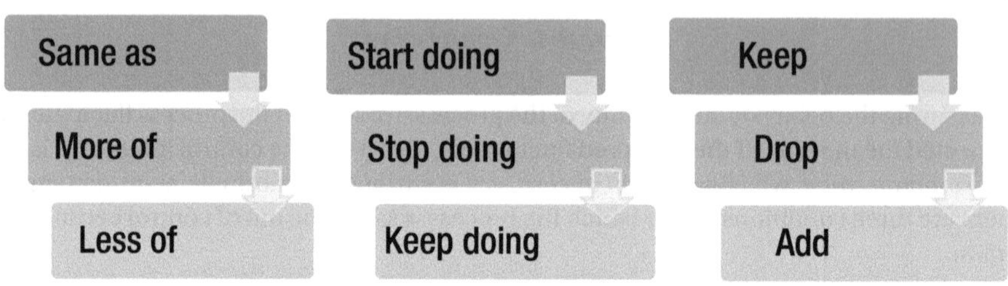

Figure 8-5. *Different styles of retrospectives*

8.3.1.1 SAMOLO - Same as – more of – less of

'Same as' are those processes and practices that the team finds value and would continue to use.

'More of' are those processes and practices that the team find value, but feels it's not doing enough of. The more they do it, the better is the expected outcome. An example of such a practice is testing automation.

'Less of' are those processes and practices that are team starting finding diminishing value and would like to discourage. The team feels the less they do it, the better is the expected outcome. An example of such a practice is the time spent in seeking clarifications from the business over emails.

8.3.1.2 Start doing – stop doing – keep doing

'Start doing' are the activities that the team feels are not done, but is worth doing because they will generate better outcomes. Maybe some of the tasks have been procrastinated on for a long time, or there is an inherent fear of the unknown associated with these tasks, although the benefits perceived are plenty.

'Stop doing' are the activities that the team feel are not useful, generally disliked, or not worth doing, so should be stopped.

'Keep doing' are the activities that are liked, adding value and the team feels are worth continuing.

The style Keep - Drop - Add is similar to Start doing - stop doing - keep doing.

8.3.2 Comparisons between lessons learned and retrospectives

In many ways, retrospectives are similar in intent to lessons learned exercises prevalent in traditional waterfall-based projects. But since in Agile projects, the emphasis is on continuous improvement, Agile teams have effectively shortened the radius of Deming's Plan-Do-Check-Act cycle by making it more frequent. For the purpose of understanding, it is worth observing some notable differences (Refer to Table 8-3), which makes retrospectives particularly more attractive than its traditional counterpart.

Table 8-3. *Comparison between lessons learned exercise and retrospectives*

Aspect	Lessons learned in traditional projects	Retrospectives in Agile projects
Timing	Conducted at the end of the project.	Conducted at the end of each iteration or after periodic intervals.
Documentation overhead	Lessons learned are stored in the organization's knowledge repository.	Very little documentation is created or stored. More of a verbal and collaborative exercise in the team.
Usage and purpose	Used for reference by future project teams, but too late for the current project team.	Benefits the current team as they work on the agreed actions from the very next iteration.
Tracking benefits	Benefits realized are hard to track.	Benefits realized are almost immediate. The project team benefits from the just-in-time feedback and can take credit from the achievement / improvement.
Team involvement and participation	More of a ceremonial exercise - the participation could be low as some team members (including the project manager himself) might have moved on or would have got allocated to another project.	The team has a vested interest in the outcome of the retrospective as it addresses the needs of the current project and the current team. There is an earnest attempt to self-introspect and contribute.
Optionality	Referring to the lessons learned repository is optional and depends on the awareness, time and interest level of the future teams. Only best practices and policies are carried over.	The team signsup to conduct retrospectives regularly and almost immediately address the relevant action items. It is engrained in the culture of the Agile team.

8.3.3 Steps of a retrospective

Retrospective meetings are generally held immediately after the iteration review meetings. At the end of the iteration review, the product owner and the stakeholders leave and then the forum is opened up for the development team to conduct the retrospective. Note that while the focus of the preceding iteration review meeting is the product, stakeholder feedback and acceptance, the focus of the retrospective meeting is process improvement. It's a collective responsibility of the team members to identify what went well in the last iteration and what could be improved from the next iteration onward. The action items determined in the retrospective meeting are fed back into the planning stage of the next iteration.

Depending on the maturity of the team, a retrospective meeting could last anywhere between 2–3 hours. There are five steps[3] that typically include the agenda of a team retrospective, as shown in Figure 8-6.

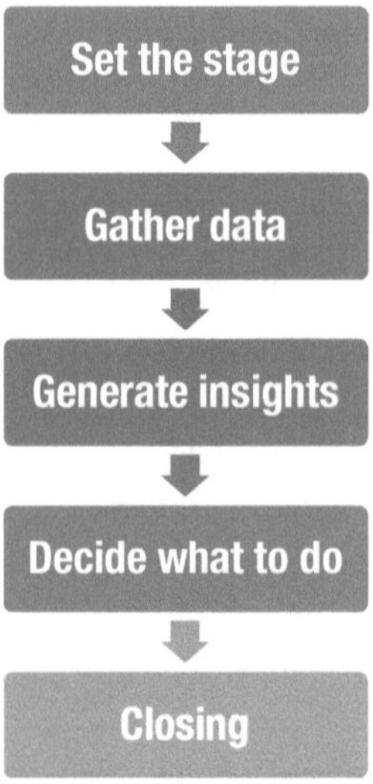

Figure 8-6. *Steps in a retrospective meeting*

8.3.3.1 Set the stage

The first step in the retrospective meeting is to set the stage by getting participants comfortable to speak openly without any fear of retribution or potential conflicts in airing concerns. The facilitator or the retrospective leader[4] also outlines the topics that will be the focus during the meeting.

There are a few activities that can help set the stage.

- **Check-in** - in this activityevery participant is asked to express in a few words about their primary concern and expectation from the retrospective. This shouldn't take more than 5–10 minutes.

[3]Refer to *Agile Retrospectives: Making Good Teams Great* by E. Derby and D. Larsen (Pragmatic Bookshelf Publishing).
[4]The retrospective leader could be someone outside the team, like a person from another team in the organization. Note that the objective of the leader is not to come up with ideas himself/herself, but to remain neutral, facilitate the session and allow the team members to get their act going.

- **Focus on / focus off** - in this activity, participants' attention is drawn to a chart showing the following:

Focus on / off
Inquiry rather than advocacy Dialogue rather than debate Conversations rather than argument Understanding rather than defending

  Participants are divided into groups and each group is asked to describe each of the lines above. They are then asked if they are willing to stick to the left-hand column during the retrospective.

- **ESVP** - in this activity every participant is asked to associate themselves anonymously with one of *Explorers, Shoppers, Vacationers, or Prisoners*. Explorers are eager participants who want to learn about the project and are likely to have whole-hearted engagement during the meeting. Shoppers look at the information available and will take away one useful idea. Vacationers are not enthusiastic about the retrospective but they are happy to be away from the regular workspace. Their engagement is relatively partial. The last category is the prisoners who feel they are coerced to attend the retrospective meeting and are unlikely to stay engaged. By plotting the anonymous responses from the participants, the facilitator is able to gauge the level of interest and energy in the meeting.

- **Working agreements** - in this activity the participants are divided into groups and asked to come up with working agreements. These are presented, clarified, voted, ranked and finally the team chooses to go with a few (5-7) of the working agreements.

8.3.3.2 Gather data

The second step in the retrospective meeting is to collate data such that team members can visualize what happened during the iteration. It is observed that the areas where the team's emotion widely fluctuates is around defects, rework, failed builds, conflicts, operational issues of tools, access restrictions, infrastructure and environment outages. Some of the activities[5] used to gather data are:

- **Timeline** - Team members write down memorable events during the iteration in chronological order.

[5]Details of the activities are not required for the PMI-ACP® exam. They are listed down here for the sake of completion of the subject, so you can really skim read this section. For further details, you should refer to the original (and excellent) source: *Agile Retrospectives: Making Good Teams Great*, by E.Derby and D. Larsen (Pragmatic Bookshelf Publishing).

- **Triple nickels** - Each team member is given five minutes and a card to recollect and write down five issues or ideas that happened during the iteration. After that, the card is passed to the next team member who then expands on the ideas of the previous person or writes new events. This is repeated five times until sufficient data is gathered.
- **Color code dots** - This is used to indicate the feelings of the team during the events depicted on the timeline. Events are color coded to indicate high energy or low energy exhibited.
- **Mad, sad, glad** - Similar to the color coded dots, team members list down their feelings in variations of mad, sad, or glad on the different events during the iteration.
- **Locate strengths** - In this technique, team members are grouped into pairs and interview each other on the highlights and positives that happened during the iteration. The goal is to determine the themes that should be carried forward into the next iteration.
- **Satisfaction histogram** - In this activity, a histogram is used to plot individual and team satisfaction with processes and practices on a scale of 1 to 5, with 5 being the highest measure of satisfaction.
- **Team radar** - In this activity, the team self-assesses how they are doing on a few factors like tools, processes. and practices that they have deemed as important.
- **Like to like** - This is used by the team to judge their personal opinions and those of the other team members about events during the iteration.

8.3.3.3 Generate insights

Once the data is gathered, the third step in the retrospective meeting is to analyze the data and generate meaningful insights and conclusions from it. Activities that help in doing so are:

- **Brainstorming** - generating ideas and filtering on specific criteria.
- **Force field analysis** - determining what factors reinforce or impede a proposed change.
- **5 why's** - asking 'why?' five times to determine the root cause of an issue.
- **Fishbone** - identify root cause of an issue.
- **Patterns and shifts** - looking for trends and patterns between the facts and feelings.
- **Prioritize with dots** - identify priority of the issues and proposals.
- **Identify themes** - determining common themes and links between the ideas generated.

8.3.3.4 Decide what to do

Insights, once generated, needs to be translated into action. This fourth step of the retrospective focuses on the highest priority items and devises an action plan that can be implemented during the next iteration itself. Note that there could be actions thatare beyond the remit of the team members to resolve themselves. In such cases, the Scrum Master or the Agile coach would need to intervene and use their authority and influence to guide toward a solution.

Let us now look at some activities that could be conducted at this stage of the retrospective:

- **Retrospective planning game** - Team members signup for tasks that are necessary to conduct the improvements or experiments.
- **SMART goals** - The action items that the team decides to pursue should have the following attributes expressed by the acronym SMART. An example of a SMART goal is "We need to achieve 80% code coverage while writing Junits for this iteration.

SMART goals
Specific
Measurable
Achievable
Relevant
Time-bound

- **Circle of questions** - in this activity, team members sitting in a circle, ask questions to each other regarding the action items, until the answers converge, a consensus is reached and everyone feels happy that they have been heard.
- **Short subjects** - The team members agree on what went well or what they would do differently next time.

8.3.3.5 Closing the retrospective

The last step of the retrospective meeting is to close gracefully with expression of appreciations of the time devoted by the participants. Team members reflect on the retrospective itself and summarize their action items. The action items could also be added to the backlog as nonfunctional items. Examples of activities include:

- **Appreciations** - The team members express their gratitude and appreciation to each other for the help and collaboration received during the iteration and the retrospective.
- **+/Delta** - in this activity, team members retrospect on the retrospective itself. They collectively decide what they want to do or change from the next retrospective meeting.
- **Helped, Hindered, Hypothesis** - similar to the previous one, the team members are given three flipcharts to list down what part of the retrospective helped, hindered them, or any new ideas for improvement.
- **Return on time invested (ROTI)** - During this activity team members are asked to rate their feedback on a scale of 0 to 4 (with 4 being highest) whether the time they devoted to the retrospective exercise was worth it or not.

Before we conclude this section, it is to be noted that teams could call for retrospectives at the end of an iteration, release,or on an adhoc basis. For example, if during a daily stand-up meeting, the Scrum Master or the team notices something wrong, they could call for an adhoc retrospective in the middle of a sprint. Such events are called *instraspectives* and are exclusively used to have a focused discussion on a particular issue or event to trigger any action to change within a sprint.

8.3.4 Process tailoring

We get to see heavier processes and methodologies integrated with each other in mature organizations. The tighter is the integration, the greater the perceived quality, integrity and resilience of the systems. However, in Agile projects, the focus is on interactions between teams and the customers, rather that processes and tools. The challenge over here is how to pare down the processes, eliminate any embellishments, such that agility is achieved, but not at the cost of quality or the integrity of the systems.

The outcome of retrospectives is a key driver for the Agile team to inspect and adapt its way of working. Agile methods, inherently, are less prescriptive, so they are quite open to tailoring. However, one should not be hasty to start tailoring straightaway. One should spend a sufficient amount of time adopting some well-known methodologies before adapting it. Otherwise, it could lead to dysfunctional behavior that will be harder to undo and course correct.

Some processes that could be tailored arehow the sprint backlog is managed and maintained by the team during the sprint; which tools should be used for issue tracking, version control, builds and deployment; which metrics to use and how to report and interpret the trends;and when and where to adopt and adapt practices like pair programming, continuous integration, exploratory testing and so on.

Just like retrospectives process tailoring could involve the following steps:

- Determine the scope - which processes to tailor based on feedback from the team.
- Determine the duration - the amount of time required to tailor and observe the impact of tailoring.
- Determine the impact - by involving and engaging stakeholders in the decision-making part.
- Determine reusable resources - like organizational process assets, best practices, industry-wide practices and see how applicable they are in the current context.
- Review and confirm that the tailored process is indeed working in the way it was envisioned to.
- Socialize the improved process to stakeholders such that it becomes well understood, accepted, relevant and consistent - not only in the context of the current project, but also for future projects.

8.3.5 Pre-mortem / pre-failure analysis

Pre-mortems are logically opposite to retrospectives thatare conducted after the iteration. In a pre-mortem, the team members are asked to determine possible reasons what can go wrong or why the project could fail *in future*. Pre-mortems, logically, are similar to risk identification and analysis, since they happen before the possible occurrence of failure in the project. Based on the ideas collected, team members can take actions to change their plan or to mitigate the causes for failure.

8.4 People

In Chapter 5: Team Performance, we have covered a lot about team building and development. We also covered the role of servant leadership skills required in Agile leaders like Scrum Masters and Agile coaches that are required for a healthy functioning of an Agile team. In this section we are going to see a few more people-oriented improvement techniques, mostly from a people-leadership perspective.

8.4.1 Feedback methods

Agile practices are characterized by rapid feedback loops at various stages. Here are some key aspects on giving feedback to people:

- Make the feedback constructive in nature. The person receiving the feedback should be receptive and feel comfortable that the feedback and suggestions are being given for their improvement.
- Positive feedback is easy to communicate. But negative feedback should be carefully delivered, otherwise it can get misconstrued very easily. One prevalent technique is the 'sandwich method' where the corrective feedback is sandwiched between layers of praise. The goal is not to sugar-coat, but to make it easier to deliver and accept, as the recipient feels that the feedback is well rounded.
- Make the feedback relevant and related to the overall goals and objectives of the individual and that of the project.
- Exhibit care as it is important that the feedback contains proper choice of words and body language. Use of negative words and judgment could have a discouraging effect.
- Be specific, back up with sufficient data and give instances of observations and examples as that is how the receiver and the feedback giver can connect better.
- Praise in public, but criticize in private - human beings feel good receiving admiration in public, but negative comments in public hurt them more deeply. A private space is the best spot to deliver corrective feedback.
- Give the feedback at the appropriate time such that the issue can be addressed promptly. Waiting too late could have a detrimental effect on the consequences.
- Let the feedback be regular. Especially in the team environment, it is helpful to have one-on-one sessions at least once every 2 weeks. Feedback twice a year during the midyear and annual performance cycles, could some with surprise, making them seldom effective.
- Followup after some time to see if the feedback has been actioned or not.

8.4.2 Self-Assessment

Self-assessment is a very powerful technique used for betterment of a product, process, or an individual. Its purpose is to stimulate learning and change, as well as demonstrate enthusiasm for positive development.

It can be applied through the project. One could use a checklist or a questionnaire from time to time to assess the health of the team.

8.4.3 Failure modes and alternatives

Alistair Cockburn, in his book *Agile Software Development - The Cooperative Game,* has described some failure modes, while determining characteristics of people that impact project outcomes.

- **Making mistakes** - it is natural that people make mistakes, so there needs to be a mechanism (like iterative delivery) to take corrective actions quickly.
- **Preferring to fail conservatively** - generally people are risk averse, but when they fail, they have a tendency to revert back to safe and suboptimal methods instead of researching further.
- **Inventing rather than researching** - refers to the tendency of people to reinvent the wheels rather than looking around for solutions that are already in place.
- **Being inconsistent creatures of habit** - making it difficult to adopt new approaches.

On the positive side, Alistair has also listed some success modes thatare positive characteristics that could contribute to project successes.

- being good at looking around
- being able to learn
- being malleable
- taking pride in work
- taking pride in contributing
- being good citizens
- taking initiative

8.4.4 Agile coaching and mentoring

One of the primary ways to continuously nurture and improve the people working in a team is through periodic coaching interventions. The type of coaching intervention varies with the maturity of the team and its growing comfort in thriving in a collaborative and synergistic environment. The Shu-Ha-Ri model that we saw in Chapter 5: Team Performance shows how the team progresses through their steps of maturity. Similarly even in the case of an Agile coach, his / her coaching skills moves the Shu-Ha-Ri levels of maturity.

During a typical coaching session, the Agile coach explores the team dynamics nonintrusively and shares their Agile experiences and ideas to the team members with an intent to encourage him or her to learn, adopt and adapt based on the demands of the situation.

Lyssa Adkins has very neatly articulated the multifaceted role of an Agile coach, illustrated pictorially in Figure 8-7. During coaching sessions, the Agile coach models the desired behaviors (like active listening, participative decision-making, adaptive leadership and confronting impediments) that lead the team to success. Coaches reach out to each individual member of the team, understand their expectations, beliefs and aspirations and help them become better and better in following the principles and practices of Agile.

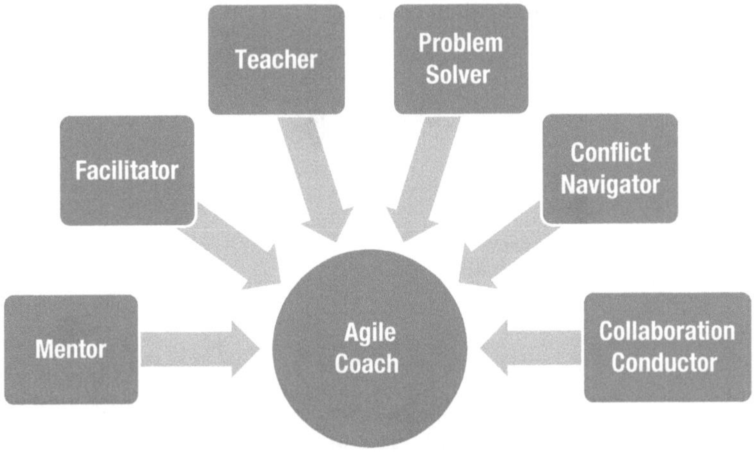

Figure 8-7. *Multifaceted role of an Agile coach*[6]

8.4.4.1 Individual coaching vs. team coaching

An Agile coach indulges in two levels of coaching simultaneously - one at an individual level and the other at the team level. Figure 8-8 is an adaptation from the illustration given by Lyssa Adkins to show how Agile coaches switch from one level to another during the sprint.

During the beginning and end of the sprints and releases, the Agile coach does the most amount of coaching at the team level. During this time, the Agile coach guides the team through the principles of Agile, often interleaving with teaching sessions on various practices to enhance effectiveness in pursuit of their goal. During this time, the teams are involved in sprint planning, sprint review and retrospectives. If there are issues discovered during the middle of the sprint, the Agile coach generally reserves them to be discussed during the retrospective, so as not to disturb the operating rhythm of the team. As we have seen earlier, the outcome of retrospectives are process improvements and this is where the Agile coach could play a very handy role in guiding the team through their decisions and practices of continuous improvement.

[6]Figure based on the content *Coaching Agile Teams* authored by Lyssa Adkins. (The Addison-Wesley 18 May 2010).

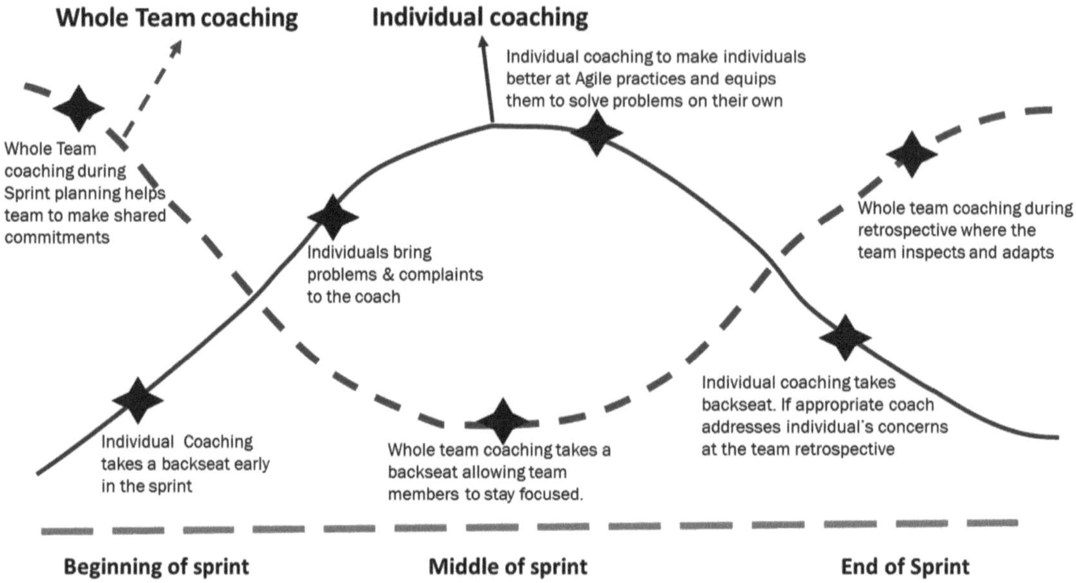

Figure 8-8. *Coaching intervention during a sprint*[7]

During the middle of the sprint, the team coaching takes a backseat. Team members approach the Agile coach with their problems and issues and mostly benefit from individual coaching or mentoring sessions on a one-on-one basis. The aspects of coaching could be conflict management, reinforcing of values, identifying skills for improvement and so on. In the next section, we shall see some of the groundwork that goes on to make one-on-one coaching effective.

8.4.4.2 Groundwork for one-on-one coaching

The conversation that the Agile coach should be having should breed trust, confidence and respect. The team members should naturally feel that the coach is always around to listen to their problems and give sound advice. Lyssa Adkins has suggested some groundwork in this context:

- **Meet them a half-step ahead** - Agile coach uses their knowledge and experience to help team members take the next step from where they are currently.
- **Guarantee safety** - Agile coaches need to maintain sensitivity and confidentiality of the coaching conversation. Team members should be able to openly share their thoughts and feelings without any fear of reprisal or retribution.
- **Partner with managers** - Often team members may be line managed by the managers of other departments. It is important for the coach to collaborate with the managers to understand their approach, rewards and strategy such that the team member is able to receive a holistic and joined-up support from the coach and the manager.
- **Create a positive regard** - Agile coach has to maintain professionality and positive regard of team members who need coaching, even if they are disliked. The focus should be on helping people improve themselves in their current roles.

[7]Adapted from Figure titled "Whole-team and individual coaching interventions during the sprint," from the book - *Coaching Agile Teams* authored by Lyssa Adkins (The Addison-Wesley 18 May 2010).

8.4.4.3 Agile coaching - failure modes

Lyssa Adkins, from her profound experience, has shared a few failure modes[8] seen in Agile coaching. For the purpose of the PMI-ACP® exam, details of each of the modes are not required. So we cover only the basics of each in Table 8-4 below.

Table 8-4. *Agile Coaching - failure modes*

Agile coaching failure modes	Characteristics
Spy mode	Agile coach plays the watch-dog role, observes the team with an intent to pick up topics for the next retrospective and then disappears. There may not be a trusted relationship between such a coach and the team.
The Seagull	Agile coach attends stands-up, offers advice to the team to resolve situations. and 'flies' back again.
The Butterfly	Agile coach hovers around from one team to another, offering advice to the team randomly, not necessarily when the team is looking for help.
The Opinionator	Agile coach expresses their opinions, rather than coaching the team to have discussions and resolve the problems on their own.
The Admin	Agile coach does less of coaching, but more of administrative tasks like arranging for logistics and other trivial jobs.
The Hub	Agile coach acts as a center for all communication and tasks in the team.
The Expert	Agile coach, because of his expertise, gets too involved in problem solving that he/she may not allow the team to learn and be on their own.
The Nag	Agile coach keeps chasing the team to complete their tasks and keep their commitment.

8.4.4.4 Agile coaching - success modes

Lyssa Adkins continues with her observations of good practices that make Agile Coaches successful. Table 8-5 below shows the various success modes.

Table 8-5. *Agile Coaching - success modes*

Agile coaching success modes	Characteristics
The Magician	Agile coach asks questions that help the team discover solutions that otherwise werenot seen or found.
The Child	Agile coach is curious about everything and looks for reasoning in everything around them.
The Ear	Agile coach patiently listens to everything from the team, but allows the team to act on their own by withholding their responses or opinions.

(*continued*)

[8]Refer to *Coaching Agile Teams* by Lyssa Adkins (The Addison-Wesley 18 May 2010).

Table 8-5. (*continued*)

Agile coaching success modes	Characteristics
The Heckler	Agile coach keeps the environment fun and light, helping the team to stay focused and productive.
The Wise fool	Agile coach asks dumb questions that help the team to learn and discover new information.
The Creeping Vine	Agile coach makes small moves for improvement that the team might not observe, but pulls them in the direction of sound Agile practices.
The Dreamer	Agile coach dreams of the future and thinks of ways to achieve it.
The Megaphone	Agile coach hears everyone to form a holistic perspective.

8.5 Agile adoption

Although many organizations understand the benefits of following Agile like higher return on investment, efficiency and customer-oriented behavior, transition into Agile is not easy. There could be situations where the top management has an intense desire to transform the way value is delivered to the customer and they see Agile and devops a means of realizing their vision. But, on the ground there could be lots of resistive forces - legacy software, documentation-heavy processes, silos in the organization and mindsets of people. The bigger the organization the more intertwined are its processes. Although the topic of adoption of Agile practices is beyond the scope of the PMI-ACP® exam and this book, it makes sense to reflect on the real world and explore a couple of points mentioned below.

8.5.1 Agile hybrid models

Some organizations adopt a model that is more of a hybrid between traditional waterfall and Agile approaches. In some literature the word Water-Scrum-Fall can be found. There are a few scenarios where the hybrid model is used to get the best of both worlds:

- **Large multi-year complex programs** - Often organizations, when they want to embark on large transformative programs, would need to predict deadlines, milestones and budgets. There is a fair degree of approximation that is required upfront to get the program kick-started. But once the program is underway, the execution happens in an Agile fashion, making use of rapid cycles of iterative delivery and feedback cycles to conform to the master plan.
- **Regulatory and compliance projects** - Such projects are characterized by lengthy requirements gathering; and detailed business, technical and data analysis stages. For example, when the Basel or Dodd-Frank regulations came into being, large financial institutions spawned several projects to understand the compliance requirements, determine the impact on their software systems, their outputs and the users and of course document it for future reference. In most cases, such projects also need to refer to a high-level architectural roadmap (business architecture and technical architecture) and a design based on that. At a more project-level, execution could still go on in an Agile fashion.

- **Dependencies between teams working at different pace** - Organizations could encounter projects that cut across multiple departments (or even vendors) who operate at different speeds or on different priorities that are not aligned to each other. For example, an Agile team is dependent on another upstream application team who delivers software increments once in a quarter. Or a team that cannot fully integrate until the vendor has released the beta version of their product on a particular release date. In such situations a purist Agile approach will fail. So a fairly detailed up-front plan that enlists the dependencies is required. Each of the teams could continue to be Agile in their own worlds. In another situation one or more of the interfacing teams could be following waterfall methodologies as well!
- **Solutions that impact legacy and 'fast-moving' technology together** - Let's envision a company that is working on a library of API-based services that can be invoked by their mobile applications. The middle tier of the solution is based on open sourced software, but the backend needs to be integrated with the legacy (say, mainframe) based solutions. In such cases, a hybrid solution that does some planning and an end-to-end strawman design upfront is required. Of course, the mobile applications can be developed in a strictly Agile manner with continuous collaboration between the development team and the end users.
- **Solutions that depend on lengthy hardware provisioning cycles** - It is seen from experience that procuring and provisioning of hardware is generally a very time-consuming affair. Projects that need their application software to be deployed on specific hardware, networking equipment, or commercial software will need to plan upfront and get their infrastructure plan approved by the infrastructure board before the procurement process can begin. Such situations call for up-front architecture and planning and the hybrid method suits particularly well.
- **Organizational hierarchy consisting of specialists and 'horizontals'** - We have often encountered organizations thatare teamed up into specialisms like architecture, design, UX designer, development and testing. Without cross-functional skills, it is really hard to transform such an organization structure to work in an Agile fashion. What such organizations start doing, is breaking the scope into manageable chunks of work items and delivering in sequential cycles of mini-waterfalls one after another. This keeps the designer, developer and the tester all busy, but with work catering to different versions. Although this makes the team utilization very high, it creates a lot of thrashing since resources needs to keep switching context if they have to troubleshoot something of the past. This also necessitates an increased level of management oversight to ensure that the arrangement keeps working effectively. This is far from being Agile.

8.5.2 Sidky Agile Maturity Index

While an increasing number of organizations are beginning to adopt Agile practices to deliver value to their businesses, they do not have a rulebook or a prescribed set of steps to transition from the traditional waterfall-based methodology to the Agile methodology. Organizations experience a very wide variation in their current-day processes; their maturity; their organization structure, culture, mindset;and also in their zeal to experiment a new way of working.

Ahmed Sidky and James D. Arthur, in 2006, came up with the Sidky Agile Measurement Index[9] (SAMI) that is used to rank the maturity of Agile practices in an organization. SAMI has been popularly adopted by the Agile community and acts like a framework thatdetermines the readiness of an organization to adopt Agile and what set of practices can and should be introduced in the organization. The different levels are listed below in Figure 8-9.

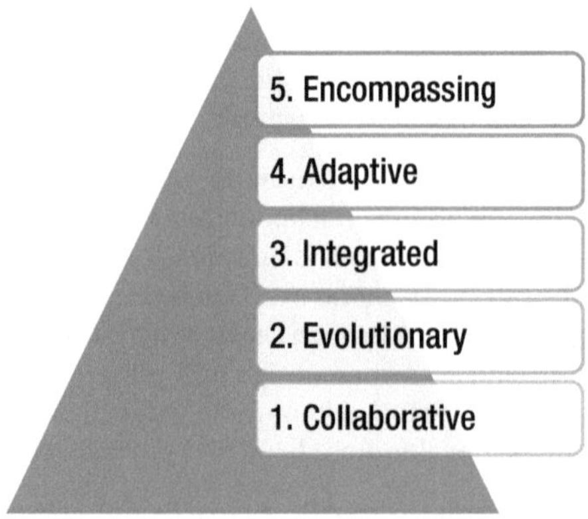

Figure 8-9. *SAMI and stages of Agile adoption*

The first level is labeled collaborative where stakeholders have an enhanced level of communication between themselves and the team is self-organized and empowered to make decisions on their own or through group consensus.

The second level is labeled as evolutionary, where the teams evolve their delivery model continuously to produce software iteratively and incrementally.

In the third stage labeled as integrated, the team works synergistically and in an integrated fashion to deliver high-quality software to the customer in an efficient and integrated manner.

The fourth stage is labeled as adaptive where there team members not only uses Agile practices efficiently, but also makes use of multiple checkpoints to receive feedback and respond to changes naturally.

The final stage is encompassing where the Agile team is able to foster agility throughout the organization in a sustainable way and not fallback into the waterfall mode of working.

8.5.3 Adopting Agile in an organization – Virginia Satir change model

Referring to Virginia Satir's model (Figure 8-10), organizations and teams go through the change curve when they transition from traditional methodologies to Agile. There could be a dip in performance for a little time, as the teams organize themselves, look to overcome resistance to change and settle down into a sustainable operating rhythm. Like all flavors of Agile, the important aspect is to start imminently and not plan too far ahead.

[9]Refer to the paper –"A Disciplined Approach to Adopting Agile Practices: The Agile Adoption Framework" by Ahmed Sidky and James Arthur, available at `https://arxiv.org/ftp/arxiv/papers/0704/0704.1294.pdf`

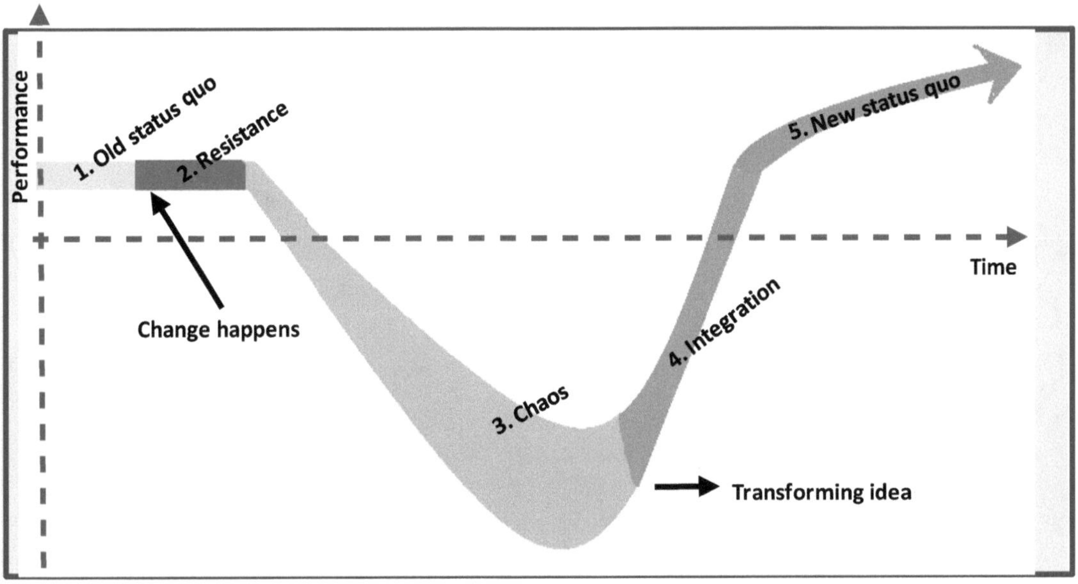

Figure 8-10. *Virginia Satir Change Model*

One way to make the transition gradual and appealing is to take some calculated risk. This can be done by teaming up a bunch of enthusiastic engineers with a handful of Agile tools and a lightweight framework like Scrum or Kanban to conduct a proof-of-concept on a small and 'fail-safe' project (let's call it a pilot project). Once the team accomplishes their goal, they should demonstrate improvements in the form of automation (let's say a reduction in headcount), quicker turnaround, efficient use of cross-functional resources, motivated manpower and a happier customer. If the demonstration is effective enough, it can make heads turn. The fear of the unknown begins to fade away as more and more projects and teams begin to follow. With more attention, executive sponsorship follows, as that is critical for any Agile transformation to succeed. The results are reflected in the performance - development teams and businesses collaborate and become more determined to pursue continuous improvement and iterative delivery. The team members on the pilot project become internal experts and begin evangelizing across teams and building more capability. This results in a paradigm shift.

8.6 Focus areas for the exam

- ✓ How knowledge sharing or knowledge dissemination happens in Agile teams?
- ✓ What is the literal meaning of the word Kaizen?
- ✓ What are Lean 5S, Fishbone, 5 Why's and Pareto techniques?
- ✓ How are control charts used for process improvement? Concept around process being out of control and rule of seven.
- ✓ What is the purpose of a retrospective?
- ✓ The five steps for a retrospective. Details of the techniques under each step may not be required that much.

- ✓ What is introspection and pre-mortem?
- ✓ What are best practices to provide feedback?
- ✓ What are the failure modes?
- ✓ Different facets of roles of an Agile coach.
- ✓ When does an Agile coach focus on individual coaching and team coaching?
- ✓ Agile coaching - success and failure modes.
- ✓ Agile adoption in an organization - basic awareness of Virginia Satir Change curve and Sidky Agile Maturity Index (SAMI).

Quizzes

1. Retrospective meeting happens after which event in an iteration?

   A. Iteration review meeting

   B. Iteration planning meeting

   C. Release planning meeting

   D. Daily stand-up meeting

2. In retrospective, Gather data stage includesactivities like ________.

   A. triple nickels, control chart, locate strengths

   B. timeline, color code dots, team strengths

   C. triple nickels, color code dots, locate strengths

   D. timeline, control charts, team strengths

3. Richard is conducting a retrospective meeting. As recommended by the Agile coach, Richard is planning on using the following agenda in the meeting:

   A. Set the stage, generate data, gather insight, decide what to do, close the retrospective.

   B. Set the stage, gather data, generate insight, decide what to do, close the retrospective.

   C. Gather data, set the stage, generate insight, decide what to do, close the retrospective.

   D. Gather data, set the stage, decide what to do, generate insight, close the retrospective.

4. Failure modes shared by Alistair Cockburn, includes all of the following except:

   A. Fail conservatively

   B. Inventing rather than researching

   C. Making mistakes

   D. Being consistent

5. An event where the team calls for an adhoc or impromptu retrospective meeting is:

   A. Retrospective meeting

   B. Adhoc retrospective meeting

   C. Intraspective meeting

   D. Daily stand-up meeting

6. __________ is a technique used to identify the root cause of a problem.

   A. Pareto chart

   B. Fishbone diagram

   C. Control chart

   D. Scatter diagram

7. In focus on / focus off exercise, the team should focus on __________ rather than advocacy.

   A. Dialogue

   B. Investigation

   C. Understanding

   D. Inquiry

8. Actions and goals that teams agree at the end of retrospectives should be SMART. The acronym stands for:

   A. Specific, measurable, achievable, realistic, time-bound

   B. Short, measurable, actionable, realistic, time-bound

   C. Specific, measurable, amendable, realistic, time-bound

   D. Short, measurable, achievable, random, time-bound

9. What is a control chart?

   A. A type of a RACI chart

   B. A chart that shows the root cause of a problem

   C. A type of a fishbone diagram

   D. A chart that shows the stability of a process

10. In SIDKY's agile maturity framework, what are the different levels to follow agile practices

    A. Collaborative, evolutionary, integrated, adaptive, encompassing

    B. Collaborative, exploratory, integrated, adaptive, encompassing

    C. Constructive, exploratory, integrated, adaptive, encompassing

    D. Consistent, evolutionary, integrated, adaptive, encompassing

11. Which of the following is a recommendation for one-on-one coaching?

    A. Guarantee safety so that the team member is able to open up.

    B. Create positive regard and show professionalism at all times.

    C. Team up with the functional manager of the team member.

    D. All of the above.

12. Retrospective is best described as:

    A. Review the software built by the team and not how the team worked and apply the learnings to the next iteration.

    B. A forum to share achievements, celebrate and identify coaching needs.

    C. Identify 5 things thatwent well and 5 things thatdid not go well or could have been better. Documents these lessons learned and save in organizational document repository for use in future projects.

    D. Review how the team worked and not on what was delivered. Take the learning on what could be improved and feedthat as input to next iteration.

13. The activity of ________________ is to analyze the current processes and make changes as per project requirements.

    A. Process Tailoring

    B. Value Stream Mapping

    C. Process analysis.

    D. Creating product backlog

14. As an agile coach, you coach at two levels - Whole-team level and Individual level. Which level is it best to coach at the start and end of an iteration?

    A. Whole-team

    B. Individual Level

    C. Both levels

    D. None of the above

15. Individual level coaching is best to provide at which stage of the sprint?

    A. Start of a sprint

    B. End of a sprint

    C. Middle of a sprint

    D. Anytime when conflicts arise

16. What does Lean 5S stands for

    A. sort, set in order, shine, standardize, sustain

    B. set in order, sort, standardize, sustain shine

    C. sustain, standardize, sort, set in order, shine

    D. standardize, sustain, sort, set in order, shine

17. During inspection, you found that the 3 consecutively selected specimens of the manufactured product have dimensions of 5.78 cm. As per the contract, the client has mentioned specification limits of 5.55 cm to 5.85 cm. And the control limits are 5.7 cm to 5.8 cm. What should you do?

    A. Reject the items as the measurement is above the lower control limit. Adjust the process.

    B. Discard the specimens as they are too close to the upper control limit.

    C. Accept the item since the measurement lies within the specification limits.

    D. Accept the item since the measurement lies within the control limits and the rule of seven is not violated.

18. There is a problem reported during process analysis. A chart with several dots showing that the process is out of control, so which tool is in use here?

    A. Pareto Diagram

    B. Control chart

    C. Burndown Chart

    D. Kanban Chart

19. Virginia Satir model depicts:

    A. The relationship between products, processes and people.

    B. The change curve in transition from the current to the future stage.

    C. The skill development requirements within the team.

    D. The prescription for Agile adoption in an organization.

20. When closing a retrospective, which activity is used?

    A. Circle of questions

    B. Brainstorming

    C. Helped, Hindered, Hypothesis

    D. Mad, sad, glad

Answer

1. A
2. C
3. B
4. D
5. C
6. B
7. D
8. A
9. D
10. A
11. D
12. D
13. A
14. A
15. C
16. A
17. D
18. B
19. B
20. C

CHAPTER 9

PMI® Code of Ethics and Professional Conduct

On matters of style, swim with the current, on matters of principle, stand like a rock.

—Thomas Jefferson

This is the final chapter on the course for the PMI-ACP® exam. One can expect up to 4 or 5 questions on the topic of ethics and professional conduct as it relates to the Agile practitioner. Questions are most likely blended with other topics, so it might be hard to pinpoint the chapter from where it is originating; and as such, that is unnecessary to know as well.

This chapter is based on the eight-page PDF document that is available for download from the PMI® site and it is recommended to be read during the course of preparation for the exam. The link to the document is given below:

`http://www.pmi.org/-/media/pmi/documents/public/pdf/governance/code-of-ethics-and-professional-conduct.pdf?la=en`

The same code is also included inside the PMI-ACP® handbook:

`http://www.pmi.org/-/media/pmi/documents/public/pdf/certifications/agile-certified-practitioner-handbook.pdf`

In this chapter we will only touch upon the topics thatcould be expected in the PMI-ACP® exam or certain guidelines and scenarios that could help one to answer the relevant questions correctly.

9.1 Purpose of the Code

The Project Management Institute is the world's leading project management organization with close to half a million members and certification holders globally. As professionals contribute to the organization, society and their personal lives, they are often confronted with dilemmas and choices that impact their projects and their involvement. PMI® has created a practical framework consisting of four key values of honesty, responsibility, respect and fairness that drive ethical conduct. PMI® believes this framework helpsone to make a wise choice when faced with difficult situations that concern ethics and conduct during pursuit of success in the real-life project management profession.

By following a uniform framework, PMI® expects all fellow practitioners belonging to the global project management fraternity to uphold the highest standards of integrity, trust, credibility and reputation earned while interacting with their people, superiors, customers, other internal and external stakeholders and the society at large.

S. Boral, *Ace the PMI-ACP® exam*, DOI 10.1007/978-1-4842-2526-4_9

9.2 For Whom Does the Code Apply?

The code of ethics and professional conduct is not meant only for PMI-ACP® certification aspirants or holders. In fact, PMI® has designed and structured the code such that this applies uniformly and consistently to a wide range of professionals of project management and members and certification holders.

As PMI® states, the code applies uniformly to:

- All members of the Project Management Institute (PMI®)
- All who hold a PMI® certification like PMP®, PMI-ACP®, PMI-RMP®, PgMP®, CAPM®
- All who are pursuing a certification from PMI®
- All volunteers of PMI® for chapter events like seminars and conferences

9.3 Structure of the Code

Each section of the code has been structured into aspirational standards and mandatory standards. The aspirational standards are the ones that we strive to uphold and adhere to at all times, while the mandatory standards are firm guidelines that limit or prohibit behavior that is deemed inappropriate. Violations to the mandatory standards are subject to disciplinary actions from PMI's Ethics Review committee.

9.4 Four Core Values of the Code

Let us now look at the four values of the code. Note that the code and its standards refer to "we" and "us," which implies the practitioners.

9.4.1 Responsibility

The code states[1] that responsibility is our duty to take ownership of the decision and actions we make or fail to make and their resulting consequences.

Here are a few standards in this regard:

- We make decisions and take actions that serve the best interests of the society and the environment.
- We accept assignments and fulfill project and professional obligations that are commensurate with our qualifications and skills.
- We fulfill commitments dutifully, maintaining professional integrity at all times.
- Wherever we notice errors or omissions, we own up, communicate asis and take appropriate corrective actions promptly.

[1]To preserve the originality, the definitions are quoted from: `http://www.pmi.org/-/media/pmi/documents/public/pdf/governance/code-of-ethics-and-professional-conduct.pdf?la=en`

- We follow rules, laws and compliance requirements; protect and respect intellectual property, proprietary, confidential and sensitive information.
- Wherever we notice unethical or illegal practices, behavior, or violations of the code, we report them to the appropriate authorities substantiated by facts of observation.

9.4.2 Respect

The code states that respect is our duty to show a high regard for ourselves, others and the resources entrusted to us that include people, money, reputation, the safety of others and natural or environmental resources.

Here are a few standards in this regard:

- Create an environment based on trust and confidence where diverse perspectives and views are encouraged, listened and valued.
- We respect cultural diversity and avoid any behaviors that areconsidered inappropriate or disrespectful.
- We confront and address conflicts directly with the persons involved in conflict and try to resolve them professionally by mutual respect and understanding each other's perspectives.
- We negotiate in good faith with our customers and vendors and try to reach a desirable win-win outcome wherever possible or applicable.
- We do not abuse our power or position to influence an outcome that is personally favorable to us.
- We refrain from any abusive behavior.

9.4.3 Fairness

The code states that fairness is our duty to make decisions transparently and act objectively with any partiality, bias, self-interest, or prejudice.

Here are a few standards in this regard:

- We make decisions in a transparent and impartial manner.
- We try to steer away from potential conflict-of-interest situations, provide full disclosure to the authorities proactively and refrain from being involved or influencing or making any decisions in such a situation.
- We provide a fair ground and equal opportunities by allowing competitors access to the same resources (e.g., data and systems) that they are entitled to.
- We act fairly during evaluating and hiring of resources and do not base decisions on personal consideration or any discrimination.
- We follow diversity and foster an inclusive workforce by removing all discriminations of gender, race, physical disability, sexual orientation, age and religion.
- We educate ourselves about cultural diversity and maintain professional sensitivity and fairness when dealing with other cultures.

9.4.4 Honesty

The code states that honesty is our duty to understand the truth and act in a truthful manner.

Here are a few standards in this regard:

- We seek truth and create an environment where truth can prevail at all times.
- We do not mislead our stakeholders by giving them delayed, partial, incomplete, or inaccurate information.
- We provide communication that is accurate, reliable and timely even if that applies to delivering bad news or news that is expected to create a negative outcome.
- We do not shift blame to others when sharing bad news.
- We give credit to the person(s) who deserve so and not take undue advantage.
- We do not resort to dishonest means (like bribe or inappropriate gifts), deceive others, or for personal gain.
- We make promises and commitments in good faith.

9.5 Core Values in Agile Perspective

In this final section of this chapter, let us have a quick look at Table 9-1. The table shows some of the Agile practices, tools and techniques that embody the four core values from the code of ethics and professional conduct.

Table 9-1. *Core values from code of ethics and Agile practices*

Core Values	Agile practices, tools and techniques that embody them
Responsibility	• Pair programming and collective code ownership - how XP teams mutually collaborate, organize themselves and take responsibility of the code, troubleshoot and resolve defects and refactor continuously to keep technical debt at a low. • Retrospectives - how team members exhibit courage and openness during retrospectives to speak up on what is going well and what is not, based on which the team agrees to act. • Value-based analysis and value-driven prioritization - how teams make decisions on value, estimates and priorities in the interest of the project and the organization.
Respect	• Group decision-making and planning poker estimation - how teams respect each other's views and take group-based decisions at the time of planning, estimation, designing and implementing incrementally. • Servant leadership- Exhibited in the role of the Scrum Master, servant leadership is about providing what the team needs to be successful, removing impediments. • Caves and commons -having open spaces for the team to openly collaborate, but at the same time respecting the need for having privacy by having 'caves.' • Participative leadership style - in contrast to command-and-control style of management, this style respects the individuality and experience of team members and empowers them to contribute their best. • Virtual teams - using various technologies and cross-cultural programs to bind distributed teams working across various locations and timezones.

(*continued*)

Table 9-1. *(continued)*

Core Values	Agile practices, tools and techniques that embody them
Fairness	• Valuing customer collaboration over negotiation - being fair to the customer by anticipating, welcoming and accommodating change even late in the day and collaborating with them to ensure realization of business value. • Agile contracting - disclosing proactively if there is any conflict of interest and negotiating in good faith to obtain a win-win outcome. • Estimation - making sure that the estimates are fair and consensus is reached within the team during the planning session and also reviewing / revising the same based on enhanced understanding as the project progresses. • Conflict management - dealing with various levels of conflicts and resolving them using the most constructive strategy.
Honesty	• Information radiators - using burndown charts and tracking velocity to transparently show the progress of the project. • Sprint demo - involving the customers and giving them an early and honest view of the result of the iteration and seeking feedback. • Retrospectives - brainstorming together as a team to identify what went well and what needs to be improved upon. • Daily stand-ups - daily forums where team members discuss and disclose what got done and what impedes their progress. • Value stream maps and CFD's - using them to show workinprogress and identifying wastes and bottlenecks in the process.

9.6 Focus Areas for the Exam

✓ Four values of the code of ethics and professional conduct.

✓ Only scenario-based questions are expected from this topic.

✓ When in doubt, always fall back to the standards stated against each of the four values.

Quizzes

1. What are the core values of the PMI® code of ethics?

    A. Responsibility, Respect, Fairness, Honesty

    B. Responsibility, Respect, Fairness, Truth

    C. Responsibility, Integrity, Confidence, Fairness, Honesty

    D. Responsibility, Respect, Openness, Honesty

2. Bill is discussing the terms and conditions of a contract with a supplier. He observes that the supplier is happy to deal verbally, but when it comes to documentation he is not taking much of an interest. As a result, the contract documentation is very flaky and impeding the sign-off process from both sides. What should Bill do now?

    A. Since you need a win-win outcome, agree to an informal way as this is how the supplier company works and is comfortable.

    B. Start documenting all conversation with this supplier as meeting minutes and keep them as a record.

    C. Back out of the contract.

    D. Insist the supplier follows all project processes including formal contracts and sign-off. Also keep senior stakeholders informed.

3. Richard is working on a project to manufacture spare parts of a vehicle. However, the customer rejected the shipmentdue to the wrong size of parts as compared to the agreed size in the contract. What should you do?

    A. The contract should be updated for the new size of the spare parts.

    B. The sunk costs can be adjusted against project contingency reserves.

    C. Quality control has been failed, resulting in the wrong size of spare parts manufactured. So take corrective actions.

    D. Blame the manufacturing team.

4. PMI® code applies to all, except:

    A. PMI® members.

    B. Holds a PMI® certification but not a PMI® member.

    C. In process to apply for a certification but not a PMI® member.

    D. Neither involved with PMI® nor a PMI® member.

5. A position is opened on your project. One of your relatives approached you for the same and requested to refer his resume for this open position in your project. You should:

   A. Submit the resume since the skillsets match but do not disclose that you are a relative.

   B. Do not submit, as this will be a conflict of interest.

   C. Submit the resume but disclose the relationship to the hiring department.

   D. Secretly give it to one of your colleagues to submit the resume so that you can avail yourself of the referral benefit.

6. You are working on new bid for your company. One of your friend's companies is in competition. He approached you trying to get some information on the bid including financial information. The information is classified as 'company internal.' What do you do?

   A. Decline the request politely.

   B. Provide the information as he is your best friend.

   C. Provide the information on condition that you will share some benefit out of it.

   D. Provide partial information, which will not harm you or your organization.

7. You understand that one of your colleagues is filing for PMI® certification but does not have relevant experience. He is filling the application with wrong information. What should you do?

   A. Remind him of PMI®'s code of ethics and professional responsibility.

   B. Escalate to his manager.

   C. Report to PMI®.

   D. Leave it for the PMI® audit team to take care of it.

8. Richard, from another department, is deputizing while the assigned project manager is on long leave. While collecting project status, Richard finds discrepancy in status from past few weeks. The project is overspent, behind schedule. and actually in RED but shown Green on reports. What should Richard do?

   A. Report to PMI®, as this is clear violation of PMI®'s code of ethics.

   B. Since Richard is filling in, continue with the data of the previous report, as no one else noticed the discrepancy.

   C. Update actual status to dashboard report and inform the management.

   D. Ask the project manager about the discrepancies when he returns.

Answer

1. A
2. D
3. C
4. D
5. B
6. A
7. A
8. C

Appendix

Advice, tips and tricks

The PMI-ACP® certification is an important step in your career to boost your proficiency in Agile practices. Like most strategic pursuits, apply the 5 R's technique:

- **Results** - First determine your 'SMART' goal. Be convinced that you want to get PMI-ACP® certified in a finite time (say 3 months).
- **Reason** - Second, have your own explanation why you want to get PMI-ACP® certified. What is your plan after getting certified? Maybe it is just to increase your knowledge in Agile, prove your proficiency, keep pace with the industry, search for a new job,or simply to meet the training targets set on your biannual goals and objectives.
- **Roadmap** - Come up with a plan how you are going to realize the results. Determine your position with respect to the eligibility criteria for the exam and see if you need to fill in any gaps. Set a target date that is feasible and in-line with your other professional and personal commitments. Define some intermediate milestones. If you need to move the milestones or the target, self-justify why you are doing so and whether the new dates are indeed achievable or not.
- **Review** - At periodic intervals review whether you are going as per the plan or not. Research the areas where you are losing marks. If you are finding a topic difficult to absorb, read and practice more. Talk to your colleague or supervisor or anyone you feel appropriate. Refer to some of the reference books I have listed. It's important that you keep up the motivation; do not get bogged down and continue to move forward to your own target.
- **Resources** - Find out what resources you need. Since you are already reading this book, the primary resource is already with you. You might need to take a few leaves from your work during the preparatory phase. You might attend the 21-hour formal training course. You might need help from family (for the time you sacrifice!) and peer colleagues. You might benefit from forming a study group with aspirants in your similar situation.

In the following section I will give you some do's and don'ts, based on my personal experience that you might consider helpful. This is the risky part, since every exam taker has his or her own style of approaching a goal. So, read it and absorb only the part that you can personally connect to. If it strikes a chord, great! If it doesn't, don't bother.

S. Boral, *Ace the PMI-ACP® exam*, DOI 10.1007/978-1-4842-2526-4_10

Before the exam

- ✓ Do prepare a plan for your preparation and stick to it. If you have sufficient Agile project experience, you will notice that the subject matter for PMI-ACP® exam is not difficult, but it needs familiarity of the vocabulary and consistent practice. At the same time you cannot take it casually.
- ✓ Do consider forming study groups. If you find one in your organization, then it is probably the best. Otherwise lookout for regional meetup groups or ones on social media. Maintain a balance on the time you spend behind your preparations versus such activities.
- ✓ Do subscribe to virtual forums like groups on LinkedIn®. You will find experts and like-minded aspirants, in various stages of preparation, over there. Often questions are discussed. Some people share their personal experiences, which could be quite useful.
- ✓ Do connect the theory with your professional experience as that will help with learning and retention. Prefer this over memorization.
- ✓ Do fill up your application form carefully and truthfully. The section on your project experience can take time to fill (up to 2-3 days). Avoid jargons and acronyms in the free-text field for the project description. Use words that appear in Agile vocabulary that anyone can easily relate to during your application review. Contact your colleague or ex-supervisor if you have named them on your previous project details. Factor in the time needed for doing that if you have moved organizations.
- ✓ Do practice the full-length mocktests religiously. The PMI-ACP® exam last 3 hours - so not only does it test your proficiency and knowledge, it tests your patience, perseverance and sustained levels of concentration for 3 hours at a stretch. Most of you would have gotten out of the habit of taking long exams, so make sure that you are physically and mentally rehearsed going through the 3-hour rigor before the real exam.
- ✓ Do schedule your exam during the first half of the day. That's when you have the highest levels of energy.
- ✓ Do take a trip to the Prometric test center a few days before the exam. If you are planning to drive, then familiarize yourself with the route, traffic conditions and parking spots. Otherwise if you are using public transportation, check for the modes and the stops you need to take. If planned in advance, the test center administrator can also give you a walking tour. If the test center is really far off and two trips may not be feasible, then it is okay. But otherwise, this trip might just add to your comfort.
- ✗ Do not overwhelm yourself with arbitrary content over the Internet. They have varied qualities of content that might confuse you. Exercise caution if you are attempting mock exams from elsewhere -if they are not at the equivalent difficulty level as the final exam, you are likely to either get a false sense of elation and confidence or get demotivated.
- ✗ Do not worry too much about mathematical formulae. There are just a few of them (given below) and the number of mathematical questions on the real exam are also going to be very few.
- ✗ Do not schedule the exam too early, like several months ago. Chances are that you might lose momentum or even something else might crop up at the last moment.

- × Do not panic if your application is picked up for audit. This is random and not a reflection of any suspicion from PMI® about your application. Respond to the audit request transparently and timely - everything should be fine.
- × Do not worry if your preparation is interrupted temporarily with a high-priority need from your family or work. But do not get stressed out or feel guilty. You should carve out a plan that works best and helps you to make your certification journey a pleasing one.
- × Do not try to reread or rehearse every material a day before the exam. Stay relaxed and focused. Get a good night's sleep.

During the exam

- ✓ Do try to reach the exam center an hour early before the scheduled start. You will have to sign some paperwork, put away your belongings (some test centers provide lockers) and take the tutorial before the exam. The important thing is to stay relaxed.
- ✓ Do make sure that you are hydrated and had enough food that does not make you desperately hungry before the exam ends. At the same time do not overeat immediately before the exam as that could make you feel sleepy.
- ✓ Do make sure that the environment around you is comfortable. The area should be well lit, well ventilated and there should not be any noise or distractions from fellow test takers (from other subjects). Talk to the test center administrator if you have any concerns.
- ✓ Do keep a watch on the clock while you are going through the exam. You need to complete 120 questions in 180 minutes. This means that you should roughly take (slightly more than) a minute for every question on an average. So, in the best case you should have completed 45-50 questions in the first hour, another 45-50 in the next hour and the remaining questions and marked questions in the last hour.
- ✓ Do consider taking a break if you need one. Take permission from the test center administrator while you leave the room and reenter. Remember your clock keeps ticking during your break, so make it short and do not get distracted.
- ✓ Do choose the best answer, even if you are deciding to 'mark' it and revisit later. Chances are that, after several weeks of preparations, your first choice is going to be the best choice. When you review later, you can stick with the initial choice or change.
- ✓ Do try to arrive at the best option by the strategy of elimination (of the incorrect ones).
- ✓ Do read through ALL the options although you may have already predecided on an option. It is important to rule out the other options to be sure.
- ✓ Do pay attention to keywords like 'Always, Never, Most, Least, First, Last, Except, Not' as they can dramatically influence your choice of the right option.
- ✓ Do use different strategies for lengthy questions, spanning several sentences. If you see one, chances are that a lot of the text in the body of the questions may be extraneous information. You might want to ready the options first in such a case to anticipate what the question might be hinting at. Another strategy could be to read the last sentence that contains the question. This is where some practice will help.

- ✗ Do not try to guess whether a question is unscored question or not. It is neither possible nor relevant.
- ✗ Do not feel distracted if the test center administrator frequently strolls or watches over your back. He will certainly not know about your question, but is simply performing his vigilant duty. You will also be constantly video monitored.
- ✗ Do not resort to any disruptive behavior or unfair means during the exam because these might be grounds for termination of your examination session or grounds for dismissal. Refer to the exam policies and procedures in the PMI-ACP® handbook for more details.
- ✗ Do not leave any questions unanswered as there is no negative marking. Make your best guess.
- ✗ Do not rush through the questions. You might hear people claiming that they are done in 2 hours or so. You can simply ignore that. Work at your own comfortable pace; use all of the time you need; and most important, be sure of the answers that you are choosing. Remember there is no gold medal if you finish in record time.
- ✗ Don't jump into an answer if you find that technically correct from a stand-alone perspective. Check for relevance of the answer in the context of the question asked.
- ✗ Do not get stuck with any question for more than 4 minutes or so. If it's a hard question then it makes sense to take an educated guess, mark it and move on. Remember that all questions, irrespective of the level of difficulty, carries equal marks.
- ✗ Do not panic or get frustrated if you face a series of tough questions, especially at the beginning. The difficulty of the questions might vary, but rest assured that you are likely to get another series of easy-to-score questions later on.
- ✗ Do not 'mark' too many questions, leaving them for later. If you are out of time, then this might just add pressure. I would recommend a thumb-rule of marking no more than 10-15% of the questions.
- ✗ Don't be worried if selecting a particular option doesn't make it grammatically correct when fitted with rest of the sentence.

After the exam

- ✓ Do return the scratch sheets that you used during the exam.
- ✓ Do take the score sheet printed out by the test center administrator with you.
- ✓ Do collect your id and belongings before you leave the exam center.
- ✓ Do celebrate your achievement. You have become certified after weeks of hard work and you certainly deserve it. Call your family, friends and colleagues. Flaunt it on your resume, email signatures, social media - wherever it's appropriate.
- ✓ Do share your experiences and mode of preparation.
- ✓ Do expect PMI® to send you a congratulatory note and a package with the hard copy of the certificate in a few weeks. Your name will also be entered into an online registry for all valid certification holders.
- ✓ Do download the soft copy of your PMI-ACP® certificate by logging into the PMI.org site.

- ✓ Do remember that your PMI-ACP® certificate is valid for 3 years. Scout around to work out a plan how you can gather 30 PDU's over the next 3 years to renew your credential. PMI® allows you to renew sooner, if you have already gathered and reported the PDU's. If you have multiple credentials from PMI® (like PMP®), then an activity could qualify for PDU's in multiple certifications simultaneously.
- ✓ Do read some of the brilliant reference books at your leisure, as they can also help you gather PDU's. If you have PMI® membership, refer to some of the member-only content available through their site.
- ✓ Do consciously try to apply the practices, tools and techniques that you have learned. Especially in contemporary organizations, we get to see software professionals working in hybrid environments where they use things from multiple Agile methods, mixed with traditional project management. As an Agile certified professional, you should be able to facilitate such an environment.
- ✗ Do not be disheartened if you failed the exam. Sometimes it might be because of overconfidence or lack of adequate preparation. You should be able to reflect what went wrong. Seek some advice from fellow practitioners and prepare with a blend of theoretical study augmented with practice tests. Remember that with serious preparation, most do pass the exam.
- ✗ Do not share any of the questions or examples to anyone outside. You have signed the nondisclosure agreement and doing so is a violation of PMI®'s code of ethics and professional conduct.

Good luck for your preparation and the exam!

Acronyms at a glance

Acronym	Expansion	Context
PMI-ACP®	PMI® Agile Certified Practitioner (PMI-ACP)®	Name of the certification
ATDD	Acceptance Test-Driven Development	Writing acceptance tests before writing code
BART	Boundary, authority, role and task	Tool for process improvement in a team
BDD	Behavior-Driven development	Customer-oriented quality practice
CFD	Cumulative Flow Diagram	Visualization to track work in progress
CI	Continuous Integration	Agile tooling
CR	Cost reimbursable	Type of contract
CRACK	Committed, Responsible, Authorized, Collaborative and Knowledgeable	Attributes of a product owner
DEEP	Detailed appropriately, estimable, emergent, prioritized	Attributes of a product backlog
DSDM	Dynamic system development method	An iterative and incremental method of software development
FDD	Feature-Driven Development	An Agile methodology
FP	Fixed Price	Type of contract
INVEST	Independent, Negotiable, Valuable, Estimable, Small, Testable	Attributes of a user story
IRR	Internal Rate of Return	An economic model for project selection
JIT	Just-in-time	A type of planning used in Agile
MMF	Minimally marketable features	Smallest piece of functionality
MoSCOW	Must-have, Should-have, Could-have, Won't-have	Value-based prioritization technique used in Agile
MVP	Minimum viable product	Product with minimum features, but still useful for users
NPV	Net Present Value	An economic model for project selection
PBI	Product Backlog Item	Each item on the product backlog
PDCA	Plan Do Check Act	Deming's cycle for continuous improvement
PESTLE	Political, Environmental, Social, Technological, Legal, Economic	Risk categorization
PMBOK®	Project Management Body of Knowledge	PMI®'s guide for project managers

(*continued*)

Acronym	Expansion	Context
PMI®	Project Management Institute	Premier institute based in the United States,which is also the certifying body for the PMI-ACP® exam
PO	Product Owner	A role in Scrum
RAD	Rapid Application Development	A precursor of Agile methods
ROI	Return on Investment	An economic model for project selection or selection of a feature for implementation
SAFE®	Scaled Agile Framework	Framework for scaling Agile for the enterprise
SMART	Specific, Measurable, Achievable, Relevant, Time-bound	Attribute of a user story or a goal from a retrospective
SOW	Statement of work	Type of contract
T&M	Time and material	Type of contract
TDD	Test-Driven Development	A technique where tests are written before code
TIA	Transparency, Inspection and Adaptation	Three pillars of Scrum
TIMWOOD	Transport, Inventory, Motion, Waiting, Overprocessing, Overproduction, defect	Seven wastes in Lean
TPS	Toyota Production System	Origin of Lean
W5H	What, Why, Who, When, Where, How	Contents of an Agile charter
WIP	Work in progress	Aim to limit in Kanban
XP	Extreme Programming	An Agile methodology
3C's	Card, Conversation, Confirmation	Aspects of a user story

Formulae in a page

Present Value $PV=FV / (1+r)^n$
Where FV = future value, r = interest rate and n = number of time periods.

NPV higher the better
IRR higher the better
BCR higher the better
ROI higher the better
Payback period lower the better

Channels of communication = n * (n -1) / 2,
where n is the number of entities in communication.

Earned Value Management
EV = Earned Value, PV = Planned Value, AC = Actual costs
Schedule Variance SV = EV – PV
Cost Variance CV = EV – AC
Schedule Performance Index SPI = EV / PV
Cost Performance Index CPI = EV / AC

SV < 0 or SPI < 1 means project is behind schedule
CV < 0 or CPI < 1 means project is over budget
SV = 0 or SPI = 1 means project is on schedule
CV = 0 or CPI = 1 means project is on budget
SV > 0 or SPI > 1 means project is ahead of schedule
CV > 0 or CPI > 1 means project is under budget

Little Law:
Work in progress (WIP) = Lead Time * Throughput.
Where Throughput = average rate at which work departs or is completed and Lead Time = average time an item spends in the system

Takt time = Available time for production / customer demand
Where available time is the total number of hours employees are working minus any time for meetings, down times and breaks.

Risk severity or risk exposure or Expected Monetary Value (EMV) = Risk Impact X Risk Probability

Mock Exam I

1. The Managing Director (MD) of the organization stops by the task board of the team and makes a suggestion of an important feature that the development team should deliver in the current iteration. What should the development team do?

   A. Since it is coming from the MD, it must be done at any cost. So drop an item of equal size from the backlog.

   B. Say yes to the MD and then ask the team members to work overtime to achieve their target.

   C. Ask the product owner so that he can discuss the value and priorities with the MD.

   D. Ignore it, the MD will most likely forget what he said a few weeks later.

2. A newly formed development team is working on Sprint zero. In terms of doing the following activities, which is false?

   A. Team completes the entire architecture and high-level design for the project, leaving out the low-level design.

   B. Develop the detailed project plan.

   C. Deliver a few stories.

   D. All of the above.

3. Who makes the final call on priority order in the Product Backlog?

   A. The Development Team

   B. The Scrum Master

   C. The Product Owner

   D. Someone in senior leadership like the MD or the CEO

S. Boral, *Ace the PMI-ACP® exam*, DOI 10.1007/978-1-4842-2526-4

4. With respect to the roles on a Scrum team, choose the odd one out?

A. Scrum Master

B. Product Owner

C. Development Team

D. Project Manager

5. The Development Team is expected to have all the skills needed to:

A. Complete the project by the given deadline and budget shared upfront with the sponsor.

B. Do analysis and development work, but leave out all forms of testing since that is handled by another specialized team.

C. Turn the Product Backlog items into potentially shippable product increments.

D. Master all state-of-the-art technology practices and tools available.

6. What is the main way that a Scrum Master contributes to maximizing the productivity in the development team?

A. By maintaining a risk-adjusted Product Backlog in priority order.

B. By making sure hygiene is maintained on meeting – agendas, start & end times, capturing and sending out minutes, etc.

C. By facilitating Development Team decisions and removing impediments.

D. By providing news about the newest technology trends in the market.

7. All of the following are Scrum artifacts except:

A. Product backlog

B. Gantt chart

C. Sprint backlog

D. Burndown chart

8. During an estimation session each team member is asked to provide an estimate. Which of the following is correct?

A. The team member provides estimates for only the story that will be assigned to him.

B. The developer provides a development estimate, the analyst provides an analysis estimate and the tester does his part. Ultimately all the estimates are aggregated.

C. The team members provide a relative estimate in units of ideal days.

D. Participation of a team member is voluntary as the Scrum Master can fillin wherever necessary.

9. A project stakeholder wants to have a look at how the Agile team is progressing in the middle of an iteration. As a member of the Agile team, you can guide him to:

   A. The most recent weekly status report.

   B. The sprint backlog.

   C. The defect log.

   D. The combined burnup and burndown charts.

10. XP teams take collective ownership of code. For such a team, _______ and _______ are the key.

    A. Definition of done and pair programming.

    B. Trust and collaboration.

    C. Velocity and co-location.

    D. Onsite customer and test-driven development.

11. Barry is a team member currently in a sprint planning session. After hearing about the requirement from the product owner, he estimates the amount of effort required by taking account that he will be working on this story and nothing else. He assumes that he will not face any interruptions. Which unit of estimate is he using?

    A. Story points

    B. T-shirt sizes

    C. Ideal days

    D. Either A or C

12. What is the primary role of a Product Owner?

    A. The PO is basically a project manager who balances scope, time, cost and risk.

    B. Maximizing the Return on Investment (ROI) of the software developed.

    C. People management for the Team.

    D. Avoiding distracting and keeping stakeholders at bay.

13. Which of the two ceremonies are executed after all development for a sprint and beginning of the next one?

    A. Sprint review and sprint retrospective

    B. Sprint review and sprint planning

    C. Daily stand-up and sprint review

    D. Sprint retrospective and sprint planning

14. Kanban board is an example of:

    A. Toyota production system

    B. Information refrigerator

    C. High-tech and low-touch system

    D. Information radiator

15. What happens during a Sprint Review?

    A. Review of what the team could do more or less off during the next sprint.

    B. Figure out the scope for the next sprint.

    C. End of the sprint demo for everyone to solicit feedback on the work done in the sprint.

    D. It is an opportunity to brainstorm and do a root cause analysis of work items that could not get done.

16. How do we know when a sprint isover?

    A. When all items in the sprint goal have met their definition of done.

    B. When the Product owner accepts all the work that was committed in the sprint planning meeting.

    C. When the timebox expires.

    D. None of the above.

17. While inspecting a release burndown chart, it is observed that the bar graph moves below its X-axis. Choose the best conclusion.

    A. This is normal. Scope could have gotten added by the product owner.

    B. This is normal. The developers would have underestimated the complexity of the story.

    C. This is abnormal and indicates poor data quality being plotted on the burndown chart. The bar graph can touch the X-axis, but not go below it.

    D. This is abnormal. The team should have completed what was committed by them.

18. Under what condition can a sprint be abnormally terminated?

    A. When the PO determines that it no longer makes sense to carry on with a sprint.

    B. The team has overcommitted and the sprint scope is too large to be achieved.

    C. A production defect needs to be addressed by priority.

    D. There is another project for which some analysis needs to be completed by the SME's in the current team.

19. During a planning session, the product owner and the team sit down together and sort the stories from the backlog into must-have, should-have, could-have and won't-have. The must-haves top the chart and along with those a few should-haves get selected for implementation during the iteration. Which prioritization technique did the team follow?

    A. Kano model analysis.

    B. Weighted prioritization technique.

    C. Simple ranking technique.

    D. MoSCoW.

20. In Agile vocabulary. a spike is a:

    A. Sudden increase in the quantum of work received.

    B. Sudden increase in the quantum of risks.

    C. Sudden increase in the resource demand.

    D. A task that the team undertakes to experiment on a hypothesis or a new technology.

21. Fill in the blanks for the following Agile principle.

    Build projects around _______ individuals. Give them the environment and _______ they need and _______ them to get the job done.

    A. cross-functional, training, trust

    B. empowered, support, believe

    C. self-motivated, support, believe

    D. motivated, morale boost, trust

22. An XP team realizes that a story is more complex than estimated earlier and so it cannot be completed in the current iteration. Which option should the team exercise?

    A. At the next daily stand-up, propose that the "definition of done" condition be relaxed to allow the partially completed story to look close to being completed.

    B. Extend the iteration by 3–4 days, as you cannot let the team's velocity go down.

    C. Discard the code and put the story back to the backlog for future prioritization and implementation in a successive sprint.

    D. Keep the code commented so it does not do any harm and tell the customer you will pick up and complete in the next iteration.

23. Some teams use a hardening sprint ahead of a release to:

    A. Train the operations team so that they can support the product post-release.

    B. Complete some of the final tasks related to productionizing of the code.

    C. Perform acceptance testing for all the previous sprints that were part of the release.

    D. Ask all programmers to check-in all the code in version control.

24. An Agile team is using relative sizing to estimate for stories on the backlog. What are the most common units of estimates used?

    A. Days / weeks / months

    B. Story points

    C. Ideal days

    D. Either B or C

25. Bill has worked hard over the last few days and finds that the build is broken because Richard has checked in code without properly unit testing it. It will mean that Bill will have to wait until Richard comes back and fixes the issue. Bill is furious at Richard and he makes statements like, "I know Richard. He is always careless and doesn't bother how others get affected by his actions."

    Which stage of conflict do you think is reflected in Bill's language?

    A. Level 1: Problem to Solve

    B. Level 2: Disagreement

    C. Level 3: Contest

    D. Level 5: World War

26. The two highest levels of conflict are Level 4: Crusade where there is hardly any direct speaking terms and Level 5: World war where the conflict is escalated to a level that is beyond repair and resolutions.

    As a manager encountering the situation, which are the best approaches you will follow to resolve conflicts?

    A. For Level 4: use shuttle diplomacy until the intensity of the conflict is lowered and team members can be brought into a table discussion. For Level 5: separate the team members such that they do not cause harm to each other or to the environment.

    B. For Level 4: use problem solving to get to the bottom of the issue. For Level 5: ask one party to compromise on a stand that they have rigidly held.

    C. For level 4: separate the team members such that they do not cause harm to each other or to the environment. For Level 5: bring in a third party and take the two team members to battle out in the court.

    D. For Level 4: remind the two members that they need to collaborate and reach consensus, even if that means that they will have to sacrifice. For Level 5: avoid the situation since nothing can be done about it.

27. What is the formula for Risk severity? And how do you expect risks to change during a project?

    A. Risk severity = Risk probability + Risk impact. We expect risks to be highest at the beginning and decrease over time.

    B. Risk severity = Risk probability x Risk impact. We expect risks to be highest at the beginning and decrease over time.

    C. Risk severity = Risk probability x Risk impact. We expect risks to be lowest at the beginning and increase over time.

    D. Risk severity = Risk probability x Risk impact. We expect risks to be highest at the beginning and remain static until the project is over.

28. The product owner is not able to commit enough time for the Scrum team. He is however, very supportive and leading the cause for the project. Who could be the best choice of a proxy user?

    A. Technical lead of the project who knows the ins and outs of the product.

    B. UX designer because they have close proximity to the business and knows how the UI is expected to behave.

    C. A business analyst reporting to the product owner since she will be able to articulate the user stories in plain business language that is free from technical jargon.

    D. A customer care representative who interacts with the real users on a daily basis and resolves support tickets.

29. Which is the odd line out of the following?

    A. Responding to change over following a plan.

    B. Customer collaboration over contract negotiation.

    C. Customer interactions over processes and tools.

    D. Working software over comprehensive documentation.

30. A reflection workshop is also called:

    A. Sprint review

    B. Sprint retrospective

    C. Backlog grooming session

    D. None of the above

31. Richard joins as an Agile coach and observes that there are a few Scrum teams working on a single product that is used by financial planners. The teams are struggling to arrive at a common "definition of done." What should Richard do?

    A. Richard should give each development team freedom to choose their definition of done. Reconcile differences only during the hardening sprint.

    B. Richard should give each development team freedom to choose their definition of done, as far as there is convergence and common ground at the time of integration such that the product is potentially releasable.

    C. Richard should ignore the situation. It's too messy too get involved in day-to-day work of the development.

    D. Richard should get hands-on, laying out the definition of done himself and teach all development teams how to follow them.

32. Agile teams use personas thatare imaginary user roles to provide a real-life flavor of the users interacting with the system. While building a persona, which of the following relevant information should they include?

    A. Age and gender

    B. Educational and Professional background

    C. A name and a picture

    D. All of the above

33. Agile teams practice value-based delivery. While determining and delivering value, who are we targeting?

    A. Users

    B. Developers

    C. Product owners

    D. Testers

34. Alistair Cockburn has introduced the Crystal family of methodologies, which consists of Crystal clear, Crystal yellow, crystal red, crystal maroon. What are the core differences between them?

    A. From left to right, they denote progressively increasing complexity of projects.

    B. From left to right, they denote progressively increasing criticality of projects.

    C. From left to right, they denote progressively increasing size of teams working on projects.

    D. All of the above.

35. A team hires you as an Agile coach to see if the team's efficiency could be enhanced and the velocity improved.What could be your recommendation to improve velocity?

    A. Have the team commit to fewer stories every sprint, so the probability of getting them completed in time are more.

    B. Reduce the daily-stand-up meetings from 15 to 10 minutes.

    C. Suggest bringing in the business representative to sit together with the development team.

    D. Compare velocities of similar projects running in the same organization and present them to the team.

36. Barry joined as an Agile coach and he wants to improve the way the team conducts retrospective meetings. He states that there are 5 stages for effective retrospectives. They follow the sequence of:

    A. Set the Stage, Gather Data, Generating Insights, Decide What to Do, Wrap up.

    B. Set the Stage, Generating Insights, Gather Data, Decide What to Do, Wrap up.

    C. Set the Stage, Decide What to Do, Generating Insights, Gather Data, Wrap up.

    D. Set the Stage, Gather Data, Decide What to Do, Generating Insights, Wrap up.

37. The Scrum team owns the sprint burndown chart. What is the primary significance of the chart?

    A. Use as a base for weekly status report for senior management.

    B. An Agile team is characterized with information radiators on team walls. A sprint burndown chart is a relevant artifact for putting up on the team wall.

    C. Team can view their daily progress and adapt based on the situation.

    D. Keep other stakeholders at bay. Those who are interested in knowing the status can view the sprint burndown chart and not bother the development team.

38. The acronym TIMWOOD is used to describe the 7 wastes in Lean. The letters T, M and D stand for:

    A. Transport, Machine, Defects

    B. Turnaround time, Motion, Defects

    C. Transport, Machine, Deliberate

    D. Transport, Motion, Defects

39. The Japanese words Muda, Kanban and Kaizen respectively mean:

    A. Waste, signboard, continuous improvement

    B. Waste, billboard, continuous integration

    C. Improvement, signboard, continuous removal of waste

    D. None of these

40. A new team member Billy, fresh from college, joins the team and sees that at every workstation two developers are sitting next to each other. One of them is typing code and the other is looking on and giving some suggestions at times. Billy thinks that privacy could be lost and discusses this with his mentor. His mentor explains that the team is following XP methodology and are involved in ___________.

    A. Sharing best practices sitting next to each other.

    B. Pair programming.

    C. One is coding and the other is deciding on test cases based on the code written.

    D. Coaching session for coding skills.

41. The ___________ is also called "the voice of the customer"?

    A. Development manager

    B. Scrum Master

    C. Product Owner

    D. Sponsor

42. An Agile team is in its formative stage. One of the first few things that they want to do is determine the length of an iteration. Which is the most important factor to make this decision?

    A. Determine the estimate of the longest story, convert from story points to man-days and then choose the iteration size to accommodate that.

    B. Look up historical data from other projects and teams.

    C. Discuss with project stakeholders on how long they can go without demonstrating progress or giving feedback.

    D. Follow guidelines from the Scrum Master since he is the most seasoned player in the team and has had a varied experience running Scrum teams elsewhere.

43. The commitments made by the product owner to the team include the following EXCEPT?

    A. Bring a prioritized list of features from the backlog to the planning meeting.

    B. Clarify requirements as and when asked by the team.

    C. Resist any temptation of changing scope midway through a sprint.

    D. Mandatorily attend every daily-standup meeting.

44. The product owner creates an elevator speech to articulate the vision of a product to the Agile team and its stakeholders. The elevator speech is expected to contain all of the following attributes EXCEPT:

A. Who is the target customer?

B. What is the key benefit that the customer will get by using the product?

C. Location and the technology where the product will be developed and tested.

D. What differentiates it from its competitors?

45. All the following are Agile methodologies EXCEPT:

A. Test-driven development

B. Feature-driven development

C. Extreme Programming

D. Scrumban

46. Who is responsible for prioritization of stories, epics and features in the product backlog?

A. Product owner

B. Product owner with inputs gathered from the team

C. ScrumMaster

D. Development team

47. The Scrum team has committed for a sprint goal. Midway during the sprint, the team discovers that there are some new tasks that need to be done before the committed stories are completed. However, given the time constraint, the team feels it cannot be done. What are the things the team should do now?

A. Abandon the sprint.

B. Bring it up during the daily-standup and then discuss proactively with the product owner.

C. Hope for the best and let the stakeholders know during the sprint review that some stories were not completed.

D. Find someone to blame.

48. The marketing team is looking for firm commitments from an Agile team based on the estimates that came out of the Affinity estimation session held by the team. What could possibly be wrong in that approach?

A. Affinity estimation is a very quick estimation technique used for release planning and generally precision of estimates is not the goal.

B. The marketing team should direct all their requirements to the product owner and not approach the Agile team directly.

C. Agile estimates are relative measure of size. They should not be treated as commitments.

D. A and C.

49. At the time of release planning, an epic was estimated to have 13 story points. However, during iteration planning, when the epic was broken down into stories and tasks, the sum of the estimates came to about 15 story points. Choose the most appropriate option below.

A. This is likely to happen as the estimates don't necessarily add up.

B. This is likely to happen as the estimates are done by different people at different times.

C. This is likely to happen as the estimates are less accurate at a release level.

D. This is a mistake, as it appears that somewhere there was a scope creep, that is, addition of 2 story points.

50. All the following could belong to the definition of done of a team EXCEPT:

A. Code has been checked into version control.

B. Code has passed through the integration test cases and regression suite.

C. Acceptance test cases have passed.

D. Daily Scrum meetings have been attended.

51. An Agile team is coming together for the first time. They have no prior experience working together, but would like to estimate an initial velocity to target.All the following options are possible EXCEPT:

A. Use historical values as the working environment and the technology used is the same as a previous project.

B. Run an iteration and observe the velocity.

C. Make a forecast by breaking stories into tasks and see what fits.

D. Use the velocity from any arbitrary project team. The level of accuracy does not matter since the team is new.

52. During a series of conflicts, you get to hear one party blaming the other by generalizing statements like, "They are always late - no surprises in that," "He has forgotten to check-in the file and again! Careless as ever!" Referring to Lea's conflict model, which stage do you think the team members are in?

A. Problem to solve.

B. Arbitration.

C. Crusade.

D. World war.

53. Which of the following statements is not true?

A. Higher the IRR the better, higher the BCR the better.

B. Higher the IRR the better, lower the payback period the better.

C. Higher the NPV the better, higher the IRR the better.

D. Higher the NPV the better, higher the payback period the better.

54. Leaving low-priority requirements at a high level, but sufficiently detailing out the high priority (and immediate) ones is called ________.

A. Incremental development.

B. Progressive elaboration.

C. Version control.

D. Continuous improvement.

55. Retrospectives can be held:

A. After an iteration.

B. After a release.

C. After an unexpected and a significant event in the project.

D. Any of the above.

56. What does the acronym MMF stand for?

A. Maximum Marketable Feature

B. Minimal Marketable Feature

C. Maximum Measurable Feature

D. Must-have and Marketable Function

57. Which of the following do you NOT expect to see on an information radiator for an Agile team?

A. Gantt chart

B. Task board

C. Burnup chart

D. Velocity trends

58. For an emergency reason Richard, the product owner could not make it to the sprint planning meeting. Who do you think could be in a position to play his role for the time being?

A. The self-organized team.

B. The development manager.

C. The Scrum Master.

D. The CEO who is closely aligned to the project.

59. Which of the following statements is false?

A. Agile projects do just-in-time planning.

B. Agile projects balance progress and flexibility.

C. Agile projects do not require a PMO.

D. Agile projects value collaboration over documentation.

60. Team A has a velocity of 20 story points and Team B has 40 story points over a 3-week iteration. What does this mean?

A. Team B is twice more efficient than Team A.

B. Team B has double the capacity (team size) than Team A.

C. Team B is more mature, uses sophisticated tools and achieves more in the same time.

D. Nothing. Velocity of two teams cannot be compared.

61. The three levels of active listening are:

A. Level I - Internal Listening, Level II - Focused Listening, Level III - Global Listening.

B. Level I - Focused Listening, Level II - Internal Listening, Level III - Global Listening.

C. Level I - Internal Listening, Level II - Global Listening, Level III - Focused Listening.

D. Varies based on the circumstances.

62. An Agile team has an average velocity of 25. During a sprint planning session, they have come up with estimates for a list of stories in priority order as follows:

Story 1 estimate of 12 story points

Story 2 estimate of 3 story points

Story 3 estimate of 8 story points

Story 4 estimate of 5 story points

Story 5 estimate of 2 story points

Story 6 estimate of 1 story points

Story 7 estimate of 1 story points

What is the choice that the team makes?

A. Choose stories 6, 7,5,2,4 and split the larger ones 1 and 3 so that maximum number of stories can be accommodated.

B. A team's velocity is subject to change. Also estimates are not absolute. Choose all stories and complete whatever is possible. After all, customer will be pleasantly surprised if the team overachieves.

C. Club stories that are dependent on each other and deliver them together.

D. Choose stories 1,2,3,5 – the highest priority ones that add up to the team's velocity.

63. After the story writing workshop the team has come up with a set of 80 story cards that need to be very quickly estimated such that the release plan can be built. The product owner is interested in getting this completed in less than 2 hours. Which estimation technique is best suited for this purpose?

A. Work breakdown structure or bottom-up estimation.

B. Planning Poker.

C. Affinity estimation.

D. Delphi.

64. The DEEP acronym is used to describe the characteristics of a product backlog. The acronym stands for

A. Detailed Appropriately, Estimated, Emergent, Prioritized.

B. Detailed Appropriately, Economic, Emergent, Prioritized.

C. Defined properly, Estimated, Emergent, Prioritized.

D. Defined properly, Estimated, Enlisted, Probabilistic.

65. Passing of acceptance test cases is an example of:

A. Definition of ready

B. Definition of done

C. Collective ownership

D. Teamwork

66. The INVEST acronym is used to describe the characteristics of user stories. The letters I, V and S in the acronym stands for:

A. Interesting, Verifiable, Small

B. Independent, Validatable, Small

C. Independent, Valuable, Specific

D. None of the above

67. Agile releases could be one of:

A. Feature-driven or Date-Driven.

B. Date-driven or Priority-driven.

C. Team-driven or feature-driven.

D. Both release dates and constituent features are variable and negotiated on the fly.

68. Sarah is joining an Agile team. On the first day she observes that the team has a task board that contains lots of sticky notes denoting tasks in various stages of progress. She is confused about the small numbers written next to column headers of the task board and asks her manager Jane about their significance. Jane explains that the numbers depict:

A. Velocity for each column in the task board.

B. Number of resources assigned for each column in the task board.

C. WIP limit.

D. Maximum number of escaped defects allowed per column.

69. XP programmers are required to continuously submit their code into the code repository and run a 10-minute build to assess whether anything has broken or not as a result of the newly made changes. This practice is called:

A. Continuous integration.

B. Continuous improvement.

C. Version control.

D. Informative team space.

70. The Lean team has understood the benefits of creating value stream maps. After a bit of effort they prepared a value stream map and proceeds to calculate the cycle time for each step and the total lead time to handover value to the business user. What is the most important next step?

A. Continuously improve on process efficiencies.

B. Amplify learning.

C. Identify non-value added activities and eliminate them.

D. Organize daily stand-up meetings.

71. The project steering board is having a meeting to evaluate and select one of the two projects being presented by their sponsors.

Project A has IRR of 6% and requires an investment of 100K USD

Project B has IRR of 7.5% and requires an investment of 150K USD

Which project should be chosen and what is the opportunity cost?

A. Project A, 100K USD

B. Project A, 150K USD

C. Project B, 100K USD

D. Project B, 150K USD

72. The _______ is best placed to author user stories.

A. Development team since they know the technical intricacies of the features.

B. Customer or business representative because they can articulate business requirements in plain language (no technical jargon).

C. The project manager because he knows what it takes to balance scope, time and cost.

D. The tester since the acceptance test cases needs to be written at the back of the story card.

73. When is it okay for a team to extend an iteration by 4-5 days to complete what they promised?

A. Use a groupdecision-making technique and agree at a daily stand-up meeting.

B. Once the Scrum Master approves.

C. Iteration length should not be changed.

D. Instead of extending the iteration, think of 'crashing' the iteration by putting in more resources or requesting overtime and weekend work.

74. As per Alistair Cockburn, Shu-Ha-Ri is a learning technique that is applied to software development methodologies. The words Shu Ha Ri means:

A. Follow the rule, break the rule and be the rule respectively.

B. Break the rule, follow the rule and be the rule respectively.

C. Be the rule, break the rule and follow the rule respectively.

D. Follow the rule, be the rule and break the rule respectively.

75. 5 Why's is an example of a/an:

A. Estimation technique

B. Retrospective technique

C. Conflict resolution technique

D. Facilitation technique

76. In the situational leadership model, the different leadership styles in ascending order of team maturity are as follows:

A. Selling, Telling, Supporting, Delegating

B. Telling, Delegating, Participating, Selling

C. Delegating, Directing, Coaching, Supporting

D. Telling, Selling, Participating, Delegating

77. Value stream mapping is a technique that has its origin in Lean. Why do we use value stream mapping?

A. Without a visualized workflow, conversations with the customers are difficult.

B. To identify and eliminate wastes in the process.

C. To charter the future roadmap.

D. To energize the development team.

78. Active listening consists of all the following EXCEPT:

A. Paying attention to the nonverbal signs of the speaker.

B. Providing feedback on what is understood.

C. Interrupting the speaker to express your personal views and perspectives.

D. Deferring judgment.

79. User stories have enough requirements that serve as a reminder to the team and they can converse to drill down to the specifics during coding. How do the developers confirm that the requirement is met?

A. Discuss with the users, write down the acceptance test cases behind the card. and execute them.

B. There is always more chances, so the team can make assumptions, demo them. and incorporate feedback later.

C. Developers expect the product owner to maintain a checklist separately.

D. Since the user stories are not sufficient, developers need to augment with comprehensive documentation behind the scenes.

80. User stories should be valuable to ________.

A. The development team

B. The Agile coach

C. The organization

D. The user or customer

81. The different stages of Test-Driven Development are

1) Red - when the test cases fail.

2) Green - when the test cases succeed with barely minimum code.

3) Refactor - when the code is evolved by considering design patterns, code quality etc.

What is the right sequence?

A. Green, Red, Refactor.

B. Red, Refactor, Green.

C. Red, Green, Refactor.

D. None of the above as the blue stage is missing.

82. XP teams conduct spike tasks. The product owner realizes that there is no direct value to the customer in conducting such tasks, but yet permits them in the iteration backlog because:

A. Through spikes teams are able to gain knowledge of an unknown technology.

B. Through spikes teams are able to prove a hypothesis.

C. Through spikes teams are able to mitigate a risk.

D. All of the above.

83. With respect to size, which is the correct order?

A. Epic, theme, story, task.

B. Story, feature, theme, subtask.

C. Story, task, subtask, feature.

D. Epic, feature, subtask, theme.

84. The Scrum Master in a team plays the following roles EXCEPT:

A. Servant leader

B. Shepherd

C. Line manager

D. Bulldozer of impediments

85. In Scrum who takes the responsibility to prioritize stories?

A. Scrum Master.

B. Product owner with the help of the whole team.

C. Exclusively product owner.

D. Whoever is knowledgeable about the stories.

86. The product owner is looking at the backlog, shuffling priorities, adding more epics and features. and removing some that are no longer necessary. The task he is doing is called:

A. Backlog grooming

B. Product roadmap creation

C. Project charter creation

D. Backlog review

87. An Agile team consists of the following attributes:

A. Self-organized

B. Generalized specialist

C. Multilingual

D. A and B

88. ________ is a unit of estimates for user stories.

A. Velocity

B. Weeks

C. Story points

D. Work breakdown structure

89. A persona is:

A. A real customer or user.

B. Imaginary representation of a user role.

C. Any stakeholder who can provide system requirements.

D. A business analyst or a domain specialist.

90. Regarding ideal days and calendar days, all of the following statements are correct EXCEPT:

A. Calendar days are the usual days at work and includes interruptions like breaks and meetings.

B. Ideal days are the days of work minus the interruptions like breaks and meetings.

C. Calendar days are valid units of estimate in Agile, since the definition of ideal days varies from one developer to another.

D. Ideal days are valid units of estimate in Agile, since the worth of work done on a calendar day varies from one developer to another.

91. Spot the statement that is incorrect as per the Agile Manifesto:

A. Individuals and interactions over processes and tools

B. Customer collaboration over vendor management

C. Working software over comprehensive documentation

D. Responding to change over following a plan

92. Which of the following could be the biggest cause for failure in an Agile project?

A. Lack of availability of the customer to collaborate closely with the team.

B. A distributed team.

C. Some team members who are not yet well versed in devops practices.

D. Resources that have fractional allocation to multiple projects at the same time.

93. You get to see all of the following practices in a, XP team except:

A. Continuous build and integration.

B. Checking in code into a single repository.

C. Onsite customer facilitating daily stand-up meetings.

D. Test-driven development.

94. Which of the following statements regarding technical debt is false?

A. The quantum of technical debt can be measured by counting the number of days of effort required to address it.

B. Technical debt can be introduced at any time, during initial development, during maintenance and enhancements.

C. XP teams continuously refactor code to reduce technical debt.

D. All of the above are true.

95. PMI®'s code of ethics applies to:

A. PMI® members.

B. PMI® certification seekers.

C. PMI® volunteers and chapter members.

D. A, B and C.

96. When should individual development team members signup for implementing a particular story?

A. At the time of estimation, when they are submitting the estimates.

B. Once the sprint goal has been agreed at the end of the planning meeting.

C. During the daily stand-up meeting.

D. At the last responsible moment and based on capacity of the team. All items are owned by the entire development team.

97. The Agile team has started working on an iteration. On the third day, a business representative comes up to you and requests another feature to be included in the same iteration. What should the Agile team do?

A. Accommodate the feature since otherwise the business representative will not accept the iteration results.

B. Accommodate the feature since otherwise the business representative will escalate that the team is not adaptable to change.

C. Accommodate the feature by putting it into the product backlog and asking the product owner to check its ROI relative to other stories in the backlog.

D. Accommodate the feature as it is a small change and self-organized team knows how to manage last-minute requirements.

98. An Agile team is working on the software for life-saving medical equipment. The product has already been in the market for about 2 months, when the product team detects a defect in the software that could be fatal to the patients being monitored. Fixing the product and rolling out the solution to all the clients who have purchased the product will be very costly and affect the balance sheets badly. What is the most important thing that the company should do?

A. Wait and watch, as the clients have not discovered the defect and have not been affected.

B. Since it is software for a life-saving medical apparatus, immediately warn all clients and stop their use.

C. Immediately sanction a project to fix the software and roll out to all clients. This is estimated to take 4–5 months.

D. Wait for the next planned release that is 6 months away and prioritize this production defect fix over anything else.

99. To eliminate duplication in code, the word DRY is used. It stands for ________:

A. Don't repeat yourself.

B. Don't refactor your code.

C. Do review your product.

D. None of the above.

100. Agile teams do emergent architecture and design. At the end of every iteration, they deliver ________.

A. Shippable product increment.

B. Vertical slice of the cake.

C. A and B.

D. Horizontal slice of the cake.

101. An Agile team is currently reviewing the proposals submitted by prospective vendors. The outcome of the review is to shortlist and award the contract to the vendor that is considered best to work on the project. Harry, a member of the team comes to know that BigFive Consulting Company, which is owned by his relative, has also bid for the project. In this situation Harry should:

A. Keep it to himself and patiently see what goes on.

B. Keep it to himself and recommend the rest of the team to go with BigFive Consulting Company since you know them all and trust their capabilities.

C. Disclose it and stay out of the seller selection process.

D. Pass on some insider information to BigFive, so that they are at an advantage during the negotiation process.

102. Which of the following is not an attribute of a product backlog?

A. Prioritized

B. Large

C. Detailed appropriately

D. Measurable

103. The Agile team is sitting together in a room. Harry asks a quick question on the build configuration and Sally responds where Harry could find it. In between, Richard, who was busy writing code, overhears and cautions that the configuration file at that location has an issue and Harry should use the one at an alternate location. Harry was able to get what he needed in no time and continued with his tasks. This type of communication between co-located teams is called?

A. Verbal communication.

B. Osmotic communication.

C. Information radiators.

D. Informal communication.

104. On the back of the story card the acceptance test cases are found. Who specifies the acceptance test cases?

A. Customer

B. The whole team

C. Test manager

D. Scrum Master

105. Which of the following represents the richest and most effective mode of communication in a team?

A. Recorded webinar

B. Video conferencing

C. Audio conferencing

D. Face-to-face meeting accompanied by a whiteboard session.

106. To launch a product in a foreign country, one needs to pay a facilitation fee required by the municipal department to get the required no objection certificate. Going by PMI®'s code of ethics and professional conduct, one should:

A. Not pay the fee since it amounts to bribe and violates the code.

B. Pay the fee.

C. Check with the legal team whether the fee is justifiable and ethical and then decide.

D. Revoke the decision to launch the product in a country that asks for such a fee.

107. Harry and Sally have been fighting for a while on the proposed design options. Harry thinks Sally's option will be very difficult to implement and will cost lots of money upfront. Sally thinks that isn't the case as some basic components could be reused from the existing code. She also thinks that Harry is stubborn and refusing to listen to her justifications. Both approaches askyou to resolve the conflict. You think that both Harry and Sally have positive intent, so you ask Sally to present a small prototype that demonstrates her design. You also ask Harry to be patient and be attentive to what Sally demonstrates and all constructive feedback should be registered. The conflict resolution technique you followed was:

A. Problem Solving

B. Avoiding

C. Compromising

D. Forcing

108. In a planning poker session, the cards used to provide estimates are numbered as:

A. T-shirt sizes S, M, L, XL, XXL, etc.

B. Odd number 1, 3, 5, 7, 9, 11, etc.

C. Fibonacci series like 1, 2, 3, 5, 8, 13, 21, 34, etc.

D. Arithmetic progression like 5, 10, 15, 20, 25, 30, etc.

109. Richard has recently joined company ABC as a senior designer. While working on the project, he faintly recollects that he had seen such a design solution in his ex-company. So he calls up his old buddy and asks him to email the design document from his previous company to his personal id. Is this action correct?

A. Yes, since Richard is reusing the design that saves time and cost.

B. Yes, since Richard is showing his prowess in networking.

C. No, since this is a violation of intellectual rights and unethical.

D. No, since he should have not still been speaking terms with colleagues in his ex-company.

110. Which of the following activities does a servant leader NOT do?

A. Remove impediments.

B. Reiterate the vision of the project.

C. Come up with a detailed project plan at the end of the planning poker session.

D. Help in logistics and facilitation.

111. A team determines its velocity to be 30 story points in a 3-week iteration. Given that there are 300 stories in the backlog, how long will the project take to complete?

A. 30 weeks.

B. 30 weeks provided the scope remains unchanged during this period.

C. 30 weeks provided the scope doesn't change and the estimates don't change.

D. 30 weeks provided the scope, estimates and the velocity of the same remains constant.

112. Richard is tasked with evaluating a few proposal received from vendors. One of the vendors met Richard over lunch to explain their value proposition and also handed over a small token of appreciation for Richard's time. Going by the gift and entertainments policy in the company, Richard should:

A. Deny the gift from the vendor and tell him that his proposal will be rejected for trying to bribe him.

B. Accept the gift because it is not expensive.

C. Accept the gift as it is not inappropriate, disclose it in the organization and continue to fairly assess rest of the proposals.

D. Call up his manager before leaving the meeting to let him decide whether the gift should be accepted or denied.

113. Which of the following conflict resolution techniques results in a lose-lose outcome?

A. Problem Solving

B. Avoiding

C. Compromising

D. Forcing

114. Which of the following conflict resolution technique results in a win-lose outcome?

A. Problem Solving

B. Avoiding

C. Compromising

D. Forcing

115. A team consumes the data produced by the software written by another team. The 'producer' team will be ready on Day 8, but to be on the safe side, the 'receiver' team inserts a buffer of 3 days and plans a start on Day 11. These 3 days between systems are called?

A. Management reserve

B. Feeding buffer

C. Backup

D. Dependency adjustments

116. Planning poker technique is NOT:

A. An estimation technique

B. A group decision-making technique

C. A variation of the Wideband Delphi technique

D. A sprint retrospective technique

117. The Agile team is during the second last stage of the retrospective meeting where the action items are being decided. Who will take ownership of the action items?

A. The whole team

B. The product owner

C. The Scrum Master

D. Whoever raised the topic in the first place

118. In MoSCoW prioritization technique, 'S' and 'C' standfor:

A. Should have, could have

B. Shouldn't have, could have

C. Should have, couldn't have

D. Shouldn't have, couldn't have

119. An Agile coach is tasked on suggesting ways to enhance the velocity of the team. Which of the following is not an option he states?

A. Remove non-value added tasks from the team.

B. Refactor code and remove technical debt.

C. Ask the customer to stay aloof and not interfere with the team at work.

D. Invest behind devops tools for version control, continuous build and integration.

120. Which of the following will not help a distributed team?

A. A kickoff meeting at the beginning of the project.

B. Sensitivity and awareness of cultural diversity of the team in multiple locations.

C. Rotations of the team members if travel budget permits.

D. Making teams sit in groups of specialism, like the BA's together, developers together, testers together.

Mock Exam II

1. ___________ is the minimum set of features in a product that the users can start using and get benefit without waiting for more.

   A. Delighters

   B. Story maps

   C. Walking skeleton

   D. MMF

2. During value-based prioritization of user stories, Wiegers' technique considers all the following aspects except

   A. Cost

   B. Risk

   C. Value

   D. Testability

3. Which of the following is part of Agile Manifesto?

   A. Contract negotiation over following a plan

   B. Working software over comprehensive documentation

   C. Process and tools over individuals and interactions

   D. Responding to change over processes and tools

4. In the 100-point method for prioritization of user stories:

   A. Each participant is given a set of 100 stories to prioritize.

   B. Participants are given 100 minutes to sort out the prioritization of a list of stories.

   C. Participants are given 100 points that they can randomly allocate to stories based on their perceived importance to them.

   D. Each participant is asked to pick the 4 most important stories and asked to divide 100 points between them.

S. Boral, *Ace the PMI-ACP® exam*, DOI 10.1007/978-1-4842-2526-4

5. Which of the following best describes the value of all the future cash inflow and outflow in today's value by factoring in the rate of interest?

   A. Net Present Value

   B. Discounted value

   C. Payback value

   D. Future value

6. As per the Lean philosophy all of the following are categorized as wastes except:

   A. Defects

   B. Transport

   C. Overprocessing

   D. Communication that lacks richness

7. A senior executive appoints a product owner for an Agile team. He explains that the key responsibility of the product owner is to:

   A. Make sure that the Agile team is operating efficiently and effectively.

   B. ROI is maximized during every iteration.

   C. Team has a sustainable pace and is not getting burned out.

   D. The number of escaped defects reaching the customer is as minimal as possible.

8. While analyzing a risk, the team came up with the following figure. Probability = 65%, Impact = 1000, Frequency = once in a week. What is the severity of this risk?

   A. $65

   B. $650

   C. 0.65

   D. 0.00065

9. As per Pareto's 80/20 principle:

   A. 80% of the defects are removed in the last 20% of the time left on the project.

   B. 80% of the users use 20% of the features in the product.

   C. 80% of the system errors can be removed by resolving 20% of the defects.

   D. 80% of the work in the team is done by 20% of the team members.

10. A servant leader:

    A. Is aware of his and his team member's emotions and controls them.

    B. Is an expert in people management and lays down ground rules that the team members must obey.

    C. Is attentive to the needs of the team and helps to remove impediments.

    D. Monitors and controls affairs of the project by using a lot of metrics that the team needs to capture and plot on a daily basis.

11. What is the Internal Rate of Return (IRR)?

    A. It is a metric that is used to calculate the amount of an investment.

    B. It is a metric that is used to calculate the profitability of an investment.

    C. It is a metric that is used to determine whether the source of return is from internal or external sources.

    D. It is a metric that is used to compare prevailing interest rates.

12. What is the purpose of a risk burndown graph?

    A. Track risk impact over iterations.

    B. Track risk probability over iterations.

    C. Track risk severity over iterations.

    D. Track risk frequency over iterations.

13. Stakeholder management is important for an Agile team because:

    A. Having stakeholders that engage and participate in the project is a critical success factor.

    B. Without that there is likely going to be scope creep.

    C. They need to be plotted on a power-interest grid.

    D. They need to be plotted on an engagement assessment matrix.

14. Which of the following practices if followed persistently and continuously increases the quality of the product?

    A. Information radiators

    B. Verification and validation

    C. Affinity estimation technique

    D. BART analysis

15. Sidky has defined SAMI (Sidky Agile Maturity index) that has five evolutionary stages of Agile maturity in an organization. In the right sequence, they are as follows:

    A. Collaborative, engaging, integrated, adaptive, encompassing.

    B. Collaborative, evolutionary, integrated, adaptive, encompassing.

    C. Integrated, collaborative, evolutionary, adaptive, encompassing.

    D. Collaborative, evolutionary, integrated, encompassing, adaptive.

16. Choose the most correct response:

    A. Two projects A and B have IRR -5% and -12% respectively. While catering for a budget cut, Project B is likely to get the axe and not Project A.

    B. IRR is the interest rate in which NPV of cash flows is equal to zero.

    C. ROI of all projects is higher if Agile is used instead of waterfall.

    D. Both A and B.

17. An Agile team is busy working with the product owner to shuffle the product backlog items based on value and risk severities that were identified so far. The team provides the inputs, but the product owner has the last say on the decisions made and keeps the accountability. The resulting list is called __________:

    A. Risk register

    B. A DEEP backlog

    C. Risk-adjusted product backlog

    D. Iteration backlog

18. What are the three parameters of the Agile triangle?

    A. Value, quality, constraints

    B. Cost, time, scope

    C. Value, cost, customer satisfaction

    D. Value, cost, quality

19. On the branch of a decision tree, you see a decision has a 60% chance of earning a $1000 profit, but also a 40% chance of a $2000 loss. What is the EMV of this branch on the decision tree?

    A. -$200 (loss)

    B. $600 (profit)

    C. -$800 (loss)

    D. None of the above

20. The Agile team has just completed the sprint review and the feedback on the product increment was mostly positive, but a few new features have been called out. What do you think the team should do first after the review meeting?

A. Start implementation for the new features requested.

B. Update the backlog and estimate for the new features requested.

C. Complete stories that were left out in the sprint.

D. Spend time to reflect on currently used processes and how they can be improved in the retrospective meeting.

21. Bill is a Java programmer and joins an Agile team that uses XP. He is new to Agile, so he tries to find out the way of working that is prevalent on the team. He is explained that the code is integrated:

A. Finally, before the planned release date.

B. Many times a day, almost after every check-in.

C. Every Monday, Wednesday and Friday.

D. Once in an iteration when it has been reviewed and unit tested.

22. A product owner decides that the amount of risks in the project has escalated so much that it does not seem feasible to continue with the project. There is no visibility of profitability in sight. Termination of such a project is which kind of risk response?

A. Avoid

B. Mitigate

C. Transfer

D. Accept

23. A user story reads: As a borrower of a book from the library, I would prefer to search a book quickly.

The user story is not good because:

A. It doesn't seem to be specific or valuable from the borrower's standpoint.

B. It does not quantify what 'quickly' means. Without a response time it's difficult to measure.

C. It is not estimable since the acceptance criteria is not specified.

D. It is too small and not detailed enough.

24. The 4th stage of a retrospective is "Decide what to do." As a part of this stage:

    A. Action items are added to the product backlog and the product owner is asked to determine the ROI and priority.

    B. The Scrum Master takes notes and allocates them to whoever is best skilled to carry out the action items.

    C. The retrospective leader starts the "Helped, Hindered, Hypothesis" activity to determine if the retrospective itself was useful.

    D. Team members self-volunteer to take specific actions from the next sprint itself.

25. Which of the following is the best Agile team?

    A. An Agile team with specialists.

    B. An Agile team that avoids conflicts.

    C. An Agile team that collaborates and self-organizes continuously.

    D. An Agile team that has no one to blame if things go wrong.

26. During sprint execution, Wilson notices that a story was missed and needs to be implemented. What would he do?

    A. Quickly estimate, design. and complete the implementation, even if that means working overtime.

    B. Ask the product owner to add the story to the product backlog for future prioritization and planning.

    C. Pick up the item during the retrospective to determine the root cause of why the item was missed during the planning stage.

    D. Extend the iteration deadline to accommodate the missed story.

27. By maintaining a constant iteration length, the team:

    A. Establishes an operating rhythm.

    B. Creates a predictive delivery schedule where the scope is variable.

    C. Allows the team to measure a trend of their velocity, thereby improving future projections.

    D. All of the above.

28. During an iteration planning meeting, the product owner has just read out a story and provided some initial set of clarifications. The team is now going to use planning poker to estimate the story. The estimates produced in round one looks like 1, 2, 3, 2 and 8. What should happen now?

    A. Go with 2 since maximum people voted for it.

    B. Take the average of the 5 estimates.

    C. Take the worst case 8 as the estimate.

    D. Have the team members who voted for 1 and 8 explain their rationale and repeat the voting round.

29. One of the core practices in XP is 'Small releases'. Following are the advantages except:

   A. Deliver value early and quickly.

   B. Mitigate risks of a 'big-bang' integration.

   C. Adapt to changes incrementally.

   D. Limit work in progress.

30. Kaizen is a Lean principle. The literal meaning of the Japanese word Kaizen is:

   A. Continuous integration

   B. Continuous improvement

   C. Frequent validation and verification

   D. Billboard

31. Which of the following is the best definition of 'definition of done'?

   A. A term defined when the project is completed and ready to be shipped to production.

   B. A term defined by the team to determine when a user story is completed and ready for shipping to a customer.

   C. A term defined to indicate acceptance of features by the end user.

   D. A term defined to indicate when the Scrum team can take credit for their accomplishment and demo their deliverables.

32. Harry is a member of the Agile team. He is not a tester, but is interested to randomly check a few things about the system behavior without a lot of up-front planning. He begins with the charter and spends an hour or so trying different things that otherwise are not documented as user stories. Harry is conducting:

   A. Refactoring

   B. Peer reviews

   C. Acceptance testing

   D. Exploratory testing

33. Which of the following statements is NOT true?

   A. It is cheaper and easier to terminate an Agile project midway than a waterfall-based project.

   B. Agile project have a continuous focus on quality and planning.

   C. Fixed price contracts are best suited in Agile.

   D. There is no need of heavy change management processes to make and track changes in an Agile project.

34. A looselyengaged stakeholder requests John the Scrum Master, to show him the latest weekly status report to check the project health and the remaining amount of work in the project. Instead, John takes the stakeholder to the team wall where a few pertinent updates are posted continuously. To address the stakeholder's query, John specifically points out to

A. Burndown chart

B. Sprint backlog

C. Task board

D. Velocity trend

35. A persona in an Agile project is:

A. The proxy user who can provide requirement in absence of the product owner.

B. The person who provides acceptance of the product increment at the end of every iteration.

C. An imaginary representation of a user role to collect requirements from his or her perspective.

D. An onsite customer or anyone he/she assigns to be co-located with the team to provide clarifications on the fly.

36. A product roadmap contains all of the following except:

A. Milestones of each release

B. Estimates of epics and themes

C. Contents of each releases

D. Depiction of value-driven delivery to the customer

37. During iteration planning stories are broken down into tasks that are entered into the iteration backlog. The tasks neither should not be too long nor too small to cause a tracking overhead. The thumb-rule of the length of each tasks is:

A. 4–16 hours

B. 0–8 hours

C. One story point

D. Less than half a day

38. Which of the following is not a valid reason to update the product backlog?

A. Change in the composition of the development team

B. Addition of new stories or risks

C. Change in priorities

D. Finding from previous sprints

39. Which is the fastest way to generate a lot of good quality requirements?

A. Surveys

B. Facilitated workshops

C. Wisdom of crowd

D. Dot voting

40. Thumb voting is a group decision-making technique. Holding a thumb sideways indicates:

A. Agreement

B. Disagreement

C. Neutrality

D. Strong support

41. At the end of the iteration, the team observes that they have completed only 50% of a story that was initially estimated for 12 story points. How many story points from this story would count toward the team's velocity?

A. 0

B. 6

C. 12

D. 18

42. The customer has provided a bunch of requirements to the Agile team. But they are not sure what the collection of the requirements will finally look like. They asked the team if they could complete the entire design and give them a preview. Since up-front design is not encouraged, the Agile team instead produced a:

A. Spike

B. Prototype

C. Persona

D. Definition of done

43. 'Remember the future' and 'Prune the product tree' are examples of __________ and used to __________.

A. Estimation techniques, determine relative size of stories

B. Prioritization techniques, determine relative priorities of stories

C. Brainstorming techniques, solve problems

D. Innovation games, collect requirements

44. As per the estimation convergence / cone of uncertainty graph, estimates produced at the beginning of the project is called __________ while that near the end of the project are called __________.

A. Budget, definitive

B. Ballpark, accurate

C. Rough order of magnitude, definitive

D. Rough order of magnitude, precise

45. During a 3-week iteration, the team completed 3 stories of 5 story points each, 2 stories of 12 story points each and completed 50% of two stories of 14 story points each. What is the team's velocity for this iteration?

A. 39

B. 53

C. 67

D. None of the above

46. Apart from story points, which of the following could be used as unit of estimates for Agile?

A. Calendar days

B. Coffee-cup sizes

C. Person months

D. Feature points

47. Jeremy, an Agile developer practices picks up a story from the sprint backlog. He begins with writing the automated unit tests before writing the code. Jeremy is following the practice of:

A. Test-first development

B. Pair programming

C. Continuous integration

D. Feature-driven development

48. Which is the best definition of escaped defect?

A. A defect that has simply escaped the attention of the tester.

B. A defect that should have been caught during exploratory testing.

C. A defect that went undetected and landed with the customer.

D. A defect that unearths inefficiencies in the processes that needs to be rectified in the next iteration.

49. During iteration planning, the Agile team comes across a story that has an iteration length that is almost 90% of the velocity of the team. What is the best suggestion that you can give to the team in this situation?

A. Reject the story since it is not small enough.

B. Split the story.

C. Extend the iteration length.

D. It is not advisable to compare estimates of a story with the team's velocity.

50. Use the Earned Value Management technique to determine the status of the project.

The parameters are EV = $4000, PV = $5000 and AC = $6000.

A. Project is behind schedule and within budget.

B. Project is behind schedule and has cost overrun.

C. Project is ahead of schedule and within budget.

D. Project is ahead of schedule and has cost overrun.

51. For the same parameters given in the previous question (#50), what is the Schedule performance index (SPI)?

A. 0.8

B. 0.66

C. 0.83

D. 1.25

52. Richard has been appointed as an Agile coach. The team is newly formed, so he has to explain a lot of Agile practices. He asks the team to practice Just-In-Time (JIT) planning as that is the followed in Agile. What is the main reason that Richard cites to support the practice of JIT planning?

A. A JIT plan is easier to create and maintain by the project manager.

B. JIT planning helps to accommodate changes far more easily instead of using change control principles.

C. JIT planning keeps the team on their toes and helps to constantly maintain focus among the team members.

D. JIT planning helps to keep stakeholders at bay, since they cannot see the overall picture.

53. The sponsor of an Agile project approaches the Scrum Master and asks him about the burn rate of the team per sprint. The team consists of 6 members each of whose billing rate is $50 per hour. Assuming a 40 hour week and an iteration length of 2 weeks, what is the burn rate per sprint?

A. $36,000

B. $20,000

C. $30,000

D. $24,000

54. An iteration started with 10 user stories to deliver. In the middle of iteration, a team member got sick and was not available to work. During a daily stand-up meeting, this was raised to the Scrum Master to seek advice as team thinks they cannot deliver all 10 user stories in the iteration. What should be the Scrum Master's advice to team?

A. Work overtime to catch up on the lost time.

B. Fastrack if possible and extend the iteration.

C. Complete what can be done and the pending items should be put in the backlog for future iterations.

D. Reduce the scope of iteration from 10 user stories to 8 user stories and deliver as per the revised commitment.

55. A team's average velocity is 40 story points per 2-week iteration. There are 600 story points left in backlog. How many iterations are needed to complete the backlog?

A. 30

B. 25

C. 20

D. 15

56. Who facilitates the sprint review?

A. Sponsor

B. Product owner

C. Anyone from the self-organized team

D. Scrum Master

57. A team's average velocity is 45 story points per 2-week iteration. There are 490 story points left in backlog. How many weeks are needed to complete the backlog?

A. 22

B. 20

C. 10

D. 11

58. Affinity estimating is the process of:

A. Averaging the best and worst case estimates.

B. Checking that the stories in the same functional areas are of equivalent magnitude.

C. Checking that the stories of the same estimated size are of equivalent complexity.

D. Checking that the stories of the same estimated size are of the same technology.

59. What does the term "Done Done" mean in Agile projects?

    A. Unit testing completed, all tests passed.

    B. Accepted by the sponsor.

    C. Development done, ready for exploratory testing.

    D. Ready for Production release and available to the end user.

60. All tasks that are to be completed before the final release of the product are called:

    A. The iteration backlog

    B. The project backlog

    C. The sprint backlog

    D. The product backlog

61. As far as whole-team coaching is concerned, the Agile coach is most active during:

    A. Beginning of the sprint.

    B. End of the sprint, during the retrospective.

    C. In the middle of the sprint.

    D. During sprint planning and retrospectives.

62. Which of the following is an Agile Manifesto value?

    A. Individuals and interactions over comprehensive documentation.

    B. Working software over following a plan.

    C. Customer collaboration over contract negotiation.

    D. Working solutions over processes and tools.

63. Agile projects unleash creativity and innovation by:

    A. Engaging customers in frequent interactions and shared ownership.

    B. Recognizing that individuals are the ultimate source of value and creating an environment where they can make a difference.

    C. Making continuous flow of value our focus.

    D. Group accountability for results and shared responsibility for team effectiveness.

64. Which of the following Agile Manifesto values deals with working closely with business or client?

    A. Individuals and interactions over processes and tools.

    B. Working software over comprehensive documentation.

    C. Customer collaboration over contract negotiation.

    D. Responding to change over following a plan.

65. Which of the following Agile principles shows "Architecture and design emerge from a collaboration between teams"?

   A. The best architectures, requirements and designs emerge from self-organizing teams.

   B. Business people and developers must work together daily throughout the project.

   C. Build projects around motivated individuals. Give them the environment and support they need and trust them to get the job done.

   D. Continuous attention to technical excellence and good design enhances agility.

66. Which of the following artifacts helps to bring product owner and team together collaboratively?

   A. Iteration Plan

   B. The Product Backlog

   C. The Iteration Backlog

   D. Burndown chart

67. During iteration planning meeting, who is responsible to commit to deliver selected user stories in the iteration?

   A. Product Owner

   B. Agile project manager

   C. Scrum Master

   D. The team

68. Which of the following is the least desirable practice in the case of a distributed team?

   A. Setting ground rules that a team in a particular time zone will have to extend their working hours to ensure overlap.

   B. Use collaboration tools and videoconferencing whenever practical.

   C. Have some time overlap between remote teams for handoffs and daily interactions.

   D. Maintain common coding rules and tools for continuous integration.

69. What is expected from a traditional Project Manager on Agile projects?

   A. People management.

   B. Responsible to pick up and estimate user stories for next iteration.

   C. Direct team on how to work, track their progress.

   D. None of the above.

70. What are the five XP values?

A. Communication, feedback, simplicity, courage and respect

B. Commitment, openness, simplicity, courage and respect

C. Commitment, openness, focus, courage and respect

D. Commitment, feedback, simplicity, courage and respect

71. An Agile leader is planning the seating arrangement for the team. He makes sure that everyone can see each other. The benefit of such a seating arrangement is that:

A. The leader will be able to exercise authority.

B. The leader is making optimum use of available space.

C. The team will be able to see what the other person is doing.

D. This helps in osmotic communication.

72. The three pillars of empirical process control are:

A. Planning, Adaption, Retrospective

B. Inspection, Transparency, Adaptation

C. Planning, Inspection, Consistency

D. Collaboration, Value-driven, Kaizen

73. Which of the following is a valid prioritization method for an Agile project?

A. Sidky maturity model

B. Monopoly money

C. Kanban

D. Value stream mapping

74. The daily stand-up meeting was scheduled to start at 9 a.m. However the team waited till 9:08 a.m. before all participants came into the meeting room. Morning greetings exchanged between the participants. By then the clock showed 9:12 a.m. There was an issue reported by a team members and team gets into brainstorming and spent another 10 minutes. Finally, the meeting was over at 9:37 a.m.

Calculate the process cycle efficiency of this process.

A. 73%

B. 57%

C. 52%

D. 68%

75. What should be the severity order of the following four risks in descending order?

Risk A has an impact of 0.3 and a probability of 0.2.

Risk B has an impact of 0.4 and a probability of 0.2.

Risk C has an impact of 0.3 and a probability of 0.5.

Risk D has an impact of 0.5 and a probability of 0.8.

A. D, C, B and A

B. D, B, C and A

C. D, C, A, B

D. D, B, A, C

76. Agile projects deliver reliable results by:

A. Engaging customers in frequent interactions and shared ownership.

B. Recognizing that individuals are the ultimate source of value and creating an environment where they can make a difference.

C. Making continuous flow of value our focus.

D. Group accountability for results and shared responsibility for team effectiveness.

77. One of the key stakeholders suggested changing the priority of a user story by making it number one on the backlog. The story was earlier placed third on the prioritized backlog. He is very influential and powerful in the department. How should you act on the suggestion made?

A. Accept the suggestion, change the prioritization order and inform all stakeholders.

B. Simply decline. Inform him that product backlog has already been prioritized and no more changes can be made.

C. Inform and discuss this with product owner.

D. Explain why this is placed at number 3 in backlog and importance of other top user stories to deliver early.

78. Which artifact is the best to display when releases of the product will be ready and what all features will be included in those releases?

A. Developer team

B. Product backlog

C. Product owner

D. Product roadmap

79. There are anumber of projects running where your company is losing money. To reduce the losses, company decides to review and terminate a project. Consequently, 3 projects were shortlisted for review. Which project should be terminated first?

Project 1 has an internal rate of return of -7%

Project 2 has an internal rate of return of -3%

Project 3 has an internal rate of return of -5%

A. Terminate project 1

B. Terminate project 2

C. Terminate project 3

D. Terminate all projects, all have negative IRR and are losing money

80. To track and report the status of schedule and cost, which tool is best to use?

A. S-curve graph

B. Gantt chart

C. Burndown and burnup chart

D. Project plan

81. You called a TV engineer to repair your faulty TV set. You spent 10 minutes explaining the problem with the TV set. It took 4 hours for the engineer to repair the TV set and then you take another 10 minutes to check if the issue is fixed or not before the engineer leaves the site.

In the whole exercise, what is the process cycle efficiency for the engineer and you? Assume that the engineer only values the repair time, whereas you value only the time explaining the issue and checking the TV set.

A. 92.3% for engineer, 7.7% for you

B. 93.7% for engineer, 6.3% for you

C. 95.8% for engineer, 4.2% for you

D. 98.3% for engineer, 1.7% for you

82. Agile project charter is different than s traditional project charter because:

A. Agile projects do not require a charter.

B. While creating an Agile project charter, what approach to be used is not clear.

C. The scope is less clearly defined on Agile projects.

D. Agile projects typically are small, so a small charter is enough.

83. Why is the presence of the customer representative made mandatory in Agile projects?

    A. The customer representative is the main judge for business value.

    B. The project leader needs to build personal rapport with the customer representative.

    C. The customer representative can dictate the project plan and suggest course corrections.

    D. All of the above.

84. When an item is blocked, Kanban teams gather around and collectively work to remove the obstacle. This is prioritized over picking up any new piece of work and ensures continuity of flow through the system. This technique is called:

    A. Collective ownership

    B. Self-organization

    C. Swarming

    D. Group decision-making

85. All are the following are helpful when performing risk management except:

    A. Risk-Based Spikes

    B. Risk-Adjusted Backlogs

    C. Risk Burndown Charts

    D. Risk Owner

86. During a project audit, it is determined that the vendor is artificially inflating the estimates of the user stories. They are on a time-and-materials contract, so the longer they stay on in the project, the more revenue they generate. On getting to know such a practice, what should you do?

    A. Report to PMI®.

    B. Halve the estimates produced.

    C. Report the unethical conduct to the appropriate parties.

    D. Drag the vendor to the court.

87. Wideband Delphi technique is best described as:

    A. A group-based estimation approach

    B. A value-driven estimation approach

    C. A negotiating estimation approach

    D. A team-based estimation approach

88. Story points are used as one of way to estimate Agile projects. These story point estimates are:

A. Absolute

B. Relative

C. The sum of the features in release

D. A fraction of the velocity of the team

89. Planning poker allows multiple rounds of estimates.Which other technique allows a similar approach?

A. Shu-Ha-Ri

B. Wideband Delphi

C. Triple nickel

D. Circle of questions

90. On an Agile project, you get to see estimates of a user story expressed as:

A. Completed by November 15th 2016.

B. Completed within 3 months from when the user story was started.

C. Completed before the start of the next user story.

D. Completed within 40 to 60 hours.

91. On a burndown chart, the top of the bar moved lower from one iteration to the next. What does that imply?

A. The team corrected some of the underestimates of the past.

B. The team completed work in the previous iteration.

C. Scope got added into the backlog.

D. Scope got removed from the backlog.

92. Which of the following qualifies to be a good MMF?

A. An online grocery shopping cart that allows you to view and save the items you want to buy and complete the purchase process.

B. A bicycle having 2 wheels along with supporter, decorative lights, a water bottle space.

C. A cell phone that allows you to make and receive calls, click photos and allows you to connect with social media and other Internet world.

D. A camera that allows you to take photos and then access the Web to add descriptions and share them with friends.

93. It is observed that the bottom of the bar in the burndown chart is raised above the X-axis. What does that mean?

A. Scope has beenremoved.

B. Scope has beenadded.

C. This could be a mistake in plotting.

D. Team is tracking ahead of the estimated velocity.

94. Drawing a tree, the participants are asked to add related features as leaves closer to the trunks and dependent features higher on the tree. This activity is called:

A. Leaves and trunks

B. Features and dependencies

C. Define the scope tree

D. Prune the product tree

95. During an internal project audit your project is marked as RED and highlighted as noncompliant as it does not have a detailed plan. You are asked to prepare the project plan and submit within 3 days instead of having plan for next 2 iterations. What should you do?

A. Ask the team to create a plan based on experience.

B. Ignore them, as this is an internal audit and has no adverse effect on you and the project.

C. Conduct a meeting with them explaining the Agile methodology and progressive planning approach.

D. Contact your management and ask for project exception from the audit.

96. You are into the 6th month of the project, which has an estimated schedule completion of 1year from start. Referring to the latest project status report submitted by you, your sponsor wants to understand why you show that the project will be completed a month earlier than the schedule project completion date. What data should you present in support of your report?

A. Velocity

B. Risk burndown chart

C. Cumulative Flow diagram

D. Risk-based spikes

97. In an Agile project charter, you will not find the:

A. Detailed project scope

B. Estimated project cost

C. Expected ROI

D. Project objective

98. In a control chart, a process is expected to be out of control:

A. When the measured parameter is below the lower control limit.

B. When the measured parameter is above the upper control limit.

C. When the rule of seven is violated.

D. Any of the above.

99. Kanban boards reflect WIP limits against each stage of the workflow. The drawbacks of WIP include the following:

A. Hides bottlenecks.

B. Results in context switching.

C. Delayed feedback.

D. All of the above.

100. Project cost calculation must include:

A. Total cost = (Time X Resource rate) + other project costs

B. Total cost = (Team velocity X average labor rate) + additional project costs

C. Total cost = (average team size X average labor rate) + non-labor project costs

D. Total cost = (team size X hourly rate) + additional project costs

101. You are managing a project and the labor cost per month for the whole team is 30,000 USD. The fixed cost for infrastructure procurement is estimated at 10,000 USD. Based on prioritized product backlog items and team velocity, the team will need 20 iterations of 1 month each to complete the work. Post backlog items are successfully delivered and a 1-month warranty period is requested for the team to remain intact before the project is closed and the team released. What would be the total cost of the project until completion?

A. $5,90,000

B. $6,60,000

C. $6,30,000

D. $6,40,000

102. What do you expect from a servant leader?

A. Tracks tasks on the Kanban board.

B. Empowers the team.

C. Collects requirements and gather user stories.

D. Hosts the iteration review meeting.

103. Which of the following is not a characteristic of high performing Agile teams?

A. Constructive disagreement

B. Plan driven

C. Empowered

D. Self-organizing

104. Which of the following is not appropriate to be discussed in a daily stand-up meeting?

A. The application developer is on vacation, so the code changes are on hold.

B. Build failed for the transaction validator. This is expected to be fixed by today evening.

C. Code upgrade for the payment module is completed.

D. That configuration fix made by Harry last week has caused a significant improvement in our batch jobs. However there is room for a bit more improvement.

105. An Agile coach is building a high-performance team. Which of the following techniques can she adopt?

A. Make all decisions on behalf of the team, saving their time.

B. Demonstrate expertize by solving problems hands-on.

C. Performing individual coaching interventions in the middle of the sprint when team members approach with problems.

D. Intervene at every possible hint of conflict within the team.

106. In a distributed team, which is the most effective tool to use for communication between team members?

A. Email

B. Wiki

C. Skype

D. Audio playback

107. A product owner MUST attend a planning poker estimation session. Without his presence:

A. The session will not be moderated.

B. The team will have a tendency to overestimate.

C. The team will not get the necessary clarifications regarding the stories getting estimated.

D. There will be no timekeeping.

108. You are managing a complex program across the globe and team members are from different regions. You have a large number of team members working on projects and reporting to the respective project manager and then each project manager is reporting to you. Currently you have 10 different project managers on a program. To have an effective communication, how many communication channels will be there between you and project managers?

A. 10

B. 45

C. 55

D. 110

109. Which of the following Emotional Intelligence pairings is correct?

A. Self-management relates to self-control.

B. Self-awareness relates to empathy.

C. Social skills relate to influence.

D. Social awareness relates to self-confidence.

110. Which is a correct pairing of adaptive leadership and team phases?

A. Directingand Storming, Coaching and Forming, Supporting and Norming, Delegating and Performing

B. Directingand Forming, Coaching and Storming, Supporting and Norming, Delegating and Performing

C. Coaching and Forming, Supporting and Storming, Directing and Norming, Delegating and Performing

D. Coaching and Forming, Supporting and Storming, Directing and Delegating, Performing and Norming

111. You should be flexible while leading and managinga team as an Agile coach and improve emotional intelligence. There are different aspects of emotional intelligence, divided into quadrants. What are they?

A. Self, Team, Regulate, Recognize

B. Self, Others, Regulate, Optimize

C. Self, Team, Regulate, Optimize

D. Self, Others, Regulate, Recognize

112. Which of the following is not a Kanban principle?

A. Limit WIP

B. Visualize work

C. Make processes explicit

D. Limit feedback loops

113. Which of the following is not a Lean principle?

A. Eliminate waste

B. Empower the team

C. Optimize learning

D. Defer decision

114. You are a program manager and taking an interview for a PMP certified project manager position in your organization. This position is for a different project that will be led by a different program manager. During the interview process, you find the person violating the standards of PMI® code of ethics and professional conduct. However, you find him a suitable candidate for the position. What you should do?

A. Confront the person.

B. Report this to PMI® to get it appropriately investigated, as you have a suspicion, but no concrete evidence.

C. Ignore it and do not recommend him to be hired him for the project manager position.

D. Ignore it and recommend him for hiring as he will not be working with you, so it is of no harm to you.

115. What are the success criteria for a methodology while performing process analysis?

A. The project got stopped, sponsorship remained intact and the team would work the same way again.

B. The project got stopped, leadership remained intact and the team would work the same way again.

C. The project got shipped, sponsorship remained intact and the team would work the same way again.

D. The project got shipped, leadership remained intact and the team would work the same way again.

116. One thing to avoid when choosing a new Agile practice over an existing process is:

A. Accepting the claims of new practice without validation.

B. Taking time to research the validity of the benefits claimed for the new practice.

C. Testing the approach on a small scale before committing to it on the project.

D. Discontinuing the activities that have led to the underlying problems we want to address.

117. In focus on / focus off activity, what is focused on rather than an argument?

A. Inquiry

B. Conversation

C. Dialogue

D. Understanding

118. As per principle of systems thinking, Agile works well when a project is:

A. Highly-complex requirements and highly-complex technology

B. Low-complex requirements and low-complex technology

C. Highly-complex requirements and highly-complex technology

D. Medium-complex requirements and medium-complex technology

119. An Agile team's velocity is 18. The team is referring to the following stories in priority order on the product backlog:

Story 1 - 4 Points

Story 2 - 1 Points

Story 3 - 5 Points

Story 4 - 2 Points

Story 5 - 13 Points

Story 6 - 5 Points

Story 7 - 5 Points

What is the best choice of stories for the next iteration assuming that stories cannot be split any further?

A. Story 1, 2, 3, 4, 6

B. Story 1, 2, 5

C. Story 1, 2, 3, 4

D. Story 3, 5

120. Which of the following is not a good idea to have in a brainstorming session?

A. Send meeting invites with a clear agenda in advance.

B. Have an experienced facilitator lead the session.

C. Allow people to vent their frustrations and criticisms openly.

D. Have a diverse group so as to consider many different perspectives.

Mock Exam III

1. What are the core values of the PMI® code of ethics?
   A. Responsibility, Respect, Fairness, Truth
   B. Responsibility, Respect, Fairness, Honesty
   C. Accountability, Integrity, Respect, Fairness
   D. Accountability, Responsibility, Respect, Honesty

2. Kano, Wiegers' and MoSCOW are techniques used for:
   A. Disaggregation
   B. Risk analysis
   C. Value-based prioritization
   D. Collecting requirements from customers

3. The letters V, S and T in the acronym INVEST (that is used to describe user stories) stands for?
   A. Valuable, small, testable
   B. Valuable, smart, time-bound
   C. Verifiable, small, testable
   D. Valuable, specific, timely

4. An Agile coach is suggesting ways for the team to increase their velocity. Which of the suggestions are valid?
   A. Increase headcount of the team if budget permits.
   B. Engage the customer closely, if possible let him/her be co-located with rest of the team.
   C. Remove technical debt by refactoring code continuously.
   D. All of the suggestions above are valid.

S. Boral, *Ace the PMI-ACP® exam*, DOI 10.1007/978-1-4842-2526-4

5. Team members are observed to be frequently conflicting with each other, even on petty issues. Referring to Bruce Tuckman's team formation model, at which stage do you think the team is in?

   A. Forming

   B. Storming

   C. Norming

   D. Adjourning

6. During an iteration, the team has committed to deliver 20 story points. As the end of the iteration nears, it appears that 4 story points cannot be completed during the iteration. Which option is the team most likely to exercise?

   A. Extend the iteration by a few days.

   B. Relax the definition of done.

   C. Terminate the sprint, because the estimated velocity cannot be achieved.

   D. Complete whatever is possible and carry over the balance to the product backlog.

7. Referring to the Agile planning onion, which of these are in the correct sequence?

   A. Strategy, product, portfolio, iteration, daily

   B. Portfolio, product, release, iteration, daily

   C. Portfolio, release, product, iteration, daily

   D. Portfolio, daily, strategy, iteration, release

8. Midway during an iteration, a team member had to go on emergency leave for personal reasons. The team is on the verge of missing the committed sprint goal. What should be the course of action now?

   A. Agile teams are self-organized, so the others should rally around and makeup for the absent team member.

   B. Agile teams are self-empowered, so they should remove the scope from the sprint goal.

   C. Agile teams are cross-functional, so the Scrum Master should help in coding and testing activities.

   D. Agile teams maintain sustainable pace, so they deliver what is possible during the sprint and leave the rest to be put back into the product backlog.

9. What are the first three steps to conduct a retrospective?

   A. Set the stage, gather data, generate insights.

   B. Gather the team, brainstorm, make decisions.

   C. Introduce, collaborate, actions.

   D. Set the stage, generate data, gather insights.

10. Which of the following statements related to different levels of coaching are true?

   A. Whole team coaching happens in the middle of the sprint, while individual coaching happens at the beginning and end of the sprint.

   B. Whole team coaching happens at the planning stage of the sprint, while individual coaching can happen throughout the whole sprint.

   C. Whole team coaching happens in the planning and retrospective sessions of the sprint, while individual coaching happens at the middle of the sprint.

   D. Whole team coaching happens throughout the whole sprint, while individual coaching can happen at the middle of the sprint.

11. The formula for Little's Law states:

   A. WIP = Lead Time * Throughput.

   B. WIP = Lead Time / Throughput.

   C. WIP = Lead Time + Throughput.

   D. Higher the WIP, greater is the flow through the system.

12. An Agile team agrees on a 3-week iteration and a planned velocity of 40 story points per iteration. The team starts with a backlog of 400 story points. In the middle of the project, 40 story points get removed and an additional 120 story points get added. How long will the project team take to complete the project?

   A. 39 weeks

   B. 36 weeks

   C. 33 weeks

   D. 36 weeks provided the average velocity of the team remains at 40 throughout the project

13. Spikes are conducted to:

   A. Mitigate risks

   B. Make better estimates

   C. Gain confidence

   D. All of the above

14. Who can terminate a sprint midway?

   A. Product owner

   B. Scrum Master

   C. Development team

   D. Anyone in the Scrum team, but not someone who is outside the team

15. Sequence the following in descending order of size:

    A. Themes, tasks, stories

    B. Epics, features, stories, sub-stories

    C. Epics, stories, tasks, subtasks

    D. Feature, tasks, stories

16. Lyssa Adkins has provided some recommendations to follow during one-on-one coaching. Which of the following is not one of them?

    A. Meet team members a half-step ahead

    B. Partner with functional managers

    C. Create positive regard

    D. Feedback and follow-up

17. "We are going too slow. Let us remove the lower priority stories #12 and #23 from the backlog." Who do you think has the right of saying this?

    A. The development team since they are observing the velocity trends.

    B. The Scrum Master since he facilitates the daily Scrum meetings and needs to escalate the impediments to the product owner.

    C. The Product Owner since he needs to balance ROI and determine what gets delivered when.

    D. The Project Manager since his job is to track scope, time and cost.

18. How doAgile teams achieve knowledge sharing?

    A. Through team participating in all ceremonies.

    B. Through practices like pair programming and continuous integration.

    C. Through use of osmotic communication and technologies across virtual teams.

    D. All of the above.

19. The vertices of the Agile triangle are labeled as:

    A. Quality, Value, Constraints

    B. Quality, Scope, Time

    C. Quality, Value, Scope

    D. Time, Cost,Scope

20. Which of the following is NOT a criterion for determining the length of an iteration for an Agile team?

    A. Maintaining focus and sense of urgency

    B. Length of the largest story in the release

    C. Risk and uncertainty in the requirement

    D. Overhead of iterating

21. A story map is meant to show the stories that are to be delivered over time. The time parameter is shown in the horizontal (X) axis. What is there on the vertical (Y) axis?

    A. Priority of the story.

    B. Estimate of the story.

    C. ROI of the story.

    D. None of the above.

22. ________ is a low-fidelity prototype that shows a mockup for a set of screen, containing the basic layout of the different widgets on it.

    A. Persona

    B. Wireframe

    C. Spikes

    D. Story map

23. A value stream map used to show:

    A. Release date and mapping to business benefits.

    B. Product backlog items mapping to risk.

    C. Current process flow.

    D. Estimates per user story in product backlog.

24. The velocity of a Scrum team is observed to be slightly below the average velocity computed over the last three sprints. The Scrum Master is concerned and asks the team to reflect and come up with a corrective action. Which do you think is a valid action?

    A. All stories needs to be reestimated to arrive at better estimates.

    B. Redo the definition of story point.

    C. Increase the length of the iteration.

    D. There is no need to be overly concerned. Such variations are naturally going to happen.

25. Which of the following is not a valid statement in the Agile Manifesto?

    A. Individuals and interactions over processes and tools.

    B. Working software over comprehensive documentation.

    C. Customer negotiation over contract collaboration.

    D. Responding to change over following a plan.

26. A distributed Agile team is more likely to use __________.

A. Work breakdown structure

B. An electronic Kanban board for tracking work in progress

C. A command and control style of leadership

D. A project manager to monitor and control day-to-day tasks.

27. Agile contracts are characterized by:

A. Ability to define scope upfront.

B. Ability to squeeze the vendor to do more for less.

C. Ability to respond to change without the need of change control procedures.

D. Ability to deliver by a fixed time and at a fixed cost.

28. All of the following hinder effective communication in a team space EXCEPT:

A. Teams seated by their skillsets, like developers together, testers together, etc.

B. Information radiators that have not been regularly updated.

C. Developers using headphones to listen to music.

D. Developers using webcams for communicating with their distant team members.

29. One uses "shuttle" diplomacy by carrying thoughts from one group to the other until they are able to de-escalate the conflict situation. At which level of conflicts do we see the use of shuttle diplomacy?

A. Level 1: Problem to solve

B. Level 2: Disagreement

C. Level 3: Contest

D. Level 4: Crusade

30. Bill and Harry belong to a XP team and are paired up for a programming session. They pick up a story from the backlog and observe the acceptance criteria mentioned at the back of the story card. They code the acceptance test cases first and then write their modules in such a way to make the test cases pass. Which technique are they using?

A. Continuous integration

B. Peer code reviews

C. Test first development

D. Refactoring

31. The __________ is the summation of labor costs for the team. This is the cost that the team incurs during each iteration.

   A. Planned Value

   B. Burn rate

   C. Earned value

   D. Indirect cost

32. Sailboat, 20/20 vision and prune the product tree are innovation games that Agile teams use to:

   A. Collect requirements

   B. Determine release plan

   C. Perform retrospective

   D. Perform estimation

33. All of the following are true about ground rules EXCEPT:

   A. They are abided by all team members.

   B. They are unwritten rules.

   C. They set clear expectations of what is or is not acceptable behavior.

   D. They are enforced by the Agile coach and all team members have to follow them.

34. A Kanban board reflects columns marked with a WIP limit of 5 for analysis and 7 for coding. This means that

   A. There are 5 analysts and 7 developers on the team.

   B. Coding cannot start until all the 5 work items are done with analysis. Similarly testing cannot start until all 7 are finished coding.

   C. The team can progress on a maximum of 5 work items for analysis and 7 work items for coding at any time. Any work item beyond that needs to wait.

   D. It should take a maximum of 5 days to complete analysis and 7 days to complete coding for a work item. Anything beyond that signifies that the work item is too complex and it must be further broken down.

35. A team member, while trying to gather more details around a user story, is not able to get hold of a particular user. He has attempted several times, but seems like the user is unable to provide his time to the team member. What should the team member do first?

   A. Escalate to the product owner and ask him to appoint a proxy.

   B. Escalate to the Scrum Master as he is supposed to remove the impediments.

   C. Escalate to the Team during the daily stand-up meeting.

   D. Remove the item from the backlog and continue with the rest.

36. The _________ is responsible for updating the Task board.

   A. Tester (when test cases pass)

   B. The Team (as they progress)

   C. The Scrum Master (after the daily Scrum)

   D. The Product owner (after the sprint review)

37. A senior member of the team Henry is negotiating with a third-party vendor on the applicable rates on the contract. Henry is passionately hearing the vendor's concerns and trying to relate to it. Which skill is Henry using?

   A. Active listening

   B. Servant leadership

   C. Emotional intelligence

   D. Empathy

38. One of the very important stories in the sprint backlog has not passed acceptance testing. The whole team has swarmed around and tried to isolate the defect, but they have not yet been successful. The sprint is almost coming to an end and the review is in another 2 days from now. It is unlikely that the 'definition of done' will be met for this particular user story. What should the team members be thinking of now?

   A. As the story is very important, they should extend the sprint deadline and defer the sprint review meeting.

   B. They should deliver the software as is (with the story that failed) and ask the customer not to use it, until it is fixed in the next sprint.

   C. They should consult with the Agile coach on the best way forward.

   D. They should deliver only the stories that have met the definition of done. All other stories that are incomplete should be removed from delivery.

39. It seems that the number of escaped defects has been rising over the last 3 iterations. As a Scrum Master what should you do?

   A. Identify which developer(s) is/are not doing things properly and schedule one-on-one meetings with them.

   B. Do nothing, but wait to vent it out in the upcoming retrospective meeting.

   C. Ask the team to print out the chart showing the escaped defects trend and post it on the team wall.

   D. Get the team to address the issue collectively.

40. You have been appointed as an Agile coach in a fairly large department. On an initial survey you notice that there are several projects implementing Agile in their own way and sometimes in different ways. Their definition of story points and velocities are also different. The team members also have varied maturity levels. What should you be doing?

    A. Ignore. You have been recently appointed and it will take some time to understand the ways of working in different teams.

    B. Express no concern. It is completely acceptable that the team implements Agile and tailor it in a way that suits them the best.

    C. Express deep concern. Pull up the Agile PMO and ask them why they have not been able to address the issue of inconsistency.

    D. Express deep concern. Ask each of the teams to email you their metrics every Friday morning.

41. The keyword SMART is used to denote attributes of a well-defined user story. The letters S and T stand for?

    A. Smart, testable

    B. Specific, testable

    C. Short, timeboxed

    D. Specific, time-bound

42. In Agile, prioritization is done on the basis of:

    A. Risk

    B. Value

    C. A and B

    D. Complexity

43. Which of the following are NOT benefits of pair programming?

    A. Collaboration within the team

    B. Collective code ownership

    C. Feedback on coding on the fly

    D. Refactoring

44. Agile teams have large walls where they display artifacts and different metrics showing progress. These are collectively called:

    A. Caves and commons

    B. Information refrigerator

    C. Information radiator

    D. Status reports

45. Which of the following is NOT a group-based technique used to arrive at a decision?

A. Nominal group technique

B. Delphi

C. Control charts

D. Wisdom of crowd

46. Undocumented knowledge that team members gather by working in close proximity to each other is called:

A. Informative workspace

B. Expert in earshot

C. Confidential information

D. Tacit knowledge

47. Which of the following is NOT a core practice in XP?

A. Test-Driven Development

B. Continuous integration

C. Value Stream mapping

D. Collective Code ownership

48. Which of the following are valid project selection methods?

A. Discounted payback period, Net present value, ROI, Benefit cost ratio

B. Planning poker, Benefit cost ratio, internal rate of return, payback period

C. Monopoly money, feasibility, value-based prioritization

D. ROI, NPV, IRR, MMF

49. Earned value management technique can be used on Agile projects, especially for tracking release. EVM is an example of:

A. Lagging metric

B. Leading metric

C. Both A and B

D. None of the above.

50. Velocity is __________ across iterations for a given team on a given project. Velocity is __________ across teams or projects.

A. Comparable, comparable

B. Comparable, not comparable

C. Not comparable, comparable

D. Not comparable, not comparable

51. During the first half of the iteration planning meeting, the product owner mentions that Feature A should be implemented since it has the highest ROI. The team argues that they think that Feature B would give the maximum benefit to a section of users as they found out during previous conversations. What should happen now?

    A. The team should use the 'force' technique of conflict resolution and go with the Feature Benefit.

    B. The team should use the 'smoothing' technique of conflict resolution.

    C. The team should use the 'withdraw' technique of conflict resolution and go with Feature A, since the product owner has the last say as far as the ROI of a feature is concerned.

    D. The team should use the 'compromise' technique of conflict resolution and do a little bit of both Features A and B.

52. The responsibility of creating the product roadmap primarily rests with:

    A. The product owner

    B. The empowered team

    C. The Scrum Master

    D. The onsite customer

53. The responsibility of fixing defects found during acceptance testing lies with:

    A. The programmer who coded it.

    B. The programmer who paired and reviewed the code.

    C. Anyone on the team.

    D. A subject matter expert.

54. The Product owner declined an invite for the sprint planning meeting indicating his unavailability. What should happen now?

    A. The Sprint planning meeting cannot happen without the PO, so it should be rescheduled.

    B. The Scrum Master should substitute for the PO and refer to the existing Product Backlog. Any questions from the team should be taken offline.

    C. The team is self-organized, so they should determine the sprint backlog themselves.

    D. The sprint should be used only for spikes and technical tasks instead of business features.

55. One of the values of XP is collective ownership. What does the team collectively NOT own?

    A. Quality of the deliverable.

    B. Code.

    C. Product backlog.

    D. Coding conventions.

56. The team is unable to decide whether it makes sense to buy an off-the-shelf from the vendor or go about building it themselves. Both options have its merits and demerits. As a Scrum Master what would be your recommendation to the team?

A. Consult with the product owner of what he is willing to sponsor.

B. Conduct a spike to evaluate both options.

C. Do a fist of five voting.

D. None of the above.

57. As per Stacey's matrix, Agile projects are best suited where there is:

A. Agile projects can be applied in all of the below situations.

B. High disagreement on requirements and high uncertainty of technology.

C. High agreement on requirements and high certainty of technology.

D. Moderate agreement on requirements and some uncertainty on technology.

58. As an outcome of the team retrospective, the team members decide to procure the Teamcity software to automate their build process. This is an example of:

A. Agile tooling

B. Refactoring

C. Information radiator

D. Emotional intelligence

59. If an XP coach asks the team to be DRY, he/she means that:

A. Team should check-in and integrate their code many times a day.

B. Team should not duplicate the same code at multiple places.

C. Team should follow test-driven deployment.

D. Team should be disciplined in their practices.

60. A release burndown chart should show a downward trend to show progress. However, if there is an upward movement, it implies that:

A. One or more team members is absent and the team has slowed down.

B. This is a glitch in data collection and it should be fixed during charting.

C. User stories were added to the backlog.

D. The team has been working on analysis, spikes and prototypes more than delivering business functionality in recent times.

61. The team has identified a new stakeholder of the project. However, the stakeholder has low power and low influence. The stakeholder requests the Scrum Master for an invite in the daily stand-up meeting such that he catches up with the latest of the project. The Scrum Master:

A. Agrees, but tells the stakeholder that he needs to participate actively in the meeting.

B. Agrees, but tells the stakeholder that he needs to listen in, but not allowed to speak in the meeting.

C. Disagrees, but tells the stakeholder to wait for the next review meeting to see if his expectations have been fulfilled or not.

D. Ignores the request stating that this is not a legitimate request.

62. The Scrum team is in a formative stage. It is learned that the team will not be co-located. What are the options available to the team?

A. Be persistent with the demand of co-location without which the project will fail.

B. Invest in collaboration tools and technologies like interactive chats, audio and video conferences.

C. Explore possibility of rotating team members such that each gets a flavor of the culture and working at the other location.

D. B or C.

63. During a sprint planning session, the team is looking at the following stories from the backlog sorted in descending order of priority. They also have the estimate of each story as mentioned below.

Story A - 12 story points

Story B - 6 story points

Story C - 2 story points

Story D - 5 story points

Story E - 7 story points

Story F - 15 story points

Story G - 8 story points

Story H - 6 story points

Story I - 2 story points

Assuming the team velocity of 20 story points and that no story can be further split, what is the most likely backlog for each sprint?

A. Sprint 1: ABC, Sprint 2: DEG, Sprint 3: FI, Sprint 4: H

B. Sprint 1: ABC, Sprint 2: DEF, Sprint 3: GHI

C. Sprint 1: ABC, Sprint 2: DEG, Sprint 3: F, Sprint 4: HI

D. None of the above

64. If you happen to hire for a new Agile team, you should prefer:

A. Developers

B. Specialists in the technologies to be used

C. Generalists with cross-functional skillsets

D. People who exhibit adaptive leadership skills

65. During the sprint planning session, the PO asks who will be developing a particular story, because he would like to have a conversation with that developer privately. What would happen?

A. A developer comes forward and volunteers.

B. It is not known who will develop a story at the planning stage. But this will be reflected in the task board during the iteration when the story is picked up for development.

C. Ask the PO to attend the daily stand-up meeting to keep a tab on who is working on which story.

D. The Scrum Master should be providing the requested information to the PO.

66. Levels two, three and five in Lea's conflict model represent:

A. Disagreement, contest, world war

B. Problem to solve, contest, world war

C. Problem to solve, contest, crusade

D. Disagreement, contest, crusade

67. All of the following are brainstorming techniques except:

A. Quiet Writing

B. Round-Robin

C. Free-for-all

D. Triple nickels

68. All of the following are techniques to gathering data during retrospectives except:

A. Mad, sad, glad

B. Timeline

C. Circle of questions

D. Team radar

69. During the iteration planning meeting, the Agile teams commit to deliver stories A, B, C and D having estimates of 20, 12, 8 and 4 story points. However the team could complete stories A, B, C and 50% of D. What is the team velocity?

A. 38

B. 40

C. 42

D. 44

70. ESVP is used during ________ while Weigers' method is used during ________.

A. Retrospectives, estimation

B. Retrospectives, prioritization

C. Meeting etiquettes, prioritization

D. Planning, estimation

71. The current size of the Agile team is increasing from 9 to 15. As a result, it is observed that the team is unable to complete their daily stand-up meetings within the stipulated 15 minutes. As a Scrum Master, which option out of the following are you most likely to explore?

A. Extend the meeting from 15 to 25 minutes to accommodate everyone.

B. Ask team members to talk about blockers only and leave the other two questions.

C. Ask only the senior team members to talk.

D. Divide the team into two subteams and have two separate daily stand-ups. The team division should be such that they are mostly independent.

72. Agile teams are self-organized and empowered to make decisions. Which of the following core value in the Agile Manifesto best relates to this?

A. Individuals and interactions over processes and tools.

B. Working software over comprehensive documentation.

C. Responding to change over following a plan.

D. None of the above.

73. The steps of TDD are as follows:

A. Write code, test code, fix defect, retest

B. Write test, write code, refactoring

C. Green, red, refactor

D. Write code, refactor and test

74. The sponsor of an Agile project:

A. Represents the user community

B. Defines the product roadmap

C. Approves the project plan

D. Provides funding for the project

75. Amplify learning is a principle of ________, while system metaphors are used in ________.

A. Lean, XP

B. Kanban, Scrum

C. DSDM, XP

D. Scrum, Lean

76. Although the acceptance test cases have passed, the team realizes that the code violates a few coding standards, which might make it difficult to maintain over the long term. This is because of some last-minute tactical changes done by the team to complete the user story. Such an issue is an example of:

A. Violation of definition of done.

B. Introduction of technical debt.

C. Violation of ground rules.

D. Violation of collective ownership.

77. In the hardening sprint, one expects the team to:

A. Continue adding features that add business value

B. Complete testing of whatever is there and make it ready for deployment to production

C. Refactor the code

D. Perform process improvements as per the last retrospective

78. As time progresses, in an Agile project you expect:

A. Cycle time to be shorter

B. Estimates to be shorter

C. Velocity to be shorter

D. Iterations to be shorter

79. The _______ manages the product backlog while the _______ manages the iteration backlog.

    A. Scrum Master, developer

    B. Product owner, Scrum Master

    C. Product owner, team

    D. Product manager, team

80. A Product owner is or could be invited in all of the following meetings except:

    A. Iteration planning

    B. Daily stand-up

    C. Iteration review

    D. Iteration retrospective

81. The Y-axis of an iteration burndown chart depicts _______.

    A. Time

    B. Story points

    C. Number of features completed

    D. Burn rate / cost of resources

82. All of the following are valid units of estimation in Agile projects except:

    A. Story points

    B. Ideal days

    C. T-shirt sizes

    D. Person-days

83. Your team agreed on a velocity of 25 story points per iteration. The Agile PMO pointed out that another team working on a project of similar complexity is more productive with a velocity of 40 story points per iteration. What should you do?

    A. Agree to go with 40 and convince the team that overtime might be necessary to catch up.

    B. Stick to 25 and convince the PMO that velocities of two teams cannot be compared to each other.

    C. Hire an Agile coach to see how to reach 40.

    D. Use an alternate estimation technique.

84. Which of the following are valid promises made by the product owner to the team and vice versa?

A. PO promises not to change the scope in the middle of the sprint, the team commits to deliver what is mentioned on the sprint goal.

B. PO promises to be available for any questions the development team might have, the team commits to implement any changes introduced in the middle of the sprint.

C. PO promises to bring in a prioritized list of backlog, the team promises to bring in their list of risks and technical tasks that compete in priority over the business requirements.

D. PO promises to deliver a world class product, the team commits to use the most sophisticated technologies available at the market.

85. An Agile project charter contains all of the following except:

A. Description of the purpose of the project.

B. A detailed project plan.

C. Identified stakeholders and the intended customer base.

D. Rough timelines when the project is likely to be delivered.

86. In the context of Agile project management, which characteristic is the odd one out in the below?

A. Iterative and incremental delivery

B. Focus on individuals and interactions

C. Tracking and monitoring with high-tech, low-touch tools

D. Value-based prioritization

87. Which of the following is going to be least effective in increasing velocity of the team?

A. Increase involvement of the customer.

B. Remove technical debt by continuously refactoring code.

C. Shield the team from interferences.

D. Use an alternate technique for estimation.

88. An Agile coach practices whole team coaching during __________ and individual coaching at __________.

A. Sprint planning, middle of sprint.

B. Middle of sprint, throughout the sprint.

C. Sprint planning and retrospective, middle of sprint.

D. Throughout the sprint, retrospective.

89. A team of 5 members has an average velocity of 20 story points. They need to deliver a backlog of 120 story points at iterations of 2 weeks duration. Assuming that weekly labor rate of each team member is 100 what would be the estimated budget of the project? Consider only labor costs.

A. $4000

B. $5000

C. $6000

D. $7000

90. The following are characteristics of exploratory testing EXCEPT:

A. Simultaneous learning and testing.

B. Testing with focus on execution rather than up-front planning.

C. Writing acceptance tests before writing code.

D. Used in conjunction with other forms of testing like automation, regression, usability and acceptance, etc.

91. One should use daily stand-up meetings to do all of the following EXCEPT:

A. Keep up peer pressure and commit to each other.

B. Highlighting issues and bottlenecks.

C. Collaborate effectively with each other.

D. Provide a status update to the Scrum Master or Product Owner.

92. Agile teams sometimes use extreme personas to collect stories. Extreme personas are helpful since:

A. Unlike other forms of personas, they are imaginary characters that one can relate to easily.

B. Considering extreme personas help to discover stories that otherwise would have been missed.

C. Extreme personas are used when all other forms of story writing is found to be noneffective.

D. None of the above.

93. Which of the following is not a preferred unit of estimation for Agile stories?

A. Function points

B. Story points

C. Ideal days

D. T-shirt sizes

94. The technique of breaking up an epic into a story, a story into a task and a task into a subtask is called:

A. Decomposition

B. Simplification

C. Disaggregation

D. Splitting

95. The progress midway in an iteration is monitored best using:

A. Working software, as per the Agile Manifesto.

B. Release burndown chart.

C. Task board.

D. Conducting demos midway between the sprints.

96. An Agile team space is characterized by a zone where maximum osmotic communication takes place and another zone where privacy prevails and the team members can take care of their needs for separation. This arrangement is called?

A. Information radiators

B. Caves and commons

C. Private and public areas

D. Informative team zones

97. You are invited to screen a few proposals from a few vendors. While doing so, you notice that one of the proposals is from a company owned by your relative. What should you do?

A. Ignore and try to evaluate as fairly as possible.

B. Contact your relative and ask them to tweak the proposal to make it sound more competitive.

C. Influence the rest of the proposal evaluators that your relative's company is the best as you know them personally.

D. Disclose it to the appropriate authorities and stay out of the selection process.

98. Which of the following is the least-recommended way to determine the initial velocity of a team?

A. Refer to historical values.

B. Make a guess.

C. Run an initial iteration as a pilot, measure and use the velocity of that.

D. Use another team's velocity.

99. In which stage of a retrospective are the techniques like 5 Why's, Fishbone and Force field analysis used?

   A. Set the stage

   B. Gather data

   C. Generate insights

   D. Decide what to do

100. XP teams use the technique of ________ to enhance code quality, while keeping its behavior unchanged.

   A. Refactoring

   B. TDD

   C. Spikes

   D. Pair programming

101. For sprint planning, the following should participate actively:

   A. Customers, analysts and developers

   B. Scrum Master, product owner and analysts

   C. Whole project team

   D. Sponsor, onsite customer, Development lead, testing leads

102. How doAgile teams manage scope?

   A. Prevent scope creep during the project.

   B. Lock down scope during a sprint.

   C. Allow scope changes to the backlog only before a sprint.

   D. B and C.

103. Which of the following statements regarding velocity is not correct?

   A. Velocity helps to correct and adjust inaccuracies in estimates.

   B. Velocity differs from team to team.

   C. Velocity can differ from one iteration to another iteration.

   D. It is impossible to determine the initial velocity, unless the team has actually worked in the project.

104. As an Agile coach, you keep reminding the team to standup during the daily Scrums, update the storyboard before leaving for the day and complete the tasks they have committed during the daily Scrum meeting. This is a description of which failure mode of Agile coaching?

A. The Expert

B. The Nag

C. The Opinionator

D. The Seagull

105. During osmotic communication between teams, we have to be careful of drafts that are__________.

A. Unwanted chatter on topics that are not useful in the context of the current working environment.

B. Gush of air from the window.

C. Negative publicity.

D. Conflicts between the storming phases of the team.

106. The pillars of Scrum are:

A. Plan, Do, Check, Act

B. Honesty, respect, fairness, responsibility

C. Transparency, Inspection and Adaptation

D. Green, red, refactor

107. During the estimation session, the team wants to compare the estimate of a new story with a small story and a medium story that has already been estimated to 1 and 5 story points. This is commonly referred to as:

A. Affinity estimation

B. Analogous estimation

C. Wideband Delphi

D. Triangulation

108. Which of the following is true for a user story card?

A. The story card is not a requirement specification, but a reminder to have a conversation between the developer and the customer.

B. The story card can be torn apart after the definition of done is achieved.

C. The acceptance criteria are written at the back of the card.

D. All of the above are true.

109. Which of the following Scrum artifacts acts as a communication bridge between the developer and the product owner as far as priorities go?

A. Product backlog

B. Release burndown charts

C. Cumulative burndown and burnup charts

D. Product increment

110. From a risk burndown chart, we get to see:

A. New risks or existing risks whose severity has changed.

B. Whether the team is able to address risks properly and the cumulative risk severity is showing a downward trend.

C. Both A and B.

D. How many spikes have been performed in the team.

111. During the Scrum meeting, Richard the Scrum Master notices there is some disagreement between Bill and Harry on the timing to change a run-time configuration of the software. The conflict was assessed at Level 1. What should Richard do?

A. Openly blast Bill and Harry in the Scrum meeting, reminding them that such conflicts are not healthy in a self-organized team.

B. Do nothing. Since it is a Level 1 conflict, Richard expects Bill and Harry to resolve it on their own.

C. Immediately after the Scrum meeting, take Bill and Harry to another room and try to mediate to resolve the problem.

D. Escalate to Bill and Harry's line managers.

112. Mute mapping is a technique used for categorizing ideas. Which of the following is true?

A. All phone lines are muted so that the speaker can continue without interruption.

B. It is used during sprint review.

C. Participants are not allowed to speak while they move related cards (topics) together and put unrelated cards separate.

D. The ideas with the maximum votes win and the others are discarded.

113. Fractional assignment is not suitable for Agile projects since:

A. Lot of time is wasted because of context switching.

B. People do not get bored because they are involved in a variety of tasks.

C. Productivity suffers.

D. A and C.

114. During which Scrum ceremony are risk audits held?

A. Sprint planning

B. Sprint execution

C. Sprint review

D. Sprint retrospective

115. If co-location is not possible, which of the following is NOT a good practice in distributed teams?

A. It is advisable to bring them team together at the beginning to conduct a kick-off meeting or get teams to work together for 1 or 2 iterations and get used to each other's styles of working.

B. Distribute the team as per job specification - such that all analysts are in one location, all developers are in another location and all testers in the third location. Such kind of horizontalization will increase osmotic communication where team members can learn from each other.

C. Invest behind communication technologies like interactive chats, webcams, audio and video conferences, collaboration tools, electronic task boards like Jira and online planning poker sites.

D. Explore if work times can be adjusted such that there is some overlap between team members located in different time zones.

116. The product owner brings all stakeholders in a common place with an intent to reach consensus on the priorities of the items on their wish list. He tells everyone to distribute 100 points across all features that are deemed valuable to them. They may even choose to give all 100 to only one feature, if that is the only one they are interested in. Once the choices are made, the product owner sums up the votes and lists the features in descending order of priority. What is the name of this prioritization technique?

A. Planning Poker

B. Delphi

C. 100-point method

D. Weigers' method

117. Which of the following roles could an Agile PMO play in a project?

A. Help in resource management, especially shared resources.

B. Help in rolling up management reporting.

C. Help in vendor and contract management.

D. All of the above.

118. By tracking velocity trends, a team can:

A. Gauge the rate of progress

B. Estimate how much longer it will take to complete

C. Correcting estimation errors

D. All of the above

119. Bob is a newbie in an Agile team. He is studying how the team is working and sieving through the artifacts that teams track to measure their progress. While looking at a burndown chart, he observes that the bar chart, instead of going down has actually risen in the current iteration, from where it was in the past. He is confused and runs to Jessica for a clarification. What is Jessica likely to explain?

A. Jessica explains that there is a mistake in the burndown chart, as the bar graphs should always show a downward trend.

B. Jessica explains that the team has corrected the estimates of a few stories based on better understanding that they have gathered recently. In the past, there was an underestimate.

C. Jessica explains that the product owner has recently added a bunch of new stories to the backlog, hence the top has moved up.

D. Jessica explains that the rise in the bar graph is because the team's progress has been slow in the last few days, as a colleague has been ill.

120. A Kanban team uses an expedite lane on their Kanban board to:

A. Slot in work items that exceed the WIP limit, but must get done on a best effort basis.

B. To tackle critical and urgent work like production issues, but are again subject to their own WIP limits.

C. To find bottlenecks in the rest of the lanes on the Kanban board.

D. The word expedite shows that the team is working expeditiously - reacting to tasks and changes as swiftly as possible at all times.

Answers

Answers – Mock Exam I

1. C
2. D
3. C
4. D
5. C
6. C
7. B
8. C
9. D
10. B
11. C
12. B
13. A
14. D
15. C
16. C
17. A
18. A
19. D
20. D
21. C
22. C
23. B
24. D
25. C
26. A
27. B
28. C
29. C
30. B
31. B
32. D
33. A
34. D
35. C
36. A
37. C
38. D
39. A
40. C
41. C
42. C
43. D
44. C
45. A
46. B
47. B
48. D
49. A
50. D
51. D
52. C
53. D
54. B
55. D
56. B
57. A
58. C
59. C
60. D
61. A
62. D
63. C
64. A
65. B
66. D
67. A
68. C
69. A
70. C
71. C
72. B
73. C
74. A
75. B
76. D
77. B
78. C
79. A
80. D
81. C
82. D
83. A
84. C
85. B
86. A
87. D
88. C
89. B
90. C
91. B
92. A
93. C
94. D
95. D
96. D
97. C
98. B
99. A
100. C
101. C
102. D
103. B
104. A
105. D
106. C
107. A
108. C
109. C
110. C
111. D
112. C
113. C
114. D
115. B
116. D
117. A
118. A
119. C
120. D

S. Boral, *Ace the PMI-ACP® exam*, DOI 10.1007/978-1-4842-2526-4

Answers – Mock Exam II

1. D
2. D
3. B
4. C
5. A
6. D
7. B
8. B
9. C
10. C
11. B
12. C
13. A
14. B
15. B
16. D
17. C
18. A
19. A
20. D
21. B
22. A
23. B
24. D
25. C
26. B
27. D
28. D
29. D
30. B
31. B
32. D
33. C
34. A
35. C
36. B
37. A
38. A
39. B
40. C
41. A
42. B
43. D
44. C
45. A
46. B
47. A
48. C
49. B
50. B
51. A
52. B
53. D
54. C
55. D
56. B
57. A
58. C
59. D
60. D
61. D
62. C
63. B
64. C
65. A
66. B
67. D
68. A
69. D
70. A
71. D
72. B
73. B
74. D
75. A
76. A
77. C
78. D
79. A
80. A
81. A
82. C
83. A
84. C
85. D
86. C
87. A
88. B
89. B
90. D
91. B
92. A
93. A
94. D
95. C
96. A
97. A
98. D
99. D
100. A
101. D
102. B
103. B
104. D
105. C
106. C
107. C
108. C
109. A
110. B
111. D
112. D
113. C
114. B
115. D
116. A
117. B
118. D
119. A
120. C

Answers – Mock Exam III

1.	B	31.	B	61.	B	91.	D
2.	C	32.	A	62.	D	92.	B
3.	A	33.	D	63.	A	93.	A
4.	D	34.	C	64.	C	94.	C
5.	B	35.	C	65.	B	95.	C
6.	D	36.	B	66.	A	96.	B
7.	B	37.	A	67.	D	97.	D
8.	D	38.	D	68.	C	98.	D
9.	A	39.	D	69.	B	99.	C
10.	C	40.	B	70.	B	100.	A
11.	A	41.	D	71.	D	101.	C
12.	D	42.	C	72.	A	102.	D
13.	D	43.	D	73.	B	103.	D
14.	A	44.	C	74.	D	104.	B
15.	C	45.	C	75.	A	105.	A
16.	D	46.	D	76.	B	106.	C
17.	C	47.	C	77.	B	107.	D
18.	D	48.	A	78.	A	108.	D
19.	A	49.	C	79.	C	109.	A
20.	B	50.	B	80.	D	110.	C
21.	A	51.	C	81.	B	111.	B
22.	B	52.	A	82.	D	112.	C
23.	C	53.	C	83.	B	113.	D
24.	D	54.	A	84.	A	114.	D
25.	C	55.	C	85.	B	115.	B
26.	B	56.	B	86.	C	116.	C
27.	C	57.	D	87.	D	117.	D
28.	D	58.	A	88.	C	118.	D
29.	D	59.	B	89.	C	119.	B
30.	C	60.	C	90.	C	120.	B

References and Bibliography

This book includes references to the 12 books that have been suggested by PMI® as reference materials for the knowledge of Agile practices and preparation for the PMI-ACP® exam.

`http://www.pmi.org/-/media/pmi/documents/public/pdf/certifications/agile-certified-practitioner-reference-materials.pdf`

These are as follows:

1) *Agile Estimating and Planning,* by Mike Cohn. [Pearson Education / Addison-Wesley Professional]

2) *User Stories Applied: For Agile Software Development,* by Mike Cohn. [Pearson Education]

3) *Agile Project Management: Creating Innovative Products* - 2nd Edition, by Jim Highsmith. [Pearson Education / Addison-Wesley Professional]

4) *Agile Retrospectives: Making Good Teams Great,* by Esther Derby, Diana Larsen, Ken Schwaber. [Pragmatic Bookshelf]

5) *Agile Software Development: The Cooperative Game* - 2nd Edition, by Alistair Cockburn. [Pearson Education]

6) *Coaching Agile Teams: A Companion for ScrumMasters, Agile Coaches and Project Managers in Transition,* by Lyssa Adkins. [Pearson Education / Addison-Wesley Professional]

7) *Effective Project Management: Traditional, Agile, Extreme,* by Robert K. Wysocki. [Wiley]

8) *Exploring Scrum: The Fundamentals,* by Dan Rawsthorne with Doug Shimp. [CreateSpace Publishing]

9) *Kanban in Action,* by Marcus Hammarberg, Joakim Sunden. [Manning Publications]

10) *Kanban: Successful Evolutionary Change for Your Technology Business,* by David J. Anderson. [Blue Hole Press]

11) *Lean-Agile Software Development: Achieving Enterprise Agility,* by Alan Shalloway, Guy Beaver, James R. Trott. [Pearson Education]

12) *The Software Project Manager's Bridge to Agility,* by Michele Sliger, Stacia Broderick. [Pearson Education]

S. Boral, *Ace the PMI-ACP® exam*, DOI 10.1007/978-1-4842-2526-4

Each of these books is brilliant and stands apart from hundreds of materials available in the market. So definitely they are all worth reading. But fortunately, my book, which you have just completed,encompasses the learnings from most of these, so if you are in a hurry, you don't need to read each of them and the contents of my book will suffice for preparing for the PMI-ACP® exam.

Apart from the above few other references, here are some additional ones:

1) *Becoming Agile: In an Imperfect World,* by Greg Smith, Ahmed Sidky. [Manning Publications]

2) *The Art of Agile Development,* by James Shore. [O'Reilly Media]

3) *Agile Project Management with Scrum,* by Ken Schwaber. [Microsoft Press US]

4) *Strategic Management and Organizational Dynamics*: The Challenge of Complexity to Ways of Thinking about Organizations, by Ralph Douglas Stacey. [Financial Times]

5) Lean Software Development: An Agile Toolkit, by Mary Poppendieck; Tom Poppendieck (2003). [Addison-Wesley Professional]

6) Co-Active Coaching: New Skills for Coaching People toward Success in Work and Life,by LauraWhitworth. [Nicholas Brealey Publishing]

7) Software Engineering Economics, by Barry Boehm. [Prentice Hal]

8) A Guide to the Project Management Body of Knowledge (PMBOK® Guide) - Fifth Edition. [Project Management Institute]

9) A Disciplined Approach to Adopting Agile Practices: *The Agile Adoption Framework* by Ahmed Sidky, James Arthur, available at `https://arxiv.org/ftp/arxiv/papers/0704/0704.1294.pdf`

Web pages that have been referred to in this book:


```
http://agilemanifesto.org/
www.pmdoi.org
https://www.atlassian.com/agile/kanban
https://kanbanflow.com/
http://Eclipse.org
http://www.scaledagileframework.com/
http://www.dict.cc/german-english/Taktzeit.html
https://confluence.atlassian.com/display/GH061/Viewing+the+Burndown+Chart
https://resources.sei.cmu.edu/asset_files/WhitePaper/2013_019_001_299139.pdf
http://jimhighsmith.com/adaptive-leadership/
https://www.greenleaf.org/what-is-servant-leadership/
https://en.wikipedia.org/wiki/Kano_model
https://en.wikipedia.org/wiki/Queueing_theory
https://en.wikipedia.org/wiki/The_Chicken_and_the_Pig
https://en.wikipedia.org/wiki/Business_Model_Canvas
http://www.sonoma.edu/users/s/swijtink/teaching/philosophy_101/paper1/goleman.htm
http://junit.org/junit4/
https://products.office.com/en-us/sharepoint/sharepoint-2013-overview-collaboration-
software-features
https://www.atlassian.com/software/confluence
http://www-03.ibm.com/software/products/en/clearcase
https://github.com/
```

https://www.planningpoker.com/
https://kanbanflow.com/
https://www.microsoft.com/en-in/download/details.aspx?id=35451
https://www.skype.com/en/meetings/
https://www.webex.co.in/
https://cucumber.io/
https://www.microsoft.com/en-in/download/details.aspx?id=23745
https://www.teamviewer.com
https://www.jetbrains.com/teamcity/
http://www.fitnesse.org/
http://jasmine.github.io/
http://www.seleniumhq.org/
http://devmts.org.uk/dreyfus.pdf
http://store.mountaingoatsoftware.com/products/planning-poker-cards
https://www.atlassian.com/software/jira
https://confluence.atlassian.com/jiraportfoliocloud/classic-plans-802170593.html
http://pomodorotechnique.com/
http://www.sonarqube.org/tag/sqale/
https://www.jfrog.com/open-source/
http://martinfowler.com/bliki/TestPyramid.html
https://tfl.gov.uk/modes/driving/red-routes
http://www.pmi.org/-/media/pmi/documents/public/pdf/governance/code-of-ethics-and-professional-conduct.pdf?la=en

Index

A

B

S. Boral, *Ace the PMI-ACP® exam*, DOI 10.1007/978-1-4842-2526-4

C

D

E

W

X

Y, Z

MIX
Papier aus verantwortungsvollen Quellen
Paper from responsible sources
FSC® C105338

If you have any concerns about our products,
you can contact us on
ProductSafety@springernature.com

In case Publisher is established outside the EU,
the EU authorized representative is:
Springer Nature Customer Service Center GmbH
Europaplatz 3, 69115 Heidelberg, Germany

Printed by Libri Plureos GmbH
in Hamburg, Germany